World
Religions

Nihil Obstat: Rev. William Becker, STD
                Censor Librorum
                August 26, 2008

Imprimatur: †Most Rev. Bernard J. Harrington, DD
              Bishop of Winona
              August 26, 2008

The nihil obstat and imprimatur are official declarations that a book or pamphlet is free of doctrinal or moral error. No implication is contained therein that those who have granted the nihil obstat or imprimatur agree with the contents, opinions, or statements expressed, nor do they assume any legal responsibility associated with publication.

The publishing team included Michael Wilt, Jerry Windley-Daoust, Amy Kuebelback, and Christine Schmertz Navarro, development editors; Barbara Allaire, John Ferrie, and Stephan Nagel, consulting editors; Lorraine Kilmartin, reviewer; Maps.com, cartographers; prepress and manufacturing coordinated by the production departments of Saint Mary's Press.

Front cover: *top left*, © Bob Krist/CORBIS; *top middle*, Medford Taylor/SuperStock; *top right*, © Christophe Boisvieux/Corbis; *middle left*, © Burstein Collection/CORBIS; *center*, Roberto M. Arakaki/Imagestate; *bottom left*, © Wolfgang Kaehler/CORBIS; *bottom middle*, Gene Plaisted, The Crosiers; *bottom right*, © Penny Tweedie/CORBIS

Printed in the United States of America

1142 (PO2629)

ISBN 978-0-88489-997-6

World Religions

A Voyage of Discovery
Third Edition

Jeffrey Brodd
With a Foreword by Gregory L. Sobolewski

Saint Mary's Press®

Contents

South Asia

Foreword

The Roman Catholic Church and Non-Christian Religions

by Gregory L. Sobolewski

My mother's Lutheran father was trouble for my father when my father first started dating her. My grandfather seldom went to church, but he complained to my Catholic dad in a heavy accent about "those damn Cadlics." Dad felt a lot better when he discovered that his future father-in-law was talking about automobiles rather than members of a religion.

Until that discovery my dad feared my grandfather, because my dad loved his fiancée deeply, and he didn't want religion to get in the way. He also never talked with my mom's father about their religious differences, and so he presumed the worst. This example of a misunderstanding in one family in particular serves as an analogy for situations often encountered in the human family at large. We sometimes fear that which we do not understand; we sometimes ignore it; we sometimes even attack it.

When our misunderstandings are about things like automobiles, little is at stake. But when matters of faith are at issue, the stakes can be high. Matters of faith are serious for those whose faith matters. Christians learn from the Bible that "all things work together for good for those who love God, who are called according to his purpose" (Romans 8:28). Thus Christians believe that love of God casts out fear, ignorance, and hostility, and transforms our lives. In a word, Christians *hope*. Christians hope that differences can be first tolerated, then understood, and finally celebrated. The inspiration offered by the Bible's promise of things working together for good, along with Christian discussions of faith, are causes of hope for good relations among the world's many religions.

Together with all Christians, Roman Catholics strive to view the truth about people and their relationships with God, with one another, and with the world, through the lens provided by the words and deeds of Jesus of Nazareth. Jesus made the outstanding claim that his very presence brought the Kingdom of God. This Kingdom is not a place or an institution, but "righteousness and peace and joy in the Holy Spirit" (Romans 14:17) that come from knowing God through Jesus. Because the Kingdom of God is all about recognizing God's reign over the world, it is also called the Reign of God.

Jesus stated: "I am the way, and the truth, and the life. No one comes to the Father except through me" (John 14:6). Jesus could see that his hearers recognized the presence of the Kingdom of God through the choices they made in their lives. He prompted them to see God more clearly and then to act accordingly, with love. Knowing that it is difficult to do this, Jesus stated further: "I will ask the Father, and he will give you another Advocate, to be with you forever. This is the Spirit of truth, whom the world cannot receive, because it neither sees him nor knows him" (John 14:16–17). Christians believe that this Holy Spirit is the actual presence of God in our lives today—even as we do things like read this page.

Through Jesus of Nazareth, the family of God (Father, Son, and Holy Spirit) became the family for all people. As God's Son, Jesus invited human beings to know God fully. In God's Holy Spirit, the family prospers with inspired acts of love. The love within those who believe in Christ heals their wounds, promotes their dreams, and guides their relationships with God, other people, and the planet. For Christians, the presence of this love is not a matter of preference—it is not the same as saying they love a certain type of automobile, video game, or nail polish more than others. For the Christian family, the presence of this love is a matter of truth, because Jesus of Nazareth is experienced through the ages as the only complete revelation of God's familial love for all people.

Together with other Christians, Roman Catholics do not negotiate God's love among life's spiritual options. Rather, Catholics accept that Jesus of Nazareth conclusively extended God's irreversible and full love out of the family of God and into the family of humanity. Thus Christians can really live hopefully, restraining fear and not being paralyzed by it. Christians are at home with God, even as they are amazed by the unsurpassable mansion that Jesus called the Kingdom of God.

Catholics believe that the Roman Catholic Church is the seed and beginning of the Reign of God preached by Jesus, and that it is therefore obligated to bring the good news of God's family of love to all people. Within the Catholic Church, the biblical promises of hope are fully preserved even as they are understood and applied freshly for people in every age. Mother Teresa of Calcutta (1910 to 1997) is a remarkable example of how the love of God hopes without fear. She cared unconditionally for society's discarded people—cast out because of poverty, disease, age, or uselessness.

Roman Catholic leaders attempt to clarify how the Kingdom of God can be seen today, and how it might become more effective. They have never been more welcoming of non-Christian religions than they have been since the Second Vatican Council (1962 to 1965). At that gathering the Catholic Magisterium (the teaching authority of Roman Catholic popes, cardinals, and bishops) stated:

The catholic church rejects nothing of those things which are true and holy in these religions. It regards with respect those ways of acting and living and those precepts and teachings which, though often at variance with what it holds and expounds, frequently reflect a ray of that truth which enlightens everyone. (*Declaration on the Relation of the Church to Non-Christian Religions,* number 2)

This insight is remarkable! The family of God includes not only people who are baptized in Jesus Christ but also those who entered into other relationships with God. Non-Christians can, and do, speak truthfully of God. Church teaching encourages Catholics to recognize that non-Christian religions strive for the common good of the human family.

In the New Testament, we read that God "desires everyone to be saved and to come to the knowledge of the truth," and that the one mediator between God and humanity is Jesus Christ (1 Timothy 2:4–5). Given the Catholic Church's respect for non-Christian religions, it should come as no surprise that the Church teaches that salvation through Christ is available to all. We would not deny the necessities of life to a member of our family simply because she or he lived in a different place or pursued a different lifestyle. So it is with God in his desire that all be saved:

There are those who without any fault do not know anything about Christ or his church, yet who search for God with a sincere heart and, under the influence of grace, try to put into effect the will of God as known to them through the dictate of conscience: these too can obtain eternal salvation. (Vatican Council II, *Dogmatic Constitution on the Church,* number 16)

The Church itself is a necessary sign of God's saving actions in Jesus Christ. The Church is Christ's body on earth, testifying to and advancing his saving actions for all people, Christians and non-Christians alike.

Having affirmed what is true and holy in non-Christian religions, as well as the availability of salvation to all, one might ask: Has Roman Catholicism traded away the truth of Jesus? Has it trampled on the memories of the Catholic missionaries who for centuries brought faith in Jesus to lands far and wide? The Gospel according to Matthew ends with the resurrected Jesus saying:

All authority in heaven and on earth has been given to me. Go therefore and make disciples of all nations, baptizing them in the name of the Father and of the Son and of the Holy Spirit, and teaching them to obey everything that I have commanded you. And remember, I am with you always, to the end of the age. (28:18–20)

With these words Jesus gave his followers, for all time, a missionary mandate. God loves all people and desires that all be saved. The Church is obligated to be missionary, to "go and make disciples," because it believes and participates in God's all-encompassing plan for salvation. This mandate goes hand in hand with the Church's respect for non-Christian religions. For example, some years ago Pope John Paul II and representatives of many religions spent a day praying for peace. It was the pope's Christian "faith conviction," he said, that made him turn to the representatives of the world's religions "in deep love and respect" ("The Challenge and the Possibility of Peace," number 2). Christian faith conviction, with its missionary mandate, promotes genuine understanding among the world's many faiths.

My grandfather and his new son-in-law, my father, may have had different tastes in automobiles, politics, and sports, but they were united in loving the woman who was daughter to one and wife to the other. They established a friendship based not on particular details of cars and sports, but on the welfare of the one woman they each loved differently. In a similar way, the Church encourages Catholics to advance the common truths of God that are recognized by different religions, even as Catholics observe their own particular and unsurpassable truth known by faith in Jesus Christ, and even as the various religions practice faith in their own unique ways.

Roman Catholics continuously offer God's familial love to all humanity when they present the love of God as taught and demonstrated by Jesus Christ. Today Catholics are required to increase their respect for the truth found in non-Christian religions. On the day John Paul II and representatives of many religions prayed for peace, the pope recognized the common ground among the religions. In the following excerpt from his address to the gathering, he highlights the importance of this common ground, which is at the heart of creating a peaceful world:

With the world religions we share a common respect for and obedience to conscience, which teaches all of us to seek the truth, to love and serve all individuals and peoples, and therefore to make peace among individuals and among nations.

Yes, we all hold conscience and obedience to the voice of conscience to be an essential element in the road toward a better and peaceful world. Could it be otherwise, since all men and women in this world have a common nature, a common origin and a common destiny?

If there are many and important differences among us, there is also a common ground whence to operate together in the solution of this dramatic challenge of our age: true peace or catastrophic war. ("The Challenge and the Possibility of Peace," number 2)

Jeffrey Brodd's exposition of our world's religions in this book is a fascinating exploration of thousands of years of humans' spiritual hunger and satisfaction. The leaders of the Roman Catholic Church encourage Catholics to honor Jesus Christ as they develop esteem for non-Christian religions. Like new in-laws, Catholics rely on the biblical promise of hope, which is that "all things work together for good for those who love God, who are called according to his purpose" (Romans 8:28).

NORTH
AMERICA

EUROPE

ATLANTIC
OCEAN

AFRICA

PACIFIC
OCEAN

SOUTH
AMERICA

ASIA

PACIFIC
OCEAN

INDIAN OCEAN

AUSTRALIA

1 Studying the World's Religions

Scan the news on any given day, and you will probably find examples of how religion influences everyday life around the world. Consider these newspaper excerpts:

Increasingly, Muslim women in Britain take their children to school and run errands covered head to toe in flowing black gowns that allow only a slit for their eyes. . . . Their appearance, like little else, has unnerved other Britons, testing the limits of tolerance [in Britain] and fueling debate over the role of Muslims in British life. . . . Many veiled women say they are targets of abuse. Meanwhile, there are growing efforts to place legal curbs on full-face Muslim veil, known as the niqab. (From "Muslims' Veils Test Limits of Britain's Tolerance")

No longer exclusive to traditionally Buddhist countries, Buddhist temples such as this one on the Hawaiian island of Oahu, are becoming more common all over the world.

IMAGE: © WOLFGANG KAEHLER/CORBIS

More than 800 people registered for the six yoga sessions held throughout the day yesterday, starting at 7:30 a.m., said Tim Tompkins, a yoga enthusiast and president of the Times Square Alliance, the sponsor of the event, which was scheduled to coincide with the summer solstice. "What better way to bring in the summer solstice in the most chaotic place in the city?" Mr. Tompkins said. (From "A Yoga Class's Path to Serenity Leads Through Times Square")

Evan Almighty, in which Steve Carell, playing a newly elected congressman from Buffalo, is commanded by God (Morgan Freeman) to build an ark, is a movie far less interesting than its premise. . . . But there is nonetheless a fruitful franchise in the making here, a potentially endless series of movies with popular, sometimes naughty comedians acting out wholesome modern-day versions of well-known Bible stories. (From "Niceness Counts in Ark-Building, Too")

The Sunnis have bad recent experiences with the Iraqi Army. The commander of Iraq's Fifth Division, a Shiite, was replaced by the government this year after American officers accused him of pursuing an overtly sectarian agenda by arresting and harassing Sunnis. (From "In Sweep of Iraqi Town, Sectarian Fears Percolate")

A Global Village

The preceding quotations are drawn from four different articles in the same newspaper on the same day—the *New York Times,* June 22, 2007: compelling evidence that the world's religions are part of people's everyday world. We cannot call ourselves informed citizens without having at least a basic knowledge of them.[A]

Today more than ever before, we live in a global village. Thumbing through the newspaper, logging on to the Internet, flying across the ocean, buying clothes and goods created by people far away, and a host of other activities have made us all, in a real sense, neighbors. This unprecedented variety of interactions offers an abundance of opportunities to enrich our lives, by connecting us with people who think and live differently than we do. But it also poses challenges. For one thing, it is more difficult than ever to be adequately informed about one's community—now that that "community" includes the entire world. And part of meeting this challenge is gaining a sound understanding of the world's religious traditions.

As the global community grows ever more close-knit, the relevance of religion in our day-to-day lives will continue to increase, not only at the level of international affairs, but locally as well. Most people already have—or soon will have—friends, classmates, or coworkers who belong to religious traditions quite different from their own.

Recognizing the need to understand the world's religions is one thing; achieving such an understanding is another. This book aims to help. In certain ways, the study of world re-

A

Search newspapers, magazines, the Internet, and other sources for at least three stories that mention religion. Answer this question: How does religion affect people's daily lives in each example?

ligions is especially challenging, as the following section explains. But it also offers a great opportunity for discovering the many ways of being human.

The Nature of a Religious Tradition

Religion begins with mystery. Being human inevitably prompts deep questions about our existence: Where did we come from? Where are we going? Why are we here? For that matter, what is "here"? That is, what is the nature of this world? What is the nature of the supreme or ultimate reality? Beset with such questions, we find ourselves confronting mystery on all sides. By responding to the questions, religion provides a way of living and dying meaningfully amid the mystery.

This book explores the various responses to mystery that are offered by the world's religions. Anything so intimately involved with mystery is bound to be difficult, so it will help if the study itself is demystified as much as possible. The process of demystification begins by probing the nature of the questions most religious traditions address.

Religious Questions

Human beings, presumably unlike any other members of the animal kingdom, have the capacity to question such fundamental things as the source and the meaning of their existence. We are self-conscious beings. Along with being physical, rational, and emotional, we have the capacity for self-reflection; we have a conscience; we can ponder our own nature. We are spiritual (although the term *spiritual* is open to interpretation). And by virtue of our spirituality, we ask—and answer—life's most basic questions. Because these questions are more or less pertinent to each religious tradition, they can be organized into a kind of framework for studying the world's religions.[B]

Not everyone chooses to answer these basic religious questions by following a religious tradition. Some people, even though they regard themselves as spiritual, are not members of a specific religion. But others find that a religion helps them grapple with religious questions. Religions offer responses that have been tested by time, in some cases by thousands of years. They are also fortified by the richness of tradition and by the shared experience of community.

Regardless of how we choose to respond to them, religious questions are inevitable. Studying these questions can help us better understand the nature of each religious tradition. Let us consider the primary ones.

What Is the Human Condition?

The initial religious question concerns the basic nature of the human condition: What is our essential nature? Are we merely what we appear to be—physical bodies somehow equipped with the capacity to think and to feel? or are we endowed with a deeper spiritual essence, some form of soul? Are human beings by nature good, or evil, or somewhere in-between, perhaps originally good but now flawed in some way?

Often a religion's view of the basic nature of the human condition is set forth in its account of human origins. The story of Adam and Eve in the Garden of Eden, told in the Jewish and Christian bibles and also in the Qur'an (or Koran, the sacred book of Islam), is one clear example.

Suffering is an important aspect of the human condition. All religions recognize that we suffer. The question is, Why do we suffer? If we are by nature good and in no need of greater perfection, then of course suffering is not our fault. But if we are evil, or somehow flawed, perhaps we deserve to suffer. A religion typically describes a means of overcoming suffering—and of responding to the human condition in general—through the

B
The terms *spiritual* and *religious* often mean different things to different people. What does each term mean to you?

attainment of some higher state of spiritual maturity.[C]

What Is Spiritual Perfection?

Almost every religion describes what is needed to fulfill our spiritual potential most perfectly. Some religions teach a form of spiritual perfection that can be attained in this life. Others teach that perfection comes only in an afterlife. In either case perfection is a difficult thing to attain; in fact some religions teach that it is impossible to attain on our own, without divine assistance. Therefore religions tend to acknowledge the goodness of being as spiritually mature and near to perfection as possible, and do not always propose that perfection is a simple all-or-none condition.

Later in this study of religions, you will encounter specific examples that explore various approaches to spiritual maturity and spiritual perfection. For now briefly consider three questions about the way a religion defines spiritual perfection: What is ethical—that is, how are we to act while living in the world? How do we transcend the human condition? And how do we attain salvation?

What is ethical? Religions typically prescribe an ethical life as a basic requirement for the journey toward spiritual perfection. Indeed teachings regarding right and wrong constitute a significant part of most religious traditions.

How do we transcend the human condition? Some forms of spiritual perfection can be attained in this life, either temporarily or eternally. Buddhist enlightenment is one example. These forms all involve a type of **transcendence,** or overcoming of the normal limitations imposed by the human condition. Of course, we can respond to the challenges of being human in a variety of ways. Some people simply try to ignore them by allowing a certain numbness of the spirit. Others become workaholics to block them out. Some hide behind a veil of drugs or alcohol. Religions normally insist on a different type of response, a form of transcendence that brings one face-to-face with the human condition, and then raises one above it or allows one to see through it. (The precise descriptions of this transcendence vary by religion.) The Buddhist who has attained enlightenment, for example, while continuing to inhabit a physical body with the usual discomforts and needs, is said to maintain a state of indescribable spiritual tranquillity and bliss.

How do we attain salvation? Most religions teach that spiritual maturity or perfection is closely related to some form of salvation from the ultimate limitation imposed by the human condition: death. Religions that emphasize forms of transcendence typically hold that there is a direct connection between the transcendence attained in this life and final salvation. Some forms of Buddhism teach that the attainment of enlightenment in this life leads to *nirvana,* the final liberation. Religions such as Christianity and Islam, which teach that salvation depends on the divine, tend to maintain that final spiritual perfection awaits in the afterlife, sometimes after the individual's salvation has already been assured. According to this view, spiritual maturation continues even in a heavenly afterlife.

C
Contemplate the human condition by comparing the situation of humans with that of a favorite animal (it could be a pet). Does the animal think or feel, like people do? Does it seem to have a spiritual essence or soul? Does it seem to be by nature good, or evil, or somewhere in-between?

In Christianity the cross is often used as a symbol of salvation. This mosaic is from a church in Ravenna, Italy.

IMAGE: SCALA/ART RESOURCE, NY

What Is Our Destiny?

As spiritual beings, we ponder our destiny. We wonder, Where are we going, ultimately? Most (though not all) religions provide answers to that question, and their answers are closely linked to the issues of spiritual perfection.

According to some religions, human beings face two possible destinies: one leads to reward, typically eternal life in paradise, and the other leads to condemnation. Individual destiny is linked to the question of spiritual maturation: the degree to which one has achieved perfection naturally corresponds to one's prospects for reward in the afterlife.

The question of destiny is more complex for religions that teach that human beings live more than one lifetime—religions such as Hinduism, Buddhism, and Jainism. In this case the immediate destiny after this life is generally not the ultimate, final destiny, but just another step toward the final destiny. Nevertheless, the need to seek spiritual maturity (if not perfection) in this life remains vital, because the level of one's maturity (or perfection) tends to determine the nature of one's future life.

What Is the Nature of the World?

Along with answering questions about human beings, religions also answer questions about the world. Where did the world come from? Is it real, or is it just some kind of cosmic illusion? Is it sacred, perhaps even living? or is it merely matter? Is it a help or a hindrance to the religious quest?

Such questions belong to the general category **cosmology**—the understanding of the nature of the universe. The answers to cosmological questions tend to determine a religion's degree of interest in the natural world. Some religions express such interest through support of scientific inquiry and theories regarding the natural world, while others tend to be suspicious of science.[D]

What Is Ultimate Reality, and How Is It Revealed?

Finally, there is the religious question of ultimate reality (or for Western traditions especially, God). Theistic religions hold a belief in God or in multiple gods. These religions teach a certain theology, or doctrine regarding the divine. The theologies of the world include a range of basic perspectives: **monotheism** (belief in only one God), **polytheism** (belief in many gods), and **pantheism** (belief that the divine reality exists in everything), to name but a few.

Nontheistic religions do not hold a belief in a god who is essentially relevant for us, although they sometimes do hold a belief in various divine or semidivine beings. Some of these religions teach that all reality is essentially one thing, and that human beings are part of the ultimate reality.

Most religions also teach that the supreme or ultimate reality, whatever form it takes, is somehow revealed to humans. This **revelation** usually takes place through sacred stories or myths, or through various types of religious experience.

Seven Dimensions of Religion

Exploring the basic questions to which religions respond helps us understand the functions of religions. Considering the elements that make up religions helps us understand the forms of religions. Scholar Ninian Smart suggests that all the religious traditions manifest seven dimensions: experiential, mythic, doctrinal, ethical, ritual, social, and material. These dimensions are not exclusive of one another: for example, myths often set forth patterns of ritual. Indeed the seven dimensions are intertwined and complementary, weaving a rich tapestry through which religions respond to humans' basic questions, offering a doctrine here, prescribing a ritual there, and so forth. All religions use the same seven elements to

D
Summarize your personal cosmology—your own understanding of the nature of the world. Focus especially on the following questions: Where did the world come from? Is the world somehow a living, organic entity, or is it merely inorganic matter?

E

Like the terms *religious* and *spiritual, faith* tends to mean different things to different people. What does *faith* mean to you?

create their own unique tapestry, often emphasizing one dimension more, another dimension less. Zen Buddhism, for example, has a strong experiential dimension but says relatively little about doctrines.

Experiential

Religions commonly begin with the religious experiences of individuals. Some of these beginnings are famous and easy to identify. When a young prince named Gautama experienced enlightenment under the *bodhi* tree, he became the Buddha, and Buddhism was born. When Muhammad began to experience revelations from Allah, Islam began to take form. Other beginnings are not so easily identified. Moreover, religious experiences can be part of anyone's religious life; they do not always result in a new religion.

Faith generally belongs to the category religious experience, although it also has doctrinal aspects. In the New Testament, for instance, the Apostle Paul describes faith as being closely related to experience of the Holy Spirit, and involving more than just intellectual belief.

The world's major religions acknowledge numerous types of religious experience, some of them astounding. Generally speaking, in theistic religions God is experienced as a holy presence who is other (that is, as a being distinct from the individual). This experience of God is often characterized by two separate emotions: awe-inspiring fear, and fascination. A well-known example of this type of experience is the revelation of God to Moses on Mount Sinai, through the burning bush. Moses was fearful of God, yet drawn in fascination toward the divine presence.

In nontheistic religions, religious experience usually takes the form of **mysticism.** In one basic type of mysticism, found in Hinduism and other religions, the individual becomes one with the divine through inward contemplation. Another form of religious experience, known as the vision quest, is found in many primal religions, which include Native American traditions.[E]

Mythic

The concept of **myth** may not be familiar to us because most people no longer hold a predominantly mythic worldview. The matter is further complicated by our tendency to use the term *myth* in various ways. Typically we equate myths with falsehoods—but in the study of world religions, myths actually convey important truths.

We Westerners tend to base our perspectives on history and science, acquiring knowl-

The religious experience of Moses is depicted in *Moses Before the Burning Bush,* by the Italian painter Raphael (1483 to 1520).

IMAGE: SCALA/ART RESOURCE, NY

edge through empirical observation and rational thinking. Myths are both nonhistorical and nonrational. But they do not necessarily conflict with history and science, nor are they necessarily false or irrational. Myths are sources of sacred truth and are therefore powerful, for they give meaning to life.

Myths take the form of sacred stories that are passed along from one generation to the next. Many are conveyed orally, though some are recorded in scripture. Myths are often set in primordial time, a period in the distant past somehow set apart from the ordinary present. They commonly tell of the origins of humans and the world. Myths set forth fundamental knowledge regarding the nature of things and the proper way to live.

The Genesis account of the world's creation is one such story or myth. It provides knowledge about a number of basic issues: the world was created by God; human beings were created in the image of God and are by nature good; humans are meant to have "dominion" over the other creatures of the world; and so forth. These mythic ideas depend neither on history nor on science, but they remain sacred truths for Jews, Christians, and Muslims alike.[F]

Doctrinal

For many people, the most obvious and basic aspect of religion is belief. Adherents of a religion believe in something, namely, the creeds, doctrines, or teachings of their religion. Christians believe, for example, in the Apostles' Creed and in the doctrine of the Trinity. The belief aspect of religion is categorized as the doctrinal dimension.

Doctrines, creeds, and other teachings commonly originate in lived religious experience. They also derive from myths. Whereas myth and experience tend in some ways to defy the rational impulses of the mind, doctrines make sense of the content of experience and myth. They are often recorded in sacred texts, or scriptures, along with the myths and the accounts of revelation and other religious experiences that serve as the foundations of religions.

Ethical

Religions tend to devote much attention to **ethics:** How are we to act while living in the world? The ethical dimension includes many sets of teachings that respond to that question: for example, the Ten Commandments in the Christian tradition, which have striking parallels in some other traditions. The ethical dimension also incorporates more general ethical principles, such as the Buddhist ideal of compassion, which is notably similar to the Christian ideal of love for one's neighbor.

Ritual

Worship is a common aspect of religions, taking a variety of forms and occupying much of an individual's religious life. Most forms of worship are carried out through some formal practice, or **ritual.** Like belief, ritual is very familiar to most of us. Many religious rituals reenact a myth or sacred story. For example, every Muslim ideally will make at least one pilgrimage to Mecca, the most holy city of Islam. Various aspects of the pilgrimage reenact the sacred story of Muhammad's original journey to Mecca, a leading event in the founding of the religion.

Social

Religions naturally involve communities, and most people consider the communal aspect of religion significant and attractive. A sense of community, of belonging to a group such as a tribe or parish or congregation is usually empowering for individuals. The shared experience of community also fortifies religions themselves, and often results in some form of organization, typically including a hierarchy of leadership. For example, religions usually recognize one level of membership for officials or priests, and another level for common adherents. Often

F
Myth is not as strong an element in the modern, scientific world as it was in earlier ages. Still, as the Creation story in Genesis suggests, some of our basic perspectives about life are derived from mythic sources. What other mythic truths—truths that are based on neither history nor science, but that give life meaning and direction—are prevalent in your society?

particular figures are thought to embody the ideals of spiritual perfection: the Taoist sage and the Christian saint are two such figures.

Material

The sacred architecture of cathedrals, temples, and other structures of worship, and the art within them, are among humanity's beautiful cultural achievements. Icons, such as the crucifix and statues of the Buddha, are part of this material dimension of religion. So too are books of scripture. Other types of sacred entities, whether natural (such as mountains) or of human construction (such as cities), also are highly significant for some religions. In India, for example, Hindus consider almost every major river sacred.[G]

Some Challenges and Rewards of Studying the World's Religions

Several issues might make studying the world's religions unsettling. For example, it would seem that by definition, ultimate reality must be the same for all humans. Certainly the monotheistic religions consider God to be the God of all. But if that is the case, can there be more than one true religion? Are the religions saying essentially the same thing, even though they are using different words filtered through different historical and cultural frameworks? Are they in basic agreement about the truth? If so, does the matter of choosing a religion simply come down to personal preference?

These are difficult questions, and it is unrealistic to hope they will all be answered satisfactorily by the end of this study. Besides, as noted at the beginning of this chapter, religion is grounded in mystery, and surely we should not expect to penetrate such mystery entirely. We can, however, make progress toward understanding, by clarifying a proper perspective from which to examine the world's religions.

Two Approaches

A study of the world's religions is enriched when it is approached in two ways. First, it should be approached using a comparative methodology. Friedrich Max Müller, one of the founders of the study of comparative religions, pointed out that to know just one religion is to know none. As we move from chapter to chapter in this book, the dimensions of religion, along with the common questions to which different religions respond, should become clearer. Studying many religions should enable us to know each one, including our own, more precisely.

Second, the study of religions should be approached with **empathy,** which is the capacity for seeing things from another's perspective. We are familiar with the saying that we should never judge a person until we have walked a mile in his or her shoes. Empathy requires the use of the imagination, and can be quite challenging. It is rewarding too, providing a needed tool for gaining insight into the ways of others. The study of religions would not advance far if it lacked such insight.[H]

Objectives

What can we hope to gain from a broad study of the world's religions? For one thing, we can strive to become knowledgeable about their responses to the most fundamental religious questions asked by human beings all over the world. All religions are treasure troves of wisdom, and everyone can benefit from exploring them. For another thing, we can try to become better acquainted with the seven dimensions of religion through the study of abundant examples. Finally, we can expect to emerge from this study with a greatly enhanced understanding of the people who follow the religions we have explored. That, in turn, can enrich us in our roles as citizens of the global village.

G

Identify at least two examples of sacred entities, art, or architecture in your community. Compare the examples in terms of how they express religious ideas and provoke emotions.

H

It is important to cultivate empathy—the capacity for seeing things from another's perspective—when studying the religions of others. Try applying the saying about empathy, that we need to walk in another person's shoes, to a family member or close friend. What do you think life looks like from that person's perspective?

Chapter Review

1. What issues do people usually address when they ask questions about the human condition?
2. How does spiritual maturity or perfection relate to the quest for salvation?
3. Briefly explain how religions differ over the question of destiny.
4. Name some ways religions perceive the nature of the world.
5. Describe the difference between theistic and nontheistic religions.
6. How do most religions teach that the ultimate reality is usually revealed?
7. Describe in general terms the religious experience of the theistic religions. Then briefly compare it with the religious experience of the nontheistic religions.
8. Briefly explain the concept of myth.
9. Identify at least two dimensions of religion, in addition to the mythic, doctrinal, and experiential.
10. What is one benefit of using a comparative approach to study the world's religions?
11. What is empathy, and how is it applied to the study of world religions?

Glossary

cosmology. The understanding of the nature of the universe.

empathy. The capacity for seeing things from another's perspective, and an important methodological approach for studying religions.

ethics. A dimension of religion that deals with how we are to act while living in the world.

faith. Experience of the divine or holy presence, sometimes involving intellectual belief and sometimes emphasizing personal trust.

monotheism. The belief in only one god.

mysticism. A category of religious experiences characterized by communing or uniting with the divine through inward contemplation.

myth. A story (often recorded in scripture) that tends to answer questions of origins and serves as a source of sacred truth.

pantheism. The belief that the divine reality exists in everything.

polytheism. The belief in many gods.

revelation. The transmission of the divine will or knowledge to human beings, typically through myths or some form of religious experience.

ritual. Formal worship practice, often based on the reenactment of a myth.

transcendence. The overcoming of the normal limitations imposed by the human condition, whether temporarily or abidingly.

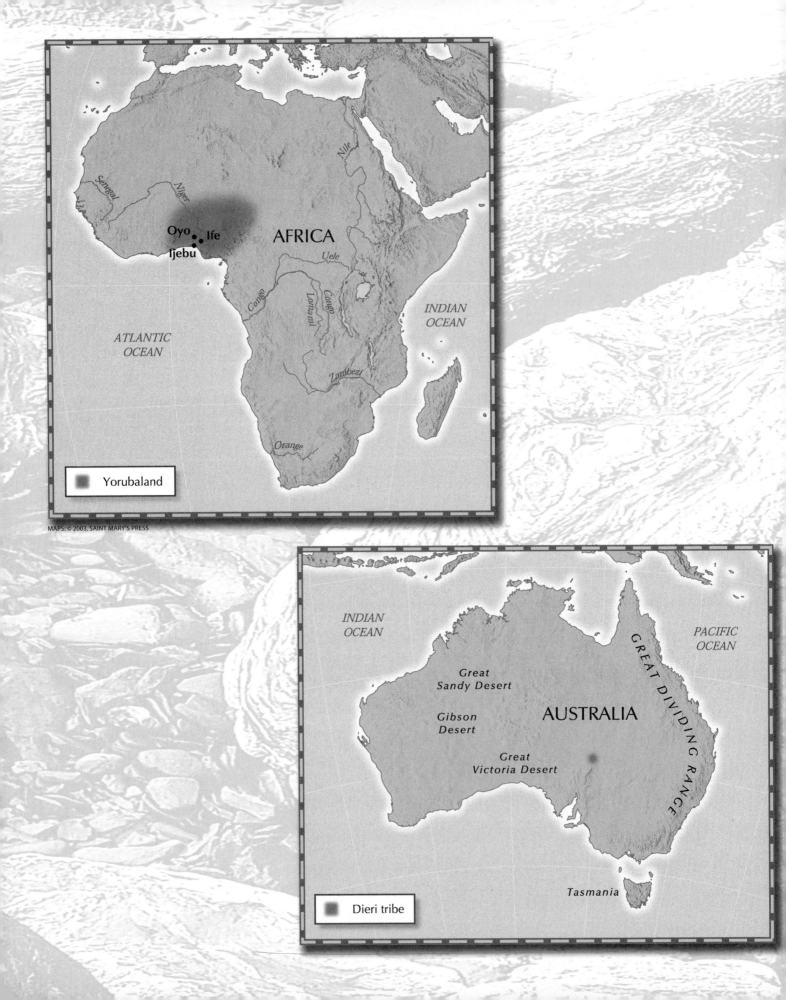

Yorubaland

Oyo
Ife
Ijebu

AFRICA

Senegal
Niger
Nile
Uele
Congo
Lomami
Congo
Zambezi
Orange

ATLANTIC OCEAN

INDIAN OCEAN

Dieri tribe

AUSTRALIA

Great Sandy Desert
Gibson Desert
Great Victoria Desert

GREAT DIVIDING RANGE

INDIAN OCEAN

PACIFIC OCEAN

Tasmania

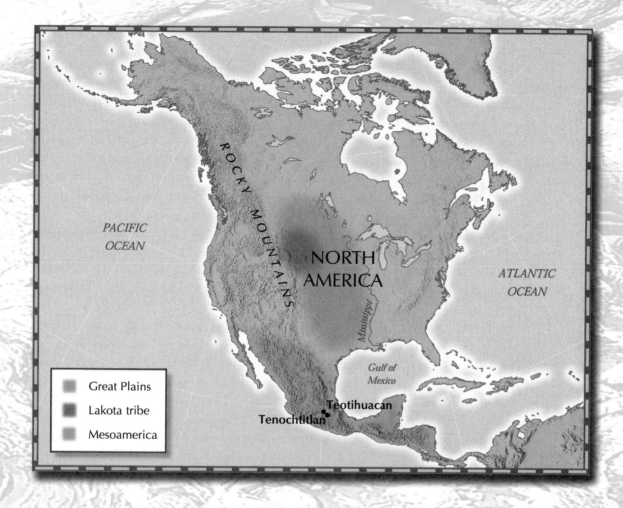

Great Plains

Lakota tribe

Mesoamerica

2 Primal Religious Traditions

The Nature of Primal Religions

Since prehistoric times small groups of people throughout the world have practiced their own unique forms of religion. Some of those religions continue to be practiced, especially among the native inhabitants of Australia, Africa, and the Americas. We refer to those religions as primal because they tended to come before the religious traditions we will study in the remaining chapters of this book.

Beginning our study with these first religions is a good idea for two reasons. One is that primal religions provide special insight into the mythic and ritual dimensions of religion. Primal peoples have tended to preserve a mythic orientation toward life. Their myths, and the rituals that reenact them, remain essential sources of knowledge and power for important aspects of their lives.

The other reason for studying primal religions first is that all religions stem, more or less directly, from primal beginnings. For example, the ancestor of Judaism, the religion of the ancient Israelites, was in its early stages a primal religion, exhibiting features similar to those discussed in this chapter. Other religions, such as Hinduism in India and Shinto in Japan, are also rooted in the primal traditions of early peoples.

Along with having originated first, primal religions generally have been the traditions of nonliterate people, which means they do not depend on scriptures or written teachings, as do most other religions. What they lack in written texts, however, they often make up for in oral material—myths or stories that are passed down from generation to generation.

Primal religions tend to be the traditions of tribal peoples, organized in small groups that dwell in villages as opposed to large cities. There are exceptions, however, including the Yoruba of Africa and the Aztecs of Mesoamerica. In this and other ways, primal traditions are diverse. It is therefore crucial that we avoid making sweeping generalizations about them.

In the light of this vast diversity, this chapter does not attempt to describe all primal religions. Instead it focuses on four rather specific examples: the Aborigines of Australia, the Yoruba, the Plains Indians of North America, and the Aztecs. Once we have considered some particular features of each of these traditions, we will reflect on general themes that tend to be common to primal religions.

In the Apache Sunrise Dance, girls entering puberty are painted white with sacred clay and cornmeal. The rite symbolizes the passage into adulthood.

Religion of the Australian Aborigines

The Aborigines, the native people of Australia, were largely unaffected by outsiders until the arrival of Europeans some two hundred years ago. The Aborigines maintained traditions extending many thousands of years into the past. In some areas, notably in the northern and central regions of Australia, those traditions remain largely intact today.

Australia is a continent of great diversity. Its geography ranges from lush forested mountains to harsh deserts, and those differences have produced a variety of social groups that speak about forty separate languages and have differing customs. Australia's primal religious life is diverse as well, but it possesses enough common elements that we can speak of one Aboriginal religion while acknowledging its varying manifestations.

The Dreaming: The Eternal Time of the Ancestors

The foundation of Aboriginal religion is the concept of the Dreaming. According to Aboriginal belief, the world was originally formless. Then at a certain point in the mythic past, supernatural beings called **Ancestors** emerged and roamed about the earth. The Ancestors gave shape to the landscape and created the various forms of life, including the first human beings. They organized humans into tribes, specified the territory each tribe was to occupy, and determined each tribe's language, social rules, and customs. When the Ancestors had finished and departed from the earth, they left behind symbols of their presence, in the form of natural landmarks, rock paintings, and so on.

This mythic period of the Ancestors is called **the Dreaming.** In a very real sense, this period lives on, for the Aborigines believe that the spiritual essence of the Ances-

Ayers Rock is a sacred place for Australian Aborigines.

tors remains in the various symbols they left behind. The sites at which these symbols are found are thought to be charged with sacred power. Only certain individuals are allowed to visit them, and they must be approached in a special way. Rather than traveling the shortest routes to the sites, visitors follow the paths that were originally taken by the Ancestors in the Dreaming. Their ritual approach reenacts the mythic events of the Dreaming, and through it the Aborigines re-create their world as it existed in the beginning. This re-creation gives them access to the endless sources of sacred power of these sites. The Aborigines inhabit a mythic geography—a world in which every notable landmark, whether it be a rock outcropping, a watering hole, or a cave, is believed to have great religious significance. Aboriginal cosmology—or understanding of the nature of the universe—thus plays a constant role in Aboriginal religion.

The spiritual essence of the Ancestors is also believed to reside within each individual. An unborn child becomes animated by a particular Ancestor when the mother or another relative makes some form of contact with a sacred site. Usually this animation involves a ritual that draws the Ancestor's spiritual essence into the unborn child.

Aboriginal rock art evokes the Dreaming.

A

Empathy—seeing something from another's perspective—helps us gain the insight we need to understand and appreciate the diversity of world religions. Striving to understand the Aboriginal concept of a mythic geography offers a good opportunity for practicing empathy.

Think of a favorite outdoor area, such as a place in the wilderness, a beach, a park, or your backyard. Imagine that every notable landmark has great religious significance and that your every move within the area is undertaken as if it were a religious ritual. Now describe the area and your experience of being there.

Through this connection each Aborigine is a living representation of an Ancestor. This relationship is symbolized by a **totem**—the natural form in which the Ancestor appeared in the Dreaming. The totem may be an animal, such as a kangaroo or snake, or a rock formation or other feature of the landscape. An individual will always be identified in certain ways with the Ancestor. The system of belief and ritual based on totems is called totemism. Totemism is a motif that is common to many primal traditions.

The Ancestors of the Dreaming also continually nourish the natural world. They are sources of life of all kinds. For a particular Ancestor's nourishing power to flow forth into the world, the human beings associated with that Ancestor must perform proper rituals.

The supernatural, the human world, and the world of nature are thus considered to be delicately interrelated. Aboriginal religious life seeks to maintain harmonious relationships among these three aspects of reality. Such harmony is itself a form of spiritual perfection.[A]

Animating the Power of the Dreaming: Aboriginal Religious Life

Aboriginal religion is the entire process of re-creating the mythic past of the Dreaming in order to tap into its sacred power. This process is accomplished primarily through ritual, the reenactment of myth. It also involves maintaining the structure of society as it was originally established by the Ancestors. This, in turn, requires the performance of certain rituals, such as those of initiation.

For Aborigines, ritual is essential if life is to have meaning. It is only through ritual that the sacred power of the Dreaming can be accessed and experienced. Furthermore, Aborigines believe that the rituals themselves were taught to the first humans by the Ancestors in the Dreaming.

Behind every ritual lies a myth that tells of certain actions of the Ancestors during the Dreaming. For example, myths that describe the creation of the kangaroo, a chief food source of the Aborigines, spell out precisely how and where the act of creation took

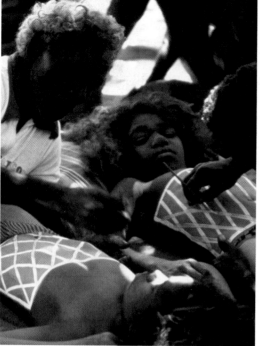

Left: Aborigine men paint initiates' bodies in preparation for ceremonies that will bring the young people to awareness of their role in tribal life.
Right: An initiation dance.

place. Rituals that reenact these myths are performed at the corresponding sacred sites in order to replenish the local population of kangaroos.[B]

Taboo:
The Basis of Aboriginal Social Structure

Aboriginal society is carefully structured. Certain people are forbidden to participate in certain rituals. The basis of this structure is the concept of **taboo,** which dictates that certain things and activities, owing to their sacred nature, are set aside for specific members of the group and are forbidden to others. Violation of this principle has on occasion been punishable by death.

The sites and rituals associated with certain Ancestors are for men only. Others, such as those connected with childbirth, are for women only. Restrictions are also based on maturity and on an individual's amount of religious training. Usually the older members of the tribe are in charge of important rituals.

Young people achieve religious maturity and training in part through the elaborate initiation rituals practiced throughout Aboriginal Australia.[C]

Initiation:
Symbolic Death, Spiritual Rebirth

Even before birth each Aborigine possesses the spiritual essence of her or his totemic Ancestor. Initiation rituals awaken young people to this spiritual identity, and at the same time redefine their social identity within the tribe. The rituals bring about the symbolic death of childhood, which prepares the way for the spiritual rebirth that is a necessary step toward adulthood. Throughout the rituals, myths of the Dreaming are taught to the young people. Through the rituals and myths, young Aborigines learn the essential truths about their world and how they are to act within it.

Both boys and girls undergo initiation, though usually the rites are especially elaborate for boys. As an example, consider the male initiation rites practiced in the nineteenth century by the Dieri tribe of south-central Australia.

The initiation rituals of the Dieri took place around a boy's ninth birthday (though the age

B
Every society has rituals that reenact origins, just as the Aborigines do. Some contemporary rituals are religious in nature, whereas others involve patriotism and other aspects of society. List as many such rituals as you can, briefly explaining how each is a reenactment of an original event.

C
To what extent does your society apply restrictions similar to those of the Aboriginal concept of taboo?

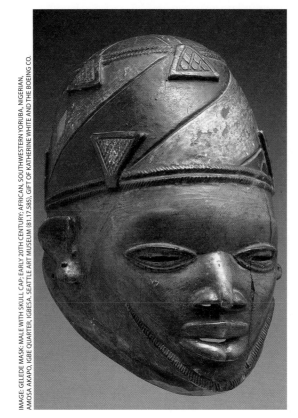

The amulets on this Yoruba mask illustrate the impact of Islam in Africa. As primal traditions develop throughout history, they incorporate elements of other religions.

IMAGE: GELEDE MASK: MALE WITH SKULL CAP: EARLY 20TH CENTURY: AFRICAN, SOUTHWESTERN YORUBA, NIGERIAN, AMOSA AKAPO, IGBE QUARTER, IGBESA. SEATTLE ART MUSEUM (81.17.585), GIFT OF KATHERINE WHITE AND THE BOEING CO.

of wood attached to a long string made from human hair. The bull-roarer re-created the sound of the deities and, because of its great power, was taboo for women.

These initiation rituals were followed by a period of months during which the boy lived alone in the wilderness, until his wounds healed and the blood wore off his skin. When he returned to his tribe, he was greeted with much rejoicing and celebration. His rites of initiation completed, the boy had become a man.

It might be difficult for an outsider to understand the reasons for these various rituals. This difficulty illustrates the great power of myth. Aboriginal myth creates a reality that is unique to the Aborigines, a world of their own in which such initiation rituals not only make sense but are essential if life is to have meaning. The power of myth, and the performance of ritual to reenact myth, are basic features of all primal traditions.^D

D
What experiences have served as rituals of initiation for you, marking your passage from childhood to adulthood?

could vary) and lasted for months. In the first ritual, intended as a symbolic death, the initiate's two lower middle teeth were knocked out and buried in the ground.

Other rituals followed, including circumcision (removal of the foreskin of the penis), which for many Aboriginal tribes is the symbolic death par excellence. According to one myth, two Ancestors had shown the Dieri in the Dreaming how to circumcise with a stone knife.

The main initiation ritual was called the Wilyaru. The initiate stood with his eyes closed as men took turns cutting their forearms and letting their blood fall on him, until he became caked with dried blood. This blood served to connect the boy symbolically with his relatives. Next, the boy's neck and back were struck with wounds that were intended to leave scars, yet another symbol of death. At this point the boy was given a bull-roarer, a sacred instrument consisting of a piece

An African Tradition: The Religion of the Yoruba

Africa, the second largest continent in terms of landmass, is home to some four hundred million people and several hundred religions, including the religion of the Yoruba. Though hardly representative of all African religions, the Yoruba tradition is similar enough to some others to serve as a good example. Yoruba society, today consisting of about ten million people, has endured for more than one thousand years. Its ancient religion has produced artwork that is famous and much admired.

The Yoruba and Their Universe

The Yoruba live in the western regions of central Africa, in Nigeria, Benin, and Togo. Yoruba designates not a unified nation, but rather a group with a common language and culture. Throughout their history the Yoruba have favored living in cities. Some of those cities, such as Ife, Oyo, and Ijebu, have been quite large. The cities have tended to maintain independence from one another. Ife has always been the center of Yoruba religion, because it was there, the Yoruba believe, that the god Orisha-nla first began to create the world.

Yoruba cosmology depicts reality as being divided into two separate worlds: heaven and earth. Heaven is the invisible home of the gods and the ancestors. Earth is the world of normal experience, the visible home of human beings, who are descended from the gods. Earth is also populated by a deviant form of human beings, witches and sorcerers, who can cause disastrous harm if not controlled.

The purpose of the Yoruba religion is to maintain the balance between the human beings of earth and the gods and ancestors of heaven, while guarding against the evil deeds of sorcerers and witches.

Gods and Ancestors: The Inhabitants of Heaven

Primal traditions commonly hold a belief in both a supreme god and a host of less powerful deities. The supreme god of the Yoruba is Olorun, and the many deities the Yoruba worship are known as **orishas** (aw-ree-shahs′). The supreme god, lesser deities, and ancestors all inhabit heaven.

Olorun, the High God

The Yoruba believe that Olorun is the primary, original source of power in the universe. All other life forms ultimately owe their existence to him. But Olorun is distant and remote, and not involved in human affairs. He is therefore worshiped hardly at all, except in prayer. No shrines or rituals are assigned to him, and no sacrifices are made on his behalf. Instead, many other gods, the *orishas,* function as mediators between Olorun and human beings.

Orishas

The *orishas* are lesser deities, compared with the supreme Olorun, but are nonetheless truly significant. All are sources of sacred power and can help or harm human beings, depending on how well the rituals designed to appease them are carried out.

Hundreds of *orishas* exist. Some are worshiped by all Yoruba, others by only one family group. An especially significant *orisha* is Orisha-nla, whom most Yoruba believe created the earth. Ogun, the god of iron and of war, has a special status. Originally he was a human being, the first king of the city of Ife. After he died he became a god, and now he inhabits the border area between the ancestors and the rest of the *orishas.* The most complex *orisha* is Esu, who contains both good and evil properties. Precisely because of this, Esu mediates between heaven and earth. Worship of Esu is included in the worship of any other *orisha,* and Esu has a place in every shrine.

IMAGE: STAFF FOR ESU (OGO ELEGBA); NIGERIAN; YORUBA, EKITI, BAMGBOYE OF ODO-OWA. SEATTLE ART MUSEUM (81.17.598), GIFT OF KATHERINE WHITE AND THE BOEING CO.; PHOTO BY PAUL MACAPIA

Esu is a Yoruba *orisha* who embodies both good and evil and mediates between heaven and earth.

Esu's dual nature as both good and evil, and his corresponding role as mediator between heaven and earth, make him a **trickster figure,** a sort of mischievous supernatural being. Tricksters are significant in many primal traditions throughout the world.

The Ancestors of the Living

The heavenly ancestors are deceased humans who have acquired supernatural status. Like the *orishas,* the ancestors possess sacred power that can help or harm the living. Therefore they too are worshiped through rituals at special shrines.

There are two types of ancestors. Family ancestors gained their supernatural status by earning a good reputation and living to an old age, and are now worshiped only by their own families. Deified ancestors were important human figures known throughout Yoruba society, and are now worshiped by large numbers of people.[E]

Connecting Heaven and Earth: Ritual Practitioners

Several types of ritual practitioners mediate between the gods and ancestors in heaven, and the human beings on earth. For whatever religious need a worshiper is attempting to fulfill, there is a specialist who can facilitate communication with the appropriate deity or ancestor.

For example: The head of a family is responsible for worshiping the family's ancestors and does so in the home at the family shrine. The king, or chief, of a city is in charge of the city's annual festivals and performs a host of other religious functions. The many priests oversee the various rituals carried out at the shrines of each *orisha.*

Among the priests who engage in specialized services are **diviners.** Those priests practice the art of **divination,** through which one's future can be learned. Becoming a diviner requires years of training, and the role is usually passed from parent to child. Divi-

nation is an extremely important aspect of Yoruba religion because knowledge of one's future is considered essential for determining how to proceed with one's life. The procedure involves an intricate system of hundreds of wisdom stories, which the diviner knows by memory. The diviner determines which of the stories are relevant for an individual, and from those stories interprets the individual's future.

Another ritual specialist mediates between the ancestors and the living. Wearing an elaborate ceremonial mask and costume, this specialist becomes a living representation of an ancestor by dancing at festivals. When an important person dies, the specialist imitates that person and conveys comforting messages from the deceased to the living.

The prevalence of these ritual practitioners clearly illustrates the importance of mediating, and thereby maintaining balance, between heaven and earth. Most primal religions share the understanding that the boundaries between the human and the supernatural realms are very thin and can easily be crossed over.

Religion of the North American Plains Indians

Interpreting the latest evidence, scholars believe that humans first came to North America some twenty thousand to thirty thousand years ago. They migrated from Asia, probably by crossing over the Bering Strait (situated between Russia and Alaska). They gradually spread out and eventually inhabited large regions of both North and South America.

Those first inhabitants of America, or Native Americans, formed many cultural groups, each with its own religion. For example, the peoples of the North American Plains comprised more than thirty tribes speaking seven distinct languages.

The Plains are vast, stretching from the Canadian provinces of Alberta, Saskatch-

Native Americans of the Northern Plains participate in a reenactment of the Battle of the Little Bighorn, in which the Lakota played a leading role. Such interest in history and other cultural aspects has become a common feature of the revitalization of Native American traditions.

ewan, and Manitoba southward to the Gulf of Mexico, bordered on the west by the Rocky Mountains and on the east by the Mississippi River. The culture we now associate with this area formed relatively recently, after the arrival of horses from Europe in the seventeenth century. Domestic horses enabled the Plains Indians to become great hunters of buffalo and other game. Numerous tribes migrated into the Plains region, exchanging ideas with one another. This exchange was aided by the use of a common sign language understood by all the tribes. The religion of the Plains is therefore somewhat representative of American Indian religion in general. Today this religion serves as the model of pan-Indian religion, a recent and popular movement uniting many tribes from across North America. As a result, Plains religion continues to be of vital interest to native peoples throughout North America.

The Plains peoples shared a number of religious features, including basic beliefs resembling those of the large and influential Lakota tribe. All the tribes performed two basic rituals, the vision quest and the Sun Dance.

Basic Beliefs of the Lakota

The Lakota are also known as the Western Sioux, although *Sioux* originated as a pejorative label, from an enemy tribe's term for "snakes." These people inhabited eastern Montana and Wyoming, the western regions of the Dakotas, and parts of Nebraska. This is an especially important tribe for a number of reasons. The Lakota are remembered for having led a confederacy of tribes that defeated Custer and his troops in the Battle of the Little Bighorn in 1876. In 1890, as the wars between Indians and whites came to an end, more than two hundred Lakota were massacred at Wounded Knee, South Dakota. Today about seventy thousand Lakota live on reservations in Manitoba, Montana, and North and South Dakota.

A Young Man's Vision Quest

John Fire / Lame Deer (1903 to 1976) was born on the Rosebud Reservation in South Dakota. In his lifetime he was a rancher, a rodeo cowboy, and a reservation police officer, but he is best known as a Lakota Sioux holy man. In this excerpt from his autobiography, Lame Deer describes his boyhood experience of a vision quest, or hanblechia *(Lakota for "crying for a vision").*

I was all alone on the hilltop. I sat there in the vision pit, a hole dug into the hill, my arms hugging my knees as I watched old man Chest, the medicine man who had brought me there, disappear far down in the valley. He was just a moving black dot among the pines, and soon he was gone altogether. (Page 11)

Night was coming on. I was still lightheaded and dizzy from my first sweat bath in which I had purified myself before going up the hill. I had never been in a sweat lodge before. I had sat in the little beehive-shaped hut made of bent willow branches and covered with blankets to keep the heat in. Old Chest and three other medicine men had been in the lodge with me. I had my back against the wall, edging as far away as I could from the red-hot stones glowing in the center. As Chest poured water over the rocks, hissing white steam enveloped me and filled my lungs. I thought the heat would kill me, burn the eyelids off my face! But right in the middle of all this swirling steam I heard Chest singing. So it couldn't be all that bad. I did not cry out "All my relatives!"—which would have made him open the flap of the sweat lodge to let in some cool air—and I was proud of this. I heard him praying for me: "Oh, holy rocks, we receive your white breath, the steam. It is the breath of life. Let this young boy inhale it. Make him strong."

The sweat bath had prepared me for my vision-seeking. Even now, an hour later, my skin still tingled. But it seemed to have made my brains empty. Maybe that was good, plenty of room for new insights. . . .

Sounds came to me through the darkness: the cries of the wind, the whisper of the trees, the voices of nature, animal sounds, the hooting of an owl. Suddenly I felt an overwhelming presence. Down there with me in my cramped hole was a big bird. The pit was only as wide as myself, and I was a skinny boy, but that huge bird was flying around me as if he had the whole sky to himself. I could hear his cries, sometimes near and sometimes far, far away. I felt feathers or a wing touching my back and head. This feeling was so overwhelming that it was just too much for me. I trembled and my bones turned to ice. . . .

Slowly I perceived that a voice was trying to tell me something. It was a bird cry, but I tell you, I began to understand some of it. . . .

I heard a human voice too, strange and high-pitched, a voice which could not come from an ordinary, living being. All at once I was way up there with the birds. The hill with the vision pit was way above everything. I could look down even on the stars, and the moon was close to my left side. It seemed as though the earth and the stars were moving below me. A voice said, "You are sacrificing yourself here to be a medicine man. In time you will be one. You will teach other medicine men. We are the fowl people, the winged ones, the eagles and the owls. We are a nation and you shall be our brother. You will never kill or harm any one of us. You are going to understand us whenever you come to seek a vision here on this hill. You will learn about herbs and roots, and you will heal people. You will ask them for nothing in return. A man's life is short. Make yours a worthy one."

I felt that these voices were good, and slowly my fear left me. I had lost all sense of time. I did not know whether it was day or night. I was asleep, yet wide awake. Then I saw a shape before me. It rose from the darkness and the swirling fog, which penetrated my earth hole. I saw that this was my great-grandfather, Tahca Ushte, Lame Deer, old man chief of the Minneconjou. I could see the blood dripping from my great-grandfather's chest where a white soldier had shot him. I understood that my great-grandfather wished me to take his name. This made me glad beyond words.

We Sioux believe that there is something within us that controls us, something like a second person almost. We call it *nagi,* what other people might call soul, spirit or essence. One can't see it, feel it or taste it, but that time on the hill—and only that once—I knew it was there inside of me. Then I felt the power surge through me like a flood. I cannot describe it, but it filled all of me. Now I knew for sure that I would become a *wicasa wakan,* a medicine man. Again I wept, this time with happiness.

I didn't know how long I had been up there on that hill—one minute or a lifetime. I felt a hand on my shoulder gently shaking me. It was old man Chest, who had come for me. He told me that I had been in the vision pit four days and four nights and that it was time to come down. He would give me something to eat and water to drink and then I was to tell him everything that had happened to me during my *hanblechia.* He would interpret my visions for me. He told me that the vision pit had changed me in a way that I would not be able to understand at that time. He told me also that I was no longer a boy, that I was a man now. I was Lame Deer.

(Lame Deer and Erdoes, *Lame Deer, Seeker of Visions,* pages 14–16)

The Lakota name for the supreme reality is **Wakan Tanka** (wah'khan tankh'ah), sometimes translated as Great Spirit or the Great Mysterious, but literally meaning "most sacred." Wakan Tanka actually refers to sixteen separate deities. The number sixteen is derived from the number four (multiplied by itself), which is the most sacred number in Plains religion. It refers to the four compass directions (north, south, east, and west), which are especially relevant to peoples living in the wide, open regions of the Plains.

The creation of the world and the arrival of the first human beings are explained in detailed myths that celebrate the activities of the various supernatural beings involved. One of those beings is Inktomi (whose name means "spider"), the Lakota trickster figure. As the mediator between the supernatural and human worlds, Inktomi taught the first humans their ways and customs. Inktomi also serves another important function. Numerous stories tell about Inktomi's mistakes and errors of judgment, and offer an important moral lesson for children: Do not behave as Inktomi did!

Basic to most religions are beliefs regarding death and the afterlife, or human destiny. The Lakota believe that four souls depart from a person at death, one of which journeys along the "spirit path" of the Milky Way. The soul meets an old woman, who judges it and either allows it to continue to the other world of the ancestors, or sends it back to earth as a ghost. Meanwhile parts of the other souls enter unborn children and are reborn in new bodies.[F]

The Vision Quest

The **vision quest** is common to many primal traditions throughout the world. It is a primary means for an individual to gain access to spiritual power that will ensure greater success in activities such as hunting, warfare, and curing the ill. Both men and women experience this quest, though men do so more frequently.

The vision quest is carried out under the supervision of a medicine man or woman, a spiritual leader who issues specific instructions beforehand and interprets the content of the vision afterward. Before setting out on the quest, the participant undergoes a ritual of purification in the sweat lodge.

The sweat lodge is used on numerous occasions, and is a common element among Plains Indians and Native American traditions in general. It is a dark and airtight hut made of saplings and covered with animal skins. The structure of the lodge is intended to represent the universe. Heated stones are placed in the center, and the medicine man or woman sprinkles water over them. The resulting hot steam causes the participant to sweat profusely, leading to both physical and spiritual purification.

Once purified in this fashion, the vision quester goes off alone to a place far from the camp, usually to a hilltop. There he or she endures the elements for a set number of days, without food or water. Depending on the instructions from the medicine man or woman, the quester might perform certain rituals, carefully structured around a central spot.

A vision comes to the quester eventually, usually near the end of the stay. It arrives in

F
Imagine yourself living in the open wilderness of the North American Plains. Why, do you suppose, did the Lakota understand their supreme reality as being closely related to the four compass directions?

For many Native American tribes, spiritual and physical purification in a sweat lodge is part of the preparation for setting out on a vision quest.

IMAGE: © BETTMANN/CORBIS

the form of an animal or some other object or force of nature. A message is often communicated along with the vision. When the individual returns to camp, the medicine man or woman interprets the vision and the message. The lessons derived from the vision quest influence the rest of the person's life.

On some occasions the participant acquires a guardian spirit, which can be in the form of an animal, an inanimate object, or a ghost. The guardian spirit continues to protect and instruct the person, especially at times of great need.

The vision quest expresses two dimensions of religion: the quest itself is a religious ritual, and the moment of receiving the vision or guardian spirit is a form of religious experience.

The Sun Dance

Whereas the vision quest focuses on the individual, the **Sun Dance,** another ritual common to all tribes of the Plains, is undertaken for the benefit of all. It occurs at the beginning of summer and is, in part, a celebration of the new year. In the past it also functioned as a preparation for the great annual buffalo hunt.

A sacred leader presides over the Sun Dance. This leader is usually a medicine man, though the Blackfeet, who inhabit Alberta, Saskatchewan, and Montana, choose a woman of out-

G
The Indians of the Northern Plains traditionally lived off the land, depending on hunting and fishing to feed themselves. What elements of the vision quest and Sun Dance rituals are related to that lifestyle?

This nineteenth-century painting on buckskin depicts the performance of a Sun Dance.

standing moral character. Leading the Sun Dance is both a great honor and a grave responsibility.

For all tribes the major task in preparing for the Sun Dance is the construction of the lodge in which the ceremony is held. A cottonwood tree is carefully selected, felled, and ritually carried to a chosen spot, where it is set upright. This tree becomes what scholars call the **axis mundi,** the axis or center of the universe—itself an important and common theme for primal traditions. As the connecting link between the earth and the heavens, the tree also represents the supreme being. The lodge is constructed of twenty-eight poles, representing the twenty-eight days of the lunar month, placed in a circle around the tree. The finished lodge is representative of the universe with its four compass directions.

The performance of the Sun Dance features long periods of dancing while facing in the direction of the sun, which is venerated for its life-giving powers. Music and drumbeats accompany the dancing. Some of the dancers skewer the flesh of their chests and attach themselves to the tree with leather thongs. They then pull back from the tree as they continue dancing, until eventually their flesh tears. Because they believe their bodies are the only things they truly own, the dancers regard bodily mutilation as the only suitable sacrifice to offer to the supreme being.

This practice of bodily mutilation once compelled the U.S. government to outlaw the Sun Dance. It is now again legal and is commonly practiced in its traditional form among tribes of the North American Plains.G

A Mesoamerican Religion: The Aztecs and Their Legacy

In some ways the Aztec tradition defies the common description of primal religious tradition. Instead of a small group of people, the

Aztecs were a highly developed civilization with a population of about fifteen million. Many Aztecs were urban, living in the city of **Tenochtitlan** (te-nohch-teet′lahn), which is now Mexico City, or in one of the four hundred towns that spread across Mesoamerica, from the Pacific Ocean to the Caribbean Sea. But like other primal traditions, Aztec religion emphasized the interrelationship between myth and ritual, as its practice of human sacrifice makes vividly clear. Aztec religion was also primal in the sense that it predated Catholicism, which came to Mesoamerica with the Spaniards in the sixteenth century. The Aztec influence can still be seen today in some modern Mexican religious practices.

The Aztecs and Mesoamerican Culture

Mesoamerica included most of present-day Mexico and extended southward to present-day Honduras, Nicaragua, and Costa Rica. Native Americans appear to have arrived there about twenty thousand years ago, although scholars lack firm evidence. From about four thousand years ago until about five hundred years ago (around the time Columbus arrived in the New World), the area was home to a sophisticated and diverse Mesoamerican culture, which included civilizations such as the Olmec (1500 to 200 BC), the Maya (AD 200 to 900), the Toltec (AD 900 to 1100), and the Aztec (AD 1325 to 1521).

The Toltec Tradition:
The Foundation of Aztec Religion

The Aztecs were relative latecomers to Mesoamerica, having migrated into the region from the northwest. By the time of their arrival, great cultural achievements had already come to pass. Those achievements offered the foundations on which the Aztecs built their own great civilization. The strongest influence came from the Toltecs. The Aztecs believed that the Toltec god **Quetzalcoatl** (kwet-suhl-kuh-wah′til) (Feathered Serpent) had presided over a golden age of cultural brilliance. The god's earthly devotee Topiltzin Quetzalcoatl (Our Young Prince the Feathered Serpent) ruled as priest-king. He provided the Aztecs with the perfect role model for their own authority figures.

The Aztecs looked back to this golden age of the Toltecs as a mythic pattern for the ideal civilization. The Toltec tradition especially influenced religion. Aztec children were taught to recite, "Truly with him it began, truly from him it flowed out, from Quetzalcoatl—all art and knowledge" (quoted in Carrasco, *Religions of Mesoamerica,* page 44). Aztec cosmology attributed the creation and ordering of the world to Quetzalcoatl.[H]

Teotihuacan: Place of Origins

It seems that even long before the rise of the Toltecs, Quetzalcoatl was worshiped in the great city of Teotihuacan (tay-oh-tee-wuh-kon′) (AD 100 to 700), whose population once exceeded two hundred thousand. Today known mainly for its monumental Pyramid of the Sun and Pyramid of the Moon, Teotihuacan is the most visited archaeological site in the Americas. Aztec myth identified Teotihuacan, located just thirty miles northeast of the Aztecs' own capital city, Tenochtitlan, as the origin of the entire cosmos, in terms of both space and time. The myth goes as follows:

It is told that when yet [all] was in darkness, when yet no sun had shone and no dawn had broken—it is said—the gods gathered themselves . . . there at Teotihuacan. They spoke . . . :
". . . Who will take it upon himself to be the sun, to bring the dawn?" (Sahagún, *Florentine Codex,* book 7, part 8, page 4)

Cosmology: Time and Space

The Aztecs' cosmology was thoroughly interrelated with their pessimistic view of time, their perspective on the human condition, and their ritual of human sacrifice.

H
The Aztecs looked back to the Toltec tradition as a kind of golden age, providing them with a mythic pattern for the ideal civilization. In what ways do you and your society look to past traditions for cultural ideals?

Age of the Fifth Sun

As indicated by the creation myth that was cited previously, the Aztecs believed that the sun was created at Teotihuacan. In fact the present sun, they thought, was the fifth sun. Four previous suns and their ages had already been destroyed, and a similar fate was anticipated for this one. The only way of delaying the end of the age was to nourish the sun continually through human sacrifices.

This remarkable pessimism was enhanced by the belief that the fifth sun was the last that would ever shine. Each of the five suns had occupied its own cosmic location: the center, the west, the north, the south, and, in the case of the fifth sun, the east. The Aztecs understood the universe to be built around this structure of the center plus four cardinal directions. Aztec cosmology thus featured a close correspondence between time and space.[1]

Four Directions and the *Axis Mundi*

The Aztecs understood the spatial world as having four quadrants extending outward from the center of the universe (the *axis mundi*), which connected the earthly realm to the many-layered heavenly realm above and the many-layered underworld below. The ancient

The Aztec cosmology is marked by a deep pessimism regarding the future. How does your society view the future? What can human beings offer to "nourish" the present so as to ensure a sound future?

city of Teotihuacan had been arranged that way, apparently with a cave as the original *axis mundi*. Following on this pattern, the Aztecs designed Tenochtitlan to be the center of their world. At the point where the four directions met stood the Great Temple, known by the Aztecs as Serpent Mountain.

It is not surprising that the Aztecs' great temple should be called a mountain—the mountain is commonly a type of *axis mundi* for primal traditions around the globe. It is also not surprising that the temple should bear the name *Serpent*: recall that the Toltec god was called Feathered Serpent. However, worship at Serpent Mountain was devoted especially to a god of rain and fertility and to a god of war and sacrifice.

The Human Role in Sustaining the Cosmos

The Aztecs understood the human condition as being vitally linked to cosmology. Two divine forces, one concentrated in the head, the other in the heart, were believed to nurture the human being with basic needs. Because of the potency of these divine forces, each human being was regarded as a sort of *axis mundi,* connecting the earthly realm to the divine. The human body, especially the head and the heart, was also regarded as potent nourishment for the sun and the cosmos.

The Ritual of Human Sacrifice

So, it was said, when he arrived . . . he ascended by himself, of his free will, to the place where he was to die. . . .

And when he had mounted all the steps, when he had reached the summit, then the priests fell upon him; they threw him on his back upon the sacrificial stone. Then [one] cut open his breast, seized his heart, and raised it as an offering to the sun.

For in this manner were all [these] captives offered up. But his body they did not roll

At the pyramid-shaped Great Temple, in the Aztec city of Tenochtitlan, worship was dedicated to a god of rain and fertility and to a god of war and sacrifice.

IMAGE: © CHARLES & JOSETTE LENARS/CORBIS

The Aztecs understood the universe to have five parts: a center and four directions. This painting portrays the founding of the city of Teotihuacan.

This illustration from an Aztec manuscript shows how the Aztecs offered up the hearts and heads of their warriors and captives in order to gain the favor of the gods and to delay the end of the Age of the Fifth Sun.

Primal Religious Traditions 35

down; rather, they lowered it. Four men carried it.

And his severed head they strung on the skull-rack. (Sahagún, *Florentine Codex,* book 2, part 3, page 68)

This account illustrates some of the ways human sacrifice fit into the Aztecs' overall cosmology and understanding of the human condition. The heart, with its abundance of divine force, was offered as nourishment to the sun. The head, similarly, was offered to the sky. The warrior's willingness to ascend the temple's stairs suggests his acceptance of his role in sustaining the fragile cosmos. According to Aztec belief, moreover, this role would allow him to enter the highest heaven upon death.

Sacrifices like this one were carried out at least once every twenty days. Usually the victims were captive warriors, as in the account cited here; in fact the need for sacrificial victims motivated much of Aztec warfare. Sometimes the victims were slaves, including, rarely, women and children.J

The Mastery of Language

Aztec religion was not fixated on human sacrifice. The rich culture of the Aztecs provided many means of fulfilling religious needs. For example, a great deal of religious power was believed to be conveyed through the mastery of language.

The Aztecs spoke Nahuatl (nay′wah-tuhl), a naturally expressive language capable of high achievements in poetry and other forms of speech. Specialists called "knowers of things" could communicate with the gods and make offerings through language, thus providing an alternative to sacrifice. The Aztecs also favored wit, commonly employing riddles in their ordinary speaking. Knowing the answers to riddles meant that one came from a good family. Here are two examples:

What is it that is a small blue gourd bowl filled with popcorn? One can see from our little riddle that it is the heavens. (Sahagún, *Florentine Codex,* book 6, part 7, page 237)

What is that which we enter in three places [and] leave by only one? It is our shirt. (Page 239)K

From Aztec Empire to Catholic Mexico

The fall of Tenochtitlan in 1521 to Hernán Cortés and his Spanish army was due in part to the religion of the Aztecs. The Aztec king Moctezuma II (commonly, though incorrectly, known as Montezuma) is said to have believed that the Spanish leader was Topiltzin Quetzalcoatl, the long-lost priest-king of the Toltecs. Our Young Prince the Feathered Serpent had disappeared from earth long ago, but was expected to return, possibly in 1519. By an amazing coincidence, Cortés—wearing a feathered helmet—arrived in Mesoamerica that year. Moctezuma welcomed Cortés as the returning Topiltzin Quetzalcoatl, providing him with gifts.

The end of the Aztec empire in no way marked the end of Aztec culture. Tenochtitlan has survived as the huge metropolis Mexico City, and Aztec culture has survived in religious forms.

The popular veneration of the Virgin of Guadalupe began, according to legend, in 1531 on the outskirts of the fallen city of Tenochtitlan when a dark-skinned apparition of the Virgin Mary appeared to an Aztec convert to Catholicism named Juan Diego. The hill on which she appeared was considered the sacred place of the Aztec mother goddess Tonantzin, who had been worshiped for centuries. Some Mexican Indians today continue to refer to the Virgin Mary as Tonantzin.

The popular Día de los Muertos, Day of the Dead, also shows the survival of Aztec religious culture. This celebration, held at the end of October and beginning of November, joins the living and the dead through festive and spiritually meaningful rituals. The Aztecs set aside time each year to perform similar rituals devoted to the same basic purpose.

J
Considering the Aztec ritual of human sacrifice offers a challenging opportunity to see things from another's perspective. Explain how human sacrifice is part of the Aztecs' ordered and sophisticated religious worldview, given their cosmology and understanding of the human condition.

K
In your experience how has the mastery of language helped to convey religious power? How does the significance of speech in the Aztec tradition compare with the significance of speech in another religious tradition with which you are familiar?

Common Themes, Diverse Traditions

Though primal religions exhibit great diversity, many of them also share specific elements, including totemism, taboo, the trickster figure, the vision quest, and the *axis mundi*.

The four examples of primal religions presented in this chapter also share certain general themes. For these religions the boundaries between the supernatural and the human worlds are thin and easily crossed. Among the Australian Aborigines, for example, the sacred power of an Ancestor of the Dreaming is believed to enter an individual at the time of conception. The Yoruba commonly turn to divination to acquire knowledge of their destinies from the *orishas*. In both traditions communication between the ancestors and the living is thought to take place regularly.

A related theme is the all-encompassing nature of religion. In primal societies the secular and the sacred are not separate. Rather, the universe is full of religious significance, and humans constantly draw on its sacred and life-giving powers. This is vividly illustrated by the lack of specific terms for religion in Native

In Mexico today Christian families decorate the graves of their ancestors on the Day of the Dead. The Aztecs practiced similar rituals.

IMAGE: © DANNY LEHMAN/CORBIS

The Seven Dimensions of Religion: Primal Religious Traditions

Dimension	Examples
Experiential	receiving a vision or guardian spirit during a vision quest
Mythic	Aboriginal Ancestors and the Dreaming, trickster figures (such as Esu and Inktomi), Teotihuacan as the place of cosmic origins
Doctrinal	totemism, Yoruba theology of Olorun and the *orishas,* Lakota belief in four souls of the dead person, Aztec belief that the Age of the Fifth Sun would soon end
Ethical	moral lessons learned from the errors of Inktomi (the Lakota trickster figure)
Ritual	Aboriginal rites of initiation, the Sun Dance, Aztec human sacrifice
Social	taboo as the basis of social structure
Material	totems, bull-roarers, Yoruba masks, the sweat lodge, the Sun Dance lodge, the Great Temple (Serpent Mountain) of Tenochtitlan

American languages; religion pervades life, so there is no need to set it apart.

Another common theme is change. Too often, students of religion have regarded primal traditions as static monoliths. In fact primal religions have constantly been changing. For example, the religions of the Plains peoples altered markedly when horses arrived from Europe in the seventeenth century. Although Aztec religion is largely a thing of the past, its legacy continues to affect Latin American religious life. Australian Aborigines are well equipped to accommodate modern changes: once a new tradition has been accepted, they agree that the Ancestors established it long ago, in the period of the Dreaming, and the innovation becomes part of their eternal reality.

One powerful consequence of this ongoing change is the remarkable adaptability of primal peoples. Though it is commonly asserted that these cultures will inevitably disappear from the face of the earth, the primal religious traditions are not necessarily doomed. On the contrary, native peoples seem to be increasing their level of participation in their traditional ways. These traditions now bear the imprint of modernity, but their ancient foundations live on.[L]

Chapter Review

1. Why are some forms of religion called primal? Describe some of the characteristics of primal religions.
2. What elements of the natural and human world did the Ancestors create or establish in the period of the Dreaming?
3. What survives in the symbols left behind by the Ancestors?
4. Explain the terms *totem* and *taboo*.
5. Why is ritual essential if Aboriginal life is to have meaning?
6. How did Aboriginal rituals originate?
7. What purposes are served by Aboriginal initiation rituals?
8. Identify two acts of Dieri initiation rituals that symbolize death.
9. In what part of Africa do the Yoruba live?
10. Why has the city of Ife always been the center of Yoruba religion?
11. Briefly describe the Yoruba understanding of the cosmos.
12. Who is Olorun, and what is his role in Yoruba religion?
13. What are the *orishas?* Explain their significance in the religious life of the Yoruba.
14. Name and briefly describe at least two of the *orishas.*
15. What is a trickster figure?
16. Describe the two types of Yoruba ancestors.
17. Describe the role of Yoruba ritual practitioners.
18. What is divination, and why do the Yoruba regard it as essential?
19. According to the interpretation of the latest evidence, when and how do scholars think human beings first came to North America?
20. Why is the religion of the Plains Indians of vital interest among native peoples throughout North America?
21. What is Wakan Tanka?
22. Who is Inktomi?
23. Briefly describe Lakota beliefs regarding death and the afterlife.
24. What do individuals try to gain access to by going on a vision quest?
25. Briefly describe the structure and function of the sweat lodge.
26. Describe a typical vision experienced by a person who undertakes a vision quest.
27. Among the Blackfeet tribe, who presides over the Sun Dance?
28. What is the *axis mundi* in general? What is the *axis mundi* in the Sun Dance?
29. Why do some participants in the Sun Dance skewer their chests and dance until their flesh tears?
30. In what two ways does the Aztec tradition defy the description of a primal religious tradition? In what ways is the Aztec tradition like other primal religious traditions?

L
In general, primal religions understand the boundaries between the human and the supernatural realms to be thin and easily crossed. Drawing from the religious traditions of the Aborigines, the Yoruba, the Indians of the Northern Plains, and the Aztecs, identify as many examples as you can that illustrate this understanding.

31. What geographical area did Mesoamerica include?

32. According to Aztec cosmology, what god created and ordered the world? What ancient city is the origin of the cosmos?

33. Who was Topiltzin Quetzalcoatl? What was his significance for the Aztecs?

34. What did the Aztecs call their present age? What did they anticipate its fate to be?

35. How did the Aztecs understand the spatial world?

36. Why did the Aztecs regard each human being as a sort of *axis mundi*?

37. What were the special religious capabilities of the Aztec knowers of things?

38. What historical coincidence contributed to the fall of Tenochtitlan to the Spaniards?

39. How does the popular Day of the Dead show the survival of Aztec religious culture?

40. What three themes are shared by the primal religions studied in this chapter?

Glossary

Ancestors. For the Australian Aboriginal religion, Ancestors are supernatural beings (or deities) who emerged and roamed the earth during the time of the Dreaming, giving shape to the landscape and creating various forms of life. When the word *ancestors* is lowercased, it refers to the deceased, who can assist the living while requiring religious devotion (as among the Yoruba, for example).

axis mundi (Latin: "axis of the universe"). Common to many religions, an entity such as a mountain, tree, or pole that is believed to connect the heavens and the earth, and is sometimes regarded as the center of the world; for example, the cottonwood tree of the Plains Indians' Sun Dance.

divination. The use of various techniques, such as throwing bones or shells and then interpreting the pattern in which they fall, for gaining knowledge about an individual's future or about the cause of a personal problem; important among many religions worldwide, including that of the Yoruba.

diviners. Ritual practitioners who specialize in the art of divination; very important among the Yoruba.

Dreaming, the. The mythic time of Australian Aboriginal religion when the Ancestors inhabited the earth.

orishas (aw-ree-shahs´; Yoruba: "head source"). The hundreds of various Yoruba deities who are the main objects of ritual attention, including Orisha-nla, the creator god; Ogun, the god of iron and of war; and Esu, the trickster figure.

Quetzalcoatl (kwet-suhl-kuh-wah´til; Nahuatl: Feathered Serpent). Mesoamerican creator god worshiped at Teotihuacan and by the Toltecs; believed by the Aztecs to have presided over a golden age. Quetzalcoatl's earthly representative was Topiltzin Quetzalcoatl (Nahuatl: Our Young Prince the Feathered Serpent), a legendary Toltec priest-king.

Sun Dance. Ritual of the Lakota and other tribes of the North American Plains that celebrates the new year and prepares the tribe for the annual buffalo hunt; performed in the late spring or early summer in a specially constructed lodge.

taboo (sometimes spelled tabu). A system of social ordering that dictates that specific objects and activities, owing to their sacred nature, are set aside for specific groups and are strictly forbidden to others; common to many primal peoples, including the Australian Aborigines.

Tenochtitlan (te-nohcht-teet´lahn). Capital city of the Aztec empire, believed to be the center of the world. Home of the Great Temple, or Serpent Mountain. Site of present-day Mexico City.

totem. A natural entity, such as an animal or a feature of the landscape, that symbolizes an individual or group and that has special significance for the religious life of that individual or group; a common motif among Australian Aborigines and other primal peoples.

trickster figure. A type of supernatural being who tends to disrupt the normal course of life, found among many primal peoples; for example, Esu among the Yoruba and Inktomi among the Lakota.

vision quest. A means of seeking spiritual power through an encounter with a guardian spirit or other medium, usually in the form of an animal or other natural entity, following a period of fasting and other forms of self-denial; common to many primal peoples, including the Lakota and other tribes of the North American Plains.

Wakan Tanka (wah´khan tankh´ah; Lakota: "most sacred"). Lakota name for the supreme reality, often referring collectively to sixteen separate deities.

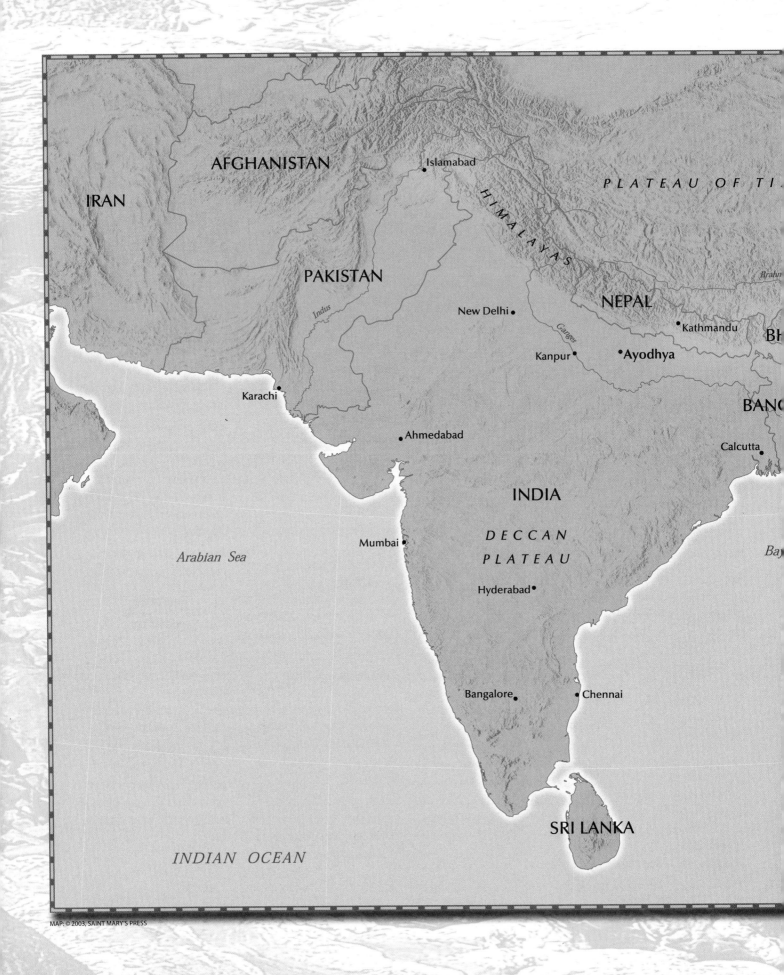

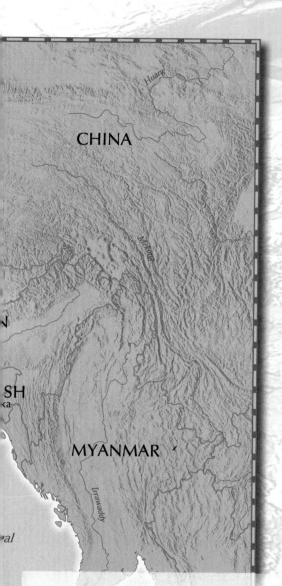

3   Hinduism

There is only one God, but endless are his aspects and endless are his names. Call him by any name and worship him in any aspect that pleases you, you are sure to see him. (Shri Ramakrishna, quoted in Prabhavananda with Manchester, *The Spiritual Heritage of India,* page 353)

Many Rivers to One Ocean

The esteemed holy man Shri Ramakrishna (1836 to 1886) speaks for most of his fellow Hindus when he emphasizes the harmony and tolerance that are characteristic of his religion. A harmony of many different beliefs and practices, all aiming for the common goal of salvation, like many rivers converging into one ocean, Hinduism also tends to be highly tolerant of other religions. True to the ideals of Hinduism, Shri Ramakrishna lived what he taught. From early boyhood he mastered a variety of Hindu paths of worship, later he became a Muslim and then a Christian, and all the while, from his own perspective, he evolved into a better Hindu.

Throughout the ages, harmony amid diversity, and tolerance toward other faiths have characterized Hinduism. The nearly four-thousand-year-old **Rig Veda** (rig vay′duh), Hinduism's oldest sacred text, declares: "God is one but men call him by many names" (1.64.46). The great twentieth-century Hindu, Mahatma Gandhi, echoes the ancient wisdom of the Rig Veda: "Even as a tree has a single trunk, but many branches and leaves, so is there one true and perfect Religion, but it

becomes many as it passes through the human medium" (*The Moral and Political Writings of Mahatma Gandhi,* volume 1, pages 542–543). Like Ramakrishna, Gandhi revered Christianity; he even placed the Sermon on the Mount from the Gospel of Matthew alongside Hinduism's Bhagavad-Gita as his favorite religious texts.

In this chapter we will consider the main aspects of the vast diversity of beliefs and practices that together form Hinduism. We will chart many rivers, but it is important not to forget that all flow eventually into one ocean.

Human Destiny: From Worldly Realms to the Divine Beyond

Learning about Hinduism depends first on understanding a perspective of reality—the universe, human beings, and the divine—that is fundamentally different from common Western perspectives. Because Hinduism emphasizes above all else the concerns of human beings, we will chart the Hindu perspective on reality by first considering human destiny. It is best to begin this story at its conclusion, for the final destiny of salvation through liberation returns the individual to the original source. Spiritual perfection amounts to a return to the beginning.

Liberation: Returning to the Sacred Source

Salvation through liberation from the constraints of the human condition is the ultimate goal of all Hindus, the ocean into which all the rivers of Hinduism eventually flow. For most it is a distant goal, not to be attained in this lifetime. Hindus believe in reincarnation (rebirth in new life-forms) and thus anticipate a long series of lifetimes, so they can afford

Mahatma Gandhi, the great Hindu political leader, is revered for his ideas on social justice. His practice of non-violent disobedience helped to free India from British rule, establishing it as an independent nation.

IMAGE: © HULTON-DEUTSCH COLLECTION/CORBIS

to be patient regarding the goal of liberation. Hinduism is not in a hurry.

The Hindu term for "liberation" is **moksha** (mohk´shuh), a Sanskrit word that also means "release." *Moksha* is a release from this ordinary, finite, limited realm of existence into the infinite ocean of the divine. It is an experience characterized by infinite being, infinite awareness, and infinite bliss. The details of this experience defy description, for it is completely beyond the experiences of this world.

Never again to be reincarnated, the Hindu who has attained *moksha* is united forever with the divine, having returned to the sacred source.

The Divine:
One Ultimate Reality, Many "Masks"

Hinduism perceives the nature of the divine very differently than do the Western monotheistic religions Judaism, Christianity, and Islam. Rather than believing in one personal God, who created all things and exists independently of them, most Hindus believe that all reality—God, the universe, human beings, and all else—is essentially one thing. At the same time, Hindus worship many gods and goddesses, appropriately thought of as the various masks of God.

Monism: All Is Brahman

Most (though not all) Hindus believe in **monism** (only-one-ism), the doctrine that all reality is ultimately one. This basic feature of the doctrinal dimension of Hinduism differs markedly from the predominant monotheism (only-one-God-ism) of the Western religions, in which God is held to be both the creator of the world, and above and independent of it.

An analogy can help make sense of the difficult concept of monism. Rivers, ponds, lakes, and oceans appear to be quite distinctive, yet they share a common essence: they all are made up of water. Monists believe that similarly all forms of reality—gods and goddesses, plants and animals, the material universe, and

humans—share a common essence. Hindus call this essence **Brahman** (brah´muhn).

Infinite and eternal, Brahman is the ground of existence and the source of the universe. It is discoverable only through the most profound contemplation, and its true nature is not revealed on the surface of things. Brahman is impersonal, without characteristics that can be seen, heard, or even intelligibly thought about. The **Upanishads** (oo-pah´ni-shuhdz), the ancient philosophical texts that form the basis of most Hindu doctrines, teach that Brahman can be described only as *neti, neti:* "not this, not that." Whatever the senses can perceive, whatever the mind can ponder, these are not Brahman, for Brahman is beyond the reach of human perception and thought. Just as atomic particles are invisible and yet are the basic building blocks of matter, so does Brahman reside beneath all surfaces, forming the essence of all things. Unlike atomic particles, however, Brahman is not material at all, but rather pure spirit.

Ultimate reality, called Brahman when referring to the essence of all things, can be described in another way as well. The Upanishads teach that ultimate reality can be understood through inward contemplation of the self. The ultimate reality within is named **Atman** (aht´muhn), the eternal Self.

The fundamental discovery of the Upanishads is that Brahman, ultimate reality understood through contemplation of the universe, and Atman, ultimate reality understood through contemplation of the inner self, are in fact one and the same. Brahman is Atman; all reality is one.

One famous passage in the Upanishads consists of a dialogue between a father and a son. Svetaketu asks his father:

"Please, sir, tell me more about this Self."

"Be it so. Put this salt in water, and come to me tomorrow morning."

Svetaketu did as he was bidden. The next morning his father asked him to bring the salt

Among Hinduism's many gods are *(clockwise from top left)* Krishna, depicted in a typical dancing pose; Agni, god of fire; Shiva, god of destruction, shown in this eleventh-century bronze ringed by a circle of flames and dancing on the back of a demon; and Ganesha, elephant god.

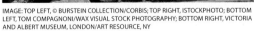

which he had put in the water. But he could not, for it had dissolved. Then said Uddalaka:

"Sip the water, and tell me how it tastes."

"It is salty, sir."

"In the same way," continued Uddalaka, "though you do not see Brahman in this body, he is indeed here. That which is the subtle essence—in that have all things their existence. That is the truth. That is the Self. And that, Svetaketu, THAT ART THOU."

(Chandogya Upanishad 6.12.3—6.13.3)

"That art thou" (*tat tvam asi* in Sanskrit) is frequently cited in Hindu literature. Brahman is Atman. This is monism. All reality—the universe, oneself, and everyone else—shares one essence. And that one is Brahman. Or that one is Atman. In the light of the understanding that all is essentially one, the terms Brahman and Atman are interchangeable.[A]

Polytheism: 330 Million Gods and Goddesses

The divine is thought ultimately to be one essence. And yet Hindus subscribe to polytheism, believing in many gods and goddesses (traditionally 330 million!). We can best understand this apparent contradiction by returning to our water analogy. We have referred to water as the common essence of rivers, ponds, lakes, and oceans. We have also noted that oceans are unique in that they are the final destination or ultimate receptacle of all of the earth's water. Though we speak of different oceans that fill separate areas of the earth's surface, there is in reality only one body of water. One person could be surfing in the Pacific while thousands of miles away her cousin is sailing on the Atlantic, each apparently enjoying a different ocean. But if you look at a map or a globe, you will see that the oceans of the world are not divided by any continuous landmasses; ultimately they form one body of water. In terms of our analogy, this one universal ocean can therefore

The Hindu god Vishnu and his consort, Lakshmi, ride on the bird Garuda.

be thought of as the ultimate ground of the common essence of reality.

Hinduism generally regards its 330 million deities as extensions of one ultimate reality, many names for one ocean, many "masks" for one God. Because the divine reality of Brahman or Atman is beyond the reach of the senses and of thought, humans need accessible points of contact with the divine. Ultimate reality must be revealed if it is to affect the individual. Hinduism's many deities provide these points of contact, each with its own personal characteristics. Hindus can freely worship whichever gods and goddesses they like. Given the vast number of deities, at least one will surely provide an effective point of contact with the divine.

Many Worlds, Many Lifetimes: Hindu Cosmology

All religious traditions set forth a cosmology—an explanation regarding the nature of the universe. Hindu cosmology, relative to the great Western religions and to modern

A

Imagine you are Svetaketu's father. Create another analogy that might answer the boy's question about the Self.

science, is noticeably distinctive in many of its aspects.

With the Hindu tradition, before examining *what* the universe is, it is appropriate to consider *why* the universe is. If everything is ultimately and originally one thing, all unified in the divine Brahman, why does there appear to be anything else? What happened in the first place that caused the human need to seek salvation? Such questions are of obvious interest, and yet they have no easy answers. Hinduism tends to regard such issues as great mysteries. Just as Brahman itself is ultimately a mystery, beyond the reach of logical explanation, so too does its creative energy flow forth mysteriously. This universe—this ordinary, finite, limited realm of existence—somehow has come to be. Humans call it home, at least for now. The important thing for Hindus is to deal with the universe as it is, to seek salvation through liberation from the world's bonds.

Cycles of Creation

The West has generally stressed the linear progression of time, from a distant beginning (such as the six days of Creation recounted in the Book of Genesis, or the big bang theory of modern astrophysics) to an eventual end of creation as we know it. Hinduism, in contrast, charts time and creation in ongoing cycles.

The cyclical cosmology of Hinduism declares that the universe undergoes long periods of creation and destruction, a rhythmic pattern that repeats itself endlessly. The end of the present period is drawing near—although millions of years remain. As the end of the cycle approaches, the destructive forces already at work will gradually gain the upper hand, eventually bringing all of creation to a deep stillness and long pause. Then the entire universe will be re-created: the galaxies will be remade; souls will arise again and come to inhabit the various life-forms; Hinduism will evolve all over again.

Reincarnation

Within the cyclical pattern of the universe, each individual is also created and re-created repeatedly, until finally attaining release from this realm through *moksha*. In its barest outline, this is the Hindu perspective on the human condition. According to the doctrine of **samsara** (sahm-sah′ruh), or "wheel of rebirth," the individual is reincarnated from one life-form to another. Accounts vary as to precisely what is reincarnated. At the very least, it is the atman, the individual "self" or "soul," the divine spark within that is destined to eventually be reunited with its source. Most aspects of the personality are generally not thought to be transmitted into the next life-form. For instance, individuals usually cannot remember past lives.

Reincarnation occurs on a vast number of levels of existence, including the various life-forms (human, animal, according to some texts even plant) of this earth and other similar worlds, gods and goddesses in the many Hindu heavens, and demons in its many hells. Traditional accounts also specify a realm of semidivine "titans" just below the heavens, and a realm of "ghosts" just above the hells. Like all realms of *samsara,* even those of the gods do not last forever—they are not Brahman. An individual might enjoy heavenly pleasures for ten thousand years, but then the wheel of rebirth is destined to continue, and the individual's atman will continue being reincarnated until *moksha* is achieved.

Reincarnation puts an interesting twist on the problem of mortality. On one hand, to die without attaining liberation must be considered a defeat, because the atman is then destined to remain on the wheel of rebirth. On the other hand, the prospect of reincarnation denies death at least some of its sting. Death is not so final for Hindus—in fact it is likely to be experienced again!

In the **Bhagavad-Gita** (buh′guh-vuhd gee′tah), Hinduism's most popular sacred text, the god Krishna teaches the great warrior Arjuna about many important religious issues, including reincarnation. As Krishna explains to Arjuna, the eternal atman (self) puts on new bodies like we put on new clothes:

Never have I not existed,
nor you, nor these kings;
and never in the future
shall we cease to exist.

Just as the embodied self
enters childhood, youth, and old age,
so does it enter another body;
this does not confound a steadfast man.

. . . .

As a man discards
worn-out clothes
to put on new
and different ones,
so the embodied self
discards
its worn-out bodies
to take on other new ones.

(Bhagavad-Gita 2:12–13,22)[B]

Law and Order:
Divine Principles in the World

Two principles, *karma* and *dharma,* connect the divine with this world. These principles form the crucial link between the realm of *samsara* and the divine source. By providing a basis for a moral life in this world, *karma* and *dharma* permeate the earthly life with spiritual significance.

Karma

Karma functions hand in hand with *samsara,* in that it determines the nature of each reincarnation. *Karma* literally means "action" or "deeds." This principle, best understood as the moral law of cause and effect, states that every action produces an outcome that is justified by the action's moral worthiness. *Karma* thus determines all the particular circumstances and situations of one's life. *Karma* functions independently of any deity or of a procedure of divine judgment. Individuals are automatically held to be morally responsible for their actions; as the old saying goes, "As you sow, so shall you reap."

This Hindu monument in Rishikesh, India, presents Krishna, the chariot driver, and Arjuna, in a scene from the Mahabharata.

Hinduism   47

C

In the right-hand column of a sheet of paper, write the main actions you have taken during the last twenty-four hours. In the left-hand column, write what caused you to take each action. Then answer these questions: Is it possible for an action to lack a cause? Why or why not?

Karma permeates the realm of *samsara*, such that an individual's *karmic* record stays with the self from reincarnation to reincarnation. *Karma* thus determines the life-form into which the atman is born, whether it be a deity or other supernatural being, a human, or an animal. Of the various life-forms, only humans have the will to affect the status of their *karma*. Therefore being human is both a privilege and a demanding responsibility.

At least in theory, *karma* secures a high degree of justice. Unlike followers of Western religions, Hindus have an easy answer to the question, Why do bad things happen to good people? Because they have committed evil deeds in their past lives and therefore deserve to be punished! The criminal can never escape justice, and the saint will never be denied a just reward. Because of this foolproof feature, the law of *karma* has been called the most logical system of divine justice the world has ever known.

Dharma

The law of *karma* holds people responsible for their actions. Applying that law requires some standard for determining the rightness or wrongness of actions. That standard is **dharma** (dahr´muh), or ethical duty based on the divine order of reality.

The significance of *dharma* can hardly be overstated. The term *dharma* is Hinduism's closest equivalent to the West's term *religion*. More than just a specific list of rights and wrongs, *dharma* is the complete rule of life. For every activity, there is a way of acting that conforms to *dharma*. Hindus look to four sources when seeking guidance about *dharma* in particular situations. These sources, in order from highest to lowest level of authority, are (1) divine revelation, as expressed in the sacred scriptures; (2) sacred tradition, as passed on from generation to generation; (3) the practices and example of those who are considered the wisest members of society; and (4) conscience.

Whenever Hindus strive to fulfill desires, *dharma* limits their pursuits. *Dharma* also shifts the focus from satisfying private cravings to caring for others. In its ultimate effect of nourishing unconditional concern for the world, *dharma* has much in common with the primary Christian ethical principle of unconditional love and with the Buddhist counterpart of infinite compassion. *Dharma* is thus a major feature of the ethical dimension of Hinduism.[C]

Hindu Society: Mapping the Individual's Identity

Despite their sometimes dizzying complexity, the many aspects of Hinduism are for the most part in harmony. Basic principles are interconnected. *Karma,* the moral law of cause and effect, is based in *dharma,* ethical duty. *Dharma,* in turn, is connected to social order. A person's particular *dharma* is determined by gender, caste, and stage of life. Within this social order, Hindus are free to choose from among four legitimate goals. Together these circumstances map an individual's identity.

The *dharma* of women, for example, has traditionally emphasized obedience toward men—first the father, then the husband, and finally the sons. The duties of caste and stage of life, which figure prominently in constituting the *dharma* of men, are less relevant for women. However women's primary role of providing for the welfare of the family has always been a basic aspect of Hindu society. By traditionally performing this role with energy and perseverance, women have tended to earn a reputation for having more integrity of character than men, who are sometimes regarded as less dependable and more prone to frivolity. On the other hand, women's domestic responsibilities have limited their educational and career opportunities compared with those of men.

Hinduism's caste system divides society into four major classes. Ricksha drivers are generally members of the *shudra,* or laborer, class.

Doing One's Job: The Caste System

Hinduism's **caste system** incorporates a traditional division of society into four distinct classes—**brahmin** (brah′min), consisting of priests; **kshatriya** (kshuht′ree-yuh), including warriors and administrators; **vaishya** (vish′yuh), made up of producers, such as farmers, merchants, and artisans; and **shudra** (sh*oo*′druh), composed of servants and laborers. The original term used for this division by class, *varna,* means "color," which is apparently related to the differences in skin tone between the darker original inhabitants of India and the fairer Aryans who migrated from the north and penetrated most of India during the centuries of Hinduism's origins (beginning about 2000 BC). The Aryans considered it important to prevent the two racial groups from intermingling, so they distinguished their own classes—the *brahmin, kshatriya,* and *vaishya*—from that of the native peoples, the *shudra.*

The original four classes of the caste system were divided and subdivided until over three thousand distinct categories emerged. These categories correspond primarily to different occupations, especially for men. For women the primary significance of caste pertains to whom they can marry; traditional *dharma* provides specific rules regarding marriage with respect to caste. An additional category consists of the "outcastes," those who are considered to be outside of society altogether. This group includes the Untouchables, who only recently have begun to enjoy some legal rights, thanks to the work of Mahatma Gandhi. He renamed the outcastes Harijan, "God's children."

In general the caste system is rigidly based on heredity. One is simply born to a lifelong caste identity, as determined by *karma,* which directs the soul into whatever situation it deserves. The Upanishads explain:

Hinduism   49

D

Hindu society is separated by caste identity. Is Western society separated in any ways that are similar to the caste system? Explain your answer.

Accordingly, those who are of pleasant conduct here—the prospect is, indeed, that they will enter a pleasant womb, either the womb of a *[brahmin],* or the womb of a *[kshatriya],* or the womb of a *[vaishya].* But those who are of stinking conduct here—the prospect is, indeed, that they will enter a stinking womb, either the womb of a dog, or the womb of a swine, or the womb of an [outcaste]. (Chandogya Upanishad 5.10.7)

Top: These women, considered Untouchables, perform lowly tasks such as sweeping and mopping streets. Gandhi called them Harijans, or "God's children." *Bottom:* This farmer selling his vegetables at market is part of the vaishya class.

In this way *karma* can be seen to justify the caste system itself. People do not just happen to be born outcastes; they deserve their lowly status because of their "stinking conduct" in previous lives. Likewise *brahmins* deserve their privileged position because of their meritorious *karma* in previous lives: they have lived in conformity to their *dharma,* and consequently are now closer to salvation.

Karma determines caste identity, and caste, in turn, determines the specific *dharma* governing a person's actions. For example, the ethical duties of a *brahmin* differ from those of a *kshatriya.* The Bhagavad-Gita presents a striking illustration of how caste identity determines *dharma.* Arjuna, a great warrior (thus of the *kshatriya* class), is poised to enter a crucial battle. As he considers the gruesome tasks that lie before him, including the killing of kinsmen and old friends, he hesitates, wondering if he should avoid battle. The god Krishna, disguised as Arjuna's charioteer, reminds Arjuna of his *dharma:*

Look to your own duty;
do not tremble before it;
nothing is better for a warrior
than a battle of sacred duty.

The doors of heaven open
for warriors who rejoice

IMAGE: TOP: © LINDSAY HEBBERD/CORBIS; BOTTOM, © JEREMY HORNER/CORBIS

to have a battle like this
thrust on them by chance.

If you fail to wage this war
of sacred duty,
you will abandon your own duty
and fame only to gain evil.

(Bhagavad-Gita 2:31–33)[D]

Acting One's Age: Four Stages of Life

Hindu society distinguishes four stages of life, each with its own set of specific duties. The stages have traditionally been especially relevant for males who belong to the *vaishya, kshatriya,* and particularly *brahmin* classes.

Upon undergoing an initiation ritual at about the time of puberty, a Hindu boy enters the first stage, that of the student. Characterized by intensive study of the Vedas (vay´duhz) and other sacred literature, this stage lasts until marriage.

Hindu marriages are traditionally arranged by the parents, and the bride and groom commonly do not know each other until the time of the wedding. Though customs such as these are changing, especially in urban areas, many Hindus adhere to the traditional way. A contemporary young woman named Vimla, whose marriage was arranged, reasons: "We don't choose the family we're born into, we

adjust to it. So why should we risk choosing our marriage? It's too important to be left up to individual choice" (quoted in Mitter, *Dharma's Daughters,* page 18).[E]

In the second stage, that of the householder, the worldly tasks of pursuing a career and raising a family are central. Women are involved in this stage along with their husbands.

The birth of the first grandchild marks the beginning of the third stage, the forest dweller stage. A man may choose to ask his wife to accompany him through this stage, which allows him to retreat from worldly bonds (sometimes literally by dwelling in the forest) in order to engage fully in a spiritual quest.

The fourth stage is that of the **sannyasin** (sun-yah´sin), or wandering **ascetic.** This stage is for forest dwellers who are ready to return to society, but remain detached from the normal attractions and distractions of social life. Engaged with the world but not attached to it, the *sannyasin* is, as described in the Bhagavad-Gita, "one who neither hates nor desires" (5:3). Women who have accompanied their husbands into the forest might naturally advance to the fourth stage as well. If they do so, the husband and wife live detached from each other, having transcended the ordinary ways of this world, including those of marriage.[F]

career, family

leave, travel, retreat

E
Who do you think should choose a person's marriage partner? How does your perspective on this issue compare with Vimla's? What aspects of Hinduism might help account for any differences in perspective?

come back to society but remain detached

F
Describe the four Hindu stages of life, comparing each stage to a similar stage in Western society.

IMAGE: © DAVID CUMMING, EYE UBIQUITOUS/CORBIS

A Hindu marriage ceremony marks the start of the householder stage of life.

Seeking One's Desire: Four Goals of Life

Liberation from *samsara,* in the Hindu view, is the summit of spiritual perfection. *Moksha* is the ultimate goal of life. But what if we enjoy this world, welcome the challenges of this life, and relish its fruits? What if we are so content in this world that we appreciate reincarnation as yet another opportunity to seek the many pleasures of existence?

Sensual Pleasure

Hinduism embraces such pleasure seeking, even as it teaches the ultimate goal of liberation. Pleasure, or **kama** (kah′muh), is

Material success, or *artha,* is a legitimate goal in Hindu life and may be signified by jewelry and gold woven into a woman's sari.

IMAGE: STEVE VIDLER/SUPERSTOCK

a legitimate aim of life. No religion denies that humans desire pleasure. Religions differ drastically, however, in their judgments as to the goodness or rightness of fulfilling that desire. Hinduism tends to surpass most religions in its outright celebration of the pursuit of pleasure. *Kama,* which refers mainly to the pleasures of sensual love, is to be embraced by whosoever desires it, provided that the lovers remain within the limits of *dharma.* So legitimate is the pursuit of *kama* that some of Hinduism's sacred literature is devoted to the enhancement of sensual love.

Material Success

Despite its complete legitimacy, the appetite for *kama* is believed to have a limit. Eventually the fulfillment found in love will no longer satisfy completely. A yearning arises for something else. For most people this yearning is for **artha,** material success and the social power and prestige that accompany it. Just as North American secular society tends to embrace the pursuit of money, Hinduism celebrates the goal of *artha.* But also like the pursuit of money, *artha* eventually proves

The Laws of Manu on *Dharma*

Some of the classical texts of Hinduism devote a great deal of attention to spelling out the details of dharma, *setting forth specific rules of conduct. The Laws of Manu, composed by about AD 200, is the most famous of these texts. Its contents continue to dictate the ways of tradition-minded Hindus to this day. Here are two examples:*

On the Proper Place of the Hindu Woman

Day and night women must be kept in dependence by the males (of) their (families), and, if they attach themselves to sensual enjoyments, they must be kept under one's control.

Her father protects (her) in childhood, her husband protects (her) in youth, and her sons protect (her) in old age; a woman is never fit for independence.

Reprehensible is the father who gives not (his daughter in marriage) at the proper time; reprehensible is the husband who approaches not (his wife in due season), and reprehensible is the son who does not protect his mother after her husband has died.

(9:2–4)

On the Student Stage of Life

Let [the student] not pronounce the mere name of his teacher (without adding an honorific title) behind his back even, and let him not mimic his gait, speech, and deportment.

By censuring (his teacher), though justly, he will become (in his next birth) an ass, by falsely defaming him, a dog; he who lives on his teacher's substance, will become a worm, and he who is envious (of his merit), a (larger) insect.

(2:199,201)

unfulfilling. In due time people experience a yearning to strive for something beyond pursuits that provide for only personal and material needs.

Harmony with *Dharma*

This yearning leads to the third goal of life, which is called *dharma*. *Dharma* as a life goal maintains its meaning as the general principle of ethical duty. But it is no longer merely a duty, begrudgingly performed. It is now that which is most desired. The deep joy of living in harmony with *dharma* is known firsthand. No one needs to tell the Hindu who pursues this goal that it is more blessed to give than to receive. The blessings of *dharma* give fuel to its fire. Yet even perfect harmony with *dharma* is a limited joy, destined eventually to lead to even deeper yearnings. After all, the world for which the ethical person has concern—even if the concern is unconditional—is still the world of this realm, afflicted with the unending pains of *samsara*.

The Bliss of *Moksha*

All Hindus are destined to seek the fourth goal of life: the infinite being, awareness, and bliss of *moksha,* the great ocean into which all rivers eventually flow. And the paths to *moksha* that are available to Hindus are as numerous and diverse as the rivers of India.[G]

✴ Three Paths to Liberation

Hinduism offers three great paths to *moksha*. People have different talents and strengths, and each of the three paths draws primarily on one of the following human tendencies: to be active, to gain knowledge, and to experience emotional attachment. The paths are not mutually exclusive; in practice Hindus usually follow more than one. All three are revered as effective means of moving closer to the ultimate goal of liberation.

✴ For the Active: *Karma Marga,* "The Path of Works"

Most people—those engaged in the day-to-day tasks of earning a living and raising a family, those for whom physical activities come naturally—prefer to seek liberation through **karma marga,** "the path of works" (also referred to as *karma yoga*). Simple to understand and to practice, this path has everything to do with living in accordance with *dharma.*

Recall that *dharma* in its most general meaning is ethical duty, and includes observance of many traditional aspects of Hinduism: household rituals, public ceremonies, and social requirements, such as conforming to dietary laws and marriage restrictions. *Dharma* also involves an ongoing concern for the world, as exemplified in the most influential modern advocate of *karma marga,* Mahatma Gandhi. For Gandhi, religion itself is none other than concern for the world expressed through social service:

I am being led to my religion through Truth and Non-violence, i.e., love in the broadest sense. I often describe my religion as religion of Truth. Of late, instead of saying God is Truth I have been saying Truth is God, in order more fully to define my religion. . . .

The bearing of this religion on social life is, or has to be, seen in one's daily social contact. To be true to such religion one has to lose oneself in continuous and continuing service of all life. Realization of Truth is impossible without a complete merging of oneself in and

IMAGE: © HOWARD DAVIES/CORBIS

G
Reflect on a major goal you have had and have achieved. Was the satisfaction of accomplishing the goal permanent? Did it cause you to desire to achieve new goals? From the experience, what did you learn about desire?

This nurse dedicates her expertise to alleviating the suffering of poor people in urban Delhi. She is following *karma marga,* "the path of works."

identification with this limitless ocean of life. Hence, for me, there is no escape from social service; there is no happiness on earth beyond or apart from it. (*The Moral and Political Writings of Mahatma Gandhi*, volume 1, page 461)

In all its aspects, *karma marga* is marked by an attitude of unselfishness. When traveling this path, one must avoid selfishly claiming credit for having accomplished an action. This is challenging, for humans are inclined to be selfish. As Krishna remarks in the Bhagavad-Gita, "Deluded by individuality, / the self thinks, 'I am the actor'" (3:27). If every accomplishment requires a pat on the back, the bondage of individuality is strengthened, and the self is further removed from the universal ocean of Atman, its true source and essence. The path of works succeeds when one does the opposite, performing the right action without needing to claim the credit.

In a similar way, selfish attachment to the results of action must be avoided. Krishna instructs Arjuna:

Be intent on action,
not on the fruits of action;
avoid attraction to the fruits
and attachment to inaction!

(Bhagavad-Gita 2:47)

Do the right thing only because it is right. Be a good student, not because being a good student will earn you a good grade, but because being a good student is right in itself. Mahatma Gandhi did great deeds, but he did not act in order to be rewarded by the praise of others or even by a sense of self-satisfaction. He simply did what he perceived to be the right thing.[H]

For the Philosophical: *Jnana Marga*, "The Path of Knowledge"

The shortest but steepest ascent to liberation follows **jnana marga** (nyah′nah mar′guh),

"the path of knowledge" (also known as *jnana yoga*). This path is intended for those with talent for philosophical reflection. It requires the follower to devote a great deal of time to learning and meditation. These demands render *jnana marga* most practical for members of the *brahmin* class.

Whereas the path of works emphasizes doing the right thing over the wrong thing, *jnana marga* emphasizes attaining knowledge over ignorance—knowledge of the true nature of reality. This is an enormous challenge because *jnana* is knowledge of a very special sort, amounting to extraordinary insight that is far beyond merely knowing about the subject matter. To attain this kind of knowledge is to live it, to be that which is known, to experience the true nature of reality. *Jnana marga* is thus primarily part of the experiential dimension of Hinduism. The knowing itself is the experience sought; it does not culminate in knowledge *about* this or that doctrine or other aspect of Hinduism. With this experience, reached through profound contemplation of the innermost self, comes a full awareness of truth, a certitude that has the power to transform the knower, thus leading to liberation.

Three Schools of Philosophy

Different teachings within *jnana marga* offer various specifics regarding the true nature of reality. The most important are those of three schools of Hindu philosophy: Vedanta, Sankhya, and Yoga. Despite their differences, the three approaches are in harmony regarding the same basic task: the attainment of knowledge over the ignorance that binds the self to *samsara*.

Vedanta. The school **Vedanta** (vay-dahn′ tuh) is most faithful to the predominant monism of Hinduism. Even within Vedanta, though, the characteristic diversity of the religion is apparent. The most prominent form of Vedanta is that espoused by the great medieval philosopher Shankara (788 to 820). Most

[H]
"Do the right thing only because it is right." Must right actions be rewarded for people to want to do them, or should they be their own reward?

The belief all reality is one.

Hindu belief on people

Hindus who traverse the path of knowledge embrace this philosophy.

Shankara's understanding of reality amounts to the basic monism predominant in Hinduism: All reality is essentially one—Brahman, the indescribable, impersonal ultimate. The world and all finite beings within it are the stuff of **maya** (mah'yah), cosmic illusion. In a state of ignorance, people are tricked into thinking of their individual selves as being ultimately real, just as the world of a dream seems real to the dreamer.

This persistent sense of individuality prevents one from experiencing the truth. Just as one might think a droplet of ocean spray exists separately from the ocean, so do individuals imagine they exist independently of Brahman. But in an instant the droplet is absorbed back into the ocean, indistinguishable from its infinite source. So too is the individual eventually absorbed back into Brahman, its infinite source. For despite the illusion of separateness, in truth all are one. The atman, the

© 2008 The M.C. Escher Company–Holland. All rights reserved. www.mcescher.com.

M. C. Escher's lithograph *Waterfall* demonstrates the Hindu concept of *maya,* or cosmic illusion. For the person viewing Escher's work, as for the individual trapped in *maya,* the world is not as it seems.

When we die we are merged with maker as well as at death with the divine

self deep within, is really the eternal Atman, the infinite Self. And Atman is Brahman.

Shankara on *Maya*

This tale is told of the great Vedanta philosopher Shankara and one of his pupils, a powerful king, who decided to test his teacher regarding the nature of maya (cosmic illusion brought about by the divine creator):

The following day, therefore, when the philosopher was coming along one of the stately approaches to the palace, to deliver his next lecture to the king, a large and dangerous elephant, maddened by heat, was let loose at him. [Shankara] turned and fled the moment he perceived his danger, and when the animal nearly reached his heels, disappeared from view. When he was found, he was at the top of a lofty palm tree, which he had ascended with a dexterity more usual among sailors than intellectuals. The elephant was caught, fettered, and conducted back to the stables,

and the great [Shankara], perspiration breaking from every pore, came before his pupil.

Politely, the king apologized to the master of cryptic wisdom for the unfortunate, nearly disastrous incident; then, with a smile scarcely concealed and half pretending great seriousness, he inquired why the venerable teacher had resorted to physical flight, since he must have been aware that the elephant was of a purely illusory, phenomenal character.

The sage replied, "Indeed, in highest truth, the elephant is non-real. Nevertheless, you and I are as non-real as that elephant. Only your ignorance, clouding the truth with this spectacle of non-real phenomenality, made you see phenomenal me go up a non-real tree."

(Zimmer, *Philosophies of India,* page 20)

When one experiences this truth, one has followed the path of knowledge to its end: liberation of the self from *samsara* into the ocean of Brahman. But as the Upanishads warn, it is an arduous path, demanding that a unique kind of knowledge be applied to a difficult lesson:

Subtler than the subtlest is this Self, and beyond all logic. Taught by a teacher who knows the Self and Brahman as one, a man leaves vain theory behind and attains to truth. (Katha Upanishad 1.2.8)

Sankhya. Contrary to Hinduism's predominant monism, **Sankhya** (sahng´kyuh) asserts that reality is composed of two distinct categories: matter, and an infinite number of eternal selves. Somehow, for reasons beyond explanation, selves get entwined with matter, thereby becoming bound to the world of *samsara*. Such is the origin and the predicament of human beings. The follower of Sankhya strives to free the eternal Self from the bondage of the personality. The basic teachings of the Sankhya school are important for the religions Jainism and Buddhism, and underlie the Hindu approach of Yoga.

Yoga. The term *yoga* has different meanings in Hinduism. In the general sense, it refers to any sort of spiritual practice—as it does in the terms for the paths to salvation, where it is substituted for *marga*, as in *jnana yoga*. In a more limited usage, it refers to a philosophical school that emphasizes physical and psychological practices.

Yoga carefully acknowledges the connection between the self and the other parts of our human makeup—the body and its sensations, the mind and its thinking, and the subconscious. The objective of the yogi, or practitioner of Yoga, is to free the eternal self from bondage by stripping away the many levels of personhood in which that self is wrapped. Note how Sankhya's teaching of the division of reality into eternal selves and eternal matter underlies Yoga. Like Sankhya, Yoga regards sensations, the mind, even the subconscious as aspects of matter.

Various versions of Yoga are based on this understanding of the human condition. The most famous sets forth eight steps:

1. Preparing morally by abstaining from five acts: harming living things, lying, stealing, acting unchastely, and being greedy
2. Preparing morally by observing five virtues: cleanliness, calmness, self-control, studiousness, and prayerfulness
3. Sitting in a posture that promotes comfort while discouraging drowsiness (Eighty-four postures are described; the most popular is the lotus position, with feet crossed and resting on the thighs, hands crossed in the lap, eyes focused on the tip of the nose.)
4. Breathing properly so that the entire body is brought into a simple rhythmic pattern

The objective of the practitioner of Yoga is to free the eternal self from bondage.

IMAGE: © DAVID SAMUEL ROBBINS/CORBIS

5. "Closing the doors of perception": withdrawing the senses from any contact with objects
6. Concentrating on one thing so the mind empties itself of all other thoughts
7. Meditating, an ever deepening state of concentration moving toward the final step
8. Going into **samadhi** (suh-mah´dee), a trancelike state in which self-consciousness is lost, and the mind is absorbed into the ultimate reality

In *samadhi* the knower becomes that which is known; the path of knowledge has been traversed to its goal. Although in practice the yogi normally comes back out of the trance, the transforming power of *samadhi* leads to final liberation. Here we have a good example of a type of spiritual perfection involving the transcendence of the human condition, eventually leading to salvation. As is typical of the climactic phenomena of the experiential dimension of any religion, *samadhi* cannot adequately be explained by way of language.

Like the final liberating experience of *moksha, samadhi* must be experienced to be fully understood.[I]

For the Emotional: *Bhakti Marga,* "The Path of Devotion"

Based in loving reverence for one's chosen god or goddess, **bhakti marga** (buhk´tee mar´guh), "the path of devotion" (also referred to as *bhakti yoga*), is most suitable for those to whom emotional attachment comes naturally. In contrast to the inward journey of *jnana marga,* this path directs spiritual energy outward, in worship of the deity. This is beneficial because the gods and goddesses favor their devotees, and answer their prayers. Most important, *bhakti marga* moves its adherents closer to liberation. Worship requires a focusing of attention on the divine, and away from the adherent's selfish concerns. Through worship, the path of devotion helps to reduce the individuality that binds the self to *samsara.*

I
What might be some differences between the knowledge sought by a Hindu on *jnana marga* and the knowledge sought by a student working on a college degree?

IMAGE: © LINDSAY HEBBERD/CORBIS

A Hindu woman follows the path of devotion by visiting a temple, where she places water on a statue of the god Nandi.

Hinduism   57

Gods and Goddesses

Stories about Hinduism's many deities form the heart of the mythic dimension of Hinduism. Some of the deities have been a part of the tradition from the beginning, whereas others are newly acknowledged.

The vast variety of gods and goddesses points to an important fact about *bhakti marga*: a typical Hindu is devoted to more than one deity, depending on the specific needs of the day. Still it is common to choose a personal deity as the object of special devotion. Some of Hinduism's most popular deities are Vishnu, Shiva, Kali, and the *avatars* Krishna and Rama.

Among the 330 million gods and goddesses is an important triad: Brahma, the Creator; Vishnu, the Preserver; and Shiva, the Destroyer. Brahma, though still highly thought of, is rarely worshiped anymore. Today, as for centuries, Vishnu and Shiva are worshiped by millions. As his role as the Preserver suggests, Vishnu, with four arms and various symbols of power and goodness, is regarded by his devotees as their supreme protector and ex-

Depictions of Krishna with his favorite consort, Radha, symbolize perfect love.

ample of moral perfection. It is notable that Shiva, a god known for destruction, should be so popular. In fact this fits logically within the Hindu cyclical cosmology, for the destruction brought about by Shiva makes way for new creation.

The cycle of destruction and creation is similarly a primary theme of the popular goddess Kali, a wife of Shiva's. Black and wearing a necklace of skulls, she is a bloodthirsty, violent destroyer of her enemies. Toward her devotees, though, she shows steadfast care and affection, providing for their needs. The great Ramakrishna was one of her millions of devotees.

Avatars

An **avatar** is an incarnation, or living embodiment, of a deity, commonly of Vishnu, who is sent to earth to accomplish a divine purpose. The relationship of the *avatar* with the deity from which he comes is illuminated in the Bhagavad-Gita. Here Krishna, an *avatar* of Vishnu, actually speaks as Vishnu when he addresses Arjuna:

Though myself unborn, undying,
the lord of creatures, I fashion nature,
which is mine, and I come into being
through my own magic.

Whenever sacred duty decays
and chaos prevails,
then, I create
myself, Arjuna.

To protect men of virtue
and destroy men who do evil,
to set the standard of sacred duty,
I appear in age after age.

(4:6–8)

Krishna has a prominent role in the epic poem *Mahabharata* (mah-hah-bah´rah-tah), of which the Bhagavad-Gita is but a small section, and also is popular in another role— that of a somewhat mischievous and always amorous male cowherd, often accompanied by adoring bands of female cowherds. Hindu art beautifully depicts scenes that symbolize the loving adoration of souls (the female cowherds) for God (Krishna). Krishna is also frequently depicted with his favorite consort, Radha. The intensity of their feelings is clearly expressed, and they function as a symbol of perfect love.

Rama is another popular *avatar*. He is the hero of the *Ramayana,* an epic poem from ancient times that continues to have enormous influence among Hindus. Like Krishna, Rama is an incarnation of Vishnu. Through the centuries he has come to be so highly regarded that many Hindus revere him as the supreme deity.

The Bhagavad-Gita

The Bhagavad-Gita contains ideas that are relevant to many aspects of Hinduism. Still it is most closely associated with *bhakti marga.* The content of the Bhagavad-Gita acknowledges the fruitfulness of the path of works and the path of knowledge, but tends to favor the path of devotion. This oft-quoted passage, in which Krishna again addresses Arjuna, especially reveals the universal appeal of that path to salvation:

Whatever you do—what you take,
what you offer, what you give,
what penances you perform—
do as an offering to me, Arjuna!

You will be freed from the bonds of action,
from the fruit of fortune and misfortune;
armed with the discipline of renunciation,
your self liberated, you will join me.

I am impartial to all creatures,
and no one is hateful or dear to me;
but men devoted to me are in me,
and I am within them.

(9:27–29)

Aspects of Daily Devotion

If we were to ask a follower of *bhakti marga* to describe Hinduism, we would most likely learn first of the various acts of worship practiced from day to day. Along with a host of individual practices, such as prayer and visits to temples and shrines, Hindu worship includes numerous household and community rituals, pilgrimages to holy places, and veneration of the ever present and much adored sacred cows. Together such acts of worship constitute to a great extent the ritual dimension of Hinduism, and the objects that are the focus of these acts enrich the material dimension.

Household and village rituals. Hindu households are home to millions of "masks" of deities. Typically they maintain shrines that honor chosen deities and contain some form of image or symbol for those deities. Domestic worship includes the tending of a sacred fire, ritual bathing, and daily devotional rites before these shrines. Though the use of material representations of deities, such as clay figurines, may appear to be a form of idolatry, or idol worship, it is not. Hindus worship not the image itself but rather the god or goddess that the image represents.

On regular occasions the village joins together in worship. Often this occurs at the local temple, where ceremonies are conducted by a priest. Villages also celebrate annual festivals in honor of certain gods; sometimes these can last for days. For example, a festival in honor of Saraswati, the goddess of wisdom and patroness of education and the arts (and hence a popular goddess at schools), can involve days of celebration before a life-size image that has been specially crafted for the festival. On the final day, the image is given a funeral and disposed of—among the cheers of smiling devotees! The cycle of creation and destruction applies to the worship of the deities as well.

Holy places. Pilgrimages to holy sites, some long and arduous, are another common form of devotion. Sometimes the destination is a temple or other site of a great festival. It can also be a natural entity, such as a river.

The Quest for Truth

Shubhabrata Dutta, known as Shuvo to his friends, is a young Hindu man now living in the United States. He offers the following thoughts on the role of Hinduism in his life:

As far as I can remember, the first time I really thought about Hinduism was in sixth grade, through some sayings of Shri Ramakrishna. Before that, although I attended all the religious festivals (there are lots of them!), I never really questioned or understood my faith. The saying of Ramakrishna that left a deep impression on me was: "If you put zeroes after a one, it makes a great number, but if you erase the one, the zeroes by themselves are not of any worth. Likewise, if we remove God from the creation, the creation, by itself, does not make any sense."

I was struck by the depth and the intelligence of the analogy. I thought that only a great scholar could have come up with this kind of simple but deep uttering. So I asked my father, himself a devotee of Shri Ramakrishna, about the scholarly career of Shri Ramakrishna, and found out to my surprise that Ramakrishna could not even sign his name properly. That was a real shock! But much later I came to realize that the unscholarly way of Shri Ramakrishna may very well answer the questions philosophers have been asking for the last three thousand years. In light of Ramakrishna's life, I understood Hinduism with all its complications; I realized that it is not that complex after all if we can just "live the life." And above all, being a "true" Hindu is no different than being a "true" Muslim or a "true" Christian. Religions are not God but many "ways" to God. One who quarrels about the ways but forgets about the destination is nothing but a fool.

Being a Hindu is very simple, actually, at least from my point of view. Being a Hindu is no more than being an *honest* human being. There are no universally held dogmas (except perhaps the prohibition against eating beef), no unanimous theological or philosophical doctrines, and no single ethical practice. From both inside and outside, Hinduism looks like a total mess, an enormous forest of ideas and practices of very dissimilar (and sometimes totally opposite) nature. What then can I believe? What path will I choose? What is the right way? A Hindu will say: "Through self-examination you will find the answers. All you need is a burning desire to know the truth, and the rest will follow automatically." I believe in this, and to my great joy, the greatest spiritual personalities of India also believed in it and showed it in their lives.

As a Hindu I grew up with certain concepts that may seem funny to other people. One of them was that all the deities are associated with particular things. So I pick up a penny from the street and touch it to my forehead because money represents the goddess Lakshmi, or I scrupulously avoid touching any paper with my feet because I fear that Saraswati, the goddess of learning, might get angry with me. Such practices are necessary sometimes and unnecessary at other times. Why? Because, as Swami Vivekananda said, "A man does not proceed from falsehood to truth, but he moves from lower truth to higher truth." As a Hindu I believe that a certain ritual or a particular belief is necessary until I reach a point where it no longer helps me toward my *moksha,* my liberation. In the famous words of Shri Ramakrishna: "First you pluck out the thorn of ignorance using the thorn of knowledge. But then you throw both of them away." What remains then? Indescribable bliss.

Most rivers are regarded as sacred. The most famous river—and the one deemed most sacred—is the Ganges. Thought to fall from its heavenly source of Vishnu's feet onto Shiva's head and out from his hair, the water of the Ganges is sacred enough to purify all sins. Pilgrims seek its banks to partake in ritual baths, and the ashes of the dead are swallowed by its life-giving water.

Cow veneration. Mahatma Gandhi referred to the protection of cows as the "central fact of Hinduism" and "one of the most wonderful phenomena in human evolution" (*Young India,* page 804). For him, and for millions of his fellow Hindus, the cow represents life. It provides for Hindus in a multitude of ways and yet suffers along with them. Therefore Hindus venerate cows, worshiping them like deities, and on regular occasions decorating them with garlands and anointing their heads with oil. In the past, the killing of a cow was sometimes a capital offense.

Gandhi describes the encompassing significance of cow veneration:

The cow to me means the entire sub-human world. Man through the cow is enjoined to realise his identity with all that lives. . . . The cow is a poem of pity. One reads pity in the gentle animal. She is the mother to millions of Indian mankind. Protection of the cow means protection of the whole dumb creation of God. (Page 804)[J]

Hinduism in the Modern World

All traditional religions are challenged by the modern world. Scientific and secular views can erode the authority of perspectives based in ancient myths. Other religious traditions can become more familiar, offering new alternatives. And new movements, some in response to those very threats, can arise within a tradition, threatening the old ways.

The modern world seems to pose an especially acute challenge for Hinduism. India, home to most of the world's Hindus, is the world's largest democracy, and sets itself apart from religion, as a secular state. It is also rapidly becoming an economic powerhouse. For its many citizens who tend to equate Hinduism with India, and whose patterns of existence are provided by the ancient principles of *dharma,* the interplay of traditional religions with the secular state and its dynamic economy is frequently unsettled and contentious.

Some familiarity with the figures and issues of modern Hinduism can help us make sense of the contemporary situation.

Those Whom Hindus Revere: Religious Leaders

Along with the pervasive caste system and all that it implies, the social dimension of Hinduism features many significant religious figures, holy people in various roles who tend to provide continual spiritual nourishment for a tradition in the grip of change. *Brahmins* tend to ancient rituals; gurus, or enlightened teachers, teach the truths of the Upanishads to the young; *sannyasins* bear the serenity of spiritual transcendence even as they walk among their fellow villagers. All nourish Hinduism, connecting it with its illustrious past and directing it toward its future.

Mahatma Gandhi

Remembered primarily for his work as a social and political reformer, Mohandas K. Gandhi (1869 to 1948), reverently called Mahatma, meaning "great souled," is also revered by many for his role as a religious reformer. His steadfast efforts to stand up to oppression through nonviolence and civil disobedience forever changed the nature of India, and of Hinduism. And yet his assassination by a Hindu extremist in 1948, just months after the accomplishment of his long-term goal to

J
Discuss the differences between your own experience of worship and the worship of a Hindu on *bhakti marga,* "the path of devotion."

A follower of Gandhi's spins thread and fasts to protest Hindu attacks on Christians and church properties. Gandhi introduced the practice of spinning to promote Indian self-sufficiency after the British cut off the thumbs of Indian tailors and forced them to buy British cloth at high prices.

IMAGE: AP IMAGES/WIDE WORLD PHOTOS

gain Indian independence from British rule, is darkly symbolic of the modern challenges that Hinduism faces, now as much as then.

Although Gandhi as a man is dead, Gandhi as a religious figure lives on. His insights continue to fuel Hinduism's tendency to accept all wisdom as lighting the way to the divine. In towns all across India, statues of Gandhi, under the protective guard of Vishnu's multiheaded cobra, remind Hindus of his revered presence.

The Sacred Among the Secular: Contemporary Issues

A seemingly countless number of pressing issues are emerging as traditional Hinduism and secular India continue their journey together in the twenty-first century. Let us consider three of them.

The Caste System

The complex social distinctions based on the caste system, especially those of the outcastes, came under careful scrutiny during the twentieth century. Significant changes have occurred, some quite recently.

In a major development, one for which Gandhi struggled for years, the Indian government in 1948 officially forbade discrimination against outcastes. Governmental programs since that time, similar to affirmative action programs in the United States, have sought to further promote the economic and social rights of those people. Among some upper-caste Indians, such programs are meeting harsh resistance. In general, attitudes based in something so deeply traditional as the caste system tend to change slowly. Such is the case as India struggles with this issue.

Women in Hindu Society

Traditional Hindu society has always been strongly patriarchal—under the domination of men. Typically women's *dharma* has required them to be obedient to men. But, as is the case with Hinduism in general, opinions on the topic of women's roles in Hinduism differ. The degree to which Hindus follow such traditional teachings varies considerably between locales, especially between cities and towns. For many urban Indians, the norms are clearly changing.

One striking example of the controversial treatment of women in Hinduism—and of the vast changes that have occurred in some cases—is the practice of **sati** (suh'tee), the burning of a widow. The following passage from a Hindu text called the Padmapurana sets forth some of the traditional teachings, both on *sati* and on the general obedience expected of a wife:

A wife must eat only after her husband has had his fill. If the latter fasts, she shall fast, too; if he touch not food, she also shall not touch it; if he be in affliction, she shall be so, too; if he be cheerful, she shall share his joy. She must on the death of her husband allow herself to be burnt alive on the same funeral pyre; then everybody will praise her virtue. (Quoted in Noss and Noss, *A History of the World's Religions,* page 119)

Although the authority of texts such as this has been questioned throughout the history of Hinduism, for centuries, *sati* was a common practice in Hindu life. Since 1829 *sati* has been officially forbidden. It does still occur, though rarely.

In some ways traditional Hinduism has been able to conform to modern norms. In others traditional practices are changing slowly. For instance, the enduring preference for raising boys rather than girls is made clear through an array of statistical evidence showing general preferential treatment of boys. One study among rural children found that more than two-thirds of those considered severely malnourished were girls (Mitter, *Dharma's Daughters,* page 116).

Hindus and Muslims

Islam and Hinduism have experienced a long history of contact, beginning in the eighth century. The contact has not always been peaceful. This is not surprising when one considers that these two religions are vastly different from each other. Still, for centuries Hindus and Muslims (adherents of Islam) have lived side by side in South Asia. For the most part, they have influenced each other's religious traditions very little, although Muslims have had a substantial effect on the artistic and scientific life of India.

In recent decades relations between Hindus and Muslims have remained uneasy, at times erupting into violence. In 1947 the Muslim community forced the partitioning of India to form the divided nation of Pakistan (the eastern part of which is now Bangladesh), thus providing a Muslim homeland. This turned into a bloody ordeal in which many followers of both religions were killed. The assassination of Gandhi occurred in its aftermath. More recently another bloody confrontation broke out in the ancient city of Ayodhya, where a Muslim mosque stood on the site traditionally regarded as the birthplace of the *avatar* Rama. In 1992, after months of tense standoffs, some three hundred thousand Hindus stormed the mosque and tore it to the ground. The challenges posed by relations between Hindus and Muslims continue to be of great concern for

IMAGE: © BALDEV/CORBIS

Residents of Ayodha, India, gather around the ruins of the mosque destroyed by Hindus in 1992.

Muslim and Hindu leaders come together in Ahmadabad, where rioting between Muslims and Hindus in February 2002 left more than one thousand people dead.

K
The secular state of India and the traditional religion Hinduism tend to disagree over some important issues. How does religion relate to the secular state in your country?

India. Now that both India and neighboring Pakistan possess nuclear capabilities, the simmering conflict between the two nations is especially dangerous.[K]

Hinduism Outside of South Asia

Most Hindus still live in India and Nepal where the Hindu population exceeds 80 percent, During the modern period, enough people have left India to give rise to significant Hindu populations throughout the world, especially in cities.

Hinduism has also moved outside of South Asia in the form of sects and philosophical societies that, though based on the teachings of Hinduism, have often been adopted and advocated by non-Indians. Beginning in the 1960s, movements such as the International Society for Krishna Consciousness (the Hare Krishna movement) and the transcendental meditation movement became popular in the West, especially among young people.

Swami Vivekananda and the World's Parliament of Religions

A follower of Shri Ramakrishna, Swami Vivekananda (1863 to 1902) took up his master's teaching on the unity of religions and established the Ramakrishna Mission, which is a significant organization within Hinduism today. Vivekananda also became the first Hindu missionary, and he achieved fame in 1893 by explaining the teachings of Hindu Vedanta to the World's Parliament of Religions in Chicago. He went on to establish the Vedanta Society in New York, San Francisco, and many other cities. Thanks largely to Ramakrishna and Vivekananda, Hinduism is alive and flourishing in the Western world today.

The Ever Changing Currents of Hinduism

The many rivers of Hindu belief and practice are more numerous today than ever. Along with the diversity that has always come so naturally, the modern world presents a vast new set of challenges, alternatives, and opportunities.

Hinduism is experiencing a great coming together of old and new. In many towns of India, the traditional ways have changed little. The temples are still in place; the festivals occur as they always have; and *brahmins* perform ancient rituals. In the cities, on the other hand, high-rise offices and apartment buildings are filled with the typical features of modernity, including the high-tech devices familiar to Westerners. And more commonly today than yesterday, India herself is responsible for developing the world's high technology.

And so these many rivers—ancient and modern, rural and urban—continue to flow toward the distant ocean of salvation, finally merging the millions of Hindus in the harmony that unites their religion.

Chapter Review

1. Explain the meaning of the term *moksha*.
2. What doctrine says all reality is ultimately one? Give an analogy that describes it.
3. Define Brahman and Atman. How are the two related?
4. What is the general function of Hinduism's many deities?
5. Give a brief explanation of the doctrine of *samsara*.
6. What is the name of Hinduism's most popular sacred text?
7. According to Hinduism, what are the two principles that connect the divine to this world? Briefly explain each.
8. Name the four classes of the caste system and describe the people who belong to each.
9. In the Bhagavad-Gita, why does Krishna encourage Arjuna to engage in war?
10. Identify and briefly explain the four stages of life.
11. Name and briefly describe the four goals of life.

The Seven Dimensions of Religion: Hinduism

Dimension	Examples
Experiential	*moksha, samadhi*
Mythic	stories and descriptions of the 330 million gods and goddesses
Doctrinal	monism, teachings of Sankhya and Yoga
Ethical	rules and ideals of *dharma*
Ritual	various forms of worship practiced by followers of *bhakti marga*
Social	the caste system; various Hindu holy figures, such as the *sannyasin*
Material	the Ganges River, clay figurines of deities, sacred cows

Top: In the villages of rural India, subsistence farming continues today as it has for centuries. *Bottom:* Mumbai, with its office complexes and apartment buildings, symbolizes modern currents in the ancient traditions of Hinduism.

12. Identify the three paths to liberation. Which type of person is best suited for each path?

13. What are the three most important schools of Hindu philosophy? What is the basic task that concerns all three?

14. Identify three important gods or goddesses of Hinduism.

15. What is an *avatar?* Name two important Hindu figures identified as *avatars.*

16. What Hindu text is most closely associated with *bhakti marga?*

17. Identify three aspects of Hindu devotional life.

18. How did Mahatma Gandhi influence Hinduism?

19. What significant changes in the caste system took place in the twentieth century?

20. What is *sati?* What is its status today?

21. What significant development occurred in relations between Hindus and Muslims in 1947?

Glossary

artha. Material success and social prestige, one of the four goals of life.

ascetic. One who renounces physical pleasures and worldly attachments for the sake of spiritual advancement; common in Hinduism and many other religious traditions, most notably Jainism.

Atman (aht´muhn). The eternal self, which the Upanishads identify with Brahman; *often lowercase:* the eternal Self or soul of an individual that is reincarnated from one body to the next and is ultimately identified with Atman.

avatar. An incarnation, or living embodiment, of a deity, usually of Vishnu, who is sent to earth to accomplish a divine purpose; Krishna and Rama are the most popular *avatars.*

Bhagavad-Gita (buh´guh-vuhd gee´tah; Sanskrit: The Song of the Blessed Lord). A short section of the epic poem *Mahabharata* in which the god Krishna teaches the great warrior Arjuna about *bhakti marga* and other ways to God; Hinduism's most popular sacred text.

bhakti marga (buhk´tee mar´guh; also *bhakti yoga;* Sanskrit: "the path of devotion"). The most popular of the three Hindu paths to salvation, emphasizing loving devotion to one's chosen god or goddess.

Brahman (brah´muhn). The eternal essence of reality and the source of the universe, beyond the reach of human perception and thought.

brahmin (brah´min). The highest of the four classes of the caste system, traditionally made up of priests.

caste system. Traditional division of Hindu society into various categories; there are four main *varnas,* or classes: *brahmin, kshatriya, vaishya,* and *shudra;* each class contains numerous subgroups, resulting in more than three thousand categories.

dharma (dahr´muh). Ethical duty based on the divine order of reality; one of the four goals of life.

jnana marga (nyah´nah mar´guh; also *jnana yoga;* Sanskrit: "the path of knowledge"). One of three Hindu paths to salvation, emphasizing knowing the true nature of reality through learning and meditation.

kama (kah´muh). Pleasure, especially of sensual love; one of the four goals of life.

karma (Sanskrit: "action"). The moral law of cause and effect of actions; determines the nature of one's reincarnation.

karma marga (also *karma yoga;* Sanskrit: "the path of works"). One of three Hindu paths to salvation, emphasiz-

ing performing right actions according to *dharma.*

kshatriya (kshuht´ree-yuh). The second of the four classes of the caste system, traditionally made up of warriors and administrators.

maya (mah´yah). Cosmic illusion brought about by divine creative power.

moksha (mohk´shuh). Liberation or release of the individual self, atman, from the bondage of *samsara;* salvation; one of the four goals of life.

monism. The doctrine that reality is ultimately made up of only one essence.

Rig Veda (rig vay´duh). A collection of 1,017 Sanskrit hymns composed about 1500 BC or earlier; Hinduism's oldest sacred text.

samadhi (suh-mah´dee). A trancelike state in which self-consciousness is lost, and the mind is absorbed into the ultimate reality; the culmination of the eight steps of Yoga.

samsara (sahm-sah´ruh). The wheel of rebirth or reincarnation; the this-worldly realm in which rebirth occurs.

Sankhya (sahng´kyuh). A system of Hindu philosophy and one approach within *jnana marga,* "the path of knowledge," asserting that reality comprises two distinct categories: matter and eternal selves.

sannyasin (sun-yah´sin). A wandering ascetic who has

advanced to the fourth and highest stage of life.

sati (suh´tee). The traditional practice of burning a widow on her husband's funeral pyre; outlawed in 1829, though it still occurs rarely.

shudra (shoo´druh). The lowest of the four classes of the caste system, traditionally made up of servants and laborers.

Upanishads (oo-pah´ni-shuhdz; from Sanskrit: "sitting near a teacher"). A collection of over two hundred texts composed between 900 and 200 BC that provide philosophical commentary on the Vedas.

vaishya (vish´yuh). The third of the four classes of the caste system, traditionally made up of producers, such as farmers, merchants, and artisans.

Vedanta (vay-dahn´tuh). A system of Hindu philosophy and one approach within *jnana marga,* "the path of knowledge," holding that all reality is essentially Brahman; most notable advocate is the medieval Hindu philosopher Shankara.

Yoga. A system of Hindu philosophy and one approach within *jnana marga,* "the path of knowledge," seeking to free the eternal self from the bondage of personhood, culminating in the experience of *samadhi; lowercase:* physical and psychological techniques for spiritual advancement.

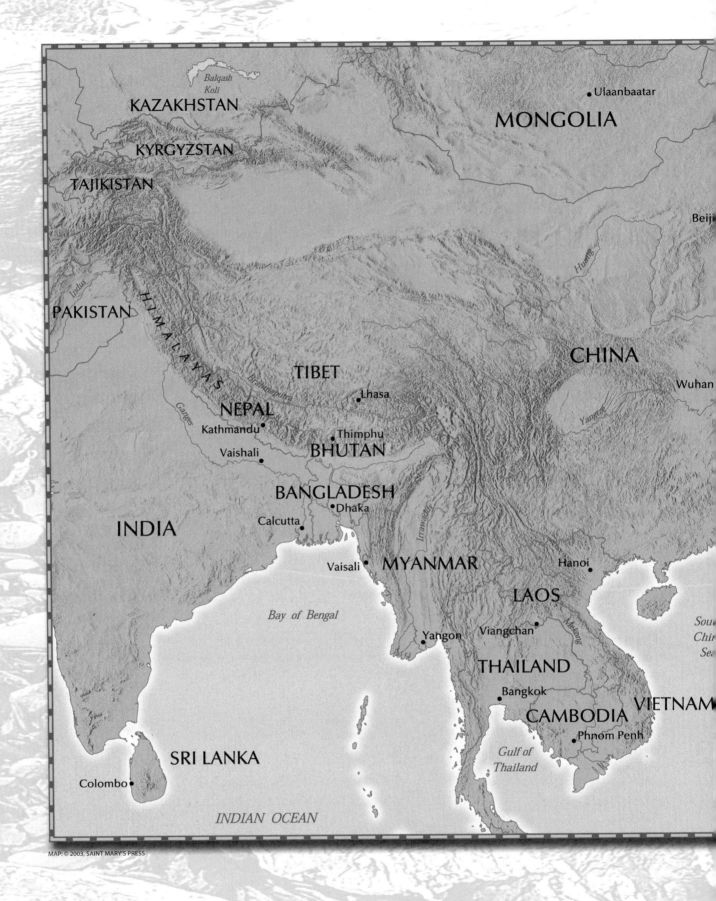

4 Buddhism

A Therapy for Living from One Who "Woke Up"

Buddhism, like Hinduism, arose in ancient India. But in stark contrast to Hinduism, with its streams of traditions converging from various sources of India's past, Buddhism began with one man. Gautama was merely a man—not a god or other supernatural being—but he was an exceptional man who underwent an extraordinary experience. To put it briefly, he "woke up"—hence acquiring the name **Buddha** (*boo*'duh), which is derived from *budh,* "to awaken." He awoke to full awareness of the nature of the human condition, and to the means of transcending it.

Buddhism teaches the discoveries attained by this man, through this experience of awakening.

Fundamental to Gautama's discoveries is that human beings are by nature prone to suffer. In other words we are in a state of disease, and we need treatment. In a manner very much like that of a physician, proceeding rationally and empirically, Gautama diagnosed the human condition and prescribed a cure. One way of understanding Buddhism, then, is as a therapy for living.

Having begun with just one man, Buddhism gradually developed into a religious tradition that includes various interpretations of the Buddha's teachings. We will explore the major divisions within Buddhism at the end of this chapter. First, let us examine the foundations—Gautama the Buddha and his teachings—which are of central significance for all forms of Buddhism.

The Life of Gautama

Like the lives of most founders of great religious traditions, that of Gautama is known

The birth of Buddha is illustrated in a Korean temple painting.

more through legend than through fact. Any attempt to produce an accurate life history of Gautama is doomed to some degree of failure. Full accounts of the Buddha's life were not written down until hundreds of years after his death, by which time legendary elements had long been established. Nevertheless, the story of Gautama is meaningful and instructive, reflecting in vivid form the issues and ideals that lie at the heart of Buddhism.

From Pampered Prince to Starving Ascetic

Born about 560 BC, the future Buddha was given the name Siddhartha. His family's name was Gautama, and so his full name is Siddhartha Gautama (though he is most commonly referred to simply as Gautama). His family belonged to the warrior *(kshatriya)* class, and his father was the ruler of a small region in northern India.

Gautama was born into a position of worldly power. According to traditional Buddhist belief, he was destined to become either a universal king (that is, a ruler over all peoples) or a Buddha, an awakened one who would offer the world salvation. The accounts of his birth tell of miraculous events befitting the arrival of such a great one. Said to have come out of his mother's side, Gautama at once strode seven paces and declared that in this lifetime he would gain enlightenment. A sage, upon seeing the boy's perfect form, affirmed that this child would gain enlightenment and become a savior.

Gautama's father wanted Gautama to become a universal king. He pampered the young prince with all the comforts of the palace. Gautama grew up in luxury, safe from the sufferings of the outside world. He was surrounded by thousands of servants and beautiful dancing girls. Eventually he married the finest maiden of the kingdom, and the two had a son. It would seem that Prince Siddhartha was enjoying a life of complete satisfaction.

The Four Passing Sights

Soon Gautama discovered that such satisfaction would not endure forever. In spite of his father's attempts to shield him from the harsh realities of the world, Gautama encountered them firsthand in an episode known as the Four Passing Sights. While he was traveling for pleasure in the countryside, his chariot passed a decrepit old man. Never before having seen old age, Gautama brooded over the implication of this sight—that such a fate was in store for everyone, himself included. On a second ride, the prince saw a diseased man, and again was dismayed and deeply disturbed. How could people enjoy life when disease threatened them all? On a third trip, Gautama saw a corpse for the first time. He was now more devastated than before, for with this sight he learned of death. Was it not senseless for people to go on living as if oblivious to the certainty of death?

These first three sights were penetrating lessons about the reality of suffering and the impermanent nature of life's pleasures. Having seen them Gautama knew he would never again find contentment in the luxuries of the palace. Nor could he again feel safe, now that he had learned the truths of old age, disease, and death. He mounted his horse and rode out from the palace, grieving as he observed the toil of peasants plowing the fields, and the destruction of living things uprooted by the plows. Eventually Gautama saw a religious ascetic, a man who had chosen to lead a homeless life of solitude and self-denial. The man explained that he was in search of salvation from this world of suffering, and then he continued on his way.

The ascetic, the fourth of the passing sights, filled Gautama with elation and hope: here was a means of overcoming his despair. Soon he would leave the palace forever, to embark on the homeless life.[A]

The Great Going Forth

At age twenty-nine, Gautama gave up his life as a prince, secretly leaving his family and palace by horseback in the dark of night. Gautama removed his jewels and dismissed his servant, sending him back with a message for the king: Gautama had not left out of resentment or lack of affection. Rather, his purpose was to put an end to old age and death. Gautama renounced a life of power and sensual enjoyment for the austere life of a mendicant (a religious person who owned nothing and begged for necessities like food and clothing). Buddhists revere this event in Gautama's life, known as the Great Going Forth, as the triumph of the spiritual over the worldly life.

IMAGE: GIRAUDON/ART RESOURCE, NY

A

How are the facts of old age, disease, and death given meaning within your religious tradition or within the religious tradition with which you are most familiar?

This Chinese painting from the ninth century depicts the Buddha and the Four Passing Sights. These sights raised religious questions that led to the founding of Buddhism.

B

Imagine yourself in Gautama's place, a pampered prince or princess with all life's worldly joys at your disposal. What would it take for you to leave it all, as Gautama did?

C

How might the doctrine of the Middle Way be relevant to the way you live? Reflect on the ways you follow (or do not follow) the Middle Way.

Gautama came upon other mendicants who taught him their versions of meditation. He learned their methods quickly, but he was not satisfied with their results. Salvation, he believed, lay beyond the meditative accomplishments of those teachings. Soon he joined a group of five mendicants who practiced asceticism to win salvation. Gautama excelled in the practice of fasting, spending the next several years on the brink of starvation. The Buddhist tradition tells of meals consisting of one piece of fruit, one sesame seed, one grain of rice. Believing that reduction of the body would increase his spiritual powers, Gautama diminished himself to skin and bones.[B]

The Middle Way

Starvation did not lead to salvation. And so, six years after leaving the palace, in another famous episode, Gautama accepted a simple meal of rice and milk. He quickly regained enough strength to proceed on his quest. His five companions left him, disgusted that he had abandoned asceticism.

A nineteenth-century Tibetan painting shows Mara's assault on Gautama as he sat beneath the fig tree seeking enlightenment.

IMAGE: RÉUNION DES MUSÉES NATIONAUX/ART RESOURCE, NY

Gautama thus discovered the important Buddhist doctrine of the **Middle Way.** Having earlier rejected a lifestyle of sensual indulgence in the palace, he now rejected the other extreme of asceticism. The Middle Way holds that a healthy spiritual life depends on a healthy physical life. Though it rejects indulgence in bodily pleasure, it does not reject the body itself. In general, the doctrine embraces the idea that contentment is a good thing. Spiritual happiness implies complete happiness—in body, in mind, and in spirit.[C]

The Enlightened One

Now Gautama, contented and strong in body, was prepared to devote all his effort to attaining salvation. Sitting in the lotus position beneath a fig tree, he resolved not to leave the spot until he had found complete and perfect fulfillment.

Traditional accounts of Gautama's enlightenment begin by depicting his encounters with the basic human shortcomings of fear and passionate desire. Mara, the god of death, noted Gautama's resolution, and was alarmed at the prospect that he might succeed. Attempting to defend his realm, Mara desperately tried to frighten Gautama from his spot. But Gautama could not be scared away. Then Mara sent forth his three daughters—the goddesses Discontent, Delight, and Desire—hoping to roust Gautama through an appeal to his passions. Again Gautama was unmoved, touching the earth to call it to be a witness to his resolve. Defeated, Mara and his daughters departed.

Enlightenment

Gautama had overcome the distractions of fear and passion, represented in legends by Mara and his daughters. Now Gautama turned his focus inward and entered a meditative trance. He ascended through levels of ever deepening awareness, until he could perceive with perfect clarity the true nature of the human condition.

During the portion of the night traditionally called the First Watch (evening), Gautama perceived his own previous lifetimes. He observed his long passage from rebirth to death to another rebirth, and so on, a continuous journey of suffering. During the Second Watch (middle of the night), he acquired the "divine eye," the ability to perceive the deaths and rebirths of all living beings. Nowhere in this world was there any safety, nowhere an escape from death. During the Third Watch (late night), Gautama discovered the Four Noble Truths, the perfect summation of the human condition and the means for transcending it.

By discovering the Four Noble Truths, Gautama had attained enlightenment—spiritual perfection in this life—and thus had won salvation. Now Gautama had become the Buddha, the Awakened One.[D]

Founding of the Sangha

Gautama the Buddha remained for many days in his spot beneath the fig tree (referred to ever since as the *bodhi,* or "wisdom," tree). In a state of perfect tranquillity and infinite wisdom, he was forever liberated from the sufferings of the human condition. He was tempted to leave his body and pass into **nirvana,** the state of eternal bliss that is ultimate salvation. His depth of compassion, however, compelled him to remain in the world and to share his discoveries with his fellow humans. True, his doctrines would be quite difficult for others to understand. Yet if just one person could comprehend them and thereby gain salvation, his effort would be well spent.

The Buddha wondered, to whom should he offer his teachings? His five former companions would perhaps grasp their meaning, he thought, and so he set off to find them. When

D
Gautama discovered the truths of Buddhism solely by looking inward, through meditation. Take a few minutes to look inward, to contemplate who you are. What truths regarding your own nature are you able to discover?

the five first saw Gautama, they decided to ignore him, convinced he was no longer worthy of their company because he had abandoned asceticism. But his spiritual presence overcame their intentions. Soon they sat listening as the Buddha, perfectly calm and radiant in his wisdom, preached his First Sermon at the Deer Park near the city of Benares. He taught the doctrines of the Middle Way and the Four Noble Truths. Gradually the five mendicants grasped his teachings and attained enlightenment, thereby becoming *arhats,* "worthy ones" or saints. The Buddha had gained his first followers; Buddhism as a religious tradition was born.

For the remaining forty-five years of his life, the Buddha continued to teach, attracting an ever growing following. The first Buddhist monastic community, or **Sangha** (sahn´guh), was formed, consisting of men and women from all walks of life. Gautama's son is said to have been among those earliest Buddhists. The Sangha was carefully organized, with specific roles for monks and nuns, and a clearly defined relationship with laypeople. For the three months of the monsoon season, the entire Sangha remained together in retreat. During the remaining nine months of the year, the Buddha and his followers traveled about the land teaching.

To this day being a Buddhist means taking refuge in the tradition's Three Jewels, or three focal elements: the Buddha, the Dharma (the Buddha's teachings), and the Sangha (the Buddhist monastic community). The act of taking refuge traditionally involves repeating a ritual formula three times. It amounts to a formal acknowledgment of the authority of the Three Jewels, and indicates a definite commitment to being a Buddhist.[E]

Death and Final *Nirvana*

At the age of eighty, in about 480 BC, the Buddha became seriously ill after eating a meal of spoiled food. To a gathering of monks and nuns, Gautama spoke his final words: "All the constituents of being are transitory; work out your salvation with diligence" (quoted in

E

As one of the Three Jewels, the Sangha obviously plays an important role in Buddhism. Describe a community (religious or otherwise) in which you participate. What is the role of community togetherness and organization? What is the relationship between community and learning?

This *stupa,* or shrine, is built on the place where the Buddha preached his First Sermon at the Deer Park.

IMAGE: © JEREMY HORNER/CORBIS

Buddhism in Translations, page 109). In this last message, the Buddha affirmed the hope of salvation for subsequent Buddhists. The physician was leaving his patients, but his prescription was to remain available for all.

After ascending through the stages of meditation to a state of perfect tranquillity, Gautama died, passing forever into *nirvana.*[F]

The Dharma: Buddhist Teachings

Most Buddhists revere Gautama and look to his life and enlightenment as the model for their own religious aspirations. But the Buddha's teachings, rather than the Buddha himself, play the predominant role in defining the religious life of Buddhism.

Buddhist teachings, or **Dharma** (dahr′muh) — not to be confused with the related Hindu doctrine of *dharma,* or "ethical duty" — are in some respects difficult to understand. They are born not of mental reflection but of insight gained through a profound meditative experience. Thus full understanding of Buddhist teachings requires an equal degree of insight gained directly through meditation. Gautama himself questioned whether anyone would comprehend his teachings, and all along he seems to have advocated Buddhism for only the few who considered themselves fit for the task.

But Buddhist teachings also have a simple aspect: they are the insights of a mere human being. Unlike many religions, Buddhism does not depend on a revelation from the divine for its truths. Buddhist truths were discovered through the inward reflections of a man, and are therefore potentially understandable by anyone. Rather than relying heavily on faith, Buddhism emphasizes the development of wisdom, or insight into the human condition. Buddhism is thus the most psychologically oriented of all the great religions.[G]

Buddhism and Hinduism: The Indian Context

Buddhism naturally shares many ideas with Hinduism because it arose in India during the period when the Upanishads were composed. But whereas Hindus have regarded Buddhism as a close relative of their own religion (many Hindus even consider the Buddha an incarnation of the god Vishnu), the Buddha himself in many ways reacted against the Hinduism of his day.

A Shared Cosmology

Buddhism and Hinduism both regard time as cyclical. They maintain that the universe is eternal, with ages of creation and destruction following one after the other. Because of this eternal time scheme, both Buddhism and Hinduism are considered eternal—are believed to have come to be and passed away many times, in cyclical fashion, along with the rest of creation. For Buddhists, then, Gautama the Buddha is not the first or only Buddha. In fact countless Buddhas preceded him, and countless Buddhas will follow him.

Many worlds exist in this eternal cyclical time scheme. Gods and goddesses inhabit various heavens, and demons inhabit various hells. Between them are the middle realms, including those of animals and humans. This scheme of multiple worlds has much in common with the Hindu universe.

Basic to this cosmology for both traditions is the doctrine of **samsara** (sahm-sah′ruh), the "wheel of rebirth," which holds that the inhabitants of all these realms are generally destined to continue being reborn in one realm or another. People can escape the cycle of rebirth only through liberation from *samsara.* That liberation is usually called *moksha* in Hinduism and *nirvana* in Buddhism. For both traditions liberation is the final goal, the end result of spiritual perfection.

F
"Work out your salvation with diligence." Use what you know about the Buddha's religious quest to elaborate on the meaning of his final words.

G
Although clearly legendary, the life story of Gautama is meaningful and instructive, reflecting the issues and ideals that lie at the heart of Buddhism. Within the story identify examples of at least five of the seven dimensions of religion.

The Buddha's Reaction Against Early Hinduism

The Buddha was discontented with many of the religious features of his day, especially the speculative philosophy and the sacrificial rituals that were the domain of the *brahmin* class. As the Upanishads illustrate, early Hinduism embraced philosophical speculation regarding the nature of the world, the human self, and the divine. The Buddha dismissed such speculation as being useless for the task of winning salvation. He insisted, instead, on direct inward observation of the human condition. He thought sacrificial rituals of devotion to gods were equally useless. Although Buddhism accepts the existence of deities, it holds that only the human mind can win salvation.

Gautama also rejected the institutional structure of Hinduism, in which only males of the *brahmin* class controlled the sacrificial rituals and sacred texts. The Buddha, himself born into the powerful warrior class, explicitly rejected the Hindu caste system. And, though apparently with some reluctance, he allowed women to join the Sangha and to become nuns.

Buddhism's tendency to accept all people is also apparent in the language of its earliest texts, which was **Pali** (pah′lee), a local dialect spoken by the common people. At the time, the sacred texts of Hinduism were all written in Sanskrit, which only the *brahmins* were expected to know. The teachings of the Buddha, though difficult to understand, were made available to everyone.

Individuals and Their Destiny

Buddhist teachings focus on the predicament of individuals and their destiny. This makes the teachings simple in the sense that their subject matter is confined to one thing, the individual. Everything the Buddha discovered is discoverable in oneself. The difficult aspect of the teachings lies mainly in this paradox:

H
"The essence of Buddhism is, there is no essence." Discuss the meaning of that saying.

To examine completely the inner realm of self leads to the discovery that the self *does not exist.* Let us attempt to make some sense of this paradox.

The Three Marks of Existence: No-Self, Impermanence, and Suffering

A main teaching of the Hindu Upanishads is that Atman, the eternal Self that resides deep within everyone, is identical to Brahman, the ultimate reality. To find Atman within and to be absorbed in it is the final aim for the Hinduism of the Upanishads.

Gautama looked deeply within, but his discovery led him to a radically different conclusion. In a word, Gautama discovered *change.* Everything, within and without, is changing, in a constant state of flux, impermanent. He summarized this changing nature of reality by noting **Three Marks of Existence.**

Anatta. Rather than finding Atman (called *atta* in Pali), the Buddha found **anatta** (uh-nat′uh), "no-self." *Anatta* means there is no ultimate reality within, no essence underlying existence, no eternal substratum that is truly real, enduring beyond the present moment. This paradox, central to Buddhist teachings, can be summarized thus: The essence of Buddhism is, there is no essence.

To gain understanding of the doctrine of *anatta,* consider your own situation. Where were you ten years ago? It may be tempting to answer, "I was in grade school," or in this or that place. But the Buddha would answer that you simply did not exist ten years ago. The you that exists now is the result of a long sequence of change. And you continue to change, literally from moment to moment. You hear a new idea from a friend or teacher, and suddenly your outlook changes; you are left with a different self. You eat a meal, and the nutrients affect the makeup of your body. Modern physiological science would generally agree with the Buddha, for not a single molecule of the bodies we inhabit were part of us more than seven years ago. Our bodies, like our selves, are continually changing.[H]

Anicca. The second mark of existence defined by the Buddha is **anicca** (uh-nee´chuh), which means "impermanence." *Anicca* is closely related to *anatta,* but it focuses on the idea that existence is constantly changing. Consider this example: Often we speak of a river flowing. The Buddha, always insistent on the precision of speech, would correct us: the flowing is the river. A river is a dynamic process, not a static entity. We may think a river is a real and unchanging thing, but actually it is an ongoing flow, a constant sequence of change. The same understanding applies to the self: it appears to be real and unchanging, but in fact it is an ongoing flow—of thoughts, perceptions, fears, hopes, and so on—that is constantly changing.[I]

Dukkha. The third mark of existence is *dukkha,* which is usually translated as "suffering." *Dukkha* is a natural result of *anicca* and *anatta.* It is one of the Four Noble Truths, and will be considered in detail later in this chapter.

Samsara: Buddhist Rebirth

The paradoxical doctrine of *anatta* raises a difficult question regarding belief in rebirth, or *samsara:* if there is no self, what is reborn? In Hinduism this is not a concern, because the eternal Atman resides within everyone. Dying is similar to discarding old clothes, and rebirth is like putting on new ones (Bhagavad-Gita 2:22).

To explain what is reborn, Buddhism also turns to analogies. For example, if a flame is passed from one candle to another, is the second candle burning with the same flame as the first? A flame, like a river, is not a static entity, but a dynamic process. It is an ever changing bundle of energy, and the passage from one candle to another is, most precisely, a transference of energy. The same can be said

of rebirth from one body to the next. It is the transference of a bundle of energy, which is patterned according to one's *karma.*[J]

Karma: Buddhist Morality and Personal Identity

The Buddhist doctrine of **karma** generally has the same meaning as the Hindu version: it is the moral law of cause and effect. *Karma* functions hand in hand with *samsara,* in that the nature of one's rebirth depends on the status of one's *karma.* Indeed, because Buddhism denies the transference of any self or soul, personal identity depends entirely on *karma.* When an individual dies, his or her

IMAGE: HTTP://EN.WIKIPEDIA.ORG/WIKI/IMAGE:TAUGHANNOCK_FALLS2.JPG

I

As you observe the natural world, do you tend to perceive things as permanent or impermanent? Could the things that you perceive as permanent really be impermanent? Give some specific examples.

J

The analogy of the flame being passed from one candle to another is the most famous one used to describe Buddhist rebirth. Invent a second analogy to help explain this doctrine.

The second mark of existence is *anicca,* or impermanence. We may see the waterfall as an unchanging thing, but it is actually an ongoing flow.

karma continues on its particular trajectory, as it were, eventually bringing about rebirth. At conception the new person is possessed of this particular status brought on by the *karma* of the previous life.

Because *karma* is constantly affected by the moral adequacy of one's actions, morality is of pressing concern for Buddhism, which therefore tends to emphasize the ethical dimension. The moral life requires observance of the **Five Precepts:**

1. Do not take life.
2. Do not take what is not given.
3. Do not engage in sensuous misconduct.
4. Do not use false speech.
5. Do not drink intoxicants.

The Five Precepts apply to all Buddhists. The following precepts are added for monks and nuns:

6. Do not eat after noon.
7. Do not watch dancing or shows.
8. Do not use garlands, perfumes, or ornaments.
9. Do not use a high or soft bed.
10. Do not accept gold or silver.

Buddhist morality emphasizes intention. The degree to which an act is immoral depends on the individual's intention to commit the act, rather than on the actual outcome. For example, for a Buddhist, intentionally shooting at a deer and missing is immoral, whereas accidentally killing a deer with a car is not immoral.[K]

The Four Noble Truths

During the Third Watch of the night of his enlightenment, upon reaching the most profound level of insight, Gautama perceived the **Four Noble Truths:**

1. To live is to suffer.
2. Suffering is caused by desire.
3. Suffering can be brought to cessation.
4. The solution to suffering is the Noble Eightfold Path.

These truths were the foundational discoveries through which the Buddha, the physician, could attend humankind: diagnosing the disease, determining its cause, issuing a prognosis, and prescribing a cure. The Buddha taught the Four Noble Truths in his momentous First Sermon. They are the central teachings of Buddhism, the heart of the tradition's doctrinal dimension.

Diagnosis of the Disease: *Dukkha*

The name of the first noble truth is **dukkha** (dook´huh), which is translated variously as "suffering," "frustration," "dislocation," or "discomfort," to name only a few possibilities. The word originally referred to disjointedness, as with a wheel not perfectly centered on its axle, or a bone slightly ajar in its socket. Generally speaking, to assert that life is *dukkha* is to imply that things are not quite as they should be, but somehow out of joint and in need of repair.

K

Some systems of morality, such as the Buddhist one, emphasize the intention of an action; other systems emphasize the outcome of an action. Which do you think has greater moral significance: intention or outcome? Explain your answer.

Buddhist precepts emphasize respect for all forms of life.

IMAGE: VERNON SIGL

That life is *dukkha* is obvious to anyone who is experiencing pain, be it physical or emotional. When we hurt or are ill, even to a slight degree, it is all too clear that things could be better. But what about the good times, when health and contentment prevail? What about the moments when we feel a deep happiness and yearn for life to continue this way forever? The problem, the Buddha would say, is that such happiness will not continue. Human life is finite, and all our experiences are of limited duration. Life's best times hasten to their end. The ordinary times, even if not hampered by illness or injury, are never quite as good as they could be.

In his First Sermon, the Buddha provided a practical list of specific life experiences during which suffering is most readily apparent. He began by citing stages of the life process: birth, old age, disease, and death. Birth entails suffering simply because it marks the beginning of life in human form, another round of existence in *samsara*. Recall that among the Four Passing Sights that prompted Gautama to leave his palace life were an old man, a diseased man, and a corpse. Although Gautama's life as a prince may have seemed ideal at the time, those sights prompted him to acknowledge the suffering that was in store even for him. Like the lives of all human beings, his was finite, of limited duration. He too would grow old, experience disease, and die.

The Buddha went on to cite three day-to-day experiences. In spite of all their efforts, people continually come into contact with unpleasant things. At the same time, people have to continually endure separation from pleasant things, along with harboring unfulfilled wishes. The problem common to these last two experiences, and one that is highly relevant to understanding Buddhism, is attachment. It is our attachment to pleasant things that sets us up to suffer when we are separated from them. What is a wish other than a mental attachment to some object or event that is not yet ours to enjoy?

The Buddha was severe in his condemnation of attachment, denouncing even such commonly cherished bonds as those between family members. In the following story, retold by Buddhist monk Thich Nhat Hanh, a woman grieving the death of a child visits the Buddha in the city of Savatthi:

The Buddha asked her, "Visakha, where have you been? Why are your clothes and hair so wet?"

Lady Visakha wept. "Lord, my little grandson just died. I wanted to come see you, but in my grief I forgot to take my hat or parasol to protect me from the rain."

"How old was your grandson, Visakha? How did he die?"

"Lord, he was only three years old. He died of typhoid fever."

"The poor little one. Visakha, how many children and grandchildren do you have?"

"Lord, I have sixteen children. Nine are married. I had eight grandchildren. Now there are only seven."

"Visakha, you like having a lot of grandchildren, don't you?"

"Oh yes, Lord. The more the better. Nothing would make me happier than to have as many children and grandchildren as there are people in Savatthi."

"Visakha, do you know how many people die each day in Savatthi?"

"Lord, sometimes nine or ten, but at least one person dies every day in Savatthi. There is no day without a death in Savatthi."

"Visakha, if your children and grandchildren were as numerous as the people of Savatthi, your hair and clothes would be as soaked as they are today every day."

Visakha joined her palms. "I understand! I really don't want as many children and grandchildren as there are people in Savatthi.

L

Reflect on the Buddha's teaching to the woman whose grandson had just died. How do you feel about this teaching? How does it compare with your perspective on family ties?

M

Have you ever performed a truly selfless act? Is such an act, completely free from any selfish motivation, even possible? (According to Buddhism it would be possible only after the actor attained enlightenment.) Explain.

The more attachments one has, the more one suffers. You have often taught me this, but I always seem to forget."

The Buddha smiled gently. (*Old Path White Clouds,* page 407)

Dukkha would seem to be unavoidable. All of life's experiences are of finite duration, and we are constantly bombarded by opportunities to become attached. Indeed the Buddha concluded in his First Sermon that human life itself, by its very nature, is unavoidably wrapped up in *dukkha*. Bodies, personalities, thoughts—all are finite, all are constantly changing. All are subject to *dukkha*. This is a grave diagnosis.[L]

Determination of the Cause: *Tanha*

The Buddha did not stop at his grave diagnosis of the diseased human condition, abandoning us to its hopelessness. Instead he proceeded to determine its cause. He identified the second noble truth as **tanha,** which is translated variously as "desire," "thirst," or "craving."

It is helpful to think of *tanha* as implying selfish desire, for it seems impossible not to desire anything—after all, the Buddha himself desired to lead others on the path to enlightenment. The distinguishing characteristic of *tanha* is its selfish orientation. It is desire for individual attainment, for private fulfillment.

Just as *dukkha* is seemingly unavoidable, so too is its cause, *tanha*. How can an individual refrain from desiring personal fulfillment? The Buddha would likely answer that she or he cannot. Individuals are destined to be selfish; *tanha* is an unavoidable aspect of being an individual. But recall what the Buddha taught about individuality. He taught the doctrine of *anatta*, "no-self." That which we regard as our self, our individuality, is not part of any ultimate reality. We are in fact changing from moment to moment. Yet we imagine that we exist as individuals, each of us unique and endowed with a self that is real and abiding and significant. But this is a falsehood. It is also another form of attachment. Attached to our false idea of being individual selves, we tend to care for ourselves diligently, all the while only adding fuel to the fire of *tanha*, and tightening the grip of *dukkha*. A British-born Buddhist teacher who went by the pen name Wei Wu Wei puts it like this:

Why are you unhappy?
Because 99.9 per cent
Of everything you think,
And of everything you do,
Is for yourself—
And there isn't one.

(*Ask the Awakened,* page 1)

It is a vicious circle! It is precisely this fictitious self that goes on thinking of itself as real. How can such a circle be broken? The great difficulty of this challenge suggests that the Buddha was not an ordinary physician, but an ingenious one who prescribed a radical cure that would forever change the world's religious landscape.[M]

A Buddha statue at Sukhothai Historical Park, in Thailand.

IMAGE: SHUTTERSTOCK

Prognosis

Critics of Buddhism often point out that focusing on suffering is an unnecessarily pessimistic approach. Surely there are alternative perspectives on life. The adage "Eat, drink, and be merry, for tomorrow you may die" calls to mind one alternative. But even if blatant indulgence in bodily pleasure is not the focus of other perspectives, philosophies and religions often place more emphasis on the joys of life than on the sorrows.

In spite of Buddhism's emphasis on suffering, the accounts of Buddhists give one the overwhelming impression that they gain a deep joy and contentment from practicing their religion. Rather than characterizing Buddhism as pessimistic, it is perhaps more accurate to label it realistic. People *do* suffer. Even happiness is yoked to suffering. Life, it would seem, can be better than it is. The Buddha understood the extreme importance of first being aware of the disease and its cause before proceeding. And he believed wholeheartedly that the disease and its cause can be rooted out from each of us. His prognosis can be described only as optimistic.[N]

Prescription for a Cure:
The Noble Eightfold Path

In the light of the pervasiveness of suffering and its cause, it is appropriate that the cure set out in the **Noble Eightfold Path** encompasses all aspects of life. In keeping with the doctrine of the Middle Way, though, the Noble Eightfold Path sets forth a life of moderation, not of extreme religious practices. Also, the eight steps constitute ongoing practices, not stages to be mastered and then left behind.

1. *Right views.* Learn the content of the Buddha's teachings, especially the Four Noble Truths.
2. *Right intentions.* Abandon the evil attitudes of greed, hatred, and delusion. Nurture the good attitudes of generosity, friendship, and insight.
3. *Right speech.* Avoid vocal wrong deeds such as gossip, lying, abusive talk, and idle talk.
4. *Right conduct.* Live morally by obeying the Five Precepts for all Buddhists, or ten precepts for monks and nuns.
5. *Right livelihood.* Abstain from occupations that harm living beings, such as selling weapons, selling liquor, butchering, hunting, or being a soldier.
6. *Right effort.* Maintain mental alertness so as to control the effect of the senses and to discriminate between wise and unwise mental activity.
7. *Right mindfulness.* Through careful attention to helpful topics, develop the mental focus needed for meditation.
8. *Right meditation.* Ascend through four levels of trance (some versions describe eight or nine levels), ultimately reaching a point of perfect tranquillity, in which the sense of individual existence has passed away. This is the state of *nirvana*.

Together the eight steps embrace the primary focal points of Buddhist training:

Young Buddhist monks in Myanmar (formerly Burma) engage in the daily tasks of monastic life.

N

Make a short list of "truths" that summarize the human condition. For each truth describe why you included it.

O

The final three steps of the Eightfold Path tend to be specifically Buddhist, whereas the first five are similar to teachings of other religions. What aspects of these first five steps strike you as being familiar? What aspects are strange to you, and how do you think they relate to Buddhist teachings in general?

A Pure Offering, Every Day

Tsechang Gonpo is a Vajrayana Buddhist living in Minneapolis. Although he and his wife, Sonam, are far from their people's native homeland, Tibet, Buddhism continues to be central to their lives. Tsechang explains what their religion means to them, and why:

Buddhism plays a very big part in our day-to-day life. It is even more important than family. A main reason for this is our belief in life after death and the wheel of rebirth, or *samsara*. When I die, I have to leave behind those who are near and dear to me, and travel on to the next life alone. It would be bad to be too attached to the things of this life, even my family.

The nature of my next life depends on the deeds I have done during this lifetime and previous lifetimes. If I have practiced Buddhism well and accumulated lots of good *karma,* then maybe I can take on a good life-form, such as a human. If not, maybe I will become a bird, or even worse, I may have to go to hell. My next life is therefore very important to me, as is the ultimate goal of escaping from the pain and suffering of *samsara* to a state we call *nirvana*. When we are enlightened, we can become a Buddha. All of us have this chance, depending on our level of practice. One can even get to Buddhahood or *nirvana* in this lifetime, if one is willing to sacrifice all worldly things and follow the tough way of intense meditation and other practices.

The reincarnation of *lamas* illustrates our beliefs in life after death. Many high lamas who maintain exceptional practice and meditation are reincarnated in their next life as previous *lamas*. The basic difference between such *lamas* and ourselves is based on the level of Buddhist practice. They can remember their previous life-form, whereas we do not remember anything because of our relatively low level of practice and our ignorance.

My father was a reincarnation of a previous *lama*. He was from the eastern part of Tibet, but came to central Tibet to master Buddhism and then to return to his people. Unfortunately he was not able to return home because of the Chinese invasion. He escaped to India, and for his own self-defense he took a weapon. Because of that he had to give back the vows of *lama,* and he became an ordinary man.

Another example of a reincarnated *lama* is His Holiness the Dalai Lama. We believe that he is the *bodhisattva* Avalokiteshvara in human form. The present Dalai Lama, Tenzin Gyatso, is fourteenth in the succession of reincarnations. He is both the temporal and spiritual leader of Tibet, and is an important figure for the Tibetan people. He had to take over the leadership at a very young age, during our most difficult period. Tibet lost its independence to communist China in 1959. Nearly two million Tibetans died during the occupation, and six thousand monasteries, temples, and other cultural and historic buildings were destroyed and their contents pillaged. But fortunately His Holiness the Dalai Lama and about eighty thousand Tibetans escaped to India.

I start each day with prayer. I pray for the well-being of all sentient beings and for the long life of His Holiness the Dalai Lama, and that I might accumulate some good *karma* during the day. Our deities are also in my prayers. Belief in deities is common among Tibetans. The majority of us believe in Nechung and Palden Lhamo, deities who give advice to us through oracles. After prayer I offer seven bowls of water to the gods, and then I burn incense. Water is offered because it is cheapest and therefore there is no sense of loss. If I felt loss due to attachment, my offering would not be pure. I then go to work, and during the day I always try to think about the most simple Buddhist teaching: "If you cannot help anybody, at least try never to harm anyone." This is really good for a common layperson like me as it is very simple and easy to follow. When the day is done and before I go to bed, I think about how I have done during the day. If I have done something bad, then I regret that and ask for forgiveness in my prayers to the Three Jewels: the Buddha, his teachings and the scriptures, and the community of monks and nuns. I meditate sometimes, but being in America it is difficult to find time to meditate every day.

wisdom (steps 1 and 2), morality (steps 3, 4, and 5), and concentration (steps 6, 7, and 8). Though all three focal points are essential, the heart of Buddhist practice lies in concentration, and specifically in the practice of meditation. The Buddha's primary teachings derive from his own meditative experience; their truths can be fully understood only when an individual attains the same level of insight through meditation. The centrality of meditation can especially be observed in the unique division of Buddhism called Zen (which will be discussed in its own chapter later in this book). The Japanese term *zen* means simply "meditation." Through this centrality of meditation and the heightened states of awareness it nurtures, Buddhism emphasizes the experiential dimension of religion.°

Enlightenment and *Nirvana*

To follow the steps of the Eightfold Path to its end is to reach *nirvana*. Just as it did for the Buddha, final *nirvana* awaits the death of the body. But the still-living **arhat** (ahr´huht), the "worthy one" who has become awakened, is forever transformed, having experienced, through the transcendent state of enlightenment, a foretaste of the final *nirvana*.

All Buddhists look forward to the same experience of *nirvana* as that of their model, Gautama the Buddha. Buddhas (recall that there have been many Buddhas in addition to Gautama) are distinct from their followers, however, in that they do not need a model to provide teachings leading to their awakening. Buddhas are able to accomplish their liberation on their own. Gautama the Buddha, then, though merely human and not above his followers in terms of the ultimate experience of *nirvana,* has a special status.

Compassion: The Enlightened *Arhat*

Having awakened, the *arhat* or "worthy one" is enlightened, fully aware of the truth of the Buddha's teachings. With this perfect wisdom, the *arhat* is now free from the imprisonment of *tanha,* and thus free from *dukkha*. The *arhat* has fully realized the truth of the doctrine of *anatta,* or "no-self," and has let go of any sense of individual existence. Spiritual perfection has been achieved. Still engaged in the affairs of this world but no longer attached to them, the *arhat* is perfectly compassionate toward all living things.

With the inward experience of enlightenment, the outward virtues of compassion, friendliness, joy, and even-mindedness are simultaneously perfected. Although the focus of Buddhist teachings is mainly on the perfection of one's inner nature, the development of qualities that benefit society is also essential.

A painting depicting the Buddha's first sermon to his first five disciples in the Deer Park, near the city of Benares. The five became enlightened *arhats*.

Buddhism   83

The ideal of compassion is especially emphasized. It is vividly illustrated in Buddhist stories, many of which depict the Buddha in former lives. One such story, originally told by Gautama, has been restated by storyteller Rafe Martin:

Once, long, long ago, the Buddha came to life as a noble prince named Mahasattva, in a land where the country of Nepal exists today.

One day, when he was grown, he went walking in a wild forest with his two older brothers. The land was dry and the leaves brittle. The sky seemed alight with flames.

Suddenly they saw a tigress. The brothers turned to flee but the tigress stumbled and fell. She was starving and her cubs were starving too. She eyed her cubs miserably, and in that dark glance, the prince sensed her long months of hunger and pain. He saw, too, that unless she found food soon, she might even be driven to devour her own cubs. He was moved to compassion by the extreme hardness of their lives. "What after all is this life for?" he thought.

Stepping forward, he calmly removed his outer garments and lay down before her. Tearing his skin with a stone, he let the starving tigress smell the blood. His brothers fled.

Hungrily, the tigress devoured the prince's body and chewed the bones. She and her cubs lived on, and for many years, the forest was filled with a golden light.

Centuries later a mighty king raised a pillar of carved stone on this spot, and pilgrims still go there to make offerings even today.

Deeds of compassion live forever.

(*The Hungry Tigress,* page 143)

This extreme example of compassion is fitting for the Buddha, who presents a role model for all Buddhist ideals. This story also illustrates that it takes many lifetimes to nurture the degree of compassion suitable for a Buddha.[P]

P

Contemplate the story of Prince Mahasattva and the tigress. What does it tell you about the nature of Buddhist compassion?

Nirvana

When the life of the *arhat,* characterized by perfect compassion, ends, he or she enters into the state called *nirvana.* The word *nirvana* literally means "blowing out." Upon the passage into *nirvana,* rather than being reborn, the life energy of the *arhat* is snuffed out, like the flame of a candle. Having extinguished all selfish desire, including desire for continued existence, the *arhat* has attained complete liberation from *samsara.*

Buddhists have always found it impossible to describe *nirvana* precisely. (The higher states of the experiential religious dimension, including the Hindu states of *moksha* and *samadhi,* are typically impossible to describe adequately.) Not even the Buddha could come up with sufficient words. *Nirvana* cannot be understood until it is experienced. It is as difficult for an ordinary human to understand *nirvana* as it would be for an unborn child to understand life outside the womb. Those still in *samsara* have never experienced anything that can even approximate *nirvana.* The most that can be said is that *nirvana* is the total cessation of suffering, and thus is absolute peace.

If *nirvana* is total cessation, does the *arhat* experience "life after death"? Because enlightenment is precisely the abandonment of one's sense of individual existence, who (or what) is left to experience the absolute peace of *nirvana?* The Buddha specifically refused to say whether a person exists or does not exist in *nirvana.* He only insisted that *nirvana* is the cessation of suffering. And this, together with the Buddha's radiant happiness born of his enlightenment, suggests that if anything is experienced in *nirvana,* it is indescribably joyful.

Three Rafts for Crossing the River: Divisions of Buddhism

Buddhists often compare the quest for salvation to the crossing of a river. On this side of the river is the realm of *samsara,* the ordinary world of suffering. On the far shore lies *nirvana,* impossible to know until it is experienced, but beckoning all Buddhists as their final destiny of absolute peace. The process of crossing the river is the task of religion. And so Buddhists think of their tradition as a raft, a means for crossing.

In fact, over the centuries Buddhism has divided into three great rafts, or "vehicles" *(yanas):* Theravada, also referred to by the somewhat derisive name *Hinayana* (the Lesser Vehicle); Mahayana (the Great Vehicle); and Vajrayana (the Vehicle of the Diamond). Some of the differences among the three vehicles are a result of regional variations, for Buddhism has spread far beyond its original homeland and is now present throughout most of Asia. Interestingly, it disappeared almost entirely from India a millennium ago.

Theravada: "The Way of the Elders"

Theravada (thay-ruh-vah´duh) Buddhism is now the prevalent form in the countries of Cambodia, Burma (the union of Myanmar), Sri Lanka, and Thailand. Theravada, whose name means "the way of the elders," follows the earliest texts, and thus tends to agree with the original teachings of the Buddha. Theravada regards the Buddha first and foremost as he who experienced enlightenment and then taught others how to accomplish the same. The Buddha is forever beyond the reach of humans, having passed into the eternal peace of *nirvana.* The teachings of Buddhism, not the figure of the Buddha, are most important.

And so Theravada focuses on the teachings: on cultivating wisdom through knowing the Four Noble Truths, and practicing the Noble Eightfold Path, especially meditation. The final aim, of course, is to enter *nirvana.* Those who succeed are the *arhats,* which for Theravada are the ideal types whom all strive to imitate (like saints in Catholicism).

Theravada's focus on meditation has led naturally to an emphasis on monastic life, because monks and nuns, unlike most laypeople, have sufficient time for meditating. In most regions where Theravada predominates, this emphasis has resulted in a religious hierarchy that differentiates the roles of laity and of religious. Even among the ordained, roles differ. Monks, who outnumber nuns by more than ten to one, have always held the most prominent position within Theravada Buddhism. In some regions all males reside in a monastery temporarily. Serving as a monk for at least three months is seen as a required step toward becoming an adult.

Young monks salute a Theravadin depiction of the reclining Buddha in Sri Lanka.

Mahayana: The Great Vehicle

By naming themselves the Great Vehicle, **Mahayana** (mah-hah-yah′nah) Buddhists are only in part asserting their superiority over Theravada Buddhism, which they named Hinayana (the Lesser Vehicle). Mahayana is indeed the largest division of Buddhism, claiming well over half the world's Buddhists. Today Mahayana is the dominant form of Buddhism in China, Japan, and Korea. But its name also indicates something of the nature of Mahayana. Whereas Theravada emphasizes the individual's path of meditation (and hence can suffice with a lesser vehicle, or raft), Mahayana is Buddhism for the masses.

For one thing, rather than concentrating on the Buddha's teachings, Mahayana focuses on the Buddha himself, celebrating him as a divine savior. This has potent popular appeal because it opens the doors to religious devotion and prayer. Rather than depending on the cultivation of wisdom through meditation on difficult teachings, this form of Buddhism offers salvation through the infinite grace of the compassionate Buddha.

And Mahayana does not stop with Gautama the Buddha, but recognizes the salvific grace of all the Buddhas of the past. More important, Mahayana reveres **bodhisattvas** (boh-dee-saht′vahs). *Bodhisattvas* are "Buddhas in the making," dedicated to attaining enlightenment. More specifically they are capable of entering into *nirvana* but, motivated by compassion, stop short of that goal so as to help others achieve it. Mahayana accepts those definitions and adds another in which *bodhisattvas* take on mythical qualities. These *bodhisattvas* exist beyond the earthly realm and are believed to dwell in one of the Buddhist heavens, from which they provide divine assistance to those who worship them. Owing to the infinite depth of their compassion, the mythical *bodhisattvas* are believed to transfer merit of their *karma* to their devotees. On occasion they appear in the world as human beings. Several *bodhisattvas* are prominent in Mahayana Buddhism, including Maitreya, whom Buddhists expect some day to be reborn into the world as the next Buddha. Along with the biography of Gautama himself, the stories and descriptions of these *bodhisattvas* make up a large portion of the mythic dimension of Buddhism.

For Mahayana Buddhists, the *bodhisattva,* rather than the *arhat,* is the ideal type. And compassion, which is perfectly embodied by the *bodhisattvas,* is the supreme virtue, regarded more highly even than wisdom. Mahayana Buddhists see Gautama's decision to preach the Dharma rather than enter immediately into *nirvana,* as proof for the primacy of compassion. They look to the *bodhisattvas* as embodiments of compassion, because the *bodhisattvas* have vowed they will wait to enter *nirvana* so they may assist others, even until "the last blade of grass" becomes enlightened.

Kuan-yin, a *bodhisattva,* is revered for compassion and assistance.

IMAGE: © BURSTEIN COLLECTION/CORBIS

Vajrayana: Tibetan Buddhism

When Mahayana Buddhists elevated the figure of the Buddha to that of divine savior, the Buddha was depicted holding the *vajra,* a diamond scepter. The Vehicle of the Diamond was named for its unique application of Buddhist teachings, resembling in their energetic rigor the strength and clarity of a diamond. The relative intensity of **Vajrayana** (vuhj-ruh-yah´nuh) is manifested in the common belief that its adherents can attain *nirvana* in this lifetime, here and now.

Vajrayana constitutes but a small minority of Buddhists, and yet it is of special interest. This interest is due in part to the situation of Vajrayana's homeland, Tibet. Now claimed as a part of the People's Republic of China, Tibet has endured much religious persecution by China's communist government. Many Vajrayana Buddhists have been killed; many others are now living in exile in India and elsewhere. But for centuries the high mountain plateaus of Tibet sheltered Vajrayana to a large extent from the rest of the world. There a full one-sixth of the male population were monks, and Buddhism pervaded life. This pervasiveness and the relatively pristine state of this form of Buddhism have also attracted special interest.

The uniqueness of Vajrayana includes the notion of fighting fire with fire. In general, Buddhist teachings prescribe shutting off the energy of desire to stop suffering. Vajrayana harnesses this energy and turns it against itself. The end goal, *nirvana,* remains the same, but the means of reaching it are remarkably different.

By harnessing the sensual energies of life, Vajrayana attempts to propel the individual toward enlightenment. Prominent among the practices used to achieve this are **mandalas** (mahn´duh-luhs), patterned icons that visually excite; **mudras** (mood´rahs), choreographed hand movements that draw on the energies

Exiled Tibetan Buddhists perform a ritual in India.

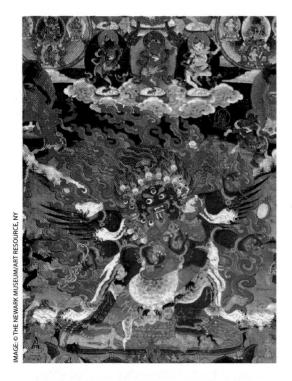

A Tibetan cloth painting displays icons of both fierce and tranquil deities. Such mandalas are used to propel Buddhists toward enlightenment.

Another important feature of Vajrayana is its institution of *lamas,* a hierarchy of clergy headed by the **Dalai Lama** (dahl′ee lahm′ah). The present Dalai Lama, who won the 1989 Nobel Peace Prize for his efforts on behalf of regaining Tibetan freedom, is the fourteenth in a direct line of succession. This line is not based on descent by natural birth, but determined through rebirth. Originating with the incarnation of a prominent *bodhisattva,* Avalokiteshvara (ah-wah-loh-ki-tesh′-wah-rah), the lineage is believed to continue through the reincarnation of one Dalai Lama into the next. Whenever a Dalai Lama dies, his successor is sought out through various means, some supernatural and others more mundane (such as noting a likely child's attraction to the former Dalai Lama's possessions).

of movement; and **mantras** (mahn′truhs), resonating chants that harness the spiritual potency of sound. Together these practices invoke sight, movement, and sound, capitalizing on the sensual energies as a way of achieving the goal of spiritual enhancement. Thanks to the willingness of Tibetan monks to share their spiritual practices with the rest of the world, many Westerners have had the opportunity to witness the making of a sand mandala or to hear the provocative intonation of mantras.

Another of Vajrayana's unique practices involves the harnessing of one of life's basic energies, that of sexuality. Whereas most Buddhists target sexual desire as especially problematic and in need of control, Vajrayana Buddhists regard sex as a potent energy for furthering spiritual progress. Through a carefully guarded set of practices known as Tantrism, some Vajrayana Buddhists engage in ritualized sex. Tantrism does not include sex merely for its own sake or sex motivated by a desire for pleasure. It is regulated by masters, and is undertaken solely to enhance spiritual energies.

The Enduring Wisdom of the Buddha

Each raft of Buddhism charts its own course, but ultimately all the rafts reach the same shore, delivering their followers into *nirvana.* A famous Buddhist mantra invokes the end of the crossing: "Gone . . . , gone, gone beyond, completely gone beyond, enlightenment hail!" (Robinson and Johnson, *The Buddhist Religion,* page 94). *Nirvana,* the ultimate goal of all Buddhists, is beyond every experience of this life. In typically paradoxical fashion, it is even beyond Buddhism itself. The raft that has ferried the Buddhist across the river to the shore of salvation must be abandoned lest the journey remain unfinished.

In other ways, too, Buddhism is paradoxical. It is indeed unique among the world's religions. Buddhism focuses on the spiritual condition of the human being, not on the supremacy of a divinity. Even more uniquely it denies the existence of a self, or soul.

Buddhism relies instead on features that are strikingly akin to the ways of the modern, scientific view of life. In fact modern scientific theory says much that is in close agreement with Gautama the Buddha's observations about the universe and the human psyche.

This is not an accident, for the Buddha, skilled physician that he was, proceeded scientifically—empirically investigating what it is to be human. People suffer. A life of moderation, as exemplified by the doctrine of the Middle Way, helps to alleviate suffering. And meditation, the Buddha's favored method of therapy, nurtures the wisdom that leads to transcendence.

His Holiness the Dalai Lama, the leader of Tibetan Buddhism.

Discovering the Dalai Lama

An excerpt from the autobiography of the fourteenth Dalai Lama provides some fascinating details about the search for the new incarnation of the deceased thirteenth lama.

When I was not quite three years old, a search party that had been sent out by the Government to find the new incarnation of the Dalai Lama arrived at Kumbum monastery. It had been led there by a number of signs. One of these concerned the embalmed body of my predecessor, Thupten Gyatso, the Thirteenth Dalai Lama, who had died aged fifty-seven in 1933. During its period of sitting in state, the head was discovered to have turned from facing south to north-east. Shortly after that the Regent, himself a senior lama, had a vision. Looking into the waters of the sacred lake, Lhamoi Lhatso, in southern Tibet, he clearly saw the Tibetan letters *Ah*, *Ka* and *Ma* float into view. These were followed by the image of a three-storeyed monastery with a turquoise and gold roof and a path running from it to a hill. Finally, he saw a small house with strangely shaped guttering. He was sure that the letter *Ah* referred to Amdo, the north-eastern province, so it was there that the search party was sent.

By the time they reached Kumbum, the members of the search party felt that they were on the right track. It seemed likely that if the letter *Ah* referred to Amdo, then *Ka* must indicate the monas-

tery at Kumbum—which was indeed three storeyed and turquoise roofed. They now only needed to locate a hill and a house with peculiar guttering. So they began to search the neighbouring villages. When they saw the gnarled branches of juniper wood on the roof of my parents' house, they were certain that the new Dalai Lama would not be far away. Nevertheless, rather than reveal the purpose of their visit, the group asked only to stay the night. The leader of the party, Kewtsang Rinpoché, then pretended to be a servant and spent much of the evening observing and playing with the youngest child in the house.

The child recognized him and called out "Sera Lama, Sera Lama." Sera was Kewtsang Rinpoché's monastery. Next day they left—only to return a few days later as a formal deputation. This time they brought with them a number of things that had belonged to my predecessor, together with several similar items that did not. In every case, the infant correctly identified those belonging to the Thirteenth Dalai Lama saying, "It's mine. It's mine." This more or less convinced the search party that they had found the new incarnation. However, there was another candidate to be seen before a final decision could be reached. But it was not long before the boy from Taktser was acknowledged to be the new Dalai Lama. I was that child. (Gyatso, *Freedom in Exile*, pages 11–12)

1. What was the name of the man who later became the Buddha and founded the religion of Buddhism?
2. What were the Four Passing Sights? Explain their significance to the origins of Buddhism.
3. Explain the doctrine of the Middle Way.
4. Describe the event of Gautama's attainment of enlightenment.
5. What is the Sangha? Who are its members?
6. What are the Three Jewels of Buddhism?
7. What features of Buddhist cosmology are shared with Hinduism?
8. Describe the Buddha's reaction against early Hinduism.
9. Identify the Three Marks of Existence. How are they interrelated?
10. What is the doctrine of *anatta?* How does it relate to the Hindu concept Atman?
11. According to the Buddhist doctrine of *samsara,* what is actually reborn? Explain the role of *karma* in the Buddhist understanding of *samsara.*
12. List the Five Precepts, which apply to all Buddhists. Then list the five additional precepts that apply to monks and nuns.
13. What are some possible English translations of the term *dukkha?* Explain its meaning in your own words.
14. What is *tanha?* How does it relate to *dukkha?*
15. List the steps of the Eightfold Path.
16. What is the difference between the Buddha and other humans who attain enlightenment?
17. Define and briefly describe the character of an *arhat.*
18. What is the literal meaning of the word *nirvana?* How does this help explain the concept of *nirvana?*
19. What are the three divisions of Buddhism?
20. What is the main focus of Theravada Buddhism?
21. What is the literal meaning of the name *Mahayana,* and what are the implications of this meaning?

The Seven Dimensions of Religion: Buddhism

Dimension	Examples
Experiential	enlightenment, *nirvana*
Mythic	biography of the Buddha, stories and descriptions of the *bodhisattvas*
Doctrinal	Middle Way, Three Marks of Existence, Four Noble Truths
Ethical	Five Precepts (and an additional five for monks and nuns), ideal of compassion
Ritual	Mahayana acts of religious devotion and prayer to the *bodhisattvas,* Vajrayana chanting of mandalas and practice of *mudras*
Social	Sangha, figure of *arhat,* Dalai Lama
Material	*bodhi* tree, mandalas

22. How does Vajrayana Buddhism "fight fire with fire"?

23. Who is the Dalai Lama? How is each Dalai Lama chosen?

24. What are the primary geographical regions of the three divisions of Buddhism?

Glossary

anatta (uh-nat´uh; Pali: "no-self"). One of the Three Marks of Existence; the Buddhist doctrine denying a permanent self.

anicca (uh-nee´chuh; Pali: "impermanence"). One of the Three Marks of Existence; the Buddhist doctrine that all existent things are constantly changing.

arhat (ahr´huht; Sanskrit: "worthy one"). One who has become enlightened; the ideal type for Theravada Buddhism.

bodhisattvas (boh-dee-saht´vahs). Future Buddhas. As the ideal types for Mahayana Buddhism, beings who have experienced enlightenment but, motivated by compassion, stop short of entering *nirvana* so as to help others achieve it.

Buddha (boo´duh; Sanskrit and Pali: "awakened one"). Siddhartha Gautama and all others who have by their own insight attained perfect enlightenment.

Dalai Lama (dahl´ee lahm´ah). The spiritual leader of Vajrayana (Tibetan) Buddhism, believed to be an incarnation of the *bodhisattva* Avalokiteshvara (ah-wah-loh-ki-tesh´wah-rah).

Dharma (dahr´muh). The teachings of the Buddha, and one of the Three Jewels of Buddhism.

dukkha (dook´huh; Pali: "suffering," "frustration," "dislocation," or "discomfort"). The first of the Four Noble Truths, the basic Buddhist insight that suffering is part of the human condition. *See also* Three Marks of Existence.

Five Precepts. The basic moral requirements that are binding for all Buddhists.

Four Noble Truths. The central teachings of Buddhism: to live is to suffer; suffering is caused by desire; the cessation of suffering can be achieved; the solution is the Noble Eightfold Path.

karma (Sanskrit: "action"). The moral law of cause and effect of actions; determines the nature of one's rebirth.

Mahayana (mah-hah-yah´nah; Sanskrit: the Great Vehicle). The largest of Buddhism's three divisions, prevalent in China, Japan, and Korea; encompasses a variety of forms, including those that emphasize devotion and prayer to the Buddhas and *bodhisattvas.*

mandalas (mahn´duh-luhs; Sanskrit: "circle"). Patterned icons that visually excite; used in Vajrayana Buddhism to enhance meditation.

mantras (mahn´truhs). Phrases or syllables chanted to evoke a deity or to enhance meditation; used in Hinduism and Buddhism, especially in Vajrayana.

Middle Way. A basic Buddhist teaching that rejects both the pleasures of sensual indulgence and the self-denial of asceticism, focusing instead on a practical approach to spiritual attainment.

mudras (mood´rahs). Choreographed hand movements used in the rituals of Vajrayana Buddhism.

nirvana (Sanskrit: "blowing out"). The ultimate goal of all Buddhists, the extinction of desire and any sense of individual selfhood, resulting in liberation from *samsara* and its limiting conditions.

Noble Eightfold Path. The fourth of the Four Noble Truths; defines the basic practices of Buddhism that lead to *nirvana.*

Pali (pah´lee). An ancient language of India, similar to Sanskrit but more commonly understood, and used in the writing of the earliest Buddhist texts; most important for Theravada Buddhism.

samsara (sahm-sah´ruh). The wheel of rebirth or reincarnation; the this-worldly realm in which rebirth occurs.

Sangha (sahn´guh; Sanskrit and Pali: "assemblage"). The Buddhist community of monks and nuns; one of the Three Jewels of Buddhism.

tanha (Pali: "desire," "thirst," or "craving"). The second of the Four Noble Truths, selfish desire, which causes *dukkha.*

Theravada (thay-ruh-vah´duh; Pali: "the way of the elders"). Prevalent form of Buddhism in Cambodia, Myanmar (formerly Burma), Sri Lanka, and Thailand; focuses on the earliest texts and emphasizes monastic lifestyle.

Three Marks of Existence. Characteristics that summarize the changing nature of reality: *anatta* (no-self), *anicca* (impermanence), and *dukkha* (suffering).

Vajrayana (vuhj-ruh-yah´nuh; Sanskrit: the Vehicle of the Diamond). Named for the *vajra,* the Buddha's diamond scepter; prevalent form of Buddhism in Tibet; emphasizes the harnessing of sensual energies to attain *nirvana.*

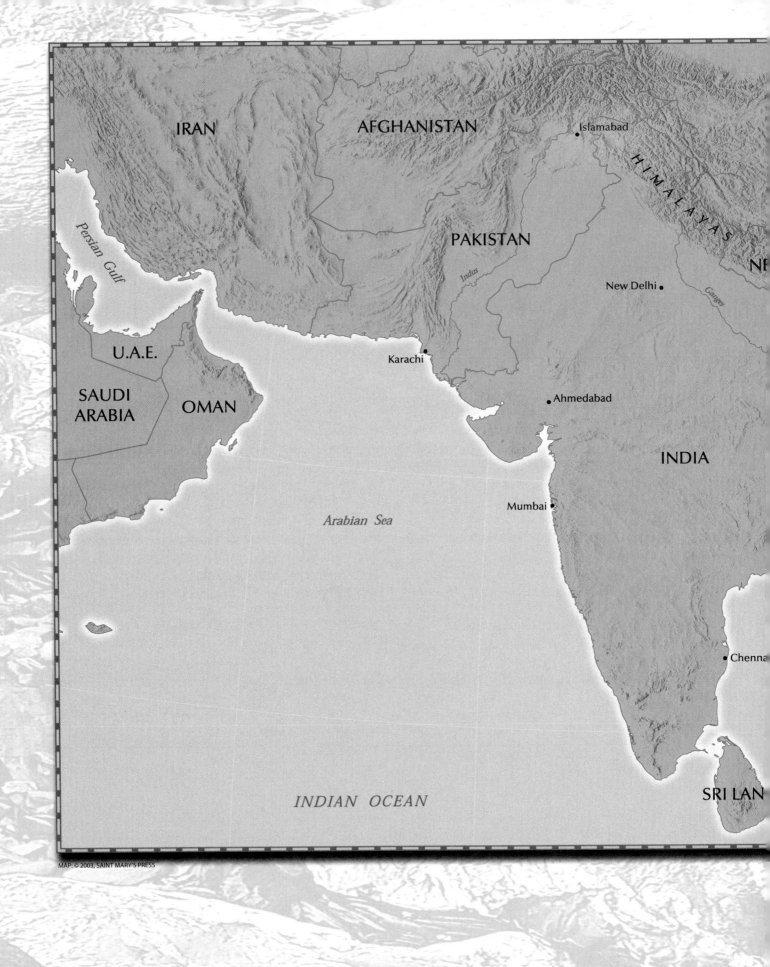

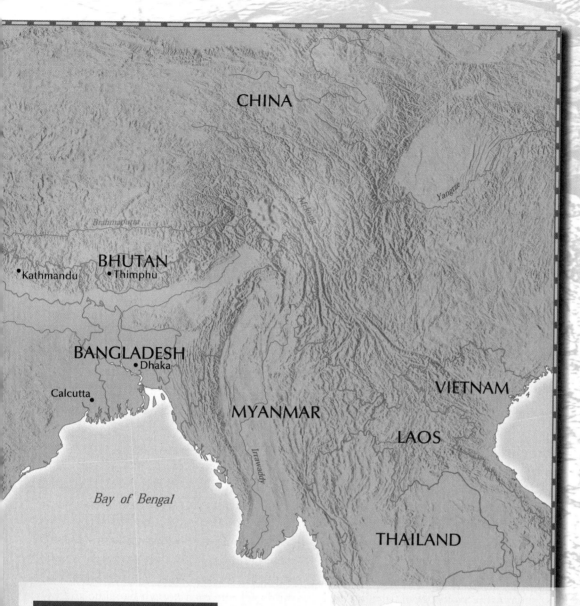

5 Jainism

All breathing, existing, living, sentient creatures should not be slain, nor treated with violence, nor abused, nor tormented, nor driven away.

This is the pure, unchangeable, eternal law, which the clever ones, who understand the world, have declared.

(Acaranga Sutra, book 1, lecture 4, lesson 1.1–2)

Ahimsa and Asceticism: Jainism's Ideals

Like Hinduism and Buddhism, Jainism originated in India, where today almost all its followers live. Jainism shares many of the basic doctrines of Hinduism and Buddhism. It holds that worlds arise and decay in an infinite series of cycles. Human beings are on a wheel called *samsara,* a long sequence of rebirths. The specific

93

Parshva, the twenty-third tirthankara, is depicted here in a ninth-century bronze statue from western India.

IMAGE: © ANGELO HORNAK/CORBIS

nature of each rebirth is determined by **karma,** the moral law of cause and effect. The ultimate religious goal, salvation, consists of liberation (called *moksha* by Jains and Hindus alike) from *samsara.*

In Hinduism and Buddhism, **ahimsa** (ah-him'suh), "nonviolence," is an important ethical principle, as indicated by the number of vegetarians among their followers. In Jainism *ahimsa* is the central principle, the "pure, unchangeable, eternal law." For all Jains religious life is primarily the avoidance of harming their fellow "sentient creatures," a broad category that comprises humans and animals (including insects). Jain monks and nuns, whom the laity revere as ideal types, expand the principle of *ahimsa* to include all life-forms, even the atomic particles that they believe are alive in such substances as wind, water, earth, and fire. They accomplish a strenuous practice of *ahimsa* through a lifestyle of rigorous self-denial, or **asceticism.**

These two features—*ahimsa* and asceticism—are the defining characteristics of Jainism. And though Jainism is a relatively small tradition (with only about four million fol-

lowers), these features ensure its importance among the religions of the world.

Makers of the River Crossing

The name *Jainism* is derived from **jina** (ji'nuh), which means "conqueror." The spiritual conquerors of the past, those who have attained salvation, are called **tirthankaras** (teert-hahn' kuhr-uhs), "makers of the river crossing." Like other Indian religions, Jainism regards rivers as symbolic of the spiritual quest. The river crossing, or ford, is especially significant, symbolizing a means of traversing the realm of *samsara* to salvation beyond. According to Jain belief, twenty-four people have established a river crossing during the present turning of the world cycle, enabling their fellow Jains to seek salvation. Jains acknowledge the authority of these *tirthankaras,* "conquerors" who have exemplified the practice of *ahimsa* and the discipline of the ascetic life.

Jains believe the sequence of world cycles is without beginning or end. *Tirthankaras* have appeared throughout this eternal process, so there is an infinite number of them. Jainism reveres all the *tirthankaras.* The twenty-four spiritual heroes of the present turning of the world cycle are each known by name and by specific symbols. Detailed stories tell of their earthly lives. However, scholars regard only the last two as historical persons. Parshva, the twenty-third *tirthankara,* lived in the eighth century BC, and continues to be a popular object of Jain devotion. Today there are more statues and other images of Parshva than of any other *tirthankara.* By far the most important *tirthankara,* though, is the most recent one, Mahavira. His life story has provided the predominant role model for Jains through the centuries.

Mahavira, the Twenty-fourth *Tirthankara*

According to the tradition followed by most Jains, Mahavira (whose name means "great hero") lived from about 599 to 527 BC, and thus would have been a contemporary of Gautama the Buddha. The two have much in common. Like the Buddhist biography of Gautama, the Jain biography of Mahavira is clearly legendary, setting forth an example of the required behavior and essential events of a perfect religious life.

Both Gautama and Mahavira were born into the *kshatriya* class of warriors and administrators. (Like Buddhism, Jainism rejected the Hindu caste system; unlike Buddhism, Jainism replaced it with a caste system of its own.) Mahavira's father was a *rajah,* or ruler, of a territory in northeastern India, not far from the home of Gautama. Mahavira grew up, married, had a daughter, and lived among the many luxuries of the palace. By his middle twenties, he was restless with his privileged lifestyle, desiring to leave it all behind and join a group of Jain ascetics, followers of Parshva. At age twenty-eight, the future *tirthankara* gave away all he possessed, said farewell to his family, and began the rigorous life of a Jain monk.

Shortly after joining the ascetics, Mahavira went off on his own. He discarded his robe as a symbol of total departure from society and wandered naked about the land for more than twelve years. He practiced the most extreme forms of asceticism. When ridiculed or physically abused by others, Mahavira passively endured the attacks. He frequently went without sleep and fasted for long periods. When not fasting he ate sparingly, begging for food and accepting only that which had been prepared without causing violence. When insects crawled on his body, he endured their bites rather than cause injury by brushing them off.

The life story of Mahavira highlights two important differences between Jainism and

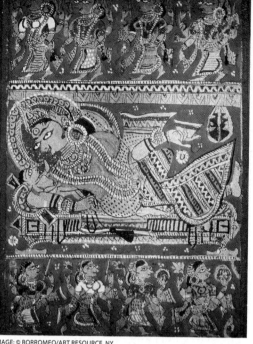

The birth of Mahavira is celebrated in this miniature painting from fifteenth-century India.

Buddhism. First, whereas Gautama rejected asceticism in favor of the Middle Way, Mahavira held fast to its most extreme form. Jains have always regarded this distinction with pride. Second, whereas Gautama discovered on his own the true practices of Buddhism while seeking enlightenment, Mahavira learned the true practices of Jainism from others. Gautama and Mahavira thus play different roles as "founders" of their respective religions.

Eventually Mahavira's asceticism led him to the supreme goal of enlightenment. After fasting without water for two and a half days in the hot sun, Mahavira squatted on his haunches in meditation, near a tree but intentionally not in its shade. (Recall that Gautama, who had accepted the Middle Way, *sat* in the lotus position *under* a fig tree.) Here Mahavira attained **kevala** (kay′vuh-luh), Jain enlightenment, which is perfect and complete knowledge, or omniscience. Like Buddhist enlightenment, *kevala* marks the point at which one is free from the negative effects of *karma,* and thus has gained release from the earthly bondage of *samsara.*

Mahavira spent the rest of his life preaching to his followers, especially to his eleven principal disciples, Hindu *brahmins* who had

A

As the last *tirthankara* to have appeared on earth, Mahavira is the most important person for Jainism. Still he is only one *tirthankara* among countless who have appeared before and who will appear in the future. From your point of view, how does the fact that Mahavira is one of many *tirthankaras* affect his status as a religious figure? In your answer try to draw on comparisons with other religious figures, such as Jesus Christ and Gautama the Buddha.

B

Jains depict the universe, or *loka,* in the shape of a giant man. Try drawing this. How does this visual representation help to illustrate the Jain teachings regarding the human condition and the quest for spiritual perfection?

converted to Jainism when they heard Mahavira's teachings. These disciples formed the basis of the Jain community that survives to this day. At the age of seventy-two, Mahavira undertook his final ascetic act, voluntarily starving himself to death. Jains believe that Mahavira's pure soul was finally freed from his physical body, ascending to its rightful place at the top of the universe, where it dwells in supreme bliss for eternity.[A]

Knowing the Universe: Cosmology and Salvation

Gautama the Buddha spoke very little about cosmology; discourse on that topic, he felt, did not serve the real concern of finding salvation. Mahavira took the opposite approach. He described the universe in abundant detail. Through the omniscience of *kevala,* he knew everything regarding the makeup of the universe. Such knowledge has always been esteemed by Jainism, which maintains that salvation of the soul depends on understanding its predicament. And the soul's predicament is based in the makeup of the universe, which is composed both of eternal souls and of infinite particles of matter.

The Jain Universe

Jains understand the universe, called the **loka** (loh´kah), to be a space that is finite yet almost indescribably vast. By one account, if a god were to fly at the speed of ten million miles per second, it would take him seven years to travel from the top of the *loka* to the bottom. Within this space are all things, both living and nonliving. Outside the *loka* is nothing but strong winds. The *loka* is eternal: it was never created and will never come to an end.

The *loka* is often depicted as having the shape of a giant man. In the center is the small but significant Middle Realm, home to several worlds (including our own) inhabited by

human beings. The soul has the opportunity to move closer to salvation only in those human worlds. Below the Middle Realm are hells inhabited by hell beings, and above are heavens inhabited by deities.

Many of the gods and goddesses of Hinduism are also acknowledged by Jains. To some extent they are believed to provide certain forms of material welfare, such as cures for illnesses, or good weather for growing crops. For this reason some Jains worship these deities. In no way, though, can the deities assist with the quest for salvation. They too are bound to *samsara* and must first be reborn as human beings to have any hope for release. Both deities and hell beings, then, are destined to experience rebirth; the torments endured by the hell beings and the bliss enjoyed by the deities are both temporary conditions.

At the very top of the *loka* is a roof in the shape of an umbrella. This is the realm of liberated souls, such as those of Mahavira and the rest of the *tirthankaras.* These souls are eternally freed, never again to be reborn.[B]

Upward and Downward Cycles

The Jain universe passes through cycles that are depicted as turnings of a wheel. As the wheel turns upward, the quality of each world improves. As the wheel turns downward, all things gradually decay, eventually reaching a state of utter destruction. At this point the next cycle begins, and the world gradually improves. The wheel continues turning like this forever.

Each upward and each downward turning of the wheel is divided into six ages, and each age lasts twenty-one thousand years. According to Jains, this world is presently in the fifth age of a downward turn. Because of the world's rampant state of decay, Jains believe, people are meaner now, and physically smaller. Moreover, people now lack the moral or spiritual competence to attain salvation. In each turning of the wheel, twenty-four *tirthankaras* appear. Mahavira was the last of this downward turn; he and his eleven disciples were the last humans of this world to attain salvation. Until conditions improve significantly, the best that Jains of this world can hope for is a good rebirth, optimally as a human in a different world, one in which salvation is presently a possibility.[C]

The Human Condition: Clean Souls in Dirty Matter

The *loka* is inhabited by two distinct types: living things, which are **jivas** (jee´vuhs), or "souls"; and the nonliving **ajiva** (uh-jee´vuh), which consists of space, time, motion, rest, and all forms of matter. *Jivas* are perfectly pure. Matter is impure. For reasons that are beyond explanation, souls have become entwined with matter, and are thus tarnished and no longer pure. The religious quest for salvation is for the *jiva* to make itself clean.

In contrast with Hinduism and its predominant doctrine of monism, which says that all reality is essentially one thing, Jainism embraces a doctrine of pluralism, which says that reality is ultimately many things, an infinity of *jivas* and an infinity of particles of matter and the other *ajiva* entities. All these entities are eternal, and all can be said to exist on their own. In simplified form, though, Jain cosmology can be divided into two categories: the soul and matter. The entire process of human destiny is based on this duality; salvation consists of liberation of the soul from the matter in which it is entwined. This understanding is similar to that of the Hindu philosophical schools of Sankhya and Yoga.

All *jivas* are, in their original purity, equal in size and quality. The soul of an ant, for instance, is identical to that of an elephant. Only the bodies they inhabit, the forms of matter in which they are entwined, differ.

Jainism is famous for its extensive classification of these various bodies, or life-forms. The

IMAGE: © CHARLES & JOSETTE LENARS/CORBIS

This painting of the cosmic wheel with Mahavira at the center portrays the Jain conception of the cyclical universe.

basic classification divides them into two categories: stationary, such as plants, and moving, such as insects and animals. A more complex scheme categorizes life-forms according to the number of senses that Jains believe they have: animals, humans, deities, and hell beings are classified as five-sensed (they can see, hear, taste, touch, and smell); flying insects are four-sensed (they lack hearing); insects such as ants and fleas are three-sensed (they lack hearing and sight); shellfish and certain insects such as worms are two-sensed (they lack hearing, sight, and smell); and plants and microbes (the simplest forms) are one-sensed (they lack every sense but touch). (Note that the Jain classifications do not always match up with those of modern biologists; for instance, biologists do not classify ants as blind.)

Much more elaborate systems further classify these life-forms according to the details that distinguish one from another. The essential point behind all these classification systems is this: All life-forms, because they are inhabited by a soul, are to be regarded as fellow creatures worthy of respect and care. Most life-forms are capable of some degree of participation in religious life. Plants can express feelings; for example, they can desire

C

Compare the Jain concept of upward and downward cycles with your own understanding of time and the cycles of growth and decay of the universe.

D

Jainism holds that plants and animals, and even some microbes, can participate to some degree in religious life. In your opinion might animals possess any form of spirituality? Discuss some specific examples.

nourishment and feel fear. Animals are able to learn simple forms of religious disciplines (lions, for instance, can learn to fast). Even some microbes, which do not have bodies but group together in the bodies of more complex life-forms, can advance spiritually. However, for a soul to obtain the potential for spiritual perfection, it must eventually be reborn in a human body.[D]

The Religious Quest: The Rise of the Fallen Soul

The Jain quest for salvation can be understood by again picturing the *loka* as a giant man. The pure, liberated souls reside at the "umbrella" at the very top of the head, while all other life-forms reside below, weighed down by the matter in which their souls are entwined. Salvation is attained when the soul cleans all matter from itself and regains its original state of purity. It is then free to bubble upward to its eternal home.

Karma is crucial to the destiny of the soul in Jainism, just as it is in Hinduism and Bud-

dhism. However, Jainism understands *karma* in a purely materialistic sense. All actions are believed to involve the various forms of matter. Whenever the soul acts, it is tarnished by matter of some kind. Immoral actions, such as injuring other life-forms, dirty the soul with thick, heavy matter. Highly virtuous actions deposit only light, fleeting bits of residue, and eventually lead toward purity. The moment in which total purification of the soul is accomplished, called *kevala,* is the Jain version of spiritual perfection. Once one has attained *kevala,* the soul is no longer subject to the tarnishing effects of *karma.* Like Mahavira, who attained *kevala* long before he died, other enlightened Jains can go on experiencing life in the body. The actual moment of death, which is carefully approached through rituals, results in the complete liberation of the soul.

For Jains of this world, in this era of continuing decline, spiritual perfection and its resulting salvation are not attainable. Under these circumstances the immediate goal of the religious life is to achieve a good rebirth.

Jain worship takes various forms, including annual festivals, pilgrimages to holy places, and acts of devotion before small domestic shrines. This is a colossal sculpture of a tirthankara.

IMAGE: © CHRIS LISLE/CORBIS

This goal, like the goal of eventually attaining salvation, is dependent on *karma,* so living a good life remains essential. The life-form into which a person is born depends on the status of the soul—whether *karma* has made it heavy or light with matter.

The Religious Life

The religious life of Jainism is divided into two categories: that of laypeople, and that of monks and nuns (collectively known as ascetics). These two styles of religious life differ greatly from each other. The vast majority of Jains remain laypeople. Among the roughly four million Jains in the world today, the ascetics number in only the low thousands. Still, the monks and nuns set forth an ideal type for all Jains. Famous for their rigorous self-denial and deliberate detachment from all aspects of everyday society, the ascetics are revered by the laity as heroic role models. Laypeople remain members of Indian society, and typically are not nearly as involved with ascetic practices. The principle of nonviolence, *ahimsa,* is the central standard of conduct for both lifestyles.

White-Robed and Sky-Clad: Jain Sects

Like all major religious traditions, Jainism is divided into different sects. The two largest are the **Shvetambaras** (shvayt-ahm´buh-ruhz), "those whose garment is white," and the **Digambaras** (dig-ahm´buh-ruhz), "those whose garment is the sky." The Digambara monks, as their name suggests, go about naked, or "sky-clad" (the nuns do not). This practice is intended to help the monks abolish any ties to society. The Shvetambaras use bowls when begging for food and eating; the Digambaras use their hands only.

Beyond these differences in practice, the sects also have certain important doctrinal differences. Although both sects include nuns, only the Shvetambaras, who are generally more liberal, believe women can attain *kevala.* The Digambaras, who are more conservative, contend that a woman must first be reborn as a man before *kevala* can be a possibility. Another difference involves beliefs concerning the physical needs of one who has attained *kevala.* The Shvetambaras believe that once one has attained *kevala,* one continues to need food to go on living; the Digambaras deny this. The Digambaras also reject the authority of Shvetambara scriptures, and hence the two

Left: A sky-clad monk of the Digambara sect sits beside the whisk he uses to clear his path of insects. *Right:* A White-robed Shveambara nun visits a Jain pilgrimage site in western India.

sects rely on slightly different accounts of the life and teachings of Mahavira and the other *tirthankaras.*

Despite these differences, the religious lives of Jains are determined not so much by sectarian distinctions as by the choice between remaining among the laity and becoming an ascetic.

Nonviolent and Ascetic: Jain Monks and Nuns

E

Imagine you are a young Jain who has decided to become an ascetic. As the day of your initiation ceremony arrives, what aspects of your former life will you miss the most? In what ways might being an ascetic improve your life?

Jains believe the extremely difficult goal of completely purifying the soul can be achieved only through an ascetic life. Because Jainism denies the existence of any deity who can offer divine assistance, monks and nuns must accomplish everything through their own human efforts. The *tirthankaras* are also entirely beyond contact; their souls are in a state of complete liberation from the material world. Their life stories and their teachings are left behind to point the way, but they cannot provide any direct assistance. The only way out of the human predicament is to set off on the arduous path of a wandering ascetic.

Once an individual has reached the minimum age (eight for the more liberal Shvetambaras; young adulthood for the more conservative Digambaras), she or he is free to decide to become an ascetic. This is a drastic choice. Family ties are severed almost completely (although Shvetambara nuns are sometimes allowed visits from relatives). The initiation ceremony that marks the transition is intentionally designed to resemble a marriage, only in this case the candidate is joined (for life) to the ascetic lifestyle itself. Generally a teacher oversees the ceremony, and the young ascetic then remains with that teacher. The ceremony involves several ritual acts: repeating the vows that are binding for all Jain ascetics; receiving an alms bowl (though this does not apply to Digambaras) and a whisk, which is used to clear insects from one's path

so they will not be stepped on; pulling out five tufts of hair, which signifies renunciation of sexual life; and fasting.

Once initiated, the ascetics own nothing and receive all their food through begging. Today they tend to wander in groups. Setting out alone, as Mahavira did, is now regarded as being especially heroic, and it rarely occurs. During the rainy season, ascetics stay with communities of lay Jains. The principle of nonviolence dictates that the ascetics try to avoid walking during this time because more life-forms appear on the paths when it rains.[E]

Five Great Vows

The vows that are binding for all ascetics define their lives in terms of both outward behavior and inward conviction. The **Five Great Vows** are these:

1. Do not injure other life-forms.
2. Avoid lying.
3. Do not take what has not been given.
4. Renounce sexual activity.
5. Renounce possession.

As is typically the case in all religions, the ethical dimension figures prominently in the quest for spiritual perfection.

Ahimsa

The first vow contains subclauses that indicate the all-encompassing nature of *ahimsa,* the principle of nonviolence. These subclauses require that ascetics be careful when walking and when laying down the begging bowl, that they inspect their food and drink before consuming them, and that they search their mind and their speech so as to avoid negative thoughts and evil words.

The centrality of *ahimsa* can also be seen in the relation of each of the other four vows to this one. For instance, the third vow, to not take what is not given, means, on the most profound level, to not take the life of another. The fifth vow, to renounce possession, rids oneself of the passion that comes from attachment to possessions; passion, in turn, is thought to be the primary cause of violence.

Despite the rigors of *ahimsa,* Jains acknowledge some important practical concessions. For instance, *ahimsa* is considered to be violated only when the injury is accompanied by lack of care. In other words, intention matters. If a nun is carefully sweeping the path before her and yet steps on a bug, she has not violated the vow of *ahimsa.* The classification of life-forms also plays a practical role: injuring a lower life-form, such as a microbe, is considered to be less immoral than injuring a higher one. Closely related to this concession is the notion that violent action damages the status of the soul to the same extent as the violence inflicted. Killing a microbe might taint a person's soul with a small amount of matter, whereas killing a mammal would severely dirty the soul with impurities. Finally, Jain nonviolence does not imply complete pacifism; Jains are generally not required to remain passive if violence is done to them, whether by a human or by some other life-form. For example, if a tiger attacks a group of ascetics, the group is allowed to kill the tiger in self-defense.[F]

Asceticism

Through minimizing the bad effects of *karma,* ascetic practices purify the soul. The close relationship between asceticism and the vow of *ahimsa* can be readily observed in most of these practices. The rigorous vegetarianism of Jains (ascetics and laity alike) is extended well beyond avoidance of meat to include avoidance of any vegetable or other food thought to contain life-forms. For example, fruits with an abundance of seeds are shunned because of the lives residing in the seeds themselves. In keeping with the rules requiring the inspection of food, water, and pathways, the ascetic is not allowed to build fires or to dig in the ground, because such actions almost inevitably injure life-forms. Bathing is carefully regulated in part to prevent injuring any microbes residing in the water.

Among these many practical concerns, most of which involve avoidance of injury, the ascetic focuses on certain religious obligations. These obligations include regular periods of fasting and meditation, along with devotional disciplines. The ascetic offers hymns of praise to the *tirthankaras,* and pays formal acts of respect to his or her teacher. A ritual of standing in silent meditation (usually for forty-eight minutes) helps the ascetic nurture an attitude of benevolence.

The most important ritual is that of repentance. Performed twice daily in the presence of one's teacher, this ritual involves acknowledgment of wrongdoing, and ends with the recitation of this famous statement from the Jain scripture known as the Avashyaka Sutra: "I ask pardon from all living creatures. May all creatures pardon me. May I have friendship for all creatures and enmity towards none" (Avashyaka Sutra 32).

F
Identify some ways in which something similar to the Jain ideal of *ahimsa* is applied in your society. Do you think these forms of nonviolence stem from religious motives or from something else? Explain your answer.

IMAGE: YASHWANT K. MALAIYA

Vegetarianism: A Jain Ideal

Although Jainism does not attempt to gain converts, it does promote ahimsa *(nonviolence), in part through advocating the universal practice of vegetarianism. A series of international conferences have given Jain participants opportunities to present their perspectives on vegetarianism and other aspects of* ahimsa, *such as disarmament and world peace. At the Third International Jain Conference in New Delhi, India, one of the presenters was Shri Nitin Mehta, of the Young Indian Vegetarians of the United Kingdom. Here is his perspective on vegetarianism:*

Violence against defenceless animals remains the greatest indictment of the human race. Our so-called modern civilization has perfected the most abominable and despicable ways of exploiting the Animal world. At no time in [the] history of [the] world have animals been treated as cruelly as they are today.

Just one example is sufficient to prove my point—as if there was not enough to eat, people in certain parts of the world have developed a love of frog's legs—and until recently India was a willing supplier of this "delicacy." In this terrible situation who else can be expected to take up this fight against barbarism but the followers of Lord Mahavira? . . .

It is well known that in this land of Dharma and Ahimsa, meat eating is spreading fast. Our youths are being brain-washed in to ape-ing all that is negative in [the] western way of life. Jains must mobilise their *resources* and drive back this horror of violence towards defenceless animals. Let the Jains "buy out" those involved in the frog trade and re-employ them usefully somewhere else. Let the whole fish-killing industry be re-employed somewhere else. Let the slaughter of cows be stopped immediately throughout India. I am told that even during the time of Akbar [1542–1605], Jains managed to halt the slaughter of the cow for a certain time. . . .

The meat industry in the West is extremely rich and powerful. Indian people should expect the international "fast-food" chains to come to India very soon—if they are not there already. Money without morals is the motto of many involved in [the] meat trade. The Jain Community should be vigilant and try to ensure that the Indian people do not "get hooked" on Western "fast foods." . . .

Millions of people in the West are giving up their meat diet and a growing number of them are working day and night to reduce the suffering of animals. I call them the "practising Jains." Many are even sent to prison when they are caught rescuing animals from laboratories where painful experiments are carried out on them. They need our moral and material support which, at present, is not available. . . .

For those who are ignorant of God's Laws, punishment is not as severe as it is to those who know it and break it. The Jains and the Hindus who eat meat are knowingly and willingly breaking God's Laws and so the punishment will be severe.

For our own sake we should re-establish the teachings of Lord Mahavira. India can set the example for the world, but time is running out.

I end with a quotation from Gandhiji [Mahatma Gandhi]:

"The greatness of a nation and its moral progress can be judged by the way it treats its animals." (*Perspectives in Jaina Philosophy and Culture*, pages 45–46)

All Jain ascetics pattern their lives after that of their great role model, Mahavira. Naturally, over the centuries certain variations have become established as normal. Thus Jains rarely practice the act of voluntary starvation that was undertaken by Mahavira. They do, however, fervently defend the act, insisting that it is not a form of suicide because it does not involve passion and violence. Quite to the contrary, Jains hold, voluntary starvation is the ideal way to die, because not eating prevents any further accumulation of *karma*.[G]

Prosperous and Moral: Jain Laypeople

Jainism is famous for the asceticism of its monks and nuns, but those people make up only a small percentage of its population. The laity, who constitute more than 99 percent of Jains, regard the ascetics with honor and respect, acknowledging their authority and tending to their needs. To a limited extent, both groups share an ascetic lifestyle. All Jains are rigorously vegetarian, and fasting is a common ritual among the laity, especially women.

For the most part, though, the Jain layperson is concerned with leading a prosperous and moral life. The ultimate aim of salvation, with its extreme ascetic requirements, is seen as a distant possibility. A more immediate concern is achieving a good rebirth by improving one's *karma* through acts like giving food and shelter to ascetics. Carefully based on codes for proper conduct, such acts of giving are the primary means of raising the status of one's *karma*.

Other means include living in accordance with certain vows and performing acts of worship. The Twelve Vows for Jain laity include the Five Lesser Vows (milder parallels to the ascetic vows):

1. Do not intentionally injure a sentient life-form (that is, a life-form having two or more senses).
2. Avoid lying.
3. Do not take what has not been given.
4. Avoid unchastity.
5. Avoid greed.

The next three vows supplement the Five Lesser Vows:

6. Avoid excessive travel.
7. Avoid excessive indulgence in things such as food or clothing.
8. Avoid any unnecessary harmful behavior (such as self-indulgence or excessive complaining).

The final four vows prescribe religious practices:

9. Restrict activities to a certain place for a period of time.
10. Regularly perform the standing meditation (as required of the ascetics).
11. Fast on certain days.
12. Give to ascetics and to charitable causes.

Jain worship takes on various forms, including annual festivals, pilgrimages to holy places, and acts of devotion before small domestic shrines. The most visible form is the temple-centered worship of images of the *tirthankaras*.

A Jain worships in the Adinath Temple complex on Mount Abu, in the state of Rajasthan, India. The temples are among the world's most magnificent artistic achievements.

G

Jain ascetic practices tend to be directly related to the ideal of *ahimsa*. Make a list of ways in which denying yourself physical and material things might help to prevent violence toward other life-forms.

H

Carefully consider the Twelve Vows taken by members of the Jain laity. Which, if any, are similar to your own religious and moral principles and practices? Which, if any, are foreign to you? How might you benefit from following the principles that seem foreign?

Some of India's most striking architectural monuments consist of Jain temples, typically coated in marble, along with gigantic statues of the *tirthankaras*. The most common act of worship involves simply gazing reverently at a statue. Another is the anointing of statues with various ritual substances. Such worship is believed to produce good *karma* owing to the attitude of devotion required. It is not in any way a petition for help, because Jains believe the *tirthankaras* are forever beyond contact with the worshipers and cannot provide any actual assistance.[H]

Jains in Today's World

In the light of the rigorous asceticism practiced by Jain monks and nuns, one might expect lay Jains not to be involved in the normal economic and social affairs of India. The situation is quite the opposite. Jains today tend to be among the country's wealthiest citizens, and are active in such philanthropic endeavors as environmental and peace movements. Indeed, though Jains make up less than one-half of 1 percent of India's population, their contributions have been known to exceed 50 percent of the total amounts given for national philanthropic efforts.

Such involvement is based, like all other aspects of the religion, in Jainism's emphasis on the principle of nonviolence. Through the centuries Jains have avoided traditional forms of agriculture, especially those involving livestock. Instead they have engaged primarily in trade, and this has proven successful. Jains generally do not seek converts, though they do advocate that all people embrace the principle of nonviolence, including the practice of vegetarianism. Helping other people comes naturally from their belief that all life-forms are, at their most basic level, equal, fellow "sentient creatures."

The Seven Dimensions of Religion: Jainism

Dimension	Examples
Experiential	*kevala*
Mythic	biography of the Mahavira; stories of other *tirthankaras,* especially Parshva
Doctrinal	descriptions of the *loka,* and of the various life-forms (*jivas*)
Ethical	practice of *ahimsa* and its related virtues (that is, the Five Great Vows)
Ritual	daily repentance before a teacher, standing in silent meditation, fasting
Social	division into sects (for example, Shvetambara and Digambara), division into ascetics and laity
Material	whisk used by ascetics to prevent injury to life-forms, statues of the *tirthankaras*

Chapter Review

1. Explain the meaning and significance of the term *tirthankara*.
2. Who was Parshva?
3. Summarize the life story of Mahavira.
4. Describe the important contrasts between the life story of Mahavira and that of Gautama the Buddha.
5. What is *kevala?*
6. In Jainism, knowledge regarding the universe and salvation is very important. Why?
7. Describe the *loka.*
8. What is the role of deities in Jainism?
9. Explain the Jain concept of upward and downward cycles. In terms of these cycles, where is the world presently?
10. Identify and briefly describe the two categories of reality and their relationship to each other according to Jain cosmology.
11. What is the Jain attitude toward all life-forms?
12. Describe the Jain quest for salvation.
13. Name the two largest Jain sects and explain their differences.
14. Describe the initiation ceremony marking the transition to an ascetic life.
15. List the Five Great Vows of Jain ascetics.
16. Briefly describe *ahimsa* and its importance to Jain ascetic life.
17. What is the relationship between Jainism's ascetics and laity?
18. What is the main concern of Jain laypeople?

Glossary

ahimsa (ah-him´suh; Sanskrit: "nonviolence," "not desiring to harm"). Both the avoidance of violence toward other life-forms and an active sense of compassion toward them; a basic principle of Jainism, Hinduism, and Buddhism.

ajiva (uh-jee´vuh). The non-living components of the Jain universe: space, time, motion, rest, and all forms of matter.

asceticism. The renunciation of physical pleasures and worldly attachments for the sake of spiritual advancement; common in many religious traditions, most notably Jainism.

Digambaras (dig-ahm´buh-ruhz; Sanskrit: "those whose garment is the sky"). The second largest Jain sect, whose monks go about naked so as to help abolish any ties to society; generally more conservative than the Shvetambaras.

Five Great Vows. The vows that are binding for Jain ascetics: do not injure other life-forms; avoid lying; do not take what has not been given; renounce sexual activity; and renounce possession.

jina (ji´nuh; Sanskrit: "conqueror"). One who has "conquered" *samsara;* synonymous with *tirthankara.*

jivas (jee´vuhs; Sanskrit: "souls"). The finite and eternal units of Life, or souls.

karma (Sanskrit: "action"). The moral law of cause and effect of actions; determines the nature of one's reincarnation; for Jainism, purely materialistic, such that all actions involve various forms of matter.

kevala (kay´vuh-luh). The perfect and complete knowledge that is Jain enlightenment; marks the point at which one is free from the damaging effects of *karma* and is liberated from *samsara.*

loka (loh´kah). The Jain universe, often depicted as having the shape of a giant man.

Shvetambaras (shvayt-ahm´buh-ruhz; Sanskrit: "those whose garment is white"). The largest Jain sect, whose monks and nuns wear white robes; generally more liberal than the Digambaras.

tirthankaras (teert-hahn´kuhr-uhs; Sanskrit: "makers of the river crossing"). The Jain spiritual heroes, such as Parshva and Mahavira, who have shown the way to salvation; synonymous with *jinas.*

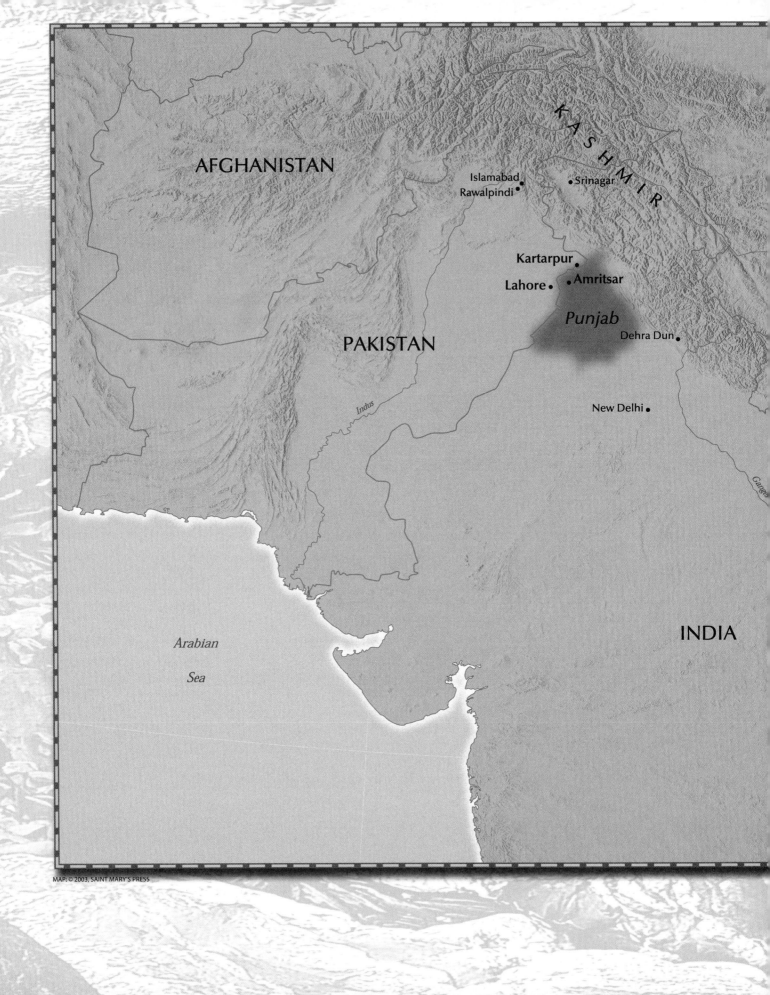

AFGHANISTAN

KASHMIR

Islamabad
Rawalpindi
Srinagar

Kartarpur
Lahore
Amritsar

PAKISTAN

Punjab

Dehra Dun

Indus

New Delhi

INDIA

Arabian

Sea

Ganges

MAP: © 2003, SAINT MARY'S PRESS

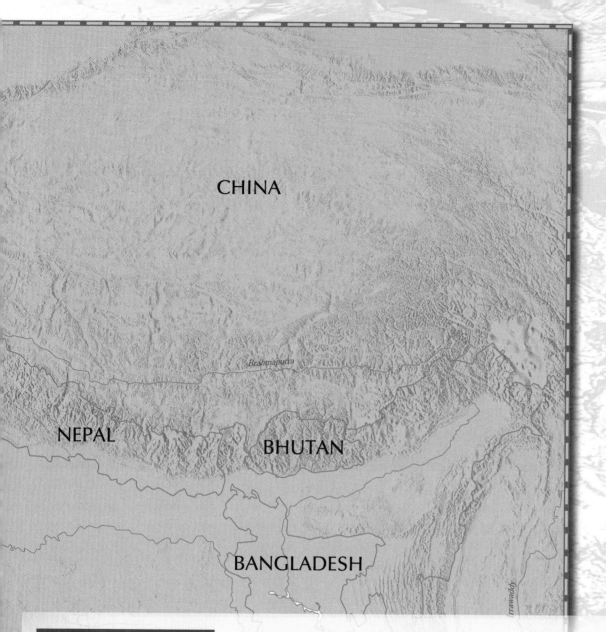

CHINA

Brahmaputra

NEPAL

BHUTAN

BANGLADESH

Irrawaddy

6 Sikhism

Identity and Community

Sikhism is a highly visible religion relative to its size. There are only about twenty-three million Sikhs today, most living in the state of Punjab in northwestern India. Still, Sikhs are familiar to many. Approximately two million Sikhs live outside of India, and Sikh communities can be found today in most of the large cities of the West. Male Sikhs are especially recognizable because of the distinctive turban they wear. A strong sense of identity, maintained through such traditional aspects as the turban, has always been a hallmark of Sikhism.

Sikhs pay homage to Guru Nanak, the founder of Sikhism, in a crowded room in Lahore, Pakistan.

IMAGE: © CHRISTINE OSBORNE/CORBIS

Sikhs also are familiar because of various other notable features of their tradition. Sikhism has long been admired as a religion that tries to reconcile the great differences between Hinduism and Islam, the two religions of medieval India, where Sikhism arose. Sikhism is monotheistic, like Islam. It maintains that there is only one God, creator of the world and sovereign ruler over all. And yet Sikhism holds that human salvation depends on a mystical union with God, the same sort of experience that is central to most forms of Hinduism.

When Sikhism was founded about five centuries ago, Muslims ruled northern India. As the centuries passed, growing hostilities led to sporadic skirmishes. In 1799 Sikh military prowess overcame the Muslims, and an independent Sikh kingdom endured for nearly half a century. More recently, Sikh conflicts with Hindus culminated in the assassination of Indira Gandhi, prime minister of India, by members of her Sikh bodyguard, in 1984. The struggle for Sikh independence that led to that incident continues today, and in some respects, Sikhism maintains an uncomfortable relationship with India's Hindu majority. On the other hand, in 2004 India elected Manmohan Singh to be Prime Minister—the first Sikh ever to hold such high office. This has given hope to many, Sikh and Hindu alike, that the sort of tensions that led to the bloody conflict of 1984 are largely in the past.

In this chapter we will address various issues of Sikh identity—their history, beliefs, and practices. In doing so we will see clearly how strong the Sikh's sense of community is, no less so now that their numbers are spreading increasingly into the world community at large.

The Development of Sikhism: From Guru Nanak to the Guru Granth Sahib

By the time Guru Nanak (1469 to 1539), the founder of Sikhism, had come on the scene, the important role of the guru had long been established in India. A **guru** (goo'roo) is a spiritual teacher. The literal meaning of the term *guru* is popularly explained by referring to its parts: *gu* means "darkness," *ru* means "enlightenment." A guru, then, is one who delivers people from the darkness of ignorance to a state of enlightenment.

Guru is an important concept for Sikhism. The word *sikh* literally means "learner" or "disciple"—that is, one who learns and follows the teachings of the Guru. The capitalized term *Guru* is used in three slightly different ways. For one, it is the title of Guru Nanak and his successors, the ten historical leaders of Sikhism. It also refers to the sacred text of Sikhism, the **Adi Granth** (ah'dee gruhnth), which is commonly referred to as the Guru Granth Sahib. Finally, it is a name for God, often in the form True Guru. In each case the Guru functions as the revealer of Truth, or God's will. (In Sikhism God lovingly reveals the divine will to humans; God too thus functions as Guru.)

The ten historical Gurus of Sikhism were revealers of truth. They are considered to be linked to one another through a sharing of the same divine essence. This association with the divine made them spiritually more adept than ordinary people, but they still were not divine incarnations of God. Hence they are not to be worshiped by Sikhs, though they are greatly revered. Guru Nanak constantly stressed his human limitations, humbly referring to himself as God's slave. All the Gurus were revered for their spiritual gifts and acquired much worldly prestige as well. The Muslim emperors who ruled northern India knew the Gurus personally and tended to respect them, in some cases developing strong friendships with them.

The Life of Guru Nanak

Nanak was born in 1469 in a small village near Lahore (in present-day Pakistan). He was born to Hindu parents of the warrior class. His parents arranged for him to marry in his teens as was customary. Soon he and his wife had two sons.

The legendary accounts of Nanak's early adult life emphasize his dissatisfaction with typical forms of employment, and his general rejection of traditional forms of Hindu worship. It seems he sought out the company of a variety of holy men, both Hindu and Muslim. His spiritual searching led him to a religious outlook that asserted the oneness of God and the need to move closer to God. The best means for increasing intimacy with God, Nanak believed, were meditating and singing hymns of praise to God. Eventually Nanak began composing his own hymns with his friend Mardana, a Muslim musician.

According to tradition Nanak was a spiritual leader even at this early stage of his life. He would rise before dawn and bathe in the river, meditate, and then lead others in singing hymns of praise. The crucial experience leading to the founding of Sikhism, though, occurred when Nanak was about thirty years old.

Receiving God's Revelation

One morning Nanak did not return from bathing in the river. He was presumed drowned, and yet his body was not found. Three days later Nanak returned to the village, but remained silent for a day. When he finally spoke, he proclaimed:

There is no Hindu and no [Muslim] so whose path shall I follow? I shall follow God's path. God is neither Hindu nor [Muslim] and the path which I follow is God's. (Cole and Sambhi, *The Sikhs*, page 10)

Nanak explained that he had been escorted to the court of God, who gave him a cup of nectar and told him:

This is the cup of the adoration of God's name. Drink it. I am with you. I bless you and raise you up. Whoever remembers you will enjoy my favour. Go, rejoice in my name and teach others to do so. I have bestowed the gift of my name upon you. Let this be your calling. (Pages 10–11)

The Journeys of Guru Nanak

Deeply moved by this revelation, Guru Nanak spent the next stage of his life, from ages thirty to about fifty, on a series of travels. The traditional account depicts four long journeys, reaching as far as Mecca and Baghdad. Although the distances and remarkable occurrences along the way may be to some extent legendary, the general nature of Nanak's travels is made clear. He visited holy sites and encountered a wide variety of religious people. He also proclaimed and practiced his own teachings, sometimes before hostile audiences.

Several incidents during Guru Nanak's travels shed light on the new message he proclaimed. On one occasion, while visiting a famous Hindu shrine, he found himself among *brahmins* throwing water toward the rising sun as an offering to their dead ancestors. Nanak turned and threw water the other way, explaining, "If you can send water to your dead ancestors in heaven, surely I can send it to my fields in the Punjab" (Singh, "Sikhism," in *The Encyclopedia of Religion,* volume 13, page 316). Such stories illustrate Nanak's consistent rejection of traditional rituals.[A]

Founding the Sikh Community

Drawing from his revelation experience and years of journeying, Guru Nanak continued proclaiming his own understanding of the truth. In doing so he attracted a large following. At about the age of fifty, Nanak built a new township called Kartarpur (whose name translates as "abode of the Creator"). Here he and his followers formed the first Sikh community, and established the lifestyle that has characterized Sikhism to this day. Sikhs refer to their community in its entirety as the **Panth.**

Guru Nanak erected a special building for worship, therefore. This provided the model of the **gurdwara** (goor′dwah-ruh), which is the central structure of any particular Sikh community. He also built a hostel to accommodate the many visitors to Kartarpur. Nanak, though in most respects a regular member of the community, sat on a special seat when addressing the community. Followers recognized the Guru as merely human and yet very spiritually advanced. Today the Adi

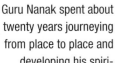

A
Guru Nanak spent about twenty years journeying from place to place and developing his spiritual perspective. In your view how might travel to distant places and encounters with foreign forms of religion nurture spiritual growth?

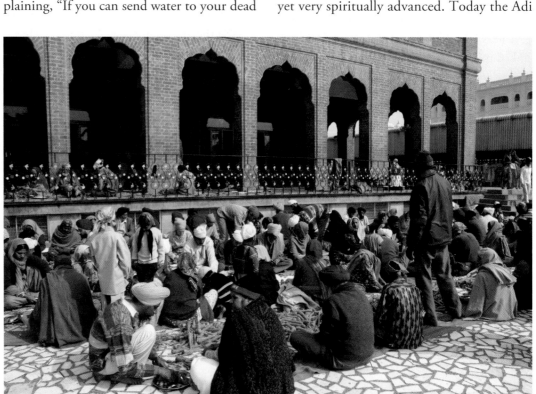

Volunteers from the Sikh community prepare food outside of the community kitchen of the Golden Temple at Amritsar. Some 40,000 people per day share in the communal meal.

IMAGE: ©JEFFERY BRODD

IMAGE: © JIM ZUCKERMAN/CORBIS

The Golden Temple at Amritsar provides Sikhs with an inspiring geographical center.

Granth, Sikhism's sacred text, occupies the role once held by the Gurus, and sits on a special seat within the *gurdwara*.

In 1539, after leading the Kartarpur community for about twenty years, Guru Nanak died. The tradition tells us that the Guru, aware of his approaching death, settled a dispute regarding the proper disposal of his body. In keeping with their respective traditions, his Hindu followers intended to cremate him, and the Muslims planned to bury him. Nanak instructed both groups that when he died, the Hindus should lay flowers at his right side, and the Muslims at his left. Those whose flowers were still fresh in the morning were to do as they wished with his body. The Guru covered himself with a sheet in preparation for death. When the sheet was removed after he died, the body was gone, and the flowers on both sides were still fresh. Even with his death, Guru Nanak helped to settle the differences between Hinduism and Islam. (Today Sikhs generally cremate their dead.)[B]

The Evolution of Sikhism: Contributions of Nanak's Successors

Guru Nanak has remained the most prominent and revered of the ten Gurus of the Sikhs. Yet his successors, each in his own way, contributed significantly to the development of the religion.

Guru Arjan

Arjan (spiritual leader from 1581 to 1606), the fifth Guru, compiled the Adi Granth, thus giving the Sikhs their sacred scripture. He also constructed at Amritsar the great *Hari Mandar* ("God's Temple"), later named *Darbar Sahib* ("Court of the Lord") and commonly called the Golden Temple. This provided the Sikhs with a geographical center. In contrast with Hindu temples, which typically have one door, the Temple of God was designed with four doors, representing Sikhism's openness to people of all four classes of the prevalent Hindu caste system, and to all four directions.

The role of the Guru as both the spiritual and temporal leader gained greater emphasis during Arjan's time. He was a worldly leader

B

Although he probably did not intend to found a new religion, Guru Nanak's life and leadership proved so inspirational that his followers united to form Sikhism. Which three or four characteristics of Guru Nanak's or events in his life do you think were most responsible for the establishment of Sikhism? Describe how those characteristics or events might have inspired his followers.

Sikhism   111

friendly with Akbar, the great Muslim emperor. Eventually, though, Arjan's participation in worldly affairs resulted in his imprisonment and death by torture. Arjan's fate led Sikhism to take on a more pronounced political and military dimension that has endured in various forms to the present day. Before Arjan died he presented his son, his successor, with two swords, one representing spiritual power and the other, worldly power.[C]

Guru Gobind Singh: The Last of the Ten Gurus

The tenth Guru, Gobind Singh (spiritual leader from 1675 to 1708), is revered as the greatest Guru after Nanak. His strength of character and spiritual adeptness made him a successful and memorable leader. Guru Gobind Singh contributed significantly to the growth of Sikh militarism. He engaged in many armed conflicts during a period when revolts against the Muslims were common.

Most notably, Guru Gobind Singh brought about two innovations that forever changed the structure of Sikhism. He instituted the Khalsa, which would redefine the Panth, or Sikh community; and he installed the Adi Granth, the sacred scripture, as Guru, radically altering the nature of the religion's leadership.

The Khalsa: The Pure Ones

In a period of great unrest and violent confrontations between Sikhs and Muslims in 1699, the Sikhs had gathered to celebrate an annual festival. Guru Gobind Singh perceived a desperate need for loyalty and cohesion among the Sikhs, so he addressed the multitude. Raising his sword he challenged any Sikh who was willing to die for him to come forward. An uncomfortable silence followed. Finally one man stepped out of the crowd and followed Guru Gobind Singh into the leader's tent. The stunned crowd heard the thud of a falling sword. Then the Guru emerged alone, with bloodstained sword in hand. Another man stepped forward, and the process was repeated. Three more men followed in turn. The crowd waited in silence. Eventually Guru Gobind Singh emerged with all five men, alive and well.

C
Guru Arjan initiated a long history of Sikh involvement in political and military affairs. Do you see any relationships between religion and political or military affairs in the world today? Try to describe two such relationships.

A Sikh teacher reviews the Adi Granth in its place of honor in the *gurdwara*.

IMAGE: © BALDEV/CORBIS SYGMA

These men have ever since been known as the beloved five. They were the original members of the **Khalsa** (khal′sah), the Pure Ones, an order within Sikhism based on the principle of loyalty exhibited by these men. The Guru had the five men initiate him into the Khalsa, and soon thousands more, both men and women, joined. All the men were given the additional name Singh, meaning "lion." All the women were given the name Kaur, which means "princess." To this day most Sikhs bear the name Singh or Kaur.[D]

Guru Gobind Singh's Successor

Guru Gobind Singh was mortally wounded by an enemy sword. Before dying, it is said, he officially installed the Adi Granth as the next Guru. This was obviously a significant step in the development of Sikhism. Until it was taken, leadership of the Sikh community passed from human hands. Ever since it occurred, the earthly authority of the religion has been the scripture.

The Adi Granth: Sikhism's Greatest Attraction

Ever since Guru Gobind Singh installed it as Guru in 1708, the Adi Granth has been regarded just as the Gurus were. Whereas the Gurus once occupied a special seat among Sikh disciples, the Adi Granth now occupies the same type of seat in any place of worship. Whereas Sikhs once looked to the Gurus as the authorities on religious matters, they now consult the Adi Granth.

Adi Granth literally means "first book." Sikhs commonly express their reverence for the scripture by referring to it as the Guru Granth Sahib (*sahib,* like *guru,* is a title of respect). Every copy is identical in script and has 1,428 pages. The Adi Granth is primarily in the Punjabi language. In recent years, English and French translations have become available.

The Adi Granth is remarkable not only for its profound theological content but also for its poetic and musical brilliance. It is made up of hymns composed by six of the Sikh Gurus along with several other religious figures of medieval India. Notable among those others is the poet Kabir (about 1440 to 1518), whose religious perspective was very similar to that of Guru Nanak.

The Adi Granth rings with brilliance when it is put to music and proclaimed in its original language, Punjabi. It has been said that "the poetic excellence, the spiritual content, and the haunting, lilting melodies of the

D
Imagine yourself as a Sikh in a crowd celebrating an annual festival in 1699. Suddenly your leader, Guru Gobind Singh, challenges anyone who is willing to die for him to come forward. What are your thoughts as you decide whether to step from the crowd?

Sikh Names

The names Singh and Kaur—for men and women, respectively—normally correspond to English last names. First names are determined shortly after birth. During a highly ritualized naming ceremony, the Adi Granth is randomly opened and a name is chosen that begins with the opening letter of the composition appearing on its left-hand page. No distinction is made between boys' first names and girls' first names; the "last names" Singh and Kaur identify gender.

hymns of the Adi Granth are Sikhism's greatest attraction to this day" (Singh, "Sikhism," in *The Encyclopedia of Religion,* volume 13, page 319).[E]

E

The Adi Granth features written material and musical accompaniment. Imagine the lyrics of a favorite song without any musical accompaniment. How does this alter their impact? How might a sacred text like the Adi Granth be strengthened by musical accompaniment?

Religious Teachings: God, Humans, and Salvation

The religious teachings of Guru Nanak and his successors, as conveyed through the Adi Granth, present a rare combination of monotheism, the predominant theology of Western religions, and mysticism, a prevalent theology among Eastern religions. They reveal that the ultimate purpose of life is to attain complete union with God. This state of spiritual perfection corresponds in an important way with Hindu *moksha* (and sometimes Sikhs use the same term to describe it), for it constitutes liberation from *samsara,* the cycle of death and rebirth, also familiar to Hinduism, Buddhism, and Jainism. The experience of union with God is eternal bliss, and it is indescribable—beyond human thought and language.

God: Formless One, Creator, True Guru

Guru Nanak's understanding of the nature of God is the center from which all Sikh teachings evolve. The Adi Granth begins with a concise summary of Sikh theology, known as the Mool Mantra:

This Being (God) is One; the truth; immanent in all things; Sustainer of all things; Creator of all things. Immanent in creation. Without fear and without hatred. Not subject to time, formless. Beyond birth and death. Self-revealing. Known by the Guru's grace. (Cole and Sambhi, *The Sikhs,* page 70)

Much of this description should sound familiar to adherents of the monotheistic traditions of the West: Judaism, Christianity, and Islam. God is one, eternal, beyond time, and beyond spatial constraints ("formless"). The last description is frequently used in the Adi Granth: God is the Formless One, beyond all attributes that humans use to describe reality. God is referred to as "he" in Sikhism because there is no neuter pronoun in the Punjabi language of the Adi Granth. Sikhs actively strive to avoid assigning to God human attributes such as gender.

Sikhs believe that for reasons beyond the grasp of human comprehension, God decided to create the world and all that is in it, including human beings. In addition to being the Creator, he is also the Preserver and the Destroyer. Here Sikhism draws from the important Hindu triad of gods: Brahma (Creator), Vishnu (Preserver), and Shiva (Destroyer). The Sikhs reject Hindu polytheism, however, insisting that their God is one. Their three names for God thus reflect different aspects of the one God.

In God's primary state, to which the Gurus refer when they use the name Formless One, God is distinct from his creation in much the same way an artist remains distinct from her or his artwork. And yet God dwells within creation—within nature and within human beings. God is thus said to be **immanent,** or indwelling (as opposed to transcendent, or beyond creation). In this state of immanence, God is personal and can be approached through loving devotion. Because of God's immanence in creation, it is possible for humans to make contact with God and come to know him. Just as one can know something of an artist by seeing the artist's works, so too can one come to know God through experiencing his creation. Indeed part of the ongoing purpose of creation is that God, through his loving grace, might reveal the divine self to human beings. It is in this capacity of immanence that God is referred to as Guru, for by revealing himself God delivers humans from darkness to enlightenment.[F]

The Human Condition: Self-Centered and Bound to *Samsara*

Human beings are especially near to God. Though Sikhism advocates kindness to living things, it also holds that other creatures are here to provide for us. (Unlike Hindus, therefore, Sikhs are not opposed to eating meat—although many prefer vegetarianism.) More important, God dwells within all human beings, and is actively concerned about their spiritual welfare. However, humans tend to neglect the need to center their lives on God.

Rather than being God-centered, humans are inclined to be self-centered. The primary shortcoming of the human condition is expressed in the Sikh term **haumai** (how′may), which is difficult to translate accurately into English but means something like "self-reliance," "pride," or "egoism." *Haumai* is humans' insistence on making do on their own rather than acknowledging dependence on God. When *haumai* dominates life, its five accompanying vices—lust, anger, greed, attachment, and pride—tend to run rampant. *Haumai* and its vices increase the distance between a person and God.

This distance from God is compounded through ignorance. Humans tend to mistake the world and its charms for the true object of attention. Rather than seeking the Creator, humans in their ignorance seek God's creation. When they do so, creation itself can be a pitfall because it presents the vices with countless attractions. Lust and greed for the world, anger and pride regarding the world, and attachment to the world: these are the evil workings of *haumai*. As long as ignorance, *haumai*, and *haumai's* vices persist, humans are destined to remain in *samsara*, the ongoing cycle of death and rebirth.

Salvation: Union with God

Despite the problem of humans' attaching to the things of creation while ignoring the

F
The image of God in Sikhism is in some ways similar to the image of God in Western religious traditions, and in some ways similar to the image of God in Hinduism. Describe the Sikh God in your own words, including references to those similarities.

Sikh children light candles as part of their loving devotion on a holy day, the birthday of one of the revered Gurus.

G

In Sikhism, God's creation can be a hindrance because of human attachment to it, but it is also necessary for salvation because it reveals God's will, or *hukam*. How does creation relate to your spiritual life? Is creation completely good? or does it present some problems?

Creator, God's creation ultimately is good and necessary for salvation. Creation allows people to move closer to God. God's immanence in creation is perceivable in **hukam** (huh´kahm), the divine order. Through *hukam* God asserts his will on the world and communicates truth to the human heart. The quest for spiritual perfection is a constant struggle between the self-centeredness to which humans are naturally inclined, and the call to live in accordance with the will of God.

God plays an essential role in determining the outcome of this struggle, for it is God's grace that enables humans to perceive God. Having received God's grace, they are called to respond in loving devotion through meditation on the nature of God. The term most often used in the Adi Granth to denote the nature of God is *nam,* the "divine Name." Meditation on the *nam* or recitation of the *nam* is repeatedly prescribed as the path to spiritual perfection. Related terms are also used to refer to the object of meditation: the Word, Truth, the Divine Order. These are all ways of expressing the immanence of God in creation.

Spiritual perfection, in Sikhism, amounts to moving beyond all human shortcomings to a state of complete union with God. This state of salvation is eternal, infinitely blissful, and forever beyond the cycle of death and rebirth.[G]

The Religious Life: Worship, Ritual, and Lifestyle

A primary aspect of Guru Nanak's teachings was the rejection of much of the traditional religious life of Hinduism and Islam. Focused as he was on seeking the indwelling God through meditation on God's nature, Nanak regarded the external forms of religion as useless.

Still, Guru Nanak instituted certain practices that amounted to a Sikh way of life. His successors continued to define that way of life, with the most notable innovations coming from the last successor, Guru Gobind Singh. The Khalsa, the order of the Pure Ones, is especially rich in symbolism and ritual practice.

Sikh Worship in the *Gurdwara*

Gurdwara literally means "doorway of the Guru." Any building that contains a copy of the Adi Granth is, technically speaking, a *gurdwara,* a Sikh house of worship. Most *gurdwaras* have a characteristic Sikh style, with minarets and chalk-white paint. Aside from

From Guru Nanak's Japjī

Guru Nanak's Japjī (juhp´jee) is among the compositions of the Adi Granth that constitute Sikhism's early morning prayers. Here is the fourth section of that prayer. Note its emphasis on meditating on the divine Name as a means to liberation through union with God.

The Eternal One whose Name is Truth speaks to us in infinite love. Insistently we beg for the gifts which are by grace bestowed. What can we offer in return for all this goodness? What gift will gain entrance to the hallowed Court? What words can we utter to attract this love? At the ambrosial hour of fragrant dawn meditate on the grandeur of the one true Name. Past actions determine the nature of our birth, but grace alone reveals the door to liberation. See the Divine Spirit, Nanak, dwelling immanent in all. Know the Divine Spirit as the One, the eternal, the changeless Truth. (Quoted in McLeod, *Sikhism,* page 272)

IMAGE: © CHRIS LISLE/CORBIS

Any building that contains a copy of the Adi Granth qualifies as a *gurdwara*, a Sikh house of worship. Here the Adi Granth is wrapped beneath a canopy.

the presence of the Adi Granth, which usually sits atop cushions and under a canopy, there are no specific requirements regarding the interior.

The *gurdwara* serves mainly as a place for Sikhs to congregate for worship. This they do frequently, on no particular day of the week. Usually worship takes place in the evening, though the early morning is also a popular time. Worship in the *gurdwara* is preceded by bathing, and consists of singing the Gurus' hymns, reading from the Adi Granth, or telling a story about one of the Gurus. No formal requirements govern the exact nature of worship. It generally ends, though, with a sharing of a special cake made of wheat, ghee (butter oil), sugar, and water. This act is symbolic of the unity of the Panth, or Sikh community.

The sharing of food is central to Sikhism. Each *gurdwara* generally has within it a com-munity kitchen, where Sikhs gather at various times to share in the preparation and consumption of a meal. This illustrates that the community is one unit, regardless of the caste status of its individual members. In addition, it provides food for those who are needy.

The Khalsa: Entry into the Community of Pure Ones

Perhaps the most vivid ritual of Sikhism is the ceremony of initiation into the Khalsa. The initiate should be at least fourteen years old. He or she must possess the Five Ks (so named because of the Punjabi terms for these requirements, each of which begins with a *k*): uncut hair, a comb, an iron wrist guard, a sword or knife, and a pair of shorts. Interpretations vary as to the precise meaning of the rich symbolism of the Five Ks, but their primary purpose is to strengthen Sikh identity.

H
Compare Sikh worship in the *gurdwara* with the forms of worship that are familiar to you. What are the similarities? What are the differences?

Sikhism   117

Sikh Ritual, Sikh Homeland

Bhai Dhanna Singh is a devoted Sikh who is engaged in the struggle to establish a Sikh homeland, to be called Khalistan. In this interview Dhanna Singh describes the ritual of initiation, or baptism, into the Khalsa.

In the morning on which a Sikh is to be baptized he is to bathe completely, including washing of his hair. And then he has to have the five articles of faith on his body when he comes to the place where the baptism is to happen. Baptism is done in the presence of the Guru Granth Sahib, and in the presence of five beloved ones *[panj piaras]*, who are already there. All of them are wearing the five articles of faith. There we express our desire, standing before those five beloved ones, to be baptized. Then we are asked about certain principles and commitments which a Sikh has to have to be baptized. Those commitments have to be met even if it comes to sacrificing oneself for the value of truth. Then the five beloved ones ask, "Are you ready for that?" and when it is nodded yes, then the Sikh is baptized. In a bowl [made] of iron, water and some sugar crystals are stirred with the double-edged sword by the five beloved ones, one by one, and as they are stirring they are reciting a hymn. Then those five hymns which are recited during the baptism ceremony become the prayer that the Sikh recites in the morning, afternoon, and night. After the *amrit* [the nectar mixed in the iron bowl] is ready the Sikh goes before the five beloved ones in a special posture, having his right knee on the ground, and one of the beloved ones takes the *amrit* and gives him five drinks, puts the *amrit* on his head five times, and sprinkles it on his eyes five times. All the time the seeker who is being baptized says "Waheguru ji ka Khalsa, Waheguru ji ki Fateh" (Khalsa belongs to God and Victory belongs to God).

After a Sikh is baptized he is told that from now on all Sikhs are brothers and sisters and there should not be any distinction on the basis of caste, color, or creed. You are all brothers and sisters, they say, and from now onwards you all belong to one Father, Guru Gobind Singh, and you will all believe in one Almighty God who is formless. Never worship any idols or anything else, never bow before graves or pseudo-saints. Guru Granth Sahib will be your holy Guru. A Sikh must say his prayers every morning and evening. A Sikh is supposed to earn his bread through the sweat of his brow, and give one-tenth of his earnings to the needy and poor. Those are the ideals of Guru Nanak which are reinforced during the baptism ceremony, which reminds the Sikh that his duty is to obey them throughout his life.
(Quoted in Mahmood, *Fighting for Faith and Nation*, pages 144–145)

Bhai Dhanna Singh envisions the Sikh homeland, Khalistan, as an ideal state . . .

What I enshrine in my soul along with most of the Sikhs is a Khalistan that is an ideal state which the world has not seen before. A place where without distinction of caste, color, or creed all the citizens will have equality. Everybody will have the right to worship as they please. Citizens of Khalistan will be prosperous, and we will contribute toward the promotion of world peace. We will see that the whole world becomes a just place to live for the people of the Lord. . . .

We don't have any malice or animosity toward the common Hindu or toward anybody. Of course there is no question that some Sikhs will take revenge on the Hindus or other innocent people, but the people who have committed heinous crimes on the Sikhs will be punished not on the street but according to the law of the land. They will be tried in the courts of Khalistan, and after their guilt is proved they will be punished according to the law. . . .

Guru Nanak's message is based on love, equality, and justice, and as Sikhs we won't be great if we don't live up to this love, equality, and justice. It's our moral duty. We can't be close-minded people. We will have to hear the viewpoints of others.
(Page 150)

The ritual is performed by five people, recalling the original initiation of Guru Gobind Singh by the beloved five. The Adi Granth is opened, and one of the five explains the basic principles of Sikhism to the initiates, who are asked if they are willing to accept them. The initiates are then served nectar made from water and sugar, which has been mixed in an iron bowl and stirred with a two-edged sword while hymns are recited. The nectar is drunk and sprinkled on the eyes and heads of the initiates who recite the Mool Mantra. The initiates are instructed about the ethical requirements of the Khalsa. Those include prohibitions against cutting one's hair, eating meat that has been improperly slaughtered, engaging in extramarital sexual relations, and using tobacco. The initiation ends with a sharing of the special cake.

The founding of the Khalsa by Guru Gobind Singh is the single most important event in the history of Sikhism since the time of Guru Nanak. Though a rather small percentage of Sikhs have undergone the traditional rites of initiation, approximately 70 percent of Sikhs are popularly considered to be members of the Khalsa, in that they typically observe the Five Ks (or at least the one they consider most important, not cutting their hair) and other central teachings. Regardless of percentages or degrees of membership, the traditional ways of the Khalsa influence to a large extent the practices and customs of the entire Panth.

Like most aspects of Sikh religious life, the Khalsa strengthens the social identity of the community. Like any religious community, however, the Panth varies from place to place. For example, in the West most Sikhs do not follow the prohibition against cutting their hair, partly because Western society considers long hair to be impractical and sometimes even because of employers' regulations.[1]

IMAGE: © FRÉDÉRIC SOLTAN/SYGMA/CORBIS

The Five Ks needed for membership in the Khalsa are uncut hair, a comb, an iron wrist guard, a sword or knife, and a pair of shorts.

Sikh Identity and Community: Work, Worship, and Charity

People who have not learned about Sikhism may wonder, Why do Sikh men typically wear turbans and refuse to shave their beards? We can now recognize that as one of the Five Ks, an uncut beard is a sign of membership in the Khalsa, and hence a symbol of Sikh identity. The turban, which is worn by almost every male Sikh in the traditional homeland, India, is another important symbol of Sikh identity.

The Five Ks of the Sikh Khalsa primarily strengthen Sikh identity. What similar symbols do you see in your own religious tradition or the traditions of people around you? How do you think those symbols strengthen a sense of identity among the members of the religions that use them?

Even in places like the United Kingdom, motorcycle helmet laws have been modified to suit the insistence of Sikhs regarding this custom (although many Western Sikhs choose not to wear the turban).

That the turban causes Sikhs to stand out in the world is no accident, nor is it regretted. Such ease of recognition nurtures social identity and a sense of community, hallmarks of Sikhism. But for such a relatively small religious community to be so easily recognized also makes it vulnerable to being misunderstood by outsiders. Some Sikhs were even mistaken for Muslim militants and became targets of persecution in the aftermath of the attacks on the World Trade Center and Pentagon on 9-11. As people around the world become more familiar with the Sikh community, one can hope that such misunderstanding will end.

The Sikh community does its own part to nurture a positive image and to make itself better known to the world at large. From its beginnings Sikhism has been on the side of religious freedom and justice for oppressed people. Justice is carried out partly through the regular donation of one-tenth of one's income to charitable causes. And though their theology resolves differences between Hinduism and Islam, Sikhs consider the uniqueness, coherence, and effectiveness of their own path to God to be most important.

The three guiding principles of Sikh life are worship, work, and charity. As members of a tradition that effectively nourishes the spirituality of the individual and also nurtures material and social welfare, Sikhs maintain their identity while playing an ever expanding role in the world community.

The Seven Dimensions of Religion: Sikhism

Dimension	Examples
Experiential	union with God and liberation (*moksha*) from *samsara*
Mythic	accounts of the life of Guru Nanak and of the founding of the Khalsa
Doctrinal	the theology of the Mool Mantra, *haumai* and *hukam*
Ethical	the four prohibitions for members of the Khalsa
Ritual	the ceremony of initiation into the Khalsa, meditation on the divine Name, worship practices in the *gurdwara*
Social	the Panth, the Khalsa
Material	the Five Ks, food served in ceremonial meals, the *gurdwara*

Chapter Review

1. Explain the literal meaning of the term *guru*.
2. What is the literal meaning of the word *sikh*?
3. List the three ways the capitalized term *Guru* is used in Sikhism.
4. Briefly describe Nanak's early life.
5. Summarize Nanak's statement upon returning from receiving God's revelation.
6. What is significant about the township called Kartarpur?
7. What is the term for the Sikh community?
8. What is the name of the Sikh scripture? Who compiled it?
9. Who is revered as the greatest Guru after Nanak?
10. What is the Khalsa?
11. Identify Guru Gobind Singh's successor.
12. What makes the Adi Granth Sikhism's "greatest attraction"?
13. What is the name of the summary of Sikh theology that begins the Adi Granth?
14. Explain what it means to say that God is immanent.
15. Why is God referred to as Guru in Sikhism?
16. What is *haumai*?
17. Why is God's creation necessary for Sikh salvation?
18. Describe the state of spiritual perfection for Sikhism.
19. Briefly describe the Sikh *gurdwara*.
20. What does the preparing and sharing of food symbolize in Sikhism?
21. Identify the Five Ks.
22. Why is the ritual of initiation into the Khalsa performed by five people?

Glossary

Adi Granth (ah´dee gruhnth; Punjabi: "first book"). Sikhism's most important sacred text and, since it was installed as Guru in 1708, Sikhism's earthly authority; also called the Guru Granth Sahib.

gurdwara (goor´dwah-ruh; Punjabi: "doorway of the Guru"). A special building that is reserved for Sikh worship and houses a copy of the Adi Granth; the central structure of any Sikh community.

guru (goo´roo). A spiritual teacher and revealer of truth, common to Hinduism, Sikhism, and some forms of Buddhism. When the word *Guru* is capitalized, it refers to the ten historical leaders of Sikhism, to the sacred text (the Guru Granth Sahib, or Adi Granth), and to God (often as True Guru).

haumai (how´may; Punjabi: "self-reliance," "pride," or "egoism"). The human inclination toward being self-centered rather than God-centered, an inclination that increases the distance between the individual and God.

hukam (huh´kahm). The divine order of the universe.

immanent. Indwelling; Sikh theology maintains that God dwells within nature and within human beings in such a way that God is personal and can be approached through worship.

Khalsa (khal´sah; Punjabi: "pure ones"). An order within Sikhism to which most Sikhs belong, founded by Guru Gobind Singh in 1699.

Panth. The Sikh community.

7 Confucianism

The Ethical Foundation of East Asia

The lands of East Asia (China, Japan, and Korea) have typically embraced a variety of religious traditions, including various strands of folk tradition. The great traditions Confucianism, Taoism, Buddhism, and, in Japan, Shinto have interwoven to form a fabric. This fabric, rather than any one particular tradition, has generally provided for the religion of the individual. So as we investigate each of those great traditions,

Left: The religions of East Asia form an interwoven fabric that provides for the religion of the individual. Worship services at the Cao Dei Temple combine elements of Confucianism, Taoism, and Buddhism.
Right: A statue of Confucius adorns a Chinese temple.

we must be careful to understand them as parts of a larger whole. Instead of expecting to find a balance of the seven dimensions of religion in any one tradition, we should try to discover how the traditions complement one another. For example, the experiential dimension is not very well developed in Confucianism, whereas it is Taoism's forte. Nor should we expect each tradition necessarily to provide answers to all the basic religious questions. For instance, when faced with questions of human destiny, East Asians are more apt to look for answers from Buddhism than to seek responses from Confucianism or Taoism.

Throughout the fabric of East Asian religion, the threads of Confucianism show prominently, especially regarding the social and ethical dimensions. For centuries Confucianism has provided the ethical foundation of East Asia, defining proper behavior from early childhood to death. In the words of one scholar, "East Asians may profess themselves to be Shintoists, Taoists, Buddhists, Muslims, or Christians, but seldom do they cease to be Confucians" (Tu Wei-ming, "Confucianism," in *Our Religions,* page 149).

As a religion that features the ethical dimension, emphasizing moral values and principles, Confucianism naturally focuses on human relationships. How should individuals behave so that families might flourish, governments may thrive, and humanity as a whole might progress toward an ever more healthy and happy state? Confucianism's answers derive from a central project: learning to be human. When individuals learn more deeply what it is to be human, then families and governments are improved, and ultimately humanity itself is improved. At the same time, the individual moves closer to realizing the full potential of human happiness.

Great Master K'ung: The Life and Legacy of Confucius

K'ung Fu-tzu (Master K'ung; 551 to 479 BC) is better known all over the English-speaking world as Confucius, from an early attempt to render his name in Latin. He is also known as China's First Teacher. His steadfast eagerness to learn to be human, and his expertise at teaching others his views have defined the lifestyle of East Asia for over two thousand years. This vast influence, affecting about one-fourth of the world's population, makes Confucius one of the most influential people ever to have lived.

Confucius

The few details we know of Confucius's life hardly suggest the eventual extent of his influence worldwide. On the surface, in fact, Confucius appears to have been a failure.

Life and Career

Confucius was born in eastern China. His family, though of noble lineage, was poor. His father died while Confucius was still a baby, leaving his mother to attend to his early education. Because of this she became a role model through the centuries for Chinese mothers, who generally are the primary nurturers of their children.

Confucius was an exceptional student, and was eager to learn. Among his favorite subjects were poetry and history. As a young man, he began a career of teaching others and quickly gained a loyal following. Along with teaching the literary and historical classics from the past, Confucius strove to apply the lessons of the ancients to the problems of his own day, including the problem of government.

At about age fifty, Confucius became a public official, securing a minor cabinet position with the duke of Lu, his home state. He apparently grew frustrated with his inability to apply his ideas in Lu, so he soon left. For the next thirteen years, Confucius wandered from state to state, trying to put his theories into practice. Eventually he gave up and returned to Lu to teach and study. When he died in 479 BC, he appeared to be a failure. The future would prove otherwise.

Eager Student, Diligent Teacher: Confucius's Character

Confucius's vast influence obviously stems from something beyond his meager accomplishments as a government official. One major source is the strength of his character. That Confucius is remembered at all is a result of the enormous influence he had on his disciples. It was they who, probably within a generation after Confucius's death, assembled his many teachings into the collection known

IMAGE: GIRAUDON/ART RESOURCE, NY

A Chinese painting from the nineteenth century depicts Confucius and his disciples.

as the **Analects.** Learned during childhood by countless Chinese and other East Asians, the sayings in the Analects are the most important source we have for the actual teachings of Confucius.

Confucius's character shines through in the Analects. Modest regarding his own talents and abilities, yet highly inspirational to his disciples, Confucius seems most of all to have been an eager student and diligent teacher, who lived a full and joyful life. That he is usually referred to simply as the Master further illustrates how deeply his disciples respected him.

The Master said, "How dare I claim to be a sage or a benevolent man? Perhaps it might be said of me that I learn without flagging and teach without growing weary." (Analects 7.34)

The Master is cordial yet stern, awe-inspiring yet not fierce, and respectful yet at ease. (Analects 7.38)

A disciple of Confucius's once found himself at a loss to describe the Master. Upon hearing of the incident, Confucius said to him:

Why did you not simply say something to this effect: he is the sort of man who forgets to eat when he tries to solve a problem that has been driving him to distraction, who is so full of joy that he forgets his worries and who does not notice the onset of old age? (Analects 7.19)[A]

China's Problems and Confucius's Solutions

Along with Confucius's strength of character, another source of his eventual influence is the brilliance of his ideas. Though Confucius's ideas were not accepted initially, history has shown that they provided potent solutions for China's problems.

Even from Confucius's vantage point in the sixth century BC, China was an ancient civilization with a glorious past. But things had begun to decline rapidly. States were warring against one another. Rulers were oppressing their subjects. Society was falling into disarray.

At roughly the same time Confucius was teaching, others were setting forth theories as solutions to China's problems. The Legalists advocated a stern rule of law enforced by severe punishments. The Mohists, following the lead of their founder, Mo Tzu (480 to 390 BC), taught universal love, even toward one's enemies. (Mo Tzu's teachings on love are similar to Jesus's teaching to love one's neighbors as one's self.) The Taoists placed more emphasis on the individual than on society. They believed the path to human happiness lay in the individualistic pursuit of harmony with nature.

Confucius took a markedly different approach. Deeply dedicated to restoring society, he embraced a vision of humanity that centered on human relationships. Though he advocated the need to love one another, Confucius did not go as far as the Mohists. He argued that justice, not love, should be the primary response when dealing with an enemy. As for the Legalists, Confucius regarded punishment as an ineffective means of nurturing lasting improvement in people. He believed that rather than being punished for making mistakes, people should be inspired by good examples.

Confucius derived his examples from the past, from rulers and sages of ancient times who perfectly embodied the ethical principles on which a healthy society must be based. Confucius was therefore concerned more with transmitting traditional ways than with inventing new theories: "I transmit but do not innovate; I am truthful in what I say and devoted to antiquity" (Analects 7.1).

One important aspect of Chinese tradition that Confucius helped to transmit was the worship of ancestors. According to archaeo-

A
The Analects show us that Confucius had a great reputation for learning and teaching; he has been revered for that in East Asia throughout the ages. Does your society revere good learners and teachers?

logical evidence, for centuries before Confucius's time, the Chinese had believed their deceased ancestors could influence the welfare of the living, for good and for ill. Through regular offerings of prayer and sacrifice, ancestor worship ensured that the dead were satisfied.

Confucius had little to say about life after death, but he advocated the continuation of ancestor worship as part of the traditional rites of the people:

When your parents are alive, comply with the rites in serving them; when they die, comply with the rites in burying them; comply with the rites in sacrificing to them. (Analects 2.5)

By transmitting traditions such as ancestor worship, Confucius sought to provide the fundamental ethical ideas with which to improve Chinese society. He believed the power of tradition would ensure their acceptance. And though he claimed he was merely a transmitter, Confucius made profound contributions in developing these ideas.[B]

Confucius's Legacy: The Confucian Tradition

The enduring reputation of Confucius's character and the brilliant content of his teachings continued to inspire new generations of disciples. These disciples have respectfully sought to understand the Master's original meaning in the teachings. Inevitably, however, different followers have offered different interpretations, some with bright innovations of their own. It would thus be a mistake to simply equate Confucianism with the teachings of Confucius.

One innovator was Mencius (about 390 to 305 BC), who is regarded as the second founder of Confucianism. He claimed that human beings are naturally good and that they commit evil acts in violation of their true nature. This eventually became accepted as a basic teaching of Confucianism. Mencius's teachings are set forth with clarity and sophistication in the **Book of Mencius,** one of the central texts of Confucianism.

B
Confucius believed strongly in the power of tradition as a means of improving Chinese society. In your society does the power of tradition play a part in improving life? or does tradition get in the way of improvement?

IMAGE: © BOHEMIAN NOMAD PICTUREMAKERS/CORBIS

A Confucian holy book, in both English and Chinese, rests on a podium in a temple in Taiwan.

C
Carefully reread Confucius's words regarding his own lifelong process of learning (see Analects 2.4). In Chinese society those words have long served as a model for lifelong learning. Are people in Western society encouraged to learn more deeply as they grow older? Discuss similarities and differences between these societies' attitudes toward learning.

For a few centuries, Confucianism was confined to philosophers and teachers like Mencius, with hardly any effect on society at large. Gradually those philosophers began to influence government officials. In 136 BC the state established a school of Confucian scholars. Soon anyone training to become an official was required to learn the Confucian texts. Since that time, almost without interruption until the beginning of the twentieth century, a formal Chinese education has included a thorough study of Confucian teachings.

An important chapter in the continuing saga of Confucianism's influence is the philosophical tradition called **Neo-Confucianism.** Arising around one thousand years ago, Neo-Confucianism was largely a response to the challenges facing Confucianism from the popular religions Taoism and Buddhism. Its most famous figure, and one of the world's greatest philosophers, is Chu Hsi (*joo shee;* AD 1130 to 1200). Chu Hsi's interpretations have since then defined the nature of Confucianism. Among his other contributions, Chu Hsi determined the Four Books from among the Confucian texts that to this day are considered most important. Along with the Analects and the Book of Mencius, these include the Great Learning and the Doctrine of the Mean.

Learning to Be Human: Confucianism's Central Project

The sayings in the Analects clearly convey Confucius's deep commitment to learning:

The Master said, "In a hamlet of ten households, there are bound to be those who are my equal in doing their best for others and in being trustworthy in what they say, but they are unlikely to be as eager to learn as I am." (5.28)

Steadfast in his own eagerness to learn, Confucius expected no less of his students:

The Master said, "I never enlighten anyone who has not been driven to distraction by trying to understand a difficulty or who has not got into a frenzy trying to put his ideas into words." (Analects 7.8)

Confucius's deep commitment to learning arose from his understanding of the nature of learning. For him, rather than being a mere gathering of information, learning was a means of discovering *what it is to be human.* Only through learning to be human can one possibly mature toward greater well-being. In the Analects, Confucius charted the ongoing nature of his maturation through ever deepening degrees of learning:

Confucius said, "At fifteen my mind was set on learning. At thirty my character had been formed. At forty I had no more perplexities. At fifty I knew the Mandate of Heaven. . . . At sixty I was at ease with whatever I heard. At seventy I could follow my heart's desire without transgressing moral principles." (2.4)

Our remaining task is to make sense of Confucius's discoveries as he advanced in his lifelong project of learning. We begin by investigating his perspective on specific qualities of being human: what it is to be mature, what the pinnacle of human virtue is, how best to behave, how to be a cultured person, and how to govern. First we consider a concept basic to all forms of Chinese religion: the Tao.[C]

Tao: The "Way" of Chinese Philosophy

The Taoist religious tradition elaborates extensively on the meaning of Tao; we will devote more time to it in the next chapter. However, Tao is also of basic significance for Confucianism.

Tao (dou) literally means "way." In Confucianism, Tao generally refers to the moral order that permeates the universe and is thus the Way that should be followed. If one can learn to know the universal Way, then one can come into harmony with it. For Confucius learning to know the Tao was of fundamental importance: "He has not lived in vain who dies the day he is told about the Way" (Analects 4.8).

The Human Ideal: *Chun-Tzu*

The Analects devotes more than eighty passages to describing the ideal human being, the **chun-tzu** (jin-dzuh). A *chun-tzu* is a person with perfect moral character, a "mature person" or "gentleman." Ancient China was a patriarchal society, organized according to male lines of descent, and Confucius seems to have assumed that only a man could become a *chun-tzu*. "Gentleman" is therefore an accurate translation, though in principle the concept of the ideal human can be applied to all, male and female.

Along with being patriarchal, the concept of the *chun-tzu* is somewhat elitist. Confucius frequently contrasted the gentleman with the "small man," assuming all along that it is the gentleman's role to lead, the small man's role to follow, and so forth. Yet Confucius also made a great contribution toward social equality. Until his teachings took hold, a man simply acquired the status of gentleman, or noble, at birth if his father happened to be of the nobility. According to Confucius one becomes a gentleman through steadfast learning. Once Confucianism was established as the official tradition, nobility was bestowed by merit rather than by birth.

Confucius's numerous references to the *chun-tzu* describe a person with such abundant virtues that he is able to contribute to the improvement of society. Like all Confucian ideals, becoming a *chun-tzu* depends first of all on learning.

Older Confucians, seeking to embody the concept of *chun-tzu,* converse during a ceremony at the Sung Kyun Kwan Temple in Korea.

The Master said, "The gentleman seeks neither a full belly nor a comfortable home. He is quick in action but cautious in speech. He goes to men possessed of the Way to be put right. Such a man can be described as eager to learn." (Analects 1.14)

The Master said of Tzu-ch'an that he had the way of the gentleman on four counts: he was respectful in the manner he conducted himself; he was reverent in the service of his lord; in caring for the common people, he was generous and, in employing their services, he was just. (Analects 5.16)

The *chun-tzu* can be said to embody spiritual perfection in the Confucian sense, although Confucius himself tended to avoid speaking of absolutes. He seems not to have envisioned a person's ever arriving at the end of life's spiritual quest. This is apparent in the previously cited passage about Confucius's own degrees of learning: "At seventy I could follow my heart's desire without transgressing

The Teacher's Place

The Confucian emphasis on learning has always implied a special respect for teachers. In this excerpt from A Chinese Childhood, *by Chiang Yee, the author tells of his gratitude toward his teacher, despite the teacher's sometimes "tyrannical" ways.*

Our teacher held a very high position in our family life in my childhood. A Chinese proverb, *I-jih-ch' ih-Ssu, Chung-sheng-wei-fu,* states that he who becomes the teacher of a child for one day is the "father" of that child's lifetime. This proverb always rang in my ears when I listened to the serious talk of my elders. In the middle of our ancestral shrine we had a big red tablet painted with five golden characters representing Heaven, Earth, Nation, Parents and Teacher. . . . The position of "Teacher" was the fifth and last, but it stood next to that of "Parents." Twice a month, on the first day and the fifteenth, one of my elders burned incense in front of the shrine and knelt down to pay respect on behalf of the family. . . .

The importance attached to the teacher's position is testified to by the fact that he stood side by side with our parents on these occasions. Confucius taught that children should be filial to their parents and respect their elders. I do not know whether the idea of setting up the tablet to Heaven, Earth, Nation, Parents and Teacher originated with him or not. If it did, he must have been an odd man—afraid, perhaps, that his own disciples might not respect him as highly as he expected!

Theoretically speaking, young people in China have always gone in awe of their elders. In my house I felt there were already enough elders to be respected without a most tyrannical teacher as well. . . .

I do not know why my elders always gave way to the teacher's tyranny. Whenever they saw him look distressed or annoyed they would ask us whether any of us had offended him or had not been working

well. Then they would apologize to him for us and endeavour to soothe him. This made us very careful of our behaviour in the family school, and also encouraged the teacher to be more tyrannical than ever. The elders seemed to think that he could not be too tyrannical. They often told us that without strict training in youth, one could not expect to achieve anything in later life. They also said that parents could not train their own children well, being influenced by affection for them: we had, therefore, to have a good teacher; and they went on to emphasize how fortunate we were to have *this* good teacher.

(Pages 79–80)

The teacher adopted different methods for each of us, according to our age and mentality. There were two sets of simple books, used for both girls and boys, composed of lines of three characters and lines of four characters with rhymes. They were universally used in China for teaching children to recognize the characters. We all learned them by heart without necessarily knowing their meaning. Then we began to read the "Four Books," with Confucius' Analects as the first book. We had to be proficient in each book before we could proceed to the next, so some of us got on faster than others. At first we were taught only to read and recite them over and over again. We could not question the "by rote" method and in those days we did not think of doing so. When we could recite the whole four books without a mistake the teacher explained the meaning of them to us passage by passage for an hour or two every day. Then we began to read the commentaries on each book by well-known Confucian scholars. (Page 83)

How strict [our teacher] was! I do not agree with his way of teaching, but I am glad that I was trained under his tyrannical rule, for otherwise I might not remember Confucius' classics as well as I do. (Page 86)

moral principles." One suspects that had Confucius lived longer, he would have attained ever higher degrees of spiritual achievement.[D]

The Supreme Virtue: *Jen*

Confucianism advocates several virtues. Wisdom, courage, trustworthiness, reverence, uprightness—all these are encouraged in the Analects and elsewhere. The supreme virtue is **jen** (ruhn). *Jen* is often translated as "goodness," "love," or "benevolence." In passages like those that follow, Confucius emphasized the fundamental importance of *jen:*

If a man sets his heart on benevolence, he will be free from evil. (Analects 4.4)

If the gentleman forsakes benevolence, in what way can he make a name for himself? The gentleman never deserts benevolence, not even for as long as it takes to eat a meal. If he hurries and stumbles one may be sure that it is in benevolence that he does so. (Analects 4.5)

We gain a more precise understanding of *jen* when we note its two primary components: doing one's best, and reciprocity (called *shu* in Chinese).

Fan Ch'ih asked about benevolence. The Master said, ". . . When dealing with others do your best." (Analects 13.19)

Tzu-kung asked, "Is there a single word which can be a guide to conduct throughout one's life?" The Master said, "It is perhaps the word *'shu.'* Do not impose on others what you yourself do not desire." (Analects 15.24)

The notion **shu** (sh*oo*) is especially intriguing, for it is essentially identical to the reciprocity taught by the Golden Rule—"Do unto others as you would have them do unto you"—a basic ethical teaching in Judaism and Christianity. Yet Confucianism does not go as far as Christianity, which teaches, "Love your

enemies." For Confucius, reciprocity works along these lines:

Someone said, "What do you think of repaying hatred with virtue?" Confucius said, "In that case what are you going to repay virtue with? Rather, repay hatred with uprightness and repay virtue with virtue." (Analects 14.36)

Jen is a perfect form of benevolence—doing one's best to treat others as one would wish to be treated. It is the central component of a perfect moral perspective.[E]

Proper Behavior as Sacred Ritual: *Li*

Confucianism's emphasis on human relationships goes hand in hand with a deep concern for proper behavior. Behaving properly is as important as having the right moral perspective, and the two are closely related. The individual who demonstrates the right moral perspective will naturally behave properly.

The Chinese term for proper behavior is **li** (lee). *Li* has two definitions. It means "rite," or "sacred ritual," and "propriety," or "behaving properly given the situation at hand." Confucianism combines both definitions, holding that behaving properly, even when performing apparently mundane routines, carries at all times the significance of a sacred ritual. Because he admired the ancient ways, Confucius looked to China's past in determining the rules of behavior that constitute *li.* His abundant store of traditional rules sets forth a complete guide to personal behavior.

The Analects contains detailed accounts of Confucius's attention to *li.* Note how carefully he regulated his own behavior, as if performing an ongoing ritual:

In the local community, Confucius was submissive and seemed to be inarticulate. In the ancestral temple and at court, though fluent, he did not speak lightly.

At court, when speaking with Counsellors of lower rank he was affable; when speak-

D Confucius taught that one becomes a *chun-tzu*—a person of perfect moral character—through steadfast learning. Explore the relation between learning and the development of moral character. Explain why you agree or disagree with this statement: It is possible to learn to be a better person.

E Compare the Confucian doctrine of *shu,* or reciprocity, with the Christian teaching to love one's enemies.

F

According to Confucianism, the cultural arts, or *wen,* play an important role in ensuring the unity and continuity of East Asian society. Explore the role of the cultural arts in your society. First identify several art forms you consider most relevant. Then explain how they help maintain the unity and continuity of your society.

ing with Counsellors of upper rank, he was frank though respectful. In the presence of his lord, his bearing, though respectful, was composed.

When he was summoned by his lord to act as usher, his face took on a serious expression and his step became brisk. When he bowed to his colleagues, stretching out his hands to the left or to the right, his robes followed his movements without being disarranged. (Analects 10.1–3)

This account illustrates a significant aspect of *li:* proper behavior is largely dependent on one's place in society. Confucians refer to this as the rectification of names. He who is called emperor ought to behave in a manner befitting the name *emperor;* counselors ought to behave as proper counselors, and so on, for every level of society. The rectification of names helps define the nature of human relationships within Confucian society.

Calligraphy is one of the skills of *wen,* the cultural arts.

IMAGE: © BOB KRIST/CORBIS

Becoming a Cultured Human Being: *Wen*

Learning to be human also involves acquiring skills of behavior that are broadly categorized as **wen,** the cultural arts. Mainly these are the arts of poetry and music, which Confucius deeply admired. He frequently referred to his love of music and to the *Book of Odes,* an anthology of Chinese poetry that preserved works from centuries before Confucius's time. *Wen* also includes other skills, of which Confucius is said to have been a master: archery, charioteering, calligraphy, and mathematics.

The cultural arts play a vital role in ensuring unity and continuity in society. For Confucianism the arts accomplish this and much more. Confucius praised art not only for its beauty but also for its moral goodness. Becoming a cultured human being—a person who appreciates and participates in the arts and skills that make up *wen*—is, in actuality, acquiring a moral education. Individuals become better people through contact with the cultural arts, and society is, in turn, improved.[F]

Leading by Power of Moral Example: *Te*

Learning to be human nurtures people's well-being. It also helps them develop the ability to lead others. Good government is a primary goal of Confucianism, as revealed in Confucius's own attempt to put his theories into practice in government service.

Good government comes about through the cultivation of **te** (day). *Te* means "virtue" or, more specifically, "virtue as shown through the power of example." It is one of the attributes of the gentleman *(chun-tzu),* and it is both the product of a life of learning and the means of educating society through example. Confucius remarked that *te* is extremely potent, with a sort of gravitational pull:

A ruler who governs his state by virtue is like the north polar star, which remains in its place while all the other stars revolve around it. (Analects 2.1)

Confucius deemed *te* a far more effective tool of leadership than laws and punishments. Laws and punishments may restrict bad behavior for the short term, but *te* has the long-term effect of nurturing moral conscience, which Confucius referred to in this passage as shame:

Guide them by edicts, keep them in line with punishments, and the common people will stay out of trouble but will have no sense of shame. Guide them by virtue, keep them in line with the rites, and they will, besides having a sense of shame, reform themselves. (Analects 2.3)[G]

Self, Family, Nation, Heaven: Confucian Harmony

The men of old who wished to make their bright virtue shine throughout the world first put in order their own states. In order to put in order their own states they first regulated their own families; in order to regulate their own families they first disciplined their own selves. (The Great Learning, quoted in Thompson, *Chinese Religion,* page 12)

This famous passage from the Great Learning (one of the Four Books of the Confucian canon) illustrates the Confucian vision of the grand harmony among human relationships. The self, the family, the nation, and the entire world of humanity are all intimately related to one another. The health of each depends on the others. The role of relationships in this vision of harmony is emphasized by the doctrine of the **Five Constant Relationships.** This doctrine is summarized in the Book of Mencius as consisting of "love between fa-

ther and son, duty between ruler and subject, distinction between husband and wife, precedence of the old over the young, and faith between friends" (3A:4).

Self

Confucianism has a unique understanding of selfhood, and therefore of the human condition. Rather than emphasizing the individuality of the self, Confucianism regards the self first and foremost as a center of human relationships. This is readily observed in the doctrine of the Five Constant Relationships. Self-identity is determined primarily by one's status as parent or child, ruler or subject, and so on. The human condition is thus conceived of largely in social terms.

The Confucian self, furthermore, is thought to be constantly changing. Through learning to be human, one continues to grow, attaining deeper and more fulfilling levels of maturity. The individual is thus engaged in an ongoing process of self-cultivation.

Learning to be human takes place with the world as classroom. The self is not withdrawn from the world, but engaged in it. And as the self is cultivated, society is improved. The realm of society that receives foremost attention from every Confucian is the family.

Family

Confucianism emerged when the family was already the center of Chinese society, and the Confucian tradition fortified that significance. Three of the Five Constant Relationships involve family. The following passage, taken from a Confucian classic on *li* (rites and propriety), elaborates on those relationships:

The father is merciful, the son filial; the elder brother is good, the younger brother submissive; the husband is upright, the wife complaisant; the adult is kind, the child obedient. (*Records of Rituals,* quoted in Thompson, *Chinese Religion,* page 11)

G
Confucius believed that *te,* virtue as shown through the power of example, is a more lasting means of improving society than is mere punishment of bad behavior. If you agree with Confucius, reflect on two situations in which the power of moral example has proved to be more effective than punishing bad behavior. If you disagree with him, reflect on two situations in which punishment has been more effective than moral example.

H

Consider the two quoted passages about the relationships within the Confucian family. Critique the structure that they describe. Be sure to comment on the Five Constant Relationships and on the virtue of being filial. Is this a good structure for family relationships?

The primary virtue in relating to one's elders is to be filial, or to act in a way suitable for a son or daughter. This virtue plays a central role in Confucianism, extending to the subject-ruler relationship as well. In the Analects, Confucius paid particular attention to being filial, pointing out that it is even more important than correcting one's parents when they are wrong:

In serving your father and mother you ought to dissuade them from doing wrong in the gentlest way. If you see your advice being ignored, you should not become disobedient but remain reverent. You should not complain even if in so doing you wear yourself out. (Analects 4.18)[H]

One's relationships with family members are defined throughout life in Confucian society. In theory this provides a clear sense of place and of purpose. In practice it is subject to abuse. The "complaisant" wife, obligated to consent to her husband's wishes, could fall victim to a domineering husband if he abandoned his duty to be "upright." The "obedient" child could be unjustly treated. And so on. Confucians themselves are fully aware of such potential abuse, and have, especially lately, maintained a critical perspective on their own system.

In any event one aspect of the Confucian family is prominent: deep respect for elders. The older people get, the more they are respected. Contemporary Western society, which tends to regard old age negatively, could perhaps learn from Confucianism on this point. Rather than having to dread the aging process, Confucians can look forward to increased social standing and to greater opportunities to share the wisdom they, through their lifelong learning, have acquired.[1]

Nation

Good government has always been of much concern in the Confucian tradition. The nation is thought of as one great family. Within the grand harmony of human relationships, the ruler plays a decisive role. The ruler is a gentleman *(chun-tzu)*, one who has acquired the necessary moral perfection so that he might lead by power of example *(te)*. The subjects, in turn, are to be filial toward their ruler. In its entirety Confucian government offers the best for all, ensuring the happiness of the people and the ongoing improvement of society.

Chi K'ang Tzu asked Confucius about government, saying, "What would you think if, in order to move closer to those who possess the Way, I were to kill those who do not follow the Way?"

Confucius answered, "In administering your government, what need is there for you to kill? Just desire the good yourself and the common people will be good. The virtue of the gentleman is like wind; the virtue of the small man is like grass. Let the wind blow over the grass and it is sure to bend." (Analects 12.19)

This Japanese print, *The Moon of the Filial Son,* highlights the virtue of being filial. It shows a model of the filial son collecting firewood when he realizes his mother needs him.

IMAGE: © ASIAN ART AND ARCHAEOLOGY, INC./CORBIS

The harmonious relationship between the nation and individuals is further described in the following passage. Here Confucius, who at the time was not officially working within the government, explained that individuals and governments nurture each other.

Someone said to Confucius, "Why do you not take part in government?"

The Master said, "The *Book of History* says, 'Oh! Simply by being a good son and friendly to his brothers a man can exert an influence upon government.' In so doing a man is, in fact, taking part in government. How can there be any question of his having actively to 'take part in government'?" (Analects 2.21)

Heaven

Confucianism says little regarding divinity or the afterlife, leading some to wonder whether it is actually a religion at all. Moreover, it places little emphasis on the experiential dimension, which normally tends to include the focal points of religious traditions (as with Hinduism's *moksha* and Buddhism's *nirvana*).

Confucius himself seems to have had little to say about the divine or supernatural, as some passages in the Analects indicate. For example:

Chi-lu asked how the spirits of the dead and the gods should be served. The Master said, "You are not able even to serve man. How can you serve the spirits?"

"May I ask about death?"

"You do not understand even life. How can you understand death?" (11.12)

However, having little to say regarding typically religious concepts is not the same thing as having no interest in them. As the following passages show, Confucius clearly understood Heaven to be a vital aspect of reality:

The Master said, "Heaven is author of the virtue that is in me." (Analects 7.23)

The Master said, ". . . When you have offended against Heaven, there is nowhere you can turn to in your prayers." (Analects 3.13)

The Master said, ". . . If I am understood at all, it is, perhaps, by Heaven." (Analects 14.35)

Also recall the previously cited passage in which Confucius declares, "At fifty I knew the Mandate of Heaven."

During the time of Confucius, Heaven was in fact China's principal deity. For Confucius,

I

In Chinese society the older people get, the more deeply respected they are. Answer the following questions:

- What differences do you see between the Confucian attitude toward aging and the attitudes of your society?
- In both societies what are the consequences for older people and for the rest of society?
- Which perspective on aging do you prefer?

J

Explain the nature and role of government in Confucianism. Then describe your own opinion of the proper nature and role of government. Finally, compare the two.

Gems of Wisdom from the Great Master K'ung

Yu, shall I tell you what it is to know. To say you know when you know, and to say you do not when you do not, that is knowledge. (Analects 2.17)

If one is guided by profit in one's actions, one will incur much ill will. (Analects 4.12)

Men of antiquity studied to improve themselves; men today study to impress others. (Analects 14.24)

Can you love anyone without making him work hard? Can you do your best for anyone without educating him? (Analects 14.7)

Not to mend one's ways when one has erred is to err indeed. (Analects 15.30)

The gentleman agrees with others without being an echo. The small man echoes without being in agreement. (Analects 13.23)

Do not worry because you have no official position. Worry about your qualifications. Do not worry because no one appreciates your abilities. Seek to be worthy of appreciation. (Analects 4.14)

K

Some people have wondered whether Confucianism can really be called a religion. What do you think? Make an argument for your position, based on what you have learned from this chapter, as well as on the discussion of religious traditions in chapter 1.

though, it seems to have represented a universal moral force, similar to, if not equivalent to, the Tao, or Way. The workings of the human world are believed to affect Heaven. In turn, Heaven, as the ultimate moral force, guides and nurtures humanity. Confucianism's grand harmony of relationships thus extends beyond humanity, involving Heaven as well. Ultimate reality is therefore at least partially dependent on its ties to human society. Confucianism is unique in this regard among the religions featured in this book.

A Legacy for East Asia, Lessons for the World

Various forms of upheaval have gripped the nations of East Asia in recent times. China, except for the small island state of Taiwan, is ruled by a communist government that has officially opposed the practice of traditional religion, including Confucianism. Korea is divided between the communist North and the westernized South. Japan, also strongly influenced by Western culture, has achieved remarkable economic success, challenging traditional ways of life.

Still, Confucianism shows signs of being a legacy that will outlast the temporary currents of government or economics in East Asia. Whatever might be declared in official decrees or encouraged by the marketplace, deeply imbedded Confucian attitudes, especially those related to family, seem destined to endure.

To people in the West, Confucianism offers ideas that have exciting prospects for improving society. Many Westerners mourn the loss of traditional "family values." In this realm Confucianism has always excelled. Confucius understood his society to be decaying largely because of a loss of such traditional values. He consciously applied the ways of the past to remedy the ills of the present, establishing rules of behavior and ideals of moral virtue to fortify the ethical foundations of his society. Could such ideas supply solutions for the West? Could a renewed widespread effort to "learn to be human" lead to improvements in

The Seven Dimensions of Religion: Confucianism

Dimension	Examples
Experiential	knowing and being in harmony with Tao or Heaven (although Confucius himself is notably vague about such concepts, leading some to question whether he is truly a "religious" figure)
Mythic	ancient accounts of the good rulers and ancestors of China's legendary past
Doctrinal	Confucius's many teachings as set forth in the Analects
Ethical	jen (the supreme human virtue), te (virtue as shown through the power of example)
Ritual	behavior resulting from the doctrine of li
Social	the Five Constant Relationships, a general emphasis on the family
Material	paintings and sculptures of Confucius, Confucian temples

self-cultivation, family togetherness, national prosperity, and harmony with Heaven?

Whatever prospects Confucianism might have for improving society, its insights on what it means to be human will remain a precious contribution to humanity.[K]

Chapter Review

1. Describe Confucius's family background.
2. At what profession was Confucius an apparent failure?
3. Using evidence from the Analects, name three adjectives that describe Confucius's character.
4. Identify and briefly describe the three schools of thought that responded to ancient China's problems with solutions different from those of Confucius.
5. What did Confucius believe about the power of tradition?
6. Who is considered the second founder of Confucianism?
7. Who was Chu Hsi?
8. Identify the Four Books of Confucianism.
9. According to Confucius, what can one discover through learning?
10. What does the term *Tao* mean for Confucianism?
11. What is a *chun-tzu?*
12. Identify and briefly describe Confucianism's supreme virtue.
13. Explain the notion *shu,* or reciprocity.
14. What is *li?*
15. What does the rectification of names mean to Confucians?
16. Name at least four of the Confucian cultural arts, or *wen.*
17. What is *te?*
18. Summarize the doctrine of the Five Constant Relationships, naming all five relationships.
19. How does Confucianism regard the self?
20. What is the primary virtue in relating to one's elders? Explain the meaning of that virtue.
21. Describe the Confucian ruler.
22. What does Heaven seem to represent for Confucius?

Glossary

Analects. The collected sayings of Confucius, one of the Four Books of Confucianism.

Book of Mencius. The collected teachings of Mencius, one of the Four Books of Confucianism.

chun-tzu (jin-dzuh; Chinese: "gentleman"). The mature person, an ideal human being with perfect moral character.

Five Constant Relationships. A doctrine summarizing the proper ethical principle for each basic human relationship, such as duty between ruler and subject.

jen (ruhn; Chinese: "goodness," "love," or "benevolence"). The supreme human virtue, doing one's best to treat others as one would wish to be treated.

li (lee; Chinese: "rite" and "propriety"). Proper behavior in any given social circumstance, as if performing a sacred ritual.

Neo-Confucianism. A major philosophical and religious tradition that developed around AD 1000 as a response to challenges facing Confucianism from Taoism and Buddhism; Neo-Confucianism's most important figure is Chu Hsi (joo shee; 1130 to 1200).

shu (shoo; Chinese: "reciprocity"). A basic principle of Confucian ethics that says not to do to others what you would not want them to do to you.

Tao (dou; Chinese: "way"). For Confucianism, the moral order that permeates the universe, the Way that should be followed. Sometimes the word *tao* is lowercased to refer more generally to an individual tao, or "way."

te (day; Chinese: "virtue"). Virtue as shown through the power of example, an attribute of the mature person.

wen. The cultural arts, skills of behavior valued by Confucius as being of moral benefit and as befitting the mature person.

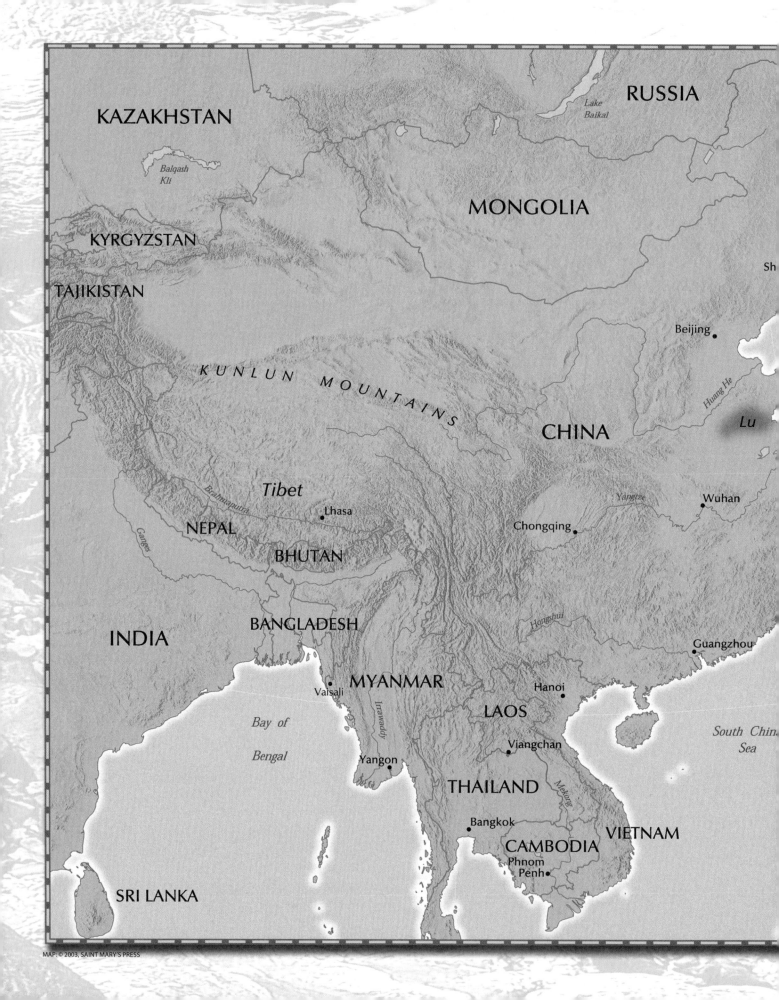

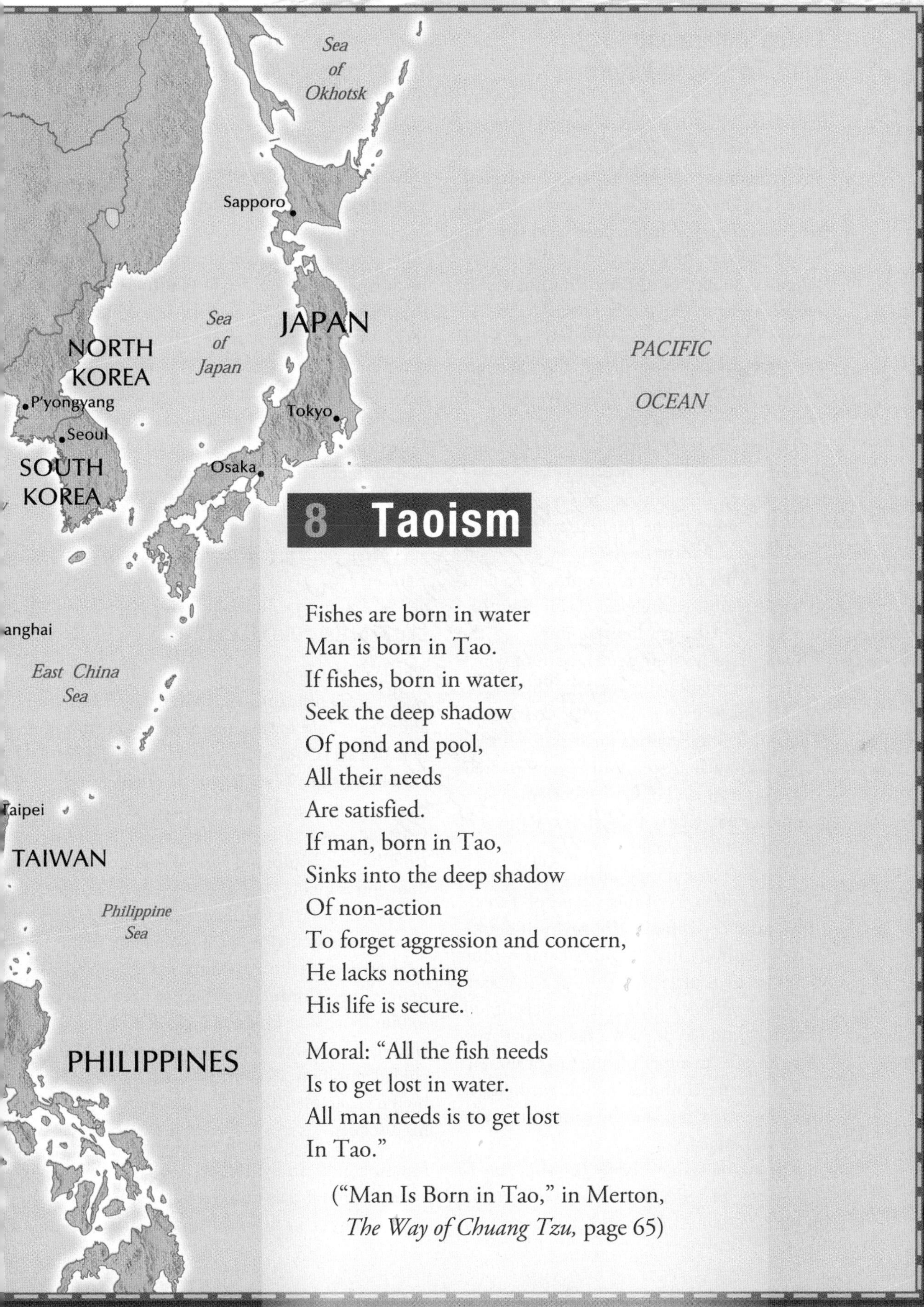

Sea
of
Okhotsk

Sapporo

Sea
of
Japan

JAPAN

NORTH
KOREA

P'yongyang

Seoul

SOUTH
KOREA

Osaka

Tokyo

PACIFIC

OCEAN

anghai

East China
Sea

Taipei

TAIWAN

Philippine
Sea

PHILIPPINES

8　Taoism

Fishes are born in water
Man is born in Tao.
If fishes, born in water,
Seek the deep shadow
Of pond and pool,
All their needs
Are satisfied.
If man, born in Tao,
Sinks into the deep shadow
Of non-action
To forget aggression and concern,
He lacks nothing
His life is secure.

Moral: "All the fish needs
Is to get lost in water.
All man needs is to get lost
In Tao."

("Man Is Born in Tao," in Merton,
The Way of Chuang Tzu, page 65)

Living in Harmony with the Way of Nature

East Asian religion is a fabric woven from various traditions. All incorporate to some extent this fundamental idea of Eastern culture: All aspects of the universe are in harmony, each part nurturing and balancing the whole. Human beings, usually regarded by Western religions as somehow distinct from the rest of nature, are considered part of this grand harmony. Taoism places special emphasis on this fundamental idea of the harmony of the universe. It teaches living in harmony with **Tao** (dou), the Way of nature.

Taoism has traditionally been understood as being composed of two distinct strands. Over the centuries both strands have complemented Confucianism, Buddhism, and (in Japan) Shinto to form the fabric of East Asian religion. One strand, philosophical Taoism, is based almost entirely on classic texts like the **Tao Te Ching** (dou day jing) and the **Chuang Tzu** (jwahng dzuh), both of which contain foundational teachings. Philosophical Taoism focuses on the great mysteries of Tao and its implications for living. This is a subject of much interest well beyond the religion's original land of China; currently there are more than eighty English translations of the *Tao Te Ching* alone.

The other strand is popular, or "religious," Taoism. Followers of this strand of Taoism strive to achieve physical longevity and, ultimately, immortality. Popular Taoism combines its own interpretation of the classic texts with various beliefs and practices of folk tradition, and has derived a fascinating array of techniques to aid in the pursuit of immortality. These techniques include meditation, breathing exercises, and the eating of certain herbs and minerals.

The classic texts *Chuang Tzu* and *Tao Te Ching* have played a vital role in both strands of the tradition. Along with documenting the basic teachings of philosophical Taoism, they also provided the foundations for the growth of popular Taoism.

Lao Tzu and Chuang Tzu: Legendary Sages, Mystical Texts

The origins of Taoism are ancient, dating back to about the time of Confucius (551 to 479 BC). They are also shrouded in mystery. We cannot even be certain whether the traditional founder of Taoism, Lao Tzu (lou dzuh), ever existed. Nor is much known about its other great founding figure, Chuang Tzu. However, we do have the texts attributed to each of them and also traditional accounts of the lives of Lao Tzu and Chuang Tzu, which, though almost entirely legendary, tell us a good deal about the mystical character of early Taoism.

Lao Tzu, the "Old Master"

The legendary flavor of the story of Lao Tzu is evident in his name, which in Chinese literally means "old master." Supposedly born in 604 BC, he is said to have been conceived by a shooting star. When his mother finally gave birth to him, Lao Tzu was already eighty-two years old, a wise man with flowing white hair. (In Chinese culture old age is a mark of wisdom and is highly respected.)

Tradition has it that Lao Tzu worked as a government archivist. More notably he was a venerated sage whose wisdom was sought by many. Even Confucius is said to have come to him for advice. One story tells of Lao Tzu's chiding Confucius for his arrogance and misguided ambition. Confucius, much impressed by the venerable Lao Tzu, withdrew and told his disciples:

I know a bird can fly; I know a fish can swim; I know animals can run. Creatures that run can be caught in nets; those that swim can

IMAGE: LEFT, NATIONAL PALACE MUSEUM, TAIPEI, TAIWAN/BRIDGEMAN ART LIBRARY; RIGHT, ISTOCKPHOTO

Left: Lao Tzu is riding his ox in this silk painting from the Ming dynasty.
Right: Taoism emphasizes living in harmony with Tao, the Way of nature.

be caught in wicker traps; those that fly can be hit by arrows. But the dragon is beyond my knowledge; it ascends into heaven on the clouds and the wind. Today I have seen Lao Tzu, and he is like the dragon! (Ssu-ma Ch'ien, *Shih Chi*)

Eventually Lao Tzu became disenchanted with the rampant corruption of government, leaving his career and his home. When he arrived at the Han-ku Pass in the western mountains separating China from Tibet, the keeper of the pass convinced him to write down his wisdom before departing. Three days later Lao Tzu handed him the *Tao Te Ching* and proceeded on his way.

The *Tao Te Ching:* Taoism's Foundational Text

Regardless of how much historical truth is preserved in the legend of Lao Tzu, it is convenient to think of him as being the author of the *Tao Te Ching.* In fact, the work was originally called the *Lao Tzu,* and it is still frequently referred to by that title. Whatever its origins, the final form of eighty-one short chapters dates to about the third century BC. Brief yet profound, the *Tao Te Ching* can be read in an afternoon, but its ideas can be pondered rewardingly for a lifetime.

The first lines of the *Tao Te Ching* display its deep and enigmatic nature:

The Tao that can be told of is not the eternal Tao;
The name that can be named is not the eternal name.

(Chapter 1)

Echoes of such mystery are repeated throughout the text:

Those who know do not speak;
Those who speak do not know.

(Chapter 56)

Give up sainthood, renounce wisdom,
And it will be a hundred times better for
everyone.

(Chapter 19)

These statements are **paradoxes**—that is, assertions that seem illogical and contradictory on the surface, yet contain deeper truths that are accessible more through intuition than through logical thinking. Paradoxes such as these are at the heart of mystical religious traditions. And the *Tao Te Ching* is a mystical sacred text par excellence. Among its paradoxes lie provocative teachings on living in harmony with nature.[A]

A
Paradoxes are found in many religious traditions, as well as in literature and poetry. Explain a paradox you have come across in religion or literature, or invent and explain a paradox based on those quoted from the *Tao Te Ching*.

Chuang Tzu: Taoism's Second Founder and His Text

Chuang Tzu, Taoism's second founder, seems to have lived from about 369 to 286 BC. The text attributed to him, called simply the *Chuang Tzu,* is not as famous as the *Tao Te Ching,* but it is equally important. It is also delightful, full of humorous yet profound lessons and stories. Though probably only parts of the text were authored by Chuang Tzu, the inspiration of his character is evident in all its pages.

Chuang Tzu was not sure if he had only dreamed he was a butterfly, or if he was a butterfly who was dreaming that he was Chuang Tzu.

A central theme of the *Chuang Tzu* is the relativity of things. Who is to say, it asks, exactly what is good, what ought to be done, or even who we are, when answers to such questions depend on particular circumstances? In one passage, Chuang Tzu (here identified by his family name, Chou) questions the nature of his existence:

Once Chuang Chou dreamt that he was a butterfly. He did not know that he had ever been anything but a butterfly and was content to hover from flower to flower. Suddenly he woke and found to his astonishment that he was Chuang Chou. But it was hard to be sure whether he really was Chou and had only dreamt that he was a butterfly, or was really a butterfly, and was only dreaming that he was Chou. (Chapter 2)

The Philosophy of Tao

The title *Tao Te Ching* literally means "the book of the Way and its power (or virtue)." The text explains the meaning of Tao and its accompanying concept, *te,* which is the power or virtue acquired by the individual through living in harmony with Tao. (A similar case of double meaning occurs in Latin: *virtus* means both "strength" and "virtue.") The *Chuang Tzu* continues this explanation, emphasizing the relative nature of all things. This relativity is based in the balance of yin and yang, twin polarities that can be likened to the opposite poles of a magnet.

Tao: The Way of Nature

The word *tao* is generally translated as "way," in the sense of a path on which one travels. Taoism deepens this general meaning considerably. The *Tao Te Ching,* which openly admits the impossibility of ever producing a full explanation, says that Tao is both the ultimate source and the principle of order in the universe. It is the Way of nature.

According to the *Tao Te Ching*, Tao is the "unified something" from which all things arise. It is not a personal creator god in the Western sense, but an unseen force that is the origin and the order of the universe. It is beyond the reach of intellectual knowledge. For lack of a better name, Lao Tzu calls this force Tao and Great:

There was something undifferentiated
   and yet complete,
Which existed before heaven and earth.
Soundless and formless, it depends on
   nothing and does not change.
It operates everywhere and is free from
   danger.
It may be considered the mother of the
   universe.
I do not know its name; I call it Tao.
If forced to give it a name, I shall call it
Great.

(*Tao Te Ching*, chapter 25)

As the unseen, incomprehensible, ultimate source, Tao is thought to exist both before and beyond all else, transcendent of humanity and the rest of creation. But Tao is also the "mother of the universe," and so is immanent; it pervades the natural world, constantly ordering and nurturing it.

The Great Tao flows everywhere.
It may go left or right.
All things depend on it for life, and it
   does not turn away from them.
It accomplishes its task, but does not
   claim credit for it.
It clothes and feeds all things but does
   not claim to be master over them.

(*Tao Te Ching*, chapter 34)[B]

The Universe in Balance: Yin and Yang

Tao can be compared to magnetism. Magnetic force is invisible and does not seem to be significant, but it actually pervades the world, constantly affecting its order. Tao is thought to be similarly invisible yet pervasive, and powerful. And just as magnetic force is accompanied by two polar opposites—negative and

B
Taoists are the first to admit that Tao can never be completely explained in words. After reading the textbook section "Tao: The Way of Nature," describe Tao as completely as you can in your own words.

The Art of Translation

Translating involves more than just converting sentences word by word from one language into another. It also requires a general process of interpretation, of determining the overall meaning of the text and expressing it accurately.

Chinese is considerably more open to varying interpretations than are European languages such as Spanish, French, and German. And the mystical character of the Tao Te Ching *makes it an especially challenging text for the translator. For example, in that text the word* tao *occurs seventy-six times, each time with a unique meaning.*

Let us consider the first line of the Tao Te Ching *as rendered by a few of the more than eighty translators. Here is a literal translation by Frederic Spiegelberg, proceeding word by word:*

Tao, insofar as it is termed tao is not the real tao.

In the translation of Wing-tsit Chan, this line reads:

The Tao that can be told of is not the eternal Tao.

And here are three more translations, by Arthur Waley, R. B. Blakney, and D. C. Lau, respectively:

The Way that can be told of is not an Unvarying Way.

There are ways but the Way is uncharted.

The way that can be spoken of
Is not the constant way.

To do justice to the wide variety of possible interpretations, one must explore a number of translations of the Tao Te Ching.

Taoism   143

positive—so too is Tao. **Yin** is the negative, passive, feminine, earthly component, characterized by darkness and weakness. **Yang** is the positive, active, masculine, heavenly component, characterized by light and strength. Like the negative and positive poles of magnetism, yin and yang are not really opponents; rather, they complement each other. Without one, the other would make no sense, just as without west, east would be indescribable. Taoist cosmology is based on this complementary balance of yin and yang.[C]

The balance of yin and yang is captured graphically as a circle in which the dark yin and the light yang curve into each other in perfect symmetry, and each contains an element of the other. Neither yin nor yang is essentially superior to the other. However, because Taoists perceive that our human condition tends to make us overindulge in the yang aspects of life, Taoism emphasizes the need to embrace the yin—the weak, the passive, the feminine. The *Tao Te Ching* describes the embracing of yin by drawing on the image of a stream, which is naturally found low in the valley:

Know the strength of man,
But keep a woman's care!
Be the stream of the universe!
Being the stream of the universe,
Ever true and unswerving,
Become as a little child once more.

(Chapter 28)

The "feminine" and "masculine" characteristics of yin and yang (here personified as woman and man) do not correspond to differences between sexes. All people are made up of both components. Many, however, manage to work themselves into a state of imbalance, usually tending toward too much yang. Taoism counters this problem by advocating virtues oriented toward yin, such as humility, noncompetition, and pacifism. These virtues are the marks of the perfectly balanced individual, which Taoism calls the sage. Because of the patriarchal nature of ancient Chinese society, the Taoist classics assume the sage to be male. Nevertheless, becoming a sage is primarily a matter of embracing the feminine yin.[D]

Relativity of Values

In keeping with its perspective of the universe as an ongoing balance of yin and yang, Taoism avoids absolute moral judgments, insisting that values are relative. For example, goodness is meaningful only because of its opposite, evil. For the Taoist, there is no such thing as absolute goodness. Just as in the symbol of yin and yang each quality contains a spot of the other, so too is goodness tinged by evil and evil by goodness. The *Tao Te Ching* demonstrates the relativity of values by noting that no value could exist if not for its opposite:

When the people of the world all know
    beauty as beauty,
There arises the recognition of ugliness.
When they all know the good as good,
    There arises the recognition of evil.

(Chapter 2)

Chuang Tzu is the master of this aspect of Taoism. We have already seen that he questioned the very nature of his existence, not sure if he was really Chuang Tzu or a butterfly. The *Chuang Tzu* contains several such insights on the relativity of values. One story points out how easily humans (or in this case, monkeys) get excessively distraught over value distinctions that seem important but are actually superficial:

In Sung there was a keeper of monkeys. Bad times came and he was obliged to tell them that he must reduce their ration of nuts. "It will be three in the morning and four in the evening," he said. The monkeys were furious. "Very well then," he said, "you shall have four in the morning and three in the evening."

C

Magnetism provides a helpful analogy for understanding Tao. Think of another helpful comparison from nature, art, or technology, and explain how it is like Tao.

D

Draw your own symbol for yin and yang. Explain its meaning.

IMAGE: SHUTTERSTOCK

The monkeys accepted with delight. (Chapter 2)[E]

Harmony of Life and Death

The problem of death and what happens afterward is of great concern to most religions. Taoism has little to say on this issue. Like yin and yang, and moral values such as good and evil, life and death are thought to be merely two harmonious parts of the same whole.

The Taoist classics say nothing of an afterlife or of the continued existence of a personal soul. The *Tao Te Ching* describes death as a return from life back into the original unity of the Tao. The *Chuang Tzu* depicts death merely as one among nature's many transformations from one state to another, as illustrated in this account:

Chuang Tzu's wife died. When Hui Tzu went to convey his condolences, he found Chuang Tzu sitting with his legs sprawled out, pounding on a tub and singing. "You lived with her, she brought up your children and grew old," said Hui Tzu. "It should be enough simply not to weep at her death. But pounding on a tub and singing—this is going too far, isn't it?"

Chuang Tzu said, "You're wrong. When she first died, do you think I didn't grieve like anyone else? But I looked back to her beginning and the time before she was born. Not only the time before she was born, but the time before she had a body. Not only the time before she had a body, but the time before she had a spirit. In the midst of the jumble of wonder and mystery a change took place and she had a spirit. Another change and she had a body. Another change and she was born. Now there's been another change and she's dead. It's just like the progression of the four seasons, spring, summer, fall, winter.

"Now she's going to lie down peacefully in a vast room. If I were to follow after her bawling and sobbing, it would show that I don't understand anything about fate. So I stopped."

(Chapter 18)[F]

Living in Accord with Tao: The Way of the Sage

Taoism emphasizes that human beings are part of the grand harmony of nature. Tao, the Way of nature, is therefore relevant in human life too. Indeed living in accord with Tao is the only way for the individual to thrive and is the Taoist form of spiritual perfection. This is the manner of living mastered by the sage, who attains oneness with Tao through apprehension of its simplicity and natural unity. Such insight is radically different from common knowledge, which tends to confuse the issue by seeing in nature a multiplicity of things, while missing nature's basic unity. The sage proceeds with an undistracted mind, in order to see the simple truth of Tao.

When trying to understand Taoism, it helps to consider the cat, with which the sage has much in common. Like the sage, the cat avoids the mistake of thinking itself into a state of distraction. By not deviating from its own nature, its tao, the cat is fully attentive to the situation at hand. Responding spontaneously and with sufficient, but not excessive, effort, the cat simply does what needs to be done, and always lands on its feet.

Because Tao is thought to pervade everything, it is always present. It is *the* Way, and there is no other. Living in accord with Tao is therefore potentially a simple thing to do. But human beings, unlike cats, are burdened with the ability to think themselves into distraction. They are able to deviate from the Way. Lao Tzu explained:

My doctrines are very easy to understand
    and very easy to practice,
But none in the world can understand or
    practice them.

(*Tao Te Ching*, chapter 70)[G]

E
Chuang Tzu points out the relativity of values in his story of the monkeys in Sung. For no apparent reason, the monkeys are furious with the first arrangement and delighted with the second. Think of a time you or someone you know got excessively distraught over a superficial distinction. What might have been the reason for that reaction?

F
Compare Chuang Tzu's perspective on the death of his wife with your own perspective on death. In what ways do you agree or disagree with Chuang Tzu?

In this print entitled *Huai River Moon,* a Chinese general encounters the Taoist sage Jiang Ziya, a man who fished with a straight hook: he was so virtuous that the fish impaled themselves voluntarily.

G

Use your own observations to expand on what the textbook has to say about the "sagely" ways of the cat. In addition, choose another type of pet, and describe what it does or does not have in common with the Taoist sage.

H

Reflect on the following topic: How might the Taoist virtue *wu-wei* be applied to the task of writing a one-page essay?

I

Imagine a stream of running water (if possible, observe a stream or river). The *Tao Te Ching* uses the stream as the ideal image of the yin—weak, passive, and feminine. Reflect on how the stream embodies the characteristics of yin.

Doing Without Acting: *Wu-Wei* and Its Related Virtues

The primary virtue of Taoism, and the means by which the sage maintains harmony with Tao, is **wu-wei** (woo-way). Suitable English translations of *wu-wei* are "actionless activity," "pure effectiveness," "yielding to win," and "creative quietude," to name but a few. *Wu-wei* literally means "inaction." But Taoists do not advocate simply doing nothing. The practice of *wu-wei* ultimately accomplishes the task at hand. "No action is undertaken, and yet nothing is left undone" (*Tao Te Ching,* chapter 48). The person who practices *wu-wei* avoids the yang tendency to act, embraces yin (the passive, the weak, the feminine), and is thereby more effective.

To practice *wu-wei* is to be so perfectly in harmony with nature that nature's energy infuses and empowers one. Unnatural action, a mistake rooted in deviation from Tao, is avoided. Instead one maintains an undistracted state, allowing the energy of Tao to accomplish the task at hand.

Act without action.
Do without ado.
Taste without tasting.
Whether it is big or small, many or few,
 repay hatred with virtue.
Prepare for the difficult while it is still easy.
Deal with the big while it is still small.
Difficult undertakings have always started
 with what is easy.
And great undertakings have always started
 with what is small.
Therefore the sage never strives for the great,
And thereby the great is achieved.
 (*Tao Te Ching,* chapter 63)[H]

Taoism is like water in its capacity to nourish and in its ordered yet constantly changing patterns. *Wu-wei* is like water in its ability to achieve without acting. A gently flowing stream can create a valley or canyon merely by staying its course. This naturally takes much time. And taking sufficient time—practicing patience—is another aspect of embracing yin.

There is nothing softer and weaker than
 water,
 And yet there is nothing better for
 attacking hard and strong things.
For this reason there is no substitute for it.
All the world knows that the weak
 overcomes the strong and the soft
 overcomes the hard.
 (*Tao Te Ching,* chapter 78)[I]

Wu-wei is at the heart of all other Taoist virtues. The virtues humility and noncompetition, naturalness and naturalism, and nonaggression and passive rule all demonstrate the basic virtue *wu-wei.*

Humility and Noncompetition

Among Taoism's many paradoxes is the outward appearance of the sage as one who is unattractive and lacks ability. Humility is one of the chief virtues of the sage. And yet, just as *wu-wei* is "actionless activity" that ends up accomplishing the task at hand with utmost efficiency, so too the humility of the sage is not a sign of weakness but one of strength. To be in accord with Tao requires humility but at the same time yields optimal results. "Therefore the sage wears rough clothing and holds the jewel in his heart" (*Tao Te Ching*, chapter 70).

The same paradox applies for a similar virtue, noncompetition. The sage chooses not to compete, but that is not at all the same as giving up the fight. On the contrary, through the virtue noncompetition, the sage emerges victorious: "It is precisely because he does not compete that the world cannot compete with him" (*Tao Te Ching*, chapter 22).

From a Western perspective, in which the competitive spirit is generally encouraged, Taoist teachings on noncompetition might appear paradoxical (as Lao Tzu intended them to appear!):

To yield is to be preserved whole.
To be bent is to become straight.
To be empty is to be full.
To be worn out is to be renewed.
To have little is to possess.
To have plenty is to be perplexed.
(*Tao Te Ching*, chapter 22)

Upon careful reflection, however, these paradoxical teachings provide wisdom for living. For example, a skilled musician chooses not to compete with the tempo of a piece, to neither rush nor lag. An athlete who sidesteps an opponent is practicing the Taoist virtue noncompetition. The martial arts demonstrate how effective refusing to compete can be. Popular images of the martial art known as judo often lead to the assumption that it is a competitive, aggressive technique of physical combat. However, the Japanese name *judo* comes from the Chinese *rou-tao*, or the "yielding way," in which the practitioner prevails by giving way. Noncompetition is also highly relevant in social situations. If someone feels especially lonely, it rarely helps if he or she tries to compete for friendship. Simply being one's self yields the best results.

Naturalness and Naturalism

Taoism also teaches the virtue naturalness—behaving as nature dictates, not as social pressure or personal pride demand. The Taoist sage, for example, would dress according to the weather, not according to the requirements of fashion. Always attentive to the Way of nature, the sage rejects showiness and pomposity:

He who stands on tiptoe is not steady.
He who strides cannot maintain the pace.
He who makes a show is not enlightened.
He who is self-righteous is not respected.
He who boasts achieves nothing.
He who brags will not endure.
(*Tao Te Ching*, chapter 24)

The Taoist sage also practices naturalism, resisting the temptation to meddle with nature. This virtue is similar in many respects to modern environmentalism. Naturalism and environmentalism both involve caring for nature. But unlike some forms of environmentalism, which strive to fix things through human ideas and efforts, Taoist naturalism is always a hands-off approach. Leave nature well enough alone, and nature will thrive:

Do you think you can take over the universe
    and improve it?
I do not believe it can be done.

The universe is sacred.
You cannot improve it.
If you try to change it, you will ruin it.
If you try to hold it, you will lose it.

(*Tao Te Ching*, chapter 29)[J]

Nonaggression and Passive Rule

The Taoist virtue of nonaggression is much like the virtue of *wu-wei*. Just as *wu-wei* produces efficient results, nonaggression ultimately allows the sage to prevail. Nonaggression is also applied to warfare. Though Taoism admits that warfare is sometimes necessary, it encourages pacifism. But even in warfare, violence and aggression should be minimized:

J
State your own solution to the following environmental dilemma. Then state the likely solution of a Taoist. Compare the two solutions.

The U.S. government has offered bounties on wolves and has operated other extermination programs that have severely reduced the wolf population. This and other circumstances have led to a great growth in the population of deer, which are natural prey for wolves. Now many deer starve to death each winter because they cannot find enough food in their overcrowded territories.

The Taoist Sage

The two most famous repositories of Taoist wisdom are its classic texts Tao Te Ching *and* Chuang Tzu. *But ever since ancient times, a third source of teachings has been prominent: the Taoist sage.*

In this excerpt from a memoir of his life in China, European Peter Goullart relates one of his first encounters with an old Taoist sage. The sage teaches through words, as well as by his actions and simple lifestyle.

Sitting one afternoon at the small temple at the base of the mountain, I saw how he came in having walked all the way from town. He was dressed in an old robe of faded blue with picturesque patches of a lighter material here and there, and wore a huge straw hat with a tip in the shape of a miniature pagoda, the usual head-covering of an itinerant Taoist. He carried a long and twisted wooden crook. We agreed to walk together to the monastery, and in spite of all my efforts I could not keep up with him. With a sly wink he continued the ascent, his immense sleeves billowing in the breeze like wings. He soon disap-

peared among the boulders while I sat down exhausted, my heart pounding, for a brief rest. I found him later in the afternoon at the back of the monastery where there was a tea plantation. Wearing only a short jacket and wide trousers, he was puttering around a tea bush loosening the soil. Wiping sweat from his rosy cheeks he sat down on a stone leaning his chin on a mattock. Now is the time to ask him something about Taoism, I decided, and I poured out my questions. He looked up at me with his innocent, childish eyes, his smile gentle but, I thought, slightly ironical.

"Take time, observe and learn," he said simply. "Words spoken in haste will not stick; a cup of water splashed into a parched field will do it no good. It is only a slow and gentle rain that will saturate the soil and produce life." He became silent ready to resume his work.

His rebuke abashed me. I saw what he meant. He probably thought I was an idle tourist, or worse, a young writer, who wanted to learn something about Taoism in an hour or so, and then write a smart article, boasting of the mysteries revealed to him. Seeing my obvious confusion, the old man relented. His face was all smiles now, but his eyes became thoughtful.

"If you want to learn about the Eternal Tao, do not be casual and in a hurry. Don't glean too much from too many books, for each book is full of opinions, prejudices and corruptions. Read only one book and only one—our Old Master's *[Tao Te Ching]*, and then try to understand it, not by juggling the words and meanings, but intuitively, through your heart and spirit. Don't ask too many questions, but patiently watch what we Taoists do, and perceive the hidden motives of our actions, and not that which is only for display. Do not be guided so much by your intellect as by faith, love and your heart, which is another name for understanding and compassion. What you need is wisdom, and not knowledge; for if one has wisdom, knowledge will come naturally. Always remember that the Eternal Tao is Infinite Wisdom, Infinite Love and Infinite Simplicity." And with this the old man took up his pickaxe and resumed his hoeing of the bush.

(*The Monastery of Jade Mountain,* pages 30–31)

The Taoist sage teaches not only through words but also through actions and a simple lifestyle.

IMAGE: © JULIA WATERLOW, EYE UBIQUTOUS/CORBIS

IMAGE: © KELLY-MOONEY PHOTOGRAPHY/CORBIS

The martial arts demonstrate the effectiveness of the virtue *wu-wei*.

A good soldier is not violent.
A good fighter is not angry.
A good winner is not vengeful.
A good employer is humble.

(*Tao Te Ching*, chapter 68)

The virtue nonaggression works hand in hand with the Taoist insistence on passive rule. The good ruler takes a passive approach through the practice of *wu-wei*. Many passages of the *Tao Te Ching* emphasize the nature of good government. Here is one example:

The best (rulers) are those whose existence is (merely) known by the people.
The next best are those who are loved and praised.
The next are those who are feared.
And the next are those who are despised.
It is only when one does not have enough faith in others that others will have no faith in him.

(Chapter 17)

Passive rule, like all Taoist teachings, functions by letting nature take its course. The best way to govern is simply to not interfere with the natural way of the people. Lao Tzu and Chuang Tzu insist Tao will prevail if well enough is let alone.[K]

Taoism in East Asia and the World

For more than two thousand years, Taoism has been central to the religious life of China and, as it spread through the centuries, all of East Asia. For one thing Taoism mixed with Buddhism to produce Zen, the subject of the next chapter in this book. More important, Taoism has functioned alongside Confucianism, and the two together have basically shaped the character of East Asia. Indeed it is commonly suggested that Taoism provides the yin to balance Confucianism's yang. For whereas Confucianism encourages conforming to the social order through rigorous activity, Taoism promotes a passive existence free from Confucian demands, celebrating the individualistic life of harmony with the Way of nature.

K
Consider carefully what chapter 17 of the *Tao Te Ching* says about good government. How does the government of your nation rate according to Lao Tzu's perspective? Do you think Lao Tzu's assertion that the best rulers are merely known to exist (and rule passively) is true for your own nation?

A centerpiece consisting of the symbol for yin and yang is placed on a "peace table" in Vietnam during the Vietnam War.

IMAGE © TIM PAGE/CORBIS

Apparently many Westerners are feeling a need for Taoist teachings. As evidence consider the numerous English translations of the *Tao Te Ching,* and the popularity of books like *The Tao of Pooh* and *The Te of Piglet,* humorous yet instructive texts that teach Taoism through Winnie-the-Pooh and his friends. (Pooh, according to author Benjamin Hoff, is a natural Taoist.)

From the Taoist perspective, it is not surprising that Taoism has gained a substantial number of admirers in the West. After all, in the grand harmony, the yin is bound to balance the yang. And even when the insights of Taoism are neglected, perhaps it is Lao Tzu who has the last laugh:

The Seven Dimensions of Religion: Taoism

Dimension	Examples
Experiential	living in accord with Tao, as perfected by the sage
Mythic	legendary account of the birth and life of Lao Tzu
Doctrinal	philosophy of Tao, *wu-wei,* cosmology based on yin and yang
Ethical	virtues of nonaggression and passive rule
Ritual	in popular, or "religious," Taoism, breathing exercises and other techniques for the pursuit of immortality; philosophical Taoism notably de-emphasizes ritual because ritual is not true to the Way of nature
Social	figure of the sage
Material	yin and yang symbol

When the highest type of men hear Tao,
  They diligently practice it.
When the average type of men hear Tao,
  They half believe in it.
When the lowest type of men hear Tao,
  They laugh heartily at it.
If they did not laugh at it, it would not be
    Tao.

(*Tao Te Ching,* chapter 41)

Chapter Review

1. Name the two founders of Taoism.
2. Which of the founders is considered the author of the *Tao Te Ching?*
3. Define the word *paradox.* Give an example of a paradox from the *Tao Te Ching.*
4. What is the *Chuang Tzu?*
5. What is the literal meaning of the title *Tao Te Ching?*
6. According to the *Tao Te Ching,* what is Tao?
7. Define the terms *yin* and *yang.*
8. Why does Taoism insist that values are relative and not absolute?
9. What does Taoism teach regarding an afterlife?
10. What is the manner of living perfected by the Taoist sage?
11. Define and briefly describe *wu-wei.* Use an analogy in your description.
12. List six Taoist virtues that demonstrate the basic virtue *wu-wei.*
13. What characteristic of Taoist naturalism distinguishes it from some forms of environmentalism?
14. What does Taoism advocate as being the best way to govern?

Glossary

Chuang Tzu (jwahng dzuh). The second foundational text of Taoism (along with the *Tao Te Ching*), containing teachings and anecdotes traditionally thought to have come from the sage Chuang Tzu, who lived in the fourth and third centuries BC.

paradoxes. Assertions that seem illogical and contradictory on the surface, and yet contain deeper truths that are accessible more through intuition than through logical thinking.

Tao (dou; Chinese: "way"). For Taoism, the Way of nature, the ultimate source and the principle of order in the universe. When the word *tao* is lowercased, it refers more generally to an individual tao, or "way."

Tao Te Ching (dou day jing; Chinese: "the book of the Way and its power [or virtue]"). Taoism's foundational text, traditionally thought to have been authored by Lao Tzu in the seventh or sixth century BC; sometimes called the *Lao Tzu.*

wu-wei (woo-way; Chinese: "non-action"). The supreme Taoist virtue, rendered in English variously as "actionless activity," "pure effectiveness," "yielding to win," "creative quietude," and so on. To practice *wu-wei* is to be so perfectly in harmony with nature that nature's energy infuses and empowers the individual.

yang. The positive, active, masculine, heavenly component of the universe, characterized by light and strength; complements yin.

yin. The negative, passive, feminine, earthly component of the universe, characterized by darkness and weakness; complements yang.

CHINA

•Harbin

•Changchun

•Shenyang

RUSSIA

W.

•Sappo

•Hakodate

NORTH
KOREA

•P'yongyang

•Seoul

SOUTH
KOREA

Sea of Japan

•Hirosaki

Akita•

•Morioka

•Sendai

JAPAN

Kanazawa•

•Nagano

Aino
Peak▲

Mount
Fuji▲

•Tokyo

•Yokohama

Tottori•

Kyoto•
•Nara

Nagoya•

Hiroshima•

•Kobe
•Osaka

Kitakyusyu•

•Matsuyama

•Aino

•Kochi

Nagasaki•

Kagoshima•

PACIF

OCEA

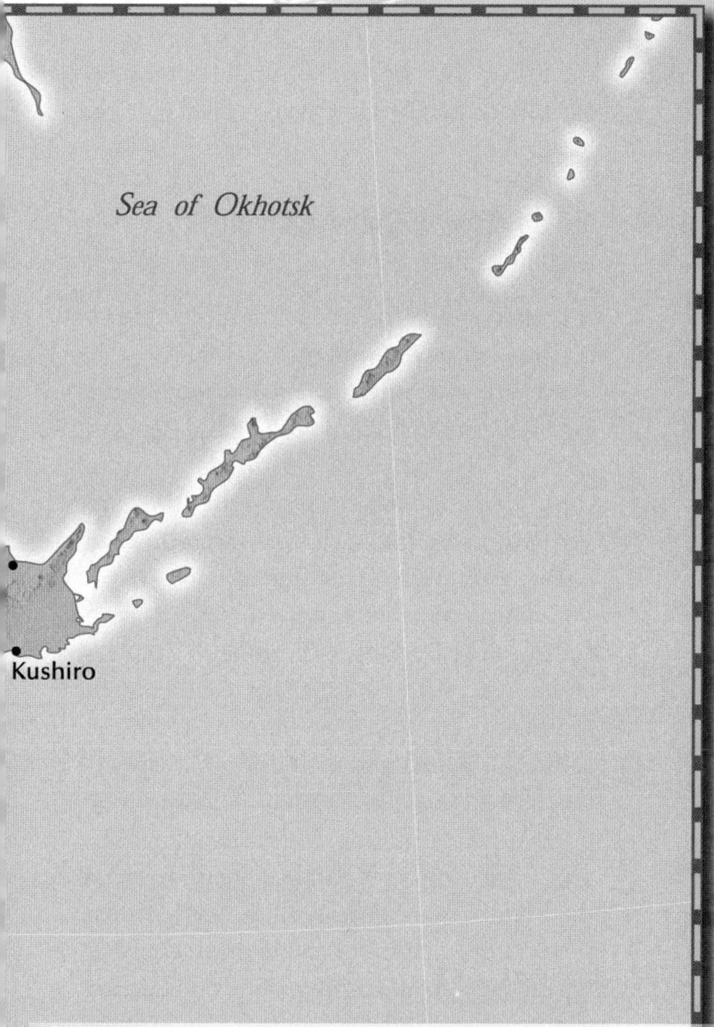

Sea of Okhotsk

Kushiro

9 Zen Buddhism

A monk told Joshu: "I have just entered the monastery. Please teach me."

Joshu asked: "Have you eaten your rice porridge?"

The monk replied: "I have eaten."

Joshu said: "Then you had better wash your bowl."

At that moment the monk was enlightened.

(*Zen Flesh, Zen Bones,* page 96)

Zen: The Spirit of Buddhism

Zen Buddhism developed within Mahayana (the Great Vehicle) Buddhism, first in China and later in Japan. For centuries Zen has had a major influence on the religious and cultural life of the people of those lands. During the past century, Zen has also received much attention in the West.

Zen is a unique form of Mahayana that focuses on what it regards as the spirit of Buddhism: the experience of enlightenment. Fixing its attention fully on this experience, Zen tends to discard most other aspects of Mahayana—devotion to Buddhas and bodhisattvas, speculations regarding the nature of reality, and philosophical elaboration on Buddhist scripture. The insight born of Zen enlightenment is profoundly simple: If you have eaten from your bowl, wash it. But such attentiveness to the situation at hand, or mindfulness, tends to get lost in the thicket of thoughts and feelings that typically crowds the mind. Those who practice Zen seek to clear the mind in order to discover the simple truth that is at the heart of things. Such a discovery can be made through direct experience only, not through thoughtful analysis.

Transmission of Zen Teachings

Focused as it is on the experience of enlightenment, Zen does not concern itself much with

Zen Buddhism focuses on the experience of enlightenment. This painting depicts Bodhidharma, the twenty-eighth Zen patriarch, meditating for nine years as walls crumble around him.

IMAGE: © ASIAN ART AND ARCHAEOLOGY, INC./CORBIS

the history of its own tradition. Still several facts about Zen's history help to shed light on its teachings.

Indian *Dhyana,* Chinese Ch'an, Japanese Zen

A brief overview of Zen can be gleaned from tracing the development of its name. The word *zen,* which means "meditation," is the Japanese pronunciation of the Chinese word *ch'an.* The word *ch'an,* in turn, comes from the Chinese attempt to pronounce the Sanskrit word *dhyana,* a term commonly used among early Buddhists in India.

Zen also traces its origins directly back to India, to the Buddha. According to Zen legend, one day the Buddha was teaching on a mountain. He wished to impart a truth too subtle for words and so, rather than speaking, he held up a flower. All his followers were puzzled except for one, Mahakasyapa, whose gentle smile indicated that he understood what the Buddha was teaching. Like much of what the Buddha taught, this subtle truth could be fully conveyed only through direct experience, not through words or analysis. The Buddha chose Mahakasyapa as his successor, thereby establishing a line of Zen patriarchs that would remain in India for several centuries.

According to legend, the twenty-eighth patriarch in this line, Bodhidharma, brought Zen to China about one thousand years after the Buddha's life, around the year AD 520. Although this legend clearly establishes the origin of Zen in India, Zen as it is known today developed mainly in China. It can be described as a mixture of Indian Buddhism and Chinese Taoism.

In China a separate line of Zen patriarchs was established, and Zen began to flourish under the influence of Hui-neng (638 to 713), the sixth patriarch of Chinese Zen, or **Ch'an** (chahn). Hui-neng came to the monastery of the fifth patriarch when he was merely a poor boy selling firewood. But his mastery of Zen quickly showed through, and he was named successor. Hui-neng's impact on Ch'an was enormous, and remains imprinted on Zen Buddhism to this day. One of his many contributions was intentionally putting an end to the traditional position of patriarchs by refusing to name a successor. Ever since, authority in Zen has been distributed among those who are competent to teach others, commonly referred to as masters, or **roshis** (roh-shees) in Japan. Hui-neng, like Bodhidharma, remains a revered Zen figure.

Ch'an continued to be an important tradition in China until about three centuries ago, when it gradually began to decline. Ch'an is a minor tradition in China today, but in Japan, Zen has flourished since the Middle Ages.

Rinzai and Soto:
Two Sects of Japanese Zen

Zen was first brought to Japan with lasting impact by two masters who had spent some years living in China. The Zen master Eisai (1141 to 1215) brought the **Rinzai** (rin-z*i*) sect, which is known as the school of sudden awakening. In general, Rinzai emphasizes the experience of awakening, called **satori** (suh-tor′ee) in Japanese. In fact, Rinzai contends that Zen training really begins only after one's first *satori*. Rinzai employs the spiritual exercise known as the **koan** (koh′ahn) as the primary means of bringing about *satori*. The *koan* is designed to frustrate the thinking process.

The other primary sect of Zen in Japan is **Soto** (soh-toh), the school of gradual awakening. It was brought by Dogen (1200 to 1253), a master revered by all Zen Buddhists, regardless of sect. Rather than focusing on the crowning achievement of *satori,* the Soto sect emphasizes the day-to-day practice of Zen, especially *zazen* (zah-zen), the method of seated meditation.

At some points in our study, the differences between these sects will prove relevant, so it is

Egyoku Hata, a modern Zen master of the Soto sect.

important to be aware of them. But they are differences in emphasis only. For example, the *koan* is not shunned completely by the Soto sect, and *zazen* is a basic method in Rinzai too. Moreover, it is common for Zen Buddhists to be involved with both sects.

Zen Teachings

Zen in its essence is the art of seeing into the nature of one's own being, and it points the way from bondage to freedom. (Suzuki, *Essays in Zen Buddhism,* page 13)

This statement by D. T. Suzuki, the person most responsible for explaining Zen to the West, points to the paradoxical nature of Zen teachings. What could be simpler than "seeing into the nature of one's own being"? After all, one's own being is always present, always there to be known. But for most people this proves very difficult in practice. The problem,

A

Because Zen is experiential, it cannot adequately be described in words. Such a problem is not unique to Zen. Describe the experience of eating your favorite food. Now repeat your description, comparing it with your memory of the actual experience. In what ways does your description fall short of adequately expressing the full experience?

B

In their conversation about death, what kind of answer do you think the emperor expected from Gudo? What might the emperor have said to encourage Gudo to elaborate?

according to Zen, is that our true nature lies hidden behind a tangle of thoughts and feelings, and behind the personality, or ego, that we mistakenly think we are. The ego is the source of selfish desire. This whole snarled mass of logical concepts and mental descriptions, of fears and longings, of self-centeredness, constantly covers up the true being—the "Zen mind" or "Buddha nature"—we really are. Hence we are in bondage. Zen offers a path to freedom.

Direct Experience, Beyond Words and Logic

A student once asked [Zen master Joshu]: "If I haven't anything in my mind, what shall I do?"

Joshu replied: "Throw it out."

"But if I haven't anything, how can I throw it out?" continued the questioner.

"Well," said Joshu, "then carry it out." (*Zen Flesh, Zen Bones,* page 39)

[Zen master] Tokusan said:

"Even though you can say something about it, I will give you thirty blows of the stick.

And if you can't say anything about it, I will also give you thirty blows of the stick."
(*The Three Pillars of Zen,* page 195, note 27)

To the outsider, Zen can appear comical, illogical, even infuriating. To the practicing Zen Buddhist, who has gained at least an initial insight into the truth Zen teaches, it all makes perfect sense. What conclusions are we to draw from this paradox, this seeming contradiction?

Zen is direct experience of truth, which is beyond the reach of thoughts and feelings about truth, and beyond the words that are used to express thoughts and feelings. The outsider who looks at Zen and fails to make sense of it is looking precisely with the mechanisms of thoughts and words. But the experience that is the focal point of Zen is beyond those mechanisms. In fact, a textbook explanation such as this one, constructed with words to communicate thoughts, is itself inadequate for imparting a full understanding of Zen. But just as a finger can point to the moon (to borrow a teaching from Zen), so too can a textbook point to true understanding. The person who chooses the way of Zen must avoid the mistake of identifying the finger with the moon, or the verbal explanation with the real truth Zen reveals.

Let us see how far words can take us toward understanding Zen. To begin we will further explore three characteristics of Zen: it is experiential, it is beyond words, and it is beyond logical thinking.[A]

Zen Is Experiential

On another day the emperor asked [Zen master] Gudo: "Where does the enlightened man go when he dies?"

Gudo answered: "I know not."

"Why don't you know?" asked the emperor.

"Because I have not died yet," replied Gudo. (*Zen Flesh, Zen Bones,* page 55)

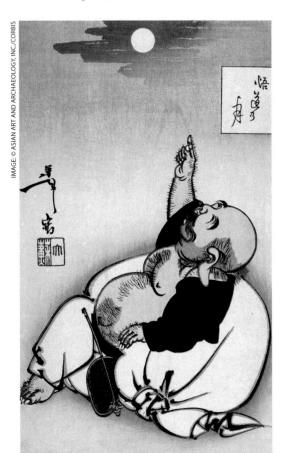

IMAGE: © ASIAN ART AND ARCHAEOLOGY, INC./CORBIS

Zen admonishes one not to confuse the pointing finger with the moon itself.

This simple conversation illustrates Zen's insistence on firsthand experience and its rejection of speculation regarding the nature of reality. The Buddha himself emphasized experience over speculation, most significantly the experience of enlightenment. And like the Buddha, Zen Buddhists regard meditation as the primary means of attaining enlightenment.[B]

Zen Is Beyond Words

The insight of Zen cannot be expressed in words. That is why the Buddha, when attempting to teach this most subtle lesson, resorted to holding up a flower rather than speaking. Zen masters have always realized the futility of trying to teach their insights in conventional ways. According to D. T. Suzuki, Zen teaches "nothing":

If I am asked, then, what Zen teaches, I would answer, Zen teaches nothing. Whatever teachings there are in Zen, they come out of one's own mind. We teach ourselves; Zen merely points the way. (*An Introduction to Zen Buddhism,* page 38)

Zen depends on direct experience of the truth. Ultimately, then, it cannot be taught.

Still Zen "points the way," and this leaves room for the usefulness of words. Like the finger pointing to the moon, words can point in the direction of the truth. For this reason Zen stops short of completely rejecting verbal teachings, including Buddhist texts. But it regards them as a ladder whose highest rung is still short of the goal. Words can assist, but they can never complete the task.[C]

Zen Is Beyond Logical Thinking

Nan-in, a Japanese master during the Meiji era (1868 to 1912), received a university professor who came to inquire about Zen.

Nan-in served tea. He poured his visitor's cup full, and then kept on pouring.

The professor watched the overflow until he no longer could restrain himself. "It is overfull. No more will go in!"

"Like this cup," Nan-in said, "you are full of your own opinions and speculations. How can I show you Zen unless you first empty your cup?" (*Zen Flesh, Zen Bones,* page 5)

Most people—not only university professors—have their "cups" filled with opinions and speculations, views born of logical thinking and of affirmations and denials regarding the nature of things. According to Zen such views clutter the mind and prevent pure insight into the truth. As long as the logical reasoning process is at work interpreting reality, direct experience is impossible. To attain such experience, to "empty your cup," is to see things as if for the first time. The Zen mind, it is often said, is a beginner's mind.

Let us approach this idea with an example. When most people look at a tree, their minds become full of affirmations and denials, of opinions and speculations: "It is an oak tree; its leaves are changing color; it is at least fifty years old. . . ." What is missed in all these observations, according to Zen, is the tree

C
Explore what you think D. T. Suzuki means when he writes that "Zen teaches nothing."

IMAGE: SHUTTERSTOCK

The essence of Zen—experiential, beyond words, beyond logical thinking—can best be expressed through the immediate beauty of the natural world. Japanese landscape design, influenced through the centuries by Zen, emphasizes the beauty of nature.

D

The next time you are outside with some free time, observe a tree. Try to see it simply for what it is, without categorizing, affirming, denying, or speculating.

itself in its most basic simplicity. To see a tree simply as a tree, as if for the first time—that is Zen.[D]

Satori: Enlightenment

The enlightenment Zen seeks is known in Japanese as *satori*. It is especially emphasized in Rinzai Zen, the sect of sudden awakening. For this sect *satori* is essential; it is both the beginning and the end of Zen practice. Until someone has had an initial experience of *satori*, they cannot fully understand the insight of Zen teachings. *Satori* is freedom from the bondage of thought, feeling, and self-centered ego; it is a pure experience in which the true nature of one's being is known directly. *Satori* is beyond the reach of verbal description and logical thinking, so it must be experienced to be known.

Most other forms of Buddhism refer to the highest spiritual experience as *nirvana*, which is thought to be a permanent state. *Satori*, however, is not permanent. The initial *satori*, which usually occurs within the first few years of Rinzai Zen training, is followed by other

The enso (Japanese for "circle") is a common Zen symbol of enlightenment.

IMAGE: SHUTTERSTOCK

satori experiences, occurring with increasing frequency and intensity. With each *satori* the person is transformed. Gradually the person attains a new, enlightened perspective.

Koans: Puzzles to Frustrate the Mind

"You can hear the sound of two hands when they clap together," said Mokurai. "Now show me the sound of one hand." (*Zen Flesh, Zen Bones,* page 25)

This is a *koan*, a puzzle designed to short-circuit the workings of the rational, logical mind. Searching every nook and cranny of its intellect for an answer that conforms to logic, the mind finds none and is eventually completely frustrated. At this point the wall of rationality can finally be broken through so that direct insight into reality can be attained.

The *koan* is emphasized in the Rinzai, or sudden awakening, sect. The master presents the student with a *koan*, and the student grapples with it in the periods between their private meetings. At such a meeting, called **dokusan** (doh-koo-sahn), the student offers an answer, and the master determines whether it is acceptable. If the answer is rejected, the student continues grappling with the *koan* and attempting new answers until one is accepted. The *koan* is not to be discussed with anyone other than the master. There are about seventeen hundred *koans*, but usually only a few are needed during the course of Zen training. Some *koans*, like "the sound of one hand clapping," are particularly famous. Others are less well known but equally, or more, perplexing:

Master Gettan said to a monk: "Keichu made a cart whose wheels had a hundred spokes. Take both front and rear parts away and remove the axle: then what will it be?" (Shibayama, *Zen Comments on the Mumonkan,* page 74)

Goso said: "To give an example, it is like a buffalo passing through a window. Its head, horns, and four legs have all passed through. Why is it that its tail cannot?" (Page 272)

Master Kyogen said: "It is like a man up a tree who hangs from a branch by his mouth; his hands cannot grasp a bough, his feet cannot touch the tree. Another man comes under the tree and asks him the meaning of Bodhidharma's coming from the West. If he does not answer, he does not meet the questioner's need. If he answers, he will lose his life. At such a time, how should he answer?" (Page 54)

Is there such a thing as a "right" answer to a *koan?* The master could deem many answers right, and many wrong. His judgment depends on the degree of insight exhibited by the student. One thing is certain: if an answer depends on logical thinking rather than direct insight into reality, it will be rejected.[E]

The Fruits of Zen

Zen's severe contention with words and logic might lead the outside observer to dismiss it as a negative, world-denying religion. However, the accounts of those who have adhered to Zen indicate that nothing could be further from the truth.

Zen Achieves a Healthy, Vigorous Mind

Zen insight, even though it flies in the face of logical thinking, is not abnormal or unhealthy. In fact, from the Zen perspective, full mental health can be attained only when the mind breaks through the bondage of thought and feeling and sees things as they really are. *Satori* is not a withdrawal from sanity; on the contrary, it is perfected sanity and complete mental health.

Zen insight, according to the tradition's followers, significantly enhances the mind's strength and vitality. When the mind is set free from the bondage of the mass of thoughts and feelings that ordinarily entangle it, it is no longer burdened by unnecessary mental activity. Its newfound vigor allows it much greater clarity and alertness.

Zen Is Practical and Attentive to This World

Zen is practical, as can be observed in Joshu's remark that triggered the enlightenment of a novice monk: "If you have eaten from your bowl, wash it." Zen is also fully attentive to this world. It does not deny the world or see everyday reality as irrelevant, but instead views the world in a new light. For example, recall that Zen sees a tree not as a bundle of observations and opinions, but fully and truly *as a tree.* The following advice of Zen master Gensha also points out Zen's attention to being in this world:

A monk once went to Gensha, and wanted to learn where the entrance to the path of truth was. Gensha asked him, "Do you hear the murmuring of the brook?" "Yes, I hear it," answered the monk. "There is the entrance," the master instructed him. (Jung, foreword, in Suzuki, *An Introduction to Zen Buddhism,* page 10)

Zen Focuses on the Here and Now

Zen neither affirms nor denies the existence of an afterlife. In this way it overcomes the duality of life and death. The focus of Zen is on the here and now. People who perceive life from the perspective of *satori* simply have no need for concern about the future, including what happens after death.

This approach is powerfully communicated in a Zen story of a man who was being chased by a tiger. Running away, the man came to a cliff. He grabbed the end of a wild vine and swung over the edge. Hanging off the cliff, he trembled as he looked up at the tiger ready to devour him; below waited a second hungry tiger. The thin vine was all that kept the man from certain death. The story continues:

E
Try to compose your own Zen *koan.* Reflect on why you find the task difficult or easy.

A Western Woman Masters Zen

At age twenty-four, an Irish American woman by the name of Maura O'Halloran traveled to Japan to study Zen at Kannonji Temple. At her first dokusan *with her master, Go Roshi, O'Halloran received the koan of mu, or "nothingness," which is designed to lead the disciple to experience her Buddha nature. Some months later O'Halloran had an initial experience of* satori, *or kensho:*

Dokusan. I did mu with all my heart and all my soul and all my being. Everything was squeezed out until my head touched the floor.

"Is it your mind or your heart or your body saying mu?"

"I don't know." Tears are flowing without reason; I laugh without reason.

"What is the difference between I don't know and mu?"

"No difference." Go Roshi whacks me.

"Ouch!"

"Who feels pain?"

"I do."

Then, when I'm not looking, he jumps up, embraces me. *"Bikkuri shita!" [You surprised me!].* I tumble backwards, laughing. He holds my hand tightly, my thumb.

"This is I don't know."

"I know."

"You must see mu in everything." I leave dokusan, crying and laughing, with Tachibana Sensei apologizing for his English translation. That's okay. He encourages me.

I go to dokusan with Kobai-san.

"Where does mu come from?"

"I don't know—how can it come from somewhere? It doesn't have a place."

Kobai-san is very fish-like, cold comfort.

"We've all struggled with the problem."

"It comes from me," I told her.

"If that's your answer, go to dokusan."

In we go again. Go Roshi says *"zenzen wakaranai" ["You don't understand at all."].*

I'm crushed, devastated. Roshi says, "Next time, come alone." . . .

. . . I'm called to dokusan. I feel so dejected, empty-minded. It doesn't even occur to me to wonder why Go Roshi wants me to come alone.

"Mu—do? [How is your mu?]"

I mu for him with all my strength, raising myself high and squeezing every bit of breath into mu until my head touches the floor.

"Once more again," he says in English. (He doesn't speak English, but I don't register surprise.)

I do so.

Then "Once more again."

My first and only thought was "He may make me do this for ages."

Then he jumped at me, grabbed me—"This body is *muji [the figure of mu],* this head, eyes, ears."

Suddenly I'm laughing and crying muji. I don't even realize "Now I am muji," but I simply was muji and everything around me.

And he hits different parts of my body. "This is muji." Count 20 in muji—20 parts of me, 20 muji in Kannonji, all around me. We're holding on to each other, laughing and laughing. "Heart muji," he says, thumping me. "And Go Roshi's heart muji," I say, belting him back. We're embracing.

"Kensho shita [You have realized your Buddha-nature]," says he.

I'm surprised. I was too self-conscious even to know that it was kensho. Only when I got outside and was looking at everything and really seeing mu did I finally know. Suddenly I understood why we must take care of things just because they exist; we are of no greater and of no lesser value.

At dinner the only words spoken aloud rang in my ears, *"Maura-san go kensho itashimashita [Maura has seen into her Buddha Nature]."*

At first I was so exhausted I felt neither joy nor sorrow, just relief. The next day I was ecstatic, couldn't stop smiling. Then all was as before—or at least, so it seems. Everyone tells me I look different. It's hard to be sure. I can't be bothered looking for big changes.

(O'Halloran, *Pure Heart, Enlightened Mind,* pages 77–79)

After another year of study, O'Halloran revealed the outgoing nature of Zen when she wrote in her journal:

I'd be embarrassed to tell anyone, it sounds so wishy-washy, but now I have maybe 50 or 60 years (who knows?) of time, of a life, open, blank, ready to offer. I want to live it for other people. What else is there to do with it? Not that I expect to change the world or even a blade of grass, but it's as if to give myself is all I can do, as the flowers have no choice but to blossom. At the moment the best I can see to do is to give to people this freedom, this bliss, and how better than through zazen? So I must go deeper and deeper and work hard, no longer for me but for everyone I can help. And still I can't save anyone. They must work themselves, and not everyone will. Thus I should also work politically, work to make people's surroundings that much more tolerable, work for a society that fosters more spiritual, more human, values. A society for people, not profits. What better way to instill the Bodhisattvic spirit in people? (Page 165)

Maura O'Halloran was killed in a traffic accident three years later. The inscription on a statue dedicated to her at Kannonji Temple declares that she is to be known by the name "Great Enlightened Lady, of the same heart and mind as the Great Teacher Buddha," and that she is "to be loved and respected forever" (page 295).

Two mice, one white and one black, little by little started to gnaw away the vine. The man saw a luscious strawberry near him. Grasping the vine with one hand, he plucked the strawberry with the other. How sweet it tasted! (*Zen Flesh, Zen Bones,* page 23)

The stories of Zen masters are full of accounts about the great teachers' awareness of the approach of death. As the masters near the end of life, many have composed poems, leaving behind their "last words" to their followers. This one is from the hand of Master Shoun:

For fifty-six years I lived as best I could,
Making my way in this world.
Now the rain has ended, the clouds are
    clearing,
The blue sky has a full moon.
            (*Zen Flesh, Zen Bones,* pages 19–20)[F]

Zen Life

The teachings of Zen invariably aim at the spirit of Buddhism: the attainment of direct insight into truth. All other aspects of religion are considered secondary to this primary goal. Still Zen is a religious tradition, and it has many of the trappings we normally associate with a religion. Those observable aspects include the formal training methods, daily practices, and cultural influences that together constitute Zen life.

The Monastic Lifestyle: Rigorous Training and Menial Tasks

Earlier we questioned whether practicing Zen is really difficult. After all, what could be simpler than "seeing into the nature of one's own being"? Probably our investigation of Zen's teachings—with their insistence on moving beyond logic, their *koans,* and their talk of a *satori* that is impossible to describe in words—

has provided proof enough that practicing Zen is not so simple a task. Zen Buddhists themselves understand fully the deep difficulty of accomplishing it. And so Zen prescribes a monastic lifestyle that is designed in every way to move the disciple closer to enlightenment. (Though this discussion speaks of monks and the monastic life, women are not excluded from Zen monastic life. There are far fewer Zen nuns than monks, but the lifestyle described as monastic applies to women as well as men.) We begin by considering the most prominent method of training, *zazen.*

Zazen: "Seated Meditation"

Zazen, whose name literally means "seated meditation," consumes most of the monks' time. Seated in rows on a slightly raised platform within the meditation hall, the monks assume the lotus posture, their eyes half-closed. Here they sit for hours each day, day after day, year after year. If ever a monk becomes sleepy or lacks concentration, an appointed attendant delivers a blow to the back

IMAGE: © OWEN FRANKEN/CORBIS

A nun meditates in a temple.

F
What does the poem written by Master Shoun tell you about his perspective on death? on life?

G

Imagine yourself practicing *zazen* in a meditation hall and getting hit in the back with an encouragement stick. Describe what it would take for you to feel actual gratitude, rather than resentment, toward the attendant who hit you.

H

Zen acknowledges the spiritual benefits of work, especially menial tasks. How does work relate to your spiritual well-being?

with an "encouragement stick." This blow is intended not to harm the monk but to refresh and focus him, and is received with a gesture of gratitude. (The blow of the encouragement stick is delivered with precision and strikes at points that are also important in the healing practice of acupuncture.)

Zazen is practiced with the intent of clearing the mind, and thereby attaining insight. But Zen does not stop with this. The insight attained through *zazen* must be taken along through the daily routines of life, and not merely confined to the meditation hall.[G]

Life in the Monastery

Work is an essential part of Zen monastic life. The physical activity of work helps to prevent the mind from becoming dull. So the monks engage in a variety of tasks, especially menial ones: preparing food in the kitchen, tending the fields, gathering firewood, and begging in local villages.

Eating and sleeping, like *zazen,* take place on small rectangular mats in the meditation hall. Meals are simple, consisting mainly of rice and vegetables. They are also structured affairs, eaten in silence and conducted with a series of hand gestures indicating if more food is desired. Every daily routine is intimately correlated with Zen teachings, so that all the routines move the monks closer to enlightenment.[H]

Zen Master, Zen Disciple

One aspect of Zen life that prevents most Westerners from ever practicing Zen in its true Chinese or Japanese form is the master-disciple relationship. The degree of confidence the disciple must invest in the master is virtually unheard of in the West, where people focus more on individualism.

The Zen master, or *roshi,* has almost complete authority over his disciples. Accounts of physical discipline abound: slapping disciples' faces, twisting their noses, pushing them to the ground. The authority and physical disci-

pline involved in the master-disciple relationship might appear strange to Western eyes. But like all aspects of Zen, they are intended to help bring about enlightenment. What might appear from the outside (and perhaps even to the disciple at the time) as unkindness, Zen intends as a nurturing concern.

Zen Beyond the Monastery

The central importance of *zazen* has, to some extent, freed Zen from the confines of the monastery. After all, a person does not need to be in a formal meditation hall to meditate. Whether in the company of others at a Zen center or on a retreat, or alone at home, men and women can practice Zen without becoming monks and nuns.

Another aspect of Zen beyond the monastery is its relevance to issues in the world at large. In the monastery the insight attained through *zazen* is applied to the daily routines of life. This holds true for Zen practice outside the monastery as well. In Japan companies commonly recommend *zazen* to their employees, sometimes offering meditation sessions as part of the normal work schedule. Zen centers also offer such sessions, along with a variety of other facilities and services for Zen laity, such as youth hostels that foster good character development in children.

Zen's concern for social justice lies at the heart of its teachings. Zen insight into reality overcomes the bondage of self-centeredness. Once that insight has been attained, the ego (the "I") and the rest of humanity are no longer distinct. The suffering of others, then, becomes one's own. In this way Zen fosters a natural impulse to alleviate suffering by working to correct social injustices.

Zen's Influence on the Cultural Arts

Zen's vast influence on East Asian cultural arts springs from its emphasis on simplicity and its overwhelming love of nature, which it inherited from Chinese Taoism. By the time of Zen's arrival in Japan, such love of nature had long been nurtured through Shinto, the traditional religion of the Japanese. This aspect of Zen was therefore very much welcomed, and today Japan's culture breathes the spirit of Zen.

The most famous example of Zen influence in the visual arts is *sumie,* or black ink painting. Aside from beautifully portraying the elements of nature, *sumie* places great significance on empty spaces, thereby conveying Zen's concern for simplicity. This concern is also evident in Japanese landscape gardening and in the pervasive art of flower arrangement, which until recently most Japanese girls were expected to learn. In all these arts, empty space is as important as filled space.

Zen has also strongly influenced physical arts, such as swordplay and archery. For centuries these have been practiced primarily as means of gaining Zen insight, not as tools for warfare. If the simplicity that comes from Zen can be applied to these arts, brilliant results follow naturally. The same spirit animates the simple but elegant Zen tea ceremony, which proceeds so spontaneously that it always seems as if it were being done for the first time.[I]

Zen's influence on literature is recognized throughout the world in the poetic form of haiku. Consisting of seventeen syllables in Japanese (the number of syllables in English translations may vary), these poems elegantly display Zen's celebration of simplicity. The following haiku was composed by Matsuo Basho (1644 to 1694), a great Zen poet:

> The sea darkening . . .
> > Oh voices of the
> > Wild ducks
> Crying, whirling, white
> > (translated by Beilenson, Japanese Haiku, page 41)[J]

In Conclusion . . .

Writing a conclusion for a chapter on Zen is something of a contradiction—but then so is writing a beginning for such a chapter. Noth-

I

Describe an aspect of your own society that might benefit from Zen teachings.

J

Compose your own haiku. In it try to capture something of the spirit of Zen.

IMAGE: © CATHERINE KARNOW/CORBIS

This temple rock garden in Japan shows the Zen emphasis on simplicity and love of nature in landscaping.

ing, after all, can be written to explain Zen completely. Zen itself diligently strives to free the mind from the bondage brought about by words. Furthermore, Zen never concludes. *Satori,* unlike *nirvana,* is not a permanent state. The Buddha himself, according to Zen, is still engaged in Zen training, still deepening his insight.

Zen refuses to affirm or to deny, even with respect to some of life's most pressing questions, such as these: What happens after we die? Does God exist? But Zen does fully affirm one thing—life itself, life lived to the fullest, in perfect awareness and direct insight into the simple truth of things. "If you have eaten from your bowl, wash it."

Like haiku, Zen is a kind of poetry, presenting methods and messages that prompt the mind to seek truth for itself. Like the finger pointing to the moon, Zen points to truth, but never is so bold as to come right out and declare it. It is perhaps fitting, then, to close this chapter with a Zen poem. Written many centuries ago, Han-shan's Cold Mountain poems seem to describe not so much a physical mountain as a spiritual ascent. This selection gives us a glimpse of the trail:

I climb the road to Cold Mountain,
The road to Cold Mountain that never ends.
The valleys are long and strewn with stones;
The streams broad and banked with
    thick grass.
Moss is slippery, though no rain has fallen;
Pines sigh, but it isn't the wind.
Who can break from the snares of the world
And sit with me among the white clouds?

(Watson, translator,
Cold Mountain, page 58)

The Seven Dimensions of Religion: Zen Buddhism

Dimension	Examples
Experiential	*satori*
Mythic	the legend of Buddha's choosing Mahakasyapa as his successor
Doctrinal	the distinction between sudden awakening and gradual awakening
Ethical	a concern for social justice
Ritual	*dokusan, zazen*
Social	the division into Rinzai and Soto (and other) sects, the master-disciple relationship
Material	the meditation hall, the encouragement stick, *sumie,* Japanese gardens

Chapter Review

1. How do the terms *dhyana* and *ch'an* relate to the name *Zen*?
2. Why did the Buddha choose Mahakasyapa as his successor?
3. What is the name of the Zen patriarch under whose influence Chinese Zen flourished?
4. Identify the two primary sects of Japanese Zen.
5. Which Zen sect is known as the school of sudden awakening?
6. For Zen Buddhists and the historical Buddha, what is the primary means of attaining enlightenment?
7. Briefly describe these three characteristics of Zen: it is experiential, it is beyond words, and it is beyond logical thinking.
8. What did Japanese master Nan-in mean by telling the university professor, "Empty your cup"?
9. What is *satori*?
10. What is the difference between *satori* and *nirvana*?
11. What is a *koan* designed to do? Give an example of a *koan*.
12. What is a *dokusan*?
13. Identify the positive effects of Zen on the mind.
14. How does the perspective of Zen alter one's view of everyday reality?
15. What does Zen teach about the existence of an afterlife?
16. What is the literal meaning of the word *zazen*?
17. What is the intent of the practice *zazen*?
18. What types of tasks do Zen monks engage in as part of their monastic training?
19. How does Zen foster the impulse to correct social injustice?
20. What is the most famous example of Zen influence in the visual arts?
21. Identify at least three other arts on which Zen has had a strong influence.

Glossary

Ch'an (chahn; Chinese: "meditation"). The Chinese sect of Buddhism that focuses on the experience of enlightenment; it began to flourish under the direction of Hui-neng in the seventh century AD; the Japanese equivalent is Zen.

dokusan (doh-koo-sahn). A periodic meeting with the master during which the disciple offers an answer to an assigned *koan*.

koan (koh´ahn). A verbal puzzle designed to short-circuit the workings of the rational, logical mind; used especially in Rinzai Zen as a means of triggering *satori*.

Rinzai (rin-z*i*). The school of sudden awakening, brought to Japan in the twelfth century AD by Eisai; one of the two major sects of Zen. *See also* Soto.

roshis (roh-shees). Zen masters who are deemed competent to teach others.

satori (suh-tor´ee). The Zen experience of enlightenment, a flash of insight in which the true nature of one's being is known directly.

Soto (soh-toh). The school of gradual awakening, brought to Japan in the thirteenth century AD by Dogen; one of the two major sects of Zen. *See also* Rinzai.

zazen (zah-zen; Japanese: "seated meditation"). The basic method of Zen meditation, traditionally practiced while seated in the lotus position in a meditation hall.

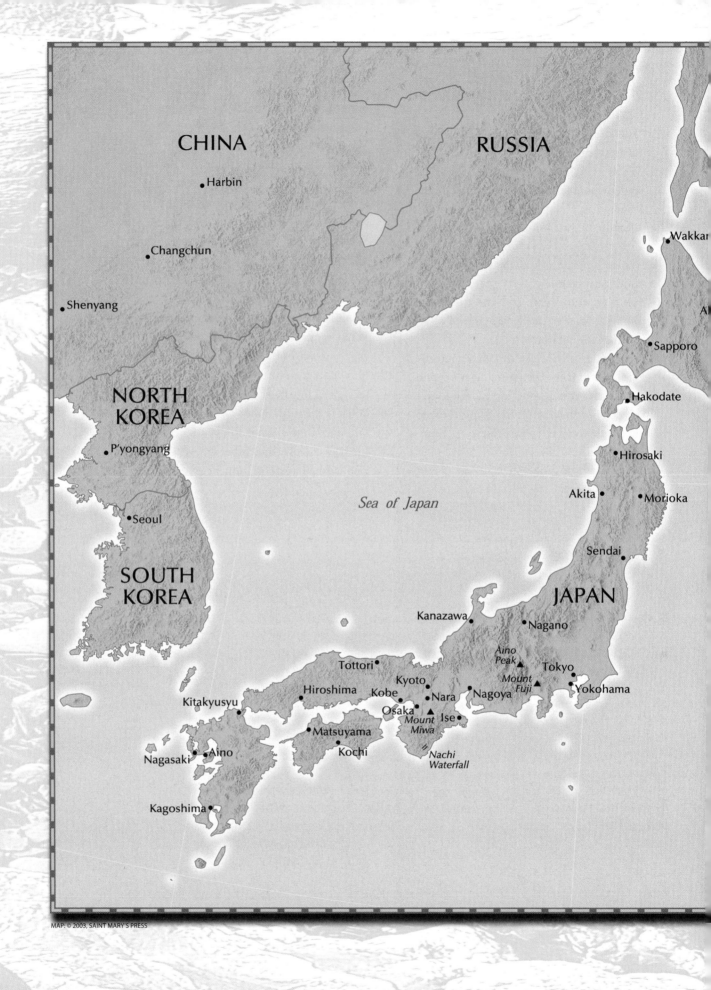

CHINA

• Harbin

RUSSIA

• Changchun

• Shenyang

NORTH
KOREA

• P'yongyang

• Wakkar

• Sapporo

• Hakodate

SOUTH
KOREA

• Seoul

Sea of Japan

• Hirosaki

Akita •

• Morioka

Sendai •

JAPAN

Kanazawa •

• Nagano

Aino
Peak ▲

Tokyo •

Tottori •

Kyoto •

Mount
Fuji ▲

• Yokohama

Hiroshima •

Kobe •

• Nara

Nagoya •

Kitakyusyu •

Osaka •

▲
Mount
Miwa

• Ise

Nagasaki •
• Aino

• Matsuyama

Nachi
Waterfall

• Kochi

Kagoshima •

Sea of Okhotsk

iro

PACIFIC

OCEAN

10 Shinto

"Way of the *Kami*"

Shinto is Japan's native religious tradition. With roots that date back to prehistoric times, Shinto has probably existed for as long as the Japanese have inhabited their islands. But Shinto has also been shaped through the ages by foreign influences. In fact, the term *shinto,* which means "way of the *kami* (kah-mee)," is from the Chinese words *shen* (divinities) and *tao* (way). It was first used by the Japanese in about the sixth century AD to distinguish their native religion from new traditions coming from China, especially Buddhism (which the Japanese call Butsudo [boo-tsoo-doh], "way of the Buddha"). Japanese religion, like East Asian religion in general, is a fabric of interwoven traditions. Shinto and Japanese folk tradition have provided native threads, and Buddhism, Confucianism, and Taoism have contributed foreign strands. The religion of most Japanese is drawn from all those traditions. For example, Japanese marriages are commonly held in Shinto shrines, and Japanese funerals are usually conducted in Buddhist temples. It would be a mistake to think of Shinto as existing independently of other traditions.

Shinto contributes to Japanese religion in a variety of ways. In one of its aspects, it is a vehicle for patriotism, conveying a long-standing respect for Japan as a nation. In another aspect Shinto attends to everyday concerns of communities and individuals, helping to secure such necessities as good crops and safe homes. Most of all Shinto is veneration of nature. A profound love of nature, which has always been a hallmark of the Japanese, is embodied in the concept that lies at the heart of Shinto, the *kami*.

Kami:
Divine Ancestors, Sacred Inhabitants

Shinto emphasizes the ritual dimension over the doctrinal. Participation in rituals means far more than holding the correct "belief" (a notion quite foreign to Shinto). Shinto therefore has not concerned itself much with theological explanations of the *kami*. Even the great scholar Motoori Norinaga (1730 to 1801), one of Shinto's most admired and influential figures, admitted, "I do not yet understand the meaning of the term, *kami*" (quoted in Earhart, *Religion in the Japanese Experience*, page 10).

Basically the **kami** are any people or things that have evoked the wonder of the Japanese. They include deities and certain human beings, such as emperors, as well as a large variety of natural entities like mountains and animals. The *kami* are numerous, and can appear anywhere. Many are also ancient, existing long before the Japanese, and even before their island home. Indeed the *kami* are Japan's divine ancestors.

A

Myths provide answers to fundamental questions about human life and history. Often they give those answers using symbolic images and events that do not have obvious meanings. With this in mind, carefully consider the Shinto myth. What fundamental questions does it answer, and how?

Divine Ancestors:
The Shinto Myth of Japan's Origins

Shinto has no sacred scripture, no bible. But it does have authoritative histories that were compiled in the eighth century AD by order of the imperial court. The histories contain a mythological account of the origins of Japan.

Known at least in outline form by virtually all Japanese, the Shinto myth tells about the divine ancestry of Japan and its people, and illustrates that the *kami* are always present and always close to Japan's land and people. It is thus a creation myth, setting forth both a cosmology and an account of human origins. Though most Japanese today would not assert its historical truth, the myth is highly significant, celebrating the greatness of Japan. It can be summarized as follows:

At the beginning of heaven and earth, seven generations of deities *(kami)* came into existence, including Izanagi and Izanami, the primal male and female. Other deities commanded these two to create land. And so, churning the sea with Izanagi's spear, they created an island from the brine that dripped from the spear.

The pair descended from heaven to earth, and Izanami gave birth to the eight islands of Japan. Izanami then gave birth to many deities, the last one being the heat god, who burned her to death as she was giving birth to him. Overcome by despair, Izanagi killed the heat god and then pursued Izanami to the underworld. Here, in spite of his wife's warnings, Izanagi beheld her decaying body. Embarrassed and outraged, Izanami pursued Izanagi, who barely managed to escape before blocking the entrance to the underworld with a huge boulder.

Izanagi, polluted from this encounter with death, waded into the ocean to purify himself. From filth in his left eye, he produced Amaterasu, the sun goddess; from filth in his right eye and his nostrils, he produced the moon god and storm god.

Eventually Amaterasu, who reigned as the chief deity, sent her grandson, Ni-ni-gi, to rule the earth as its emperor, and Ni-ni-gi's grandson became the first human emperor. The imperial line was thereby established, descended directly from Amaterasu.

In the meantime, elsewhere on the islands, the Japanese were descending from other deities.

It is easy to understand why the Japanese have revered the Shinto myth over the centuries. After all, because of the myth, they can claim divine ancestry and can take pride in the divine origins of their homeland.[A]

Two examples of *kami:* Mount Fuji and a statue of a Shinto goddess.

Shinto   169

Sacred Inhabitants:
"Eight Hundred Myriads" of *Kami*

The Shinto myth introduces some of the *kami,* including Amaterasu, who is still regarded as the most important deity, and Ni-ni-gi, Amaterasu's grandson and Japan's first emperor. The Japanese have traditionally regarded their emperors as *kami,* even while the emperors are still living. (After Japan's defeat in World War II, Emperor Hirohito was forced to announce publicly that he was not divine; many Japanese were likely shocked by that.)

Not only deities and emperors are sacred to the Japanese, however. The great scholar Motoori Norinaga writes that a wide variety of things can be considered *kami:*

Speaking in general . . . it may be said that *kami* signifies, in the first place, the deities of heaven and earth that appear in the ancient records and also the spirits of the shrines where they are worshipped.

It is hardly necessary to say that it includes human beings. It also includes such objects as birds, beasts, trees, plants, seas, mountains and so forth. In ancient usage, anything whatsoever which was outside the ordinary, which possessed superior power or which was awe-inspiring was called *kami.* (Quoted in Earhart, *Religion in the Japanese Experience,* page 10)

Motoori goes on to cite thunder, dragons, echoes, foxes, tigers, wolves, peaches, and a necklace as *kami.* The list is seemingly endless. The ancient histories, in fact, assert that the *kami* number "eight hundred myriads," or eight million. This is to be regarded not as a literal figure, but as a recognition that the islands of Japan abound with the sacred forces that the *kami* embody.

In general, it is helpful to think of *kami* as that which is sacred, whatever the specific form it takes. The importance of *kami* clearly relates to the Japanese love of nature. Nature, in all its manifestations, is considered sacred. This sacredness is celebrated and worshiped in its embodied form of *kami.*[B]

B

The concept of *kami* is central to Shinto. After reading the descriptions and examples of *kami,* close your textbook and describe *kami* in your own words.

IMAGE: © CORBIS

Japan's Emperor Hirohito, seen here shortly after World War II, renounced his divine status and broke with tradition by meeting directly with the Japanese people.

Shinto in the Religious Life of Japan

Given the abundance and variety of *kami,* it is natural that Shinto includes many forms of worship practice and of institutional organization.

Shinto Worship: Revering the *Kami*

Shinto worship focuses on simple expression of respectful gratitude to the *kami,* and to the experience of unity with them. Worship can take place in the home, at shrines, or during large and joyous seasonal festivals in which entire communities join together in colorful pageantry.

Worship at Home: The *Kamidana*

The focal point of Shinto worship in the home is a small altar called the **kamidana** (kah-mee-dah-nah), or "*kami* shelf." The *kamidana* can contain a wide variety of items, depending on the family's particular objects of worship. Usually it holds the names of deceased ancestors. Statues of favorite deities, and items brought back from shrines are also common. These objects tend to be regarded as symbols of the presence of *kami,* although for the more traditional Japanese, they are thought to actually contain *kami.*

Worship at the *kamidana* is simple and commonly occurs daily. First, family members purify themselves by washing their hands and faces. Then they present offerings such as food or flowers, clap their hands to signify their presence to the *kami,* and say prayers. The *kamidana* can also serve as the focal point for more elaborate celebrations, such as weddings.

Ceremonial Worship at Shinto Shrines

Shinto shrines have a natural beauty and are found almost everywhere in Japan. Originally the *kami* were worshiped in natural places, such as groves, waterfalls, and mountains. Some such places, like Nachi Waterfall and Mount Miwa, still function as shrines. Today the *kami* are typically worshiped in wooden structures featuring a naturalness that expresses Shinto's profound veneration of its surroundings (for instance, the wood is often left unpainted).

A visit to a Shinto shrine removes the worshiper from ordinary, everyday surroundings. The entrance to the sacred confines of the shrine is marked by a **torii** (toh-ree-ee), an archway formed by two upright pillars and a cross beam, usually fortified with horizontal supports. The *torii* is recognized worldwide as the symbol of Shinto.

The shrine is usually rectangular and surrounded by a fence. Often a grove of trees or a park can be found nearby. Having passed through the *torii,* the worshiper finds a basin with water for the rite of purification. In this rite water is splashed on the hands and the face, symbolically preparing the worshiper to appear before the *kami.* Next, the visitor enters the worship hall, the space reserved for

The rope tied around this tree is a means of showing reverence for the presence of *kami.*

Bushido: "Way of the Warrior"

Many people continue to be unsettled by the Japanese kamikaze (divine wind) pilots who willingly crashed their warplanes into enemy ships in World War II. The suicidal attitude of the kamikaze attack stems from a deeply rooted Japanese tradition established in medieval times: **bushido** (boo-shee-doh), "way of the warrior."

Bushido is Japanese through and through. It resulted from the combined teachings of three of Japan's prevalent religions: Shinto nationalism, Confucian respect for one's superiors, and Zen self-discipline and transcendence of the duality of life and death. These teachings formed the code of conduct for the **samurai** (sam´uh-ri), Japan's medieval knights.

Bushido is similar to the code of chivalry practiced by Europe's medieval knights. Its primary virtues are these:

- loyalty to one's master
- courage to fight, and to die if necessary
- honor, preferring death to dishonor
- politeness toward those in higher social positions
- justice; as a doer of just and benevolent deeds, the samurai protected victims of injustice

Most striking among the ways of the samurai—and glaringly different from the ways of Europe's knights—is the willingness to commit suicide. In fact, a samurai carried two weapons—a sword to use against the enemy, and a dagger to use against himself. The ritual suicide, known as **seppuku** (sep-poo-koo) in Japan, and commonly called hara-kiri (hair-i-kihr´ee) in the West, was a painful death brought about by cutting open the abdomen.

Bushido is illustrated vividly in the medieval Japanese tale "The Forty-seven *Ronin*." A nobleman, angered by repeated abuse from his superior, attempted to murder the superior. In response, the courts required the nobleman to commit *seppuku*, which he did. His forty-seven samurai attendants thus became *ronin*, or samurai whose superior is dead and who are bound by the code of *bushido* to avenge his death. Eventually, through cunning and great courage, the forty-seven *ronin* captured the man their superior had tried to kill, whom they held responsible for their superior's death. With politeness and humility, the forty-seven explained their duty and told the man that he must now commit *seppuku*. The man hesitated, afraid to take his own life. And so one of the forty-seven attacked, cutting off the enemy's head with a dagger. The *ronin* then washed the head, and carried it to the grave of their deceased superior and offered it to his spirit. There they waited for several days, until the courts ordered that they must now commit *seppuku* for having murdered their superior's enemy. This they calmly did. Ever since, the forty-seven *ronin* have been revered for having perfectly embodied *bushido*, the way of the warrior.

C

For Shinto, purification is necessary to allow the light of one's inborn divine essence to shine through. Think about the purification rituals of other religions, and explain why religions practice purification.

worshipers during the ceremony. A second building, the chief sanctuary, can be entered only by priests. Within that building lies the *kami* body, usually a common object such as a mirror or a sword. The *kami* of the shrine is believed to descend into the *kami* body during the ceremony. The *kami* body is an extremely sacred object, and is rarely seen even by the priests. Once a priest has invoked the presence of the *kami,* prayers are offered on behalf of the worshipers. A typical shrine ceremony culminates in an experience of unity with the *kami.*

Most of Shinto's shrines conform to this description, though the details vary. The most notable shrines are considerably more elaborate. The Grand Imperial Shrine at Ise, dedicated to the sun goddess Amaterasu, is the grandest and most famous of all. Rebuilt every twenty years to ensure its purity, the Grand Imperial Shrine houses the three sacred regalia of Japan's imperial line: a bronze mirror, a sword, and a string of jewels. According to the Shinto myth, these were sent to earth with Ni-ni-gi by his grandmother, the sun goddess Amaterasu.

The entrance to this shrine is guarded by a *torii*, a gate that is the symbol of Shinto.

Seasonal Festivals

Festivals abound in Japan. Including local and regional festivals, they number well into the hundreds. Shinto, along with Buddhism, is a significant presence at many of the festivals.

Shinto has always been closely tied to the agricultural life of Japan, and many of its festivals reflect this. For example, in October and November, festivals celebrate the new rice harvest. The first grains of rice are offered to Amaterasu. Festivals like these are especially important in rural areas.

Of Shinto's many seasonal celebrations, the most notable are the Great Purification and the festival of the New Year.

The Great Purification. The Great Purification is performed in shrines throughout Japan twice a year, in June and December. For a month before each ceremony, the priests engage in a number of practices and disciplines intended to enhance their purity. During the ceremony a priest waves a cleansing wand over a gathering of people. Participants rub paper dolls on their bodies to transfer impurities from themselves to the dolls. The priests then throw the dolls away.

Such emphasis on purification pervades Shinto. In the Shinto myth, Izanagi washes himself in the ocean after being polluted in the underworld. Worship of *kami,* whether at home before the *kamidana* or in the community at a shrine, always begins with a rite of purification. The rebuilding of the Grand Imperial Shrine at Ise every twenty years also stems from this stress on purification. Nevertheless, humans are not regarded as naturally sinful or impure. On the contrary, as descendants of the original deities, they are thought to be born with a divine essence. Purification is needed, though, to allow the light of this essence to shine through with its true luster. The Japanese reputation for cleanliness is directly related to this perspective on the human condition.[c]

The festival of the New Year. The most spectacular annual festival celebrates the New Year. The December Great Purification ceremony helps to prepare the people for this festival. Another ritual, cleaning their houses, allows them to begin the year with purified dwellings. The festival begins on January 1 and lasts for several days. During this time the people are on vacation and are free to worship at Shinto shrines and Buddhist temples. On January 7 a great feast marks the beginning of the New Year and the return to an ordinary lifestyle.

Priestess of the Shrine

A young woman named Mine, from Aino, Japan, is a priestess of the Suwa Shrine in Nagasaki. Although the Shinto priesthood is made up primarily of men, women have always played significant roles in shrine life. Mine discusses her experience as a contemporary Japanese woman who is also a member of the Shinto priesthood:

I like the feeling of being able to walk down the street, looking just like any other woman my age, and to have this little secret that I'm a Shinto priestess. . . . I'm proud to be who I am, even though it is a bit unusual for a woman in this day and age.

My family is a Shinto family and has been in charge of the village shrine at Aino for longer than anyone can remember. When I was in high school, I promised my grandfather to study Shinto when I got older, thinking at the time that it would be a good way to get to Tokyo from my little village down in Kyushu. I was like anyone else who watched TV and had their favorite singers and shows; I thought that Tokyo was where it was all happening. . . .

At one point during my university days, we had to undergo a training period. You know, the kind that is supposed to make you tough and pure and bright. We had to get up at 4:30 in the morning and thoroughly clean the shrine and gardens surrounding it, then study hard all day, even doing some meditation, and weren't allowed to sleep until 11:00 at night. The worst part was having to perform the *misogi* purification in the ocean while reciting the Oharae prayer about all the impurities and evils that we were washing away. . . . When we did it first in winter I was absolutely frozen to the bone. . . . Other than that intense training session, it was all pretty much routine study.

When I got out of school, I kept my promise to my grandfather and returned to Aino, and through his connections to Suwa Shrine, it was agreed that I [would] come and further my studies. Now that I'm out in society, meeting a variety of people all the time, when they ask me what I do and I answer that I'm a priestess, their reaction is usually the same. "Incredible!" they say. But this is my career and it seems very normal to me. I'm sure I'll have a relationship with a shrine all my life, even after marriage. If you ask what my career goals are I'd have to say that they're not easy to pinpoint in the way other young people talk about becoming the head of the department or making lots of money or marrying some up-and-coming young executive or doctor. No, for me, what I'd like to do is to make whatever shrine I'm involved with a place where people can come and feel like they are "home" and want to linger. . . .

I guess the biggest problem I face now is the old attitudes about women and what their role is supposed to be at a modern shrine such as this one. I don't have hard training or anything like that, other than the juvenile tasks I'm expected to perform because of my rank, which I suppose are similar to pouring tea or making copies in an office. It just seems that other priests, the men, who are licensed the same as me and of my rank do much more than I do. Maybe it's because people might be put off when they come to the shrine and see a woman officiating. They might say, "Hey, there are men priests here—what's a woman doing at the ritual I'm paying for?" This is discrimination of course, and in a place like Nagasaki, which is still conservative and old-fashioned and where men are believed to be superior to women, I can't escape it, even here at the shrine.

But you know, women have always had an important role in Shinto, right from the very beginning. . . .

If I could change something about Shinto . . . I'd like to somehow restore the presence of the Kami to a more direct feeling or contact. It seems that people feel the Kami is something far away, that they have to go to a shrine or be at the family altar before they can share things with the deities. But for me, I think it's a fundamental part of Shinto to have a sense that the Kami is with you, so that if something happens or you need guidance, you can communicate with it immediately, wherever you are. This closeness to the Kami is something our modern civilization and society have completely lost.

(Quoted in Nelson, *A Year in the Life of a Shinto Shrine,* pages 125–129)

Types of Shinto

Shinto has had a long and varied history and has taken on different forms through the centuries. Today three main types of Shinto can be identified, though they tend to overlap somewhat. Shrine Shinto is an organized institution, with officially designated shrines and priests. Sect Shinto is also organized but consists of a large variety of separate institutions, or "sects." Popular Shinto, though including many of the practices of the other types, lacks any formal organization.

Shrine Shinto

The Japanese government officially coined the term *Shrine Shinto* during the nineteenth century. However, the roots of Shrine Shinto extend into the distant past, when foreign religions first became prominent in Japan.

Already in the seventh century AD, Buddhism had become a significant tradition for the Japanese. Through the ages Buddhism and Shinto became closely intertwined. From the Buddhist perspective, the *kami* were local Japanese manifestations of universal Buddhist truths. Followers of Shinto, in turn, came to regard the Buddhas and *bodhisattvas* as *kami*.

Buddhism was not embraced by everyone, however. Shortly after it first appeared in Japan, the imperial government began to take measures to preserve Shinto as the national tradition. It recorded Shinto's mythology, organized its priesthood, and began caring for its shrines. In the eighteenth century, Motoori Norinaga established himself as Shinto's most admired figure by purifying the religion of all Buddhist and other foreign elements.

Tensions between Shinto and foreign influences reached a climax in the nineteenth century. In 1868, challenged by the United States and other nations to enter the modern age, Japan commenced the Meiji Restoration, a crucial project that transformed Japan into a modern nation. Massive political, economic, and religious transformations occurred. The religious transformation can be summarized briefly: Buddhism lost state support, while Shinto gained it. In 1882 Shrine Shinto was officially recognized as the state religion.

The period from 1868, the beginning of the Meiji Restoration, to 1945, the end of World War II, was both prosperous and tragic for Shinto. Adopted by the state as a vehicle for patriotism, Shinto was purified of its Buddhist elements. The state acquired authority over most of the shrines and over the priests who served them. It became the duty of every Japanese citizen to attend the shrines as a means of expressing patriotism. The Shinto myth of Japan's divine origins became a required part of every child's education so that students might learn loyalty to the emperor and his nation.

With Japan's defeat in World War II, the state support of Shinto ended in disaster. Japan's ancient and splendid tradition had been misused as a tool to fan the flames of extreme nationalism and militarism. This is not to say that Shinto somehow caused Japanese aggression. It was no more to blame than were Buddhism, Confucianism, and even Christianity, which were just as supportive of the nation's policies. On the contrary, the state's misuse of Shinto, not Shinto itself, fueled Japanese aggression.

Shrine Shinto, and Shinto in general, suffered a severe setback. Japanese tended to blame Shinto for the humiliating defeat of World War II. Nevertheless, Shrine Shinto continues to play a vital part in Japan's religious landscape. The shrines still stand, though they are assisted through the private funding of the nationwide Shrine Association rather than through government involvement. And interest in Shinto has been growing in recent years.[D]

Sect Shinto

When the Japanese government recognized Shrine Shinto in 1882, it categorized the leftover elements of organized Shinto as sect

D
Until the end of World War II, Shrine Shinto was involved with nationalism to an extreme degree. Such involvement, usually on a smaller scale, has been common throughout world history. What kind of connection do you detect between your nation and religion? What forms does this association take? In general, what do you think should be the relation between religion and a nation?

Shinto. Thirteen sects were officially included. The government designated these as religions, along with other faiths such as Buddhism and Christianity. The sects were then required to call their places of worship churches, to distinguish them from the shrines that were under the control of the state.

Many of these sects were founded and led by women. This could be a reflection of ancient times, when women were likely to have had prominent roles in Japanese religion.

Popular Shinto

Popular, or folk, Shinto has hardly been affected by the government's categorizing of Shinto into Shrine and sect. Indeed popular Shinto defies classification, for it has never been organized.

Popular Shinto includes a wide array of traditional practices, and in many instances can best be understood as Japanese folk religion. Virtually all forms of Shinto worship that do not require a priest or a formal shrine are practiced in popular Shinto. Rituals of purification are emphasized. Personal blessings are sought for protection from harm and for help in times of crisis. For example, students commonly seek assistance on examination days. People also seek blessings at major stages of life, such as birth and marriage. Certain rites help to secure the successful growing of crops, especially rice. Such agricultural concerns have been central to Shinto through the ages.

A businessman bows before a small Shinto shrine in the courtyard of the Tokyo Stock Exchange. The shrine is said to house the deity of business and commerce.

IMAGE: AP IMAGES/WORLD WIDE PHOTOS

Traditional Shinto in Modern Japan

Shinto thrived for centuries in a Japan that was predominantly rural. Its deep veneration of nature and close ties to the agricultural life of the islands were in harmony with the rural lifestyle. Then, during the twentieth century, Japan rapidly became predominantly urban. It would seem that Shinto would have been

The Seven Dimensions of Religion: Shinto

Dimension	Examples
Experiential	unity with the *kami*
Mythic	an account of the origins of Japan
Doctrinal	beliefs regarding the nature of the *kami*
Ethical	the primary virtues of *bushido*
Ritual	worship at the *kamidana* and at shrines, the Great Purification
Social	Shinto priests
Material	*kamidana, torii,* the Grand Imperial Shrine at Ise, Nachi Waterfall, Mount Miwa

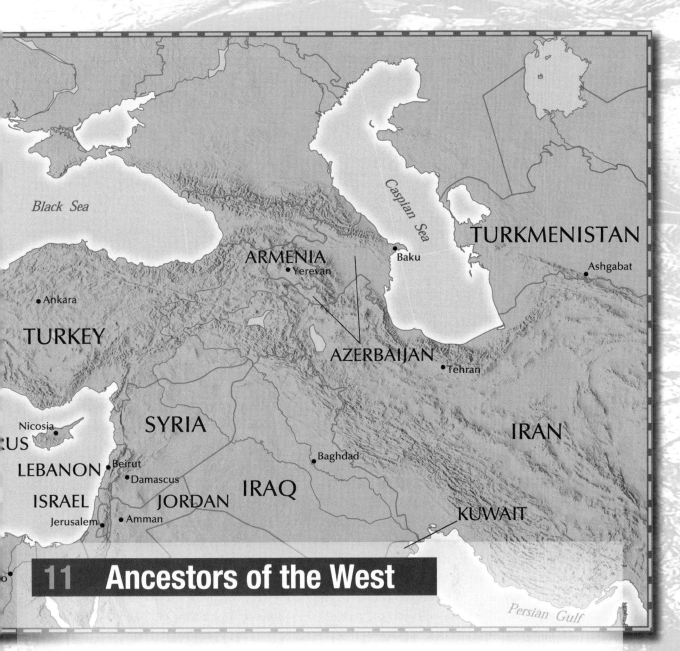

11 Ancestors of the West

The "Cradle" of the West

The region surrounding the eastern part of the Mediterranean Sea is commonly referred to as the cradle of the West. Here were born the religious beliefs and practices from which Judaism, Christianity, and Islam would eventually emerge. This chapter presents some of the religious aspects of early Western civilization. We have to be selective, because the religious traditions of the ancient West were numerous and diverse, and they endured for ages.

We will examine the traditions of Iran, Greece, and Rome for two reasons. First, they include a variety of the beliefs and practices typical in the ancient West, such as polytheism (belief in many gods) and rituals of animal sacrifice. Second, these

179

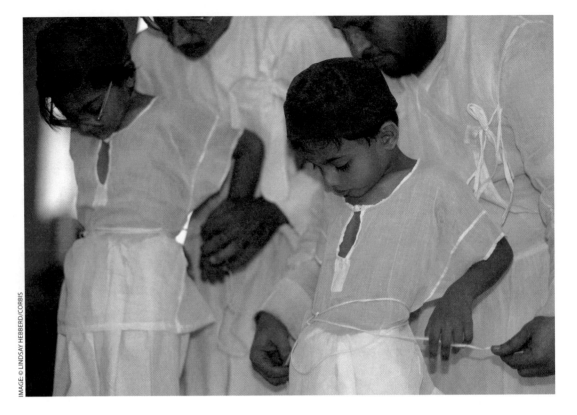

Today Zoroastrianism is practiced mainly by the Parsis of India. Here Parsi priests lead boys in a Zoroastrian ritual.

IMAGE: © LINDSAY HEBBERD/CORBIS

traditions had a strong influence on the emergence of Judaism, Christianity, and Islam. We will note many familiar features of these traditions that have been carried to modern times. Still it is important to remember that these religions are not of value merely because of their influences on Judaism, Christianity, and Islam. They are significant subjects of study in their own right. In addition, the religion of ancient Iran—Zoroastrianism—is still alive today.

Religion in Ancient Iran: Zoroastrianism

Zoroastrianism is one of the world's oldest living religions. It arose and flourished in ancient Iran, which was known as Persia. Its present followers are few, mainly the Parsis (Persians) of India.

Zoroastrianism has undergone a number of major changes since the time of its founder, Zarathustra (called Zoroaster by the Greeks). This ongoing transformation has amounted to an incredibly diverse tradition with different features at different times. Let us begin by looking at Zarathustra and the Zoroastrianism of ancient times, when the religion exerted great influence on the formation of Judaism and Christianity. A list of the religious innovations of Zarathustra and the early Zoroastrians is both impressive and familiar: judgment of the soul after death, followed by an afterlife of heaven or hell; a universe pervaded by forces of both good and evil; and monotheism.

The Origins and Early Development of Zoroastrianism

Zoroastrianism originated in an area now occupied by the nations of Iran and Afghanistan. Although we do not know for certain when Zarathustra lived, it was most likely during the sixth or fifth century BC. According to Persian tradition, he was born in 660 BC.

Zoroastrianism began to flourish throughout Iran during the Persian Empire, which was at the height of its power and influence in the fifth and fourth centuries BC. The Jews who remained in Babylon after having been forced into exile there (from 587 to 538 BC) lived in direct contact with the Persians who had gained control of the region. After Persia was conquered by the Greek general Alexander the Great in 328 BC, aspects of Persian culture, including Zoroastrianism, spread far and wide.

The Life of Zarathustra

Zarathustra's life story is shrouded in mystery. He seems to have been a son of a priest in a rural area. The traditional religion of Iran at this time was polytheistic, and a close relative of Hinduism. Zarathustra eventually initiated a large-scale religious conversion from polytheism to monotheism.

Legend has it that when Zarathustra was about thirty years old, he had an astonishing religious experience. An angel called Good Thought appeared to him and brought him, as a disembodied soul, before **Ahura Mazda** (ah'hoo-reh maz'dah), the Wise Lord. Zarathustra recognized Ahura Mazda as the one true God. After this experience Zarathustra went around preaching the radical message of monotheism to his polytheistic society. With the help of a king who had converted to Zoroastrianism, Zarathustra overcame hostile opposition and firmly established his religion. He is said to have died at the age of seventy-seven.

Although Zarathustra's life story is legendary, his teachings are verifiable. His seventeen hymns, or **Gathas** (gah'thuhs), are the oldest part of the sacred text of Zoroastrianism, the **Avesta** (a-ves'tuh). Altogether the Avesta is a diverse set of writings spanning a period of perhaps one thousand years. In the Gathas we can observe Zarathustra's innovative religious ideas.

Ahura Mazda, the One God of Zarathustra

Monotheism is a notion so familiar today that its uniqueness can pass unnoticed. But in the polytheistic society of ancient Iran, Zarathustra's innovation was truly radical and courageous. The same can be said of the monotheism of the Hebrews (the ancestors of the Jews). We do not know whether Zarathustra and the ancient Hebrews influenced each other's thinking on this issue. In any event the monotheism of both religions was a remarkable departure from the norm of the ancient world.

For Zarathustra the one true God was Ahura Mazda, the Wise Lord. Ahura Mazda is eternal and universal goodness, controlling the cosmos and the destiny of human beings. In the following passages from the Gathas, Zarathustra celebrates Ahura Mazda's role as creator:

IMAGE: © CHARLES & JOSETTE LENARS/CORBIS

A relief sculpture of Ahura Mazda stands among the ruins of Persepolis in Iran.

Who is by generation the Father of Right, at the first? Who determined the path of sun and stars? Who is it by whom the moon waxes and wanes again? . . .

Who upheld the earth beneath and the firmament from falling? Who the water and the plants? Who yoked swiftness to winds and clouds? . . .

What artist made light and darkness? What artist made sleep and waking? Who made morning, noon, and night, that call the understanding man to his duty? . . .

I strive to recognise by these things thee, O Mazdah, creator of all things through the holy spirit.

(44.3–7)[A]

A
Review the Gathas passage on Ahura Mazda. To what extent does this strike you as a familiar description of God?

Choosing Between Good and Evil: Ethical Dualism

Ethical dualism, the belief in universal forces of good and evil, is Zoroastrianism's most distinctive feature. In Zarathustra's theology the one God, Ahura Mazda, who is universal goodness, is opposed by the Lie, depicted by Zarathustra as an evil, cosmic force.

With this approach Zarathustra offered a straightforward solution to the problem of evil: evil really exists, and manifests itself in the world. On the other hand, the belief in a cosmic force of evil challenges monotheism. For if evil really exists, is Ahura Mazda, who is perfect goodness, truly the only God? Similar questions always challenge monotheistic theology, whatever the religion. Zarathustra's theology of good and evil attempted to answer those questions.

According to Zarathustra, Ahura Mazda had twin children, a beneficent spirit and a hostile spirit. (The hostile spirit later came to be known by the name Shaitan, which is related to the Hebrew name Satan.) Because both were born of Ahura Mazda, even the hostile spirit was not essentially evil. But both were free to choose between the forces of good and evil. The beneficent spirit chose truth, and the hostile spirit chose the Lie, the evil force.

For Zarathustra, the universe was a cosmic battleground of good and evil forces, depicted as angels and demons (the demons were identified as the many gods of Iranian polytheism). This belief had a major influence on Judaism, Christianity, and Islam. Zarathustra believed this cosmic battle would eventually be won by the good, angelic forces. He hinted at the doctrine of a future savior who would come to help restore goodness to the world. This doctrine was richly elaborated by later Zoroastrians, and it also seems to have influenced Judaism and its belief in the coming of a messiah.

This cosmic scheme of good and evil is crucial for human beings. For while the world awaits the ultimate triumph of goodness, humans must choose between truth and the Lie, between the beneficent spirit and the hostile spirit. Each person's choice has eternal consequences. In the Gathas, Zarathustra states the matter this way:

Hear with your ears the best things. Reflect with clear purpose, each man for himself, on the two choices for decision, being alert indeed to declare yourselves for Him before the great requital. Truly there are two primal Spirits, twins renowned to be in conflict. In thought and word, in act they are two: the better and the bad. And those who act well have chosen rightly between these two, not so the evildoers. And when these two Spirits first came together they created life and not-life, and how at the end Worst Existence shall be for the wicked, but (the House of) Best Purpose for the just man. (30.2–4)

This passage shows how the dualism of Zoroastrianism unites ethics with human destiny. At the "great requital," or day of judgment, the wicked will suffer the pains of "Worst Existence" (hell), while the just will enjoy the

"House of Best Purpose" (heaven). Humans determine their own destiny by choosing either truth, goodness, and life, or falsehood, evil, and "not-life." This ethical dualism is the basis of Zoroastrianism.[B]

Human Destiny

Zoroastrianism's doctrines regarding human destiny—resurrection and judgment of the dead, and vivid portrayals of heaven and hell—are among its most important and influential features. Zarathustra's own understanding of human destiny seems to have been as follows:

Shortly after death individuals undergo judgment. This requires crossing the Bridge of the Separator, which goes over an abyss of horrible torment but leads to paradise. The ethical records of individuals are read and judged. The good are allowed to enter paradise, while the evil are cast down to the abyss. In the Gathas, Zarathustra emphasizes the individual responsibility for failing to pass the judgment:

Their own soul and their own self shall torment them when they come where the Bridge of the Separator is, to all time dwellers in the House of the Lie. (46.11)

Zoroastrians also believe in a final bodily resurrection of everyone, good and evil alike. Once resurrected all will undergo a test by fire and molten metal; the evil will burn, while the good will pass through unharmed. It is not clear whether Zarathustra himself believed in resurrection, or if this belief developed later. We therefore do not know if Zoroastrianism's doctrine of resurrection was adopted by Judaism or vice versa.

In any event many aspects of the early Zoroastrian perspective on human destiny, such as descriptions of heaven and hell, were adopted by other religions. Heaven, or the House of Best Purpose, is said to be forever in sunshine, and its inhabitants enjoy the company of the saved. Hell, the Worst Existence, is a foul-smelling, dark place where the tormented are forced to remain completely alone.[C]

B
Does the Zoroastrian explanation for the existence of evil account for the evil you have experienced and observed? Why or why not?

A king receives his crown directly from Ahura Mazda in this relief sculpture from Iran.

IMAGE: SEF/ART RESOURCE, NY

C

Fire is often used as a symbol. Recall several ways you have seen fire used as such. Then think about what fire represents for you personally. How does this relate to what fire represented for the Zoroastrians?

Zoroastrian Life: Ethics and Worship

The traditional life of Zoroastrianism is centered on agriculture. Its ethical demands include such principles as caring for livestock and fields. Generally one is to lead a simple life, always telling the truth and doing what is right. Great care should be taken to avoid those on the side of evil, the followers of the demons for whom the Lie prevails.

Worship practices include prayer, which is to be done five times a day. (This seems to have influenced Islam, which sets forth a similar requirement.) The most famous form of Zoroastrian worship is the fire ritual. Fire is a symbol of the purity of Ahura Mazda. In the fire ritual, Zoroastrians worship not fire itself, but rather Ahura Mazda's perfect purity. This ritual has always been central to Zoroastrian worship. According to tradition Zarathustra himself was killed while tending the sacred fire.

Modern Zoroastrians continue to emphasize the fire ritual. A fire burns continually within the inner sanctuary of a temple. The priests who tend the fire are extremely careful to maintain ritual purity, covering their mouths with special cloths to avoid contaminating the fire. Worshipers wash themselves before approaching the fire, and bring offerings of sandalwood and money. In turn they receive ashes, which they rub on their faces.

Zoroastrianism Today: The Parsis

Once Islam had gained control of Iran in the tenth century, Zoroastrians began leaving. Very few remain in Iran today. Most of the world's Zoroastrians now live in India, where they are known as the Parsis.

The Parsis combine a wide variety of features from the Zoroastrian tradition. Basically, though, they maintain the monotheism of its founder and continue to revere the Avesta as their sacred text.

Top: Ruins of an ancient Zoroastrian temple. *Bottom:* Modern Zoroastrians continue to emphasize the fire ritual, in which they worship the perfect purity of Ahura Mazda.

IMAGE: © EARL NAZIMA/CORBIS

Parsis dispose of their dead by leaving them atop a tower of silence such as this one.

One well-known feature of the Parsis' religious practice is their manner of disposing of the dead. To avoid polluting the sacred elements of soil and fire, the Parsis neither bury nor cremate the body of someone who has died; rather, they place the corpse on a tower of silence, which is situated on a hilltop, out of view. Within hours vultures pick the bones clean. After several days the bones are gathered and thrown into a central well.

The Parsis are a rather closed society. Conversion to Zoroastrianism is generally not allowed, and marriages outside the faith are denounced. The Parsis are highly respected in Indian society because of their economic prosperity and great emphasis on education. They also have a reputation for being philanthropic, devoting a good share of their wealth to societal needs.

Religion in Ancient Greece

Western culture in general owes an enormous debt to ancient Greece. Democracy, drama, philosophy, and many forms of science and medicine were first developed by the ancient Greeks. In this respect ancient Greek culture is familiar to us. In the religious sphere too, along with more exotic features, are some familiar aspects. Both Judaism and Christianity developed within a cultural environment that was heavily influenced by Greek ideas. Christian theology, especially, drew a great deal directly from Greek thought.

The greatest cultural advancements were made during the period that began about 700 BC with the epic poet Homer, and ended with the death of Alexander the Great in 323 BC. The era known as the Hellenistic or classical period, from 479 BC to 323 BC, is especially noteworthy due to its great flowering of artistic and intellectual achievements. Alexander, who conquered a vast territory stretching from Greece and Egypt eastward to India, imported classical Greek culture to the entire region.

The Religious World of Homer

Sometime around the end of the eighth century BC, Homer, or perhaps two poets or even more (for simplicity's sake we refer to "Homer") composed the *Iliad* and the *Odyssey,* epic poems concerning the affairs of gods and

Ancestors of the West   185

humans in the Trojan War and its aftermath. For the next thousand years, Homer's influence was so great that he was known simply as the poet. The *Iliad* and the *Odyssey* are commonly regarded as having been the Bible of the Greeks.

The nature of the religious teachings in the work of Homer differs greatly from that of the teachings in the Jewish and Christian Bibles. The *Iliad* and the *Odyssey* do, nevertheless, contain an abundance of significant religious teachings.

The Olympian Pantheon

The most important of Homer's religious contributions is his portrayal of the Greek **pantheon,** or group of gods. The gods and goddesses inhabit the heavenly realm of Olympus (and so are called the Olympian pantheon) and form a loose-knit family. Zeus, the gatherer of clouds and bringer of storms, reigns as the father of the gods. When angered by the wrongful doings of mortals on earth, he is known to strike with thunderbolts. He has a number of consorts, including his sister and wife, Hera (marital relations between family members is common in mythology). Hera is the goddess of marriage and of women. Homer often depicted quarrels between Zeus and Hera, but the Greeks came to look upon their marriage as ideal. Zeus and Hera are the parents of Hephaestus, the god of fire, and of Ares, the god of war.

One basic feature of Homeric religion is already clear: it is polytheistic (*polytheistic* is a Greek word meaning "of many gods"). Other important deities include Poseidon, god of the ocean, and Hades, god of the underworld. Both are brothers of Zeus. Offspring of Zeus by goddesses other than Hera include Hermes, messenger god; Aphrodite, goddess of love; Apollo, god of the lyre and of the bow (among other things); and Athena, goddess of wisdom.

Along with being polytheistic, Homeric religion is notably **anthropomorphic** (*anthropomorphic* is another Greek word, meaning "of human form"). The gods have human attributes. No deity, not even Zeus, is all-powerful or all-knowing; rather, all the gods and goddesses have their own specific talents, functions, and limitations. Also, their moral behavior is much more humanlike than godlike (as we are accustomed to thinking of godlike behavior, that is). Examples of this abound. Zeus and Hera quarrel frequently. Ares and Aphrodite commit adultery. In general, the Greek gods fail to maintain consistent principles of justice, both toward one another and toward human beings.

How could gods be plagued by such human shortcomings? This problem was addressed by many innovative Greek thinkers of the classical period.[D]

Religious Innovations by the Greek Dramatists

Among the people who contributed new ideas to Homeric religion were the dramatists of fifth-century Athens. Aeschylus (about 525 to 456 BC) was especially concerned with the ideal of divine justice. Rather than focusing on the anthropomorphic characteristics of Zeus, Aeschylus celebrated Zeus's great power and wisdom. His works portray Zeus as ruling with order and justice. For example, the play *Agamemnon* explains human suffering as being a necessary part of the divine plan of Zeus:

Now Zeus is lord; and he
Who loyally acclaims his victory
Shall by heart's instinct find the universal
    key:

Zeus, whose will has marked for man
The sole way where wisdom lies;
Ordered one eternal plan:
Man must suffer to be wise.

(Lines 174–178)

Artistic depictions of some Greek gods and goddesses *(clockwise from top left):* Hermes, the messenger god, with the infant Dionysus on his arm; Apollo, the god of the lyre and of the bow, crowned with myrtle; Athena, the goddess of wisdom and defensive warfare, with her warrior's helmet; Hera, the wife of Zeus.

This ancient amphitheater at Epidaurus in Greece was the site of dramas that featured the intervention of the gods in human affairs.

This kind of direct and lofty theology is not found in Homer. The Olympian pantheon, and Zeus especially, takes on a new dignity. Zeus is no longer merely a god of tremendous power; he is now the source and the enforcer of universal moral principles. Sophocles (about 496 to 406 BC), another of the great Athenian dramatists, followed Aeschylus in celebrating the justice of Zeus and also emphasized the god's mercy.

Piety and Worship

The anthropomorphism of the Homeric deities is reflected in the way they are worshiped. As parents demand respect from their children, the gods and goddesses demand piety and proper worship. The mortals in Homer's poems are diligent in their prayers and words of praise, to which the deities respond favorably. On the other hand, the gods are quick and steadfast in punishing the impious. In the *Odyssey,* for example, the soldiers of Odysseus (also known by his Latin name, Ulysses) are all killed by Zeus for butchering and eating the sun god's cattle. Only Odysseus is spared, for resisting this impious act in spite of his great hunger.

The Greek deities, much like human beings, relish receiving gifts, especially the gift of sacrifice. Cattle, sheep, and other animals are ritually slaughtered, and the meat is cooked and offered to the gods (it is then eaten by the worshipers). Wine is poured out in libations, or acts of sacrifice. Armor and other precious items are placed in temples as gifts. All such forms of sacrificial giving are pleasing to the gods, who in turn are believed to look out for the welfare of the worshipers.

Festivals

Along with daily worship practices, lavish festivals gave the Greeks, throughout the classical period and beyond, opportunities to honor their gods. Most of those celebrations were local events, specific to each city-state. Athens, for example, worshiped its patron goddess, Athena, in an annual celebration of her birthday.

Other festivals were not limited to specific city-states but involved Greeks from across the land. One such festival developed in Olympia (a small village in southwestern Greece, not to be confused with the heavenly realm of Mount Olympus). Founded in 776 BC, the Olympic

Games were held every four years. The games endured for more than one thousand years, until the Roman emperor Theodosius I abolished them in AD 393. They were revived in their modern form in the late nineteenth century.

Like our modern version, the Olympic Games featured athletic contests such as running, wrestling, and boxing, but the festival was primarily religious. Because Theodosius was a Christian, he could not tolerate the games because of the religious focus on honoring Zeus. The games attracted the best athletes from the ancient Mediterranean world. The athletic prowess of the participants was a form of sacrificial gift, offered to Zeus through the performance of the various contests. A victorious performance was deemed an especially worthy gift. The first and final days of the five-day festival were devoted to sacrifices and ceremony. Olympia, situated in a beautiful valley among wooded hillsides, was the main sanctuary of Zeus. Temples of both Zeus and Hera occupied the area adjacent to the stadium and other sites of athletic contests.[E]

Oracles

The Greeks believed the gods communicated their desires and intentions to mortals. In Homer's poems the gods frequently converse directly with heroes such as Achilles and Odysseus. The gods also reveal their will through dreams and ominous signs, such as the clap of thunder or the flight of birds. And, according to ancient Greek belief through the centuries, the gods communicate through oracles.

An **oracle** was a sanctuary favored by a particular god, who communicated in some manner to those who visited the site. (The word *oracle* refers also to the god's message itself, or the medium through which it is communicated.) At one oracle, for example, the will of Zeus could be heard through the whispering leaves of its sacred oak grove. The most famous oracle was at Delphi, where the Greeks sought the wisdom of the god Apollo. Situated on the slopes of Mount Parnassus, high above the Gulf of Corinth, Delphi had been considered a sacred site from very early times and was thought to be the center of the earth.

The temple of Apollo stood in an elaborate complex of structures, including a theater, a stadium, and a number of treasury buildings owned by the various city-states throughout Greece. The god communicated through the Pythia, a woman who sat on a tripod within the temple. The Pythia breathed in vapors that arose from the earth and brought on an ecstatic state, and may also have ingested bay leaves or some other intoxicating plant material. In her state of ecstasy, she uttered the will of Apollo in speech that was intelligible only

E
Today's emphasis on sports makes athletes into heroes and awards them with fan adoration and large sums of money. Some scholars of religion have even suggested that sports are a religious phenomenon. Discuss the similarities between sports and religion that might have led to this suggestion.

IMAGE: © SHELDAN COLLINS/CORBIS

Ruins of the temple of Apollo, where the oracle of Delphi sat and made her prophecies.

to the oracle's priests. They, in turn, translated her utterances into Greek.

The oracle at Delphi was consulted on issues ranging from private matters to far-reaching public concerns. Major political and military decisions were sometimes based on its revelation of the god's will. Apollo was considered to favor philosophy, and he was credited with pronouncing at Delphi the influential Greek sayings "Know thyself" and "Nothing to excess"; both were engraved on the temple. The oracle also proclaimed the philosopher Socrates to be the wisest of all people.

Like the Olympic Games, the oracle at Delphi endured for centuries. It too was abolished by Emperor Theodosius I, in about AD 390. But by then the voice of Apollo had almost been silenced. The oracle had announced its own decline a short time before.[F]

F

Suppose you were to travel back through time to ancient Greece and visit the oracle at Delphi. What question would you ask? Given your modern perspective, what concerns would you have regarding the oracle's accuracy?

Homer's Perspective on Death and the Afterlife

Homer also set forth a view of death and the afterlife. When a person dies in the *Iliad* and the *Odyssey,* the soul departs from the body, entering the dark and dreary underworld ruled by the god Hades and his queen, Persephone (puhr-se'fo-nee). The House of Hades, through which flows the River Styx, offers little hope for happiness. The souls, or "shades," lack physical substance and strength, and yet remember their earthly lives with regret and longing.

In the *Odyssey* Odysseus journeys to the realm of Hades to consult a famous seer, now dead. While there he encounters the shades of his fallen comrades. His conversation with his friend Achilles, the greatest of all Greek warriors, leaves no doubt as to the gloominess of the afterlife envisioned by Homer:

"But you, Achilles,
there's not a man in the world more blest
    than you—
there never has been, never will be one.
Time was, when you were alive, we Argives
honored you as a god, and now down here,
    I see,
you lord it over the dead in all your power.
So grieve no more at dying, great Achilles."

I reassured the ghost, but he broke out,
    protesting,
"No winning words about death to *me*,
    shining Odysseus!
By god, I'd rather slave on earth for another
    man—
some dirt-poor tenant farmer who scrapes to
    keep alive—
than rule down here over all the breathless
    dead."

(Book 11, lines 548–559; quoted in Fagles, translator, *The Odyssey,* page 265)

The Homeric conception of the afterlife left little room for optimism in the face of death. Homer makes brief mention of a paradise, the Elysian fields, but he identifies only one mortal, King Menelaus, who is destined to go there after death. For the Greeks of Homer's time, the emphasis was clearly on living a good and honorable life, not on the prospects of a happy afterlife.

Alternatives to Homer: The Mystery Religions

Homer's influence on Greek religion was great, but he did not tell the entire story. Other forms of religion, some already gaining popularity by Homer's time, also flourished. Deities such as Demeter and Dionysus, who are barely mentioned in Homer's poems, rivaled the other gods in popularity. Such deities were worshiped in a diverse group of beliefs and practices that are now referred to as the **mystery religions.**

The word *mystery* is derived from a Greek term meaning "to cover," and the initiates of these religions did an extraordinary job of keeping their secrets under wraps. As a result we know very little about the actual rites. It is clear, however, that the mysteries included three basic aspects:

1. Individuals had to choose to become initiates, and they went through some form of initiation ritual.
2. Initiates experienced a personal encounter with the deity.
3. Initiates gained spiritual renewal through participation in the religion and, as with most mystery religions, hope for a better afterlife.

The mystery religions therefore offered important alternatives to the Homeric religion, especially to its dreary prospects for the afterlife in the dark realm of Hades.

The great and long-lived popularity of the mystery religions, together with the joyous pageantry of the days surrounding their initiation rites, bear witness to their power for enhancing the lives of those who followed them. Various mystery religions would play a central role in the religious life of Rome. Indeed for people of the ancient Roman world, Christianity must have appeared to be something like a mystery religion, offering a community of initiates, a deeply personal relationship with Christ, and hopes for spiritual renewal and a blessed afterlife.

The Eleusinian Mysteries

The mystery religion par excellence, celebrated at Eleusis, near Athens, honored the grain goddess Demeter and her daughter, Persephone. Along with being very popular for centuries, the Eleusinian mysteries set forth a basic form that influenced the development of later mystery religions in the Roman world.

Mystery religions were typically based on a myth celebrating the theme of new life arising from death. The myth of Demeter and Persephone goes as follows: One day Persephone was gathering flowers in a meadow. Hades sprang from beneath the earth and took her away with him to his dark, subterranean realm. Demeter searched everywhere but could not find her beloved daughter. In her grief and anger, Demeter prevented crops from growing on the land. The famine grew so quickly that humanity was threatened. Zeus feared that his worshipers would all perish, so he sent Hermes to the underworld to order Hades to let Persephone go. Hades did as he was told, but as Persephone was leaving, he gave her a taste of pomegranate, a fruit symbolic of marriage. Persephone and her mother were joyfully reunited, and the goddess made the crops grow abundantly. But because Persephone had eaten of the pomegranate, Zeus forced her to spend one-third of every year in the underworld as Hades's wife; the rest of the year she could be with her mother.

This myth clearly correlates with the agricultural cycle. For the four months that Persephone is in the underworld, the fields lie dormant. When she returns to earth, new life is born and flourishes for the duration of her eight-month stay. The initiates of the Eleusinian mysteries experienced a similar sort of new life. Through their initiation rites, they enjoyed spiritual renewal, along with the hope of a blessed afterlife, because they had gained the favor of Persephone, queen of the underworld.[G]

The Cult of Dionysus

Another popular mystery religion, especially among women, was devoted to Dionysus,

In a typical scene showing Dionysian worship, a woman devotee is followed by two satyrs, mythic beings of the wilderness, and by a panther, the animal consort of the god.

G

The theme of life arising from death, celebrated in classic fashion by the Eleusinian myth of Demeter and Persephone, is universal. It is being expressed all around us, sometimes in myth and other literary and artistic forms, sometimes in nature, and sometimes even within our own personal and social worlds. Think of three ways you have seen this theme expressed. Briefly describe each.

a god of fertility, vegetation, and specifically the vine (and hence wine). Dionysus is often depicted in Greek art with vines and grapes, and there are accounts of him miraculously turning water into wine.

Worship of Dionysus usually occurred in the remote countryside, among the wild vegetation of the hills and mountains. As in other mystery religions, it aimed at attaining union with the deity. Its goal was primarily accomplished through ritual drinking of wine and eating of animal flesh, in which the god was believed to reside.

Worship of Dionysus was often untamed, ecstatic, and, at its extreme, frenzied. Devotion to Dionysus also played a role in a tamer religious worldview, Orphism.

Orphism: Freeing the Soul from the Body

Orphism is named for the legendary Orpheus, famous in Greek mythology as a gifted musician and singer. According to the Orphics, Dionysus, the son of Zeus, was eaten by the evil Titans. In anger Zeus struck the Titans with his thunderbolts, burning them to death. From their ashes the first human beings were born.

The Greek philosopher Plato (about 428 to 347 BC) embraced the Orphic notion of the body and the soul as two distinct realms of human nature.

IMAGE: © GIANNI DAGLI ORTI/CORBIS

For the Orphics this myth established that humans possess a dual nature: the evil, bodily, Titanic aspect, and the good, spiritual, Dionysian aspect. The body, the Orphics believed, is the tomb of the soul (expressed in Greek as *soma sema* [soh´mah say´mah], "body [is] tomb"). The religious task of Orphism was to lead a pure life, through vegetarianism and other ascetic practices, so that the soul might eventually escape the body and fully realize its divine, Dionysian nature. This task was thought to take many lifetimes; the Orphics believed in reincarnation of the soul. (We do not know whether these ancient Greeks were influenced by the Hindu doctrine of reincarnation.)

Orphic Influence on Plato

Orphism remained an important part of Greek religion for centuries. Its influence on the intellectual history of Western civilization is still being felt, for the great philosopher Plato adopted some of its primary beliefs.

Though reincarnation, or the transmigration of souls, has never become a widely popular belief in the West, it was an important part of Plato's philosophy, closely related to his theory of knowledge. Plato believed that we know things in this life partly because we have experienced them in previous lives. Knowledge, therefore, is *recollection.*

Plato also embraced the Orphic notion of the dual makeup of human nature: body and soul (or mind). According to Plato, truth exists independently of any bodily, or material, evidence, consisting of Forms, or Ideas, which are eternal and perfect. Wisdom lies in identifying oneself with the truth of the Forms, rather than with the changing and imperfect material world. The influence of this **Platonic dualism** can be observed even today. For example, it can be seen in Christianity because important early Christian theologians were well educated in the philosophy of Plato and incorporated his dualism of mind and body into their understanding of Christianity. The great theologian Saint Augustine of Hippo was first attracted to Christianity largely because of its similarities to Platonic philosophy.[H]

The Healing Cult of Asclepius

The ancient Greeks commonly turned to religion for healing from sickness or injury. This was the special domain of Asclepius (a-sklee'pee-uhs). Homer described Asclepius as an able, yet mortal, physician, but the Greeks came to regard him as a god. He was thought to be the son of the god Apollo, who also was revered for his healing powers. Hygeia, the daughter of Asclepius, was closely associated with him. Her name means "health," and it is the root of the word *hygiene.*

The cult of Asclepius was very popular. In fact, for a time Asclepius was one of the most popular of all Greek deities. Unlike the gods of the Olympian pantheon, Asclepius offered the joy of a close relationship between worshiper and god. Like any good doctor, Asclepius cared dearly for every individual who sought his aid.

Asclepius was believed to have tremendous powers of healing, and according to the mythic account of his life, he even had the ability to bring the dead back to life. The great sanctuaries in which he was worshiped were really ancient health spas, where strict diets were enforced, and baths, gyms, and theaters were available for physical and recreational activities. Most of the actual healing occurred while the patient lay in a sacred chamber sleeping, when Asclepius was thought to visit in a dream and administer a cure. Patients commonly left offerings to the god, sometimes in the form of replicas of ailing body parts.

When people of the ancient Mediterranean world first heard about Christianity, Jesus seemed to have much in common with the ancient healer Asclepius. Both were called Savior, and the intimacy of the worshipers' relationship with Asclepius bore a strong resemblance to the relationship with Christ celebrated by Christians.[I]

Religion in the Roman World

Our word *religion* is derived from the Latin word *religio.* The two terms do not mean the same thing, however. In ancient Roman usage, *religio* referred to the ensuring of divine favor through scrupulous observance of ritual. Roman religion was based on the notion that life is enhanced through bonding with the divine powers inhabiting the world. All Romans, no matter their social status, strove to improve their lives through *religio.*

The major features of Roman religion as they were known in later centuries seem to have been in place from at least the time of the founding of the Roman Republic in 509 BC, and they endured the fourth century AD. Over time Roman religion was influenced by the Greek religion. Like the Greeks of Homer's time, the early Romans did not have reason to hope for a blessed afterlife. Their religion was oriented toward achieving things in this world. But the Romans eventually sought more from religion. Such alternatives as the mystery religions became popular throughout the Roman Empire.

Numina: Supernatural Powers

The Roman gods and goddesses eventually took on many characteristics of their Greek counterparts, but in early times they seem to have differed from those Olympian deities. The Romans tended not think of their gods in human terms, as Homer had done; rather, they defined their gods vaguely. For example, Venus, who later became famous as the goddess of love (and was identified with the Greek goddess Aphrodite), was not originally assigned a gender.

H

The influence of Plato, especially of his dualism of body and soul (or mind), is deeply ingrained in Christian thought, and in Western culture generally. Reflect on Plato's notion of the body as being distinct from the mind. Do you tend to look at yourself as Plato would have? Do you think this is necessarily the correct perspective? Why or why not?

I

Ancient societies normally viewed the healing of the body as a religious concern. In primal cultures healings were (and sometimes still are) typically performed by a witch doctor, medicine man or woman, shaman, or other religious figure. Do you think modern Western society treats the healing of the body as a religious concern?

Songs for the Gods

Aelius Aristides was an accomplished public speaker and writer of Greek literature who lived in the second century AD. He was frequently ill, so he spent many of his days at the Asclepium—the healing sanctuary of the god Asclepius—at Pergamum, a city in Asia Minor (modern-day Turkey). His Sacred Tales *record the events surrounding his many bouts with illness, especially the constant care he received from Asclepius, the god of healing. According to the* Sacred Tales, *Asclepius appeared often to Aristides, usually in dreams. In those revelations the god would prescribe methods of curing whatever ailed Aristides.*

Along with providing important evidence regarding medical practices in antiquity, the Sacred Tales *offer elaborate and personal accounts of religious experience in ancient Greece and Rome. In this passage Aristides gives something of an introduction to his* Sacred Tales, *which he wrote as an expression of gratitude to "the God," Asclepius:*

To narrate what came next is not within the power of man. Still I must try, as I have undertaken to recount some of these things in a cursory way. But if someone wishes to know with the utmost precision what has befallen us from the God, it is time for him to seek out the parchment books and the dreams themselves. For he will find cures of all kinds and some discourses and full scale orations and various visions, and all of the prophecies and oracles about every kind of matter, some in prose, some in verse, and all expressive of my gratitude to the God, greater than one might expect. (Quoted in Behr, *Aelius Aristides and the Sacred Tales,* page 224)

Aristides asserts that Asclepius himself approved the project by naming the writings the Sacred Tales, *and then goes on to recall what he refers to as "strange events"—his dream visions of Asclepius and miraculous healings of various types. Aristides also credits Asclepius, along with other gods, for having inspired him to produce hymns. The follow-*

ing passage makes clear the polytheistic nature of Aristides's religion, which was typical of the ancient West:

Tale follows tale, and let us say again that along with other things, Asclepius, the Savior, also commanded us to spend time on songs and lyric verse, and to relax and maintain a chorus of boys. . . . The children sang my songs; and whenever I happened to choke, if my throat were suddenly constricted, or my stomach became disordered, or whenever I had some other troublesome attack, the doctor Theodotus, being in attendance and remembering my dreams, would order the boys to sing some of my lyric verse. And while they were singing, there arose unnoticed a feeling of comfort, and sometimes everything which pained me went completely away.

And this was a very great gain, and the honor was still greater than this, for my lyric verse also found favor with the God. He ordered me to compose not only for him, but also indicated others, as Pan, Hecate, Achelous, and whatever else it might be. There also came a dream from Athena, which contained a hymn to the Goddess. . . .

And another dream came from Zeus, but I cannot remember which of these was first or second, and another again from Dionysus, which said to address the God, as "curly haired."

And Hermes was also seen with his dog skin cap, and he was marvellously beautiful and extraordinarily mobile. And while I was singing of him and feeling pleased that I had easily said the proper things, I awoke. . . .

But most things were written for Apollo and Asclepius through the inspiration of my dreams, and many of these nearly from memory, as whenever I was riding in a carriage, or even was walking.

(Pages 261–262)

The deities belonged to a larger category known as **numina** (n*oo*′men-uh). The *numina* were supernatural powers, each in charge of a specific function. These powers were thought to populate Roman homes, towns, and the countryside, and to inhabit a wide variety of spaces, such as fields, streams, trees, doorways, altars, and shrines. The gods possessed **numen** (n*oo*′men), or supernatural power, in great abundance. By securing the favor of the gods through *religio*, Romans could hope to benefit from this divine power.

The Roman Pantheon

The most powerful of all Roman deities was Jupiter (also known as Jove), the sky god. Jupiter was one of a triad of deities that also included Juno, the goddess who looked after women, and Minerva, goddess of handicrafts. Vesta, goddess of the hearth, and Janus, god of doorways, were especially venerated within the home. Because he presided over the crossing of the threshold, Janus came to be associated in general with beginnings. That is why the first month of the year is named January.

Once the Romans had come under the influence of Greek culture (especially during Roman conquests of Greek territory in the second century BC), their pantheon quickly took on the characteristics Homer had conveyed about the Olympians. Most of Rome's important deities became identified with Greek counterparts: Jupiter with Zeus, Juno with Hera, Minerva with Athena, Venus with Aphrodite, and so on.

In many ways the Roman pantheon is more familiar to the modern world than the Greek. For example, the names of six of the eight planets in our solar system are derived from Roman deities. In addition to Jupiter and Venus, there are Mars, god of war (identified with the Greek god Ares); Neptune, god of the sea (identified with Poseidon); Mercury, god of traders (identified with Hermes, the messenger god); and Saturn, god of sowing (identified with Cronos, father of Zeus).

Greek influence can also be seen in the adoption into the Roman pantheon of some Greek gods, such as Apollo and Asclepius (called Aesculapius in Latin). Another Greek religious figure the Romans worshiped extensively was Heracles, the great hero known to the Romans as Hercules. He was especially popular among merchants because of his success at making long journeys through perilous lands.

IMAGE: TOP: RÉUNION DES MUSÉES NATIONAUX/ART RESOURCE, NY; BOTTOM, © GIANNI DAGLI ORTI/CORBIS

This first-century statue of the Roman god Jupiter throwing thunderbolts *(top)* is strikingly similar to one of Zeus crafted six centuries earlier *(bottom).*

Proper worship of the gods was thought to ensure *pax decorum*, "The peace of the gods." *Pax decorum*, in turn, was believed to help ensure the welfare of the Roman state, which thus maintained official worship practices. The state assigned priests for various religious duties. The priests were highly respected and deeply devoted. They were kept very busy attending to their tasks, because the gods were worshiped regularly and with utmost precision. By the later centuries of the Roman period, more than one hundred official ceremonies are known to have occurred each year, sometimes accompanied by large public festivals, other times carried out by the assigned priest in solitude.

A Multicultural World: Mystery Religions of Rome

J

The initiates of the mystery religions were forbidden to reveal the secrets of their rites. Apuleius's description of Lucius's moments within the inner sanctuary is therefore especially intriguing to specialists attempting to discover the secrets of the cult of Isis. You have read about the Greek and Roman mysteries, as well as Apuleius's brief—and intentionally sketchy— account of the rites of the inner sanctuary. Now come up with your own description of the rites. Include the elements described by Apuleius, but add details you think Apuleius may have left out. Use your imagination!

By the end of the first century BC, Rome had conquered most of the regions surrounding the Mediterranean Sea. As a result, it imported many cultures, each with its own religious forms. Most Romans freely adopted foreign ideas and practices. Mystery religions became especially popular. Along with the Greek mysteries, important new religions from Egypt, Syria, and Asia Minor gained widespread popularity. By the middle of the first century AD, another new religion, this one from Palestine, had begun to attract followers. For the next three centuries, Christianity would vie with the mystery religions for the religious allegiance of the Roman populace.

The mystery religions had a universal appeal. Though the Eleusinian mysteries were located in a specific place, most mystery religions could be celebrated locally. It was also perfectly common to be an initiate of more than one mystery religion, and most of the religions welcomed members of any social class, ethnic background, or gender. One religion that did not embrace this inclusiveness was Mithraism—the favored cult of the Roman army—which allowed only men. In spite of

that restriction, Mithraism had an enormous following and was one of the two main rivals of Christianity in the later Roman Empire. The other rival was the mystery religion celebrating the goddess Isis.

Goddess of Many Names: The Cult of Isis

The cult of Isis drew from an ancient Egyptian tradition about the goddess Isis and her husband, Osiris. According to the myth, Osiris was killed and hacked into pieces by his evil brother. Isis searched far and wide, finally finding Osiris's body parts. She mummified him, which brought him back to life. Osiris became god of the underworld.

The theme of life overcoming death through the power of Isis was central to the goddess's cult. Osiris's powerful position as god of the underworld likewise contributed. A blessed afterlife was one of the rewards the worshipers of Isis and Osiris anticipated.

Many aspects of the cult of Isis were preserved in a delightful novel from the second century AD called *The Metamorphoses* (also known as *The Golden Ass*), by Apuleius, himself apparently an initiate of the cult. The hero of the story, Lucius, is magically transformed into an ass, only to be changed back into a human through his devotion to Isis. The novel contains a long and detailed description of the ceremony associated with initiation into the religion. Most crucially, its author has Lucius describe the moments within the inner sanctuary of the temple of Isis:

I approached the confines of death. I trod the threshold of [Persephone]; and borne through the elements I returned. At midnight I saw the Sun shining in all his glory. I approached the gods below and the gods above, and I stood beside them, and I worshiped them. (Quoted in *The Ancient Mysteries,* page 158)

Whatever we are to make of Lucius's being "borne through the elements," it is clear that the initiation rite leads to his "rebirth" (as his transformation is described later in the novel) after a ritual death. Life is renewed and enhanced through the symbolic overcoming of death. This theme is common to all the mystery religions of ancient Greece and Rome.

The cult of Isis seems to have influenced Christian veneration of the Virgin Mary. The ancient Romans recognized important similarities between those two women. Artistic representations of Isis holding her son Horus are very similar to those of Mary with the infant Jesus.[J]

Emperor Worship

The mystery religions influenced the development of Christianity because of the characteristics they had in common with it. Emperor worship influenced Christianity because of the violent persecution that sometimes resulted when the Christians refused to participate in it.

Like so many facets of Roman religion, emperor worship had its roots in Greece and other nations in the ancient Mediterranean world. For instance, when Alexander the Great conquered the lands of Egypt and Persia, he was worshiped as a god by their inhabitants.

Among the Romans, leaders such as Julius Caesar flirted with the idea of being worshiped; some, such as Caligula, Nero, and Domitian, openly declared their divinity. Emperor Augustus (who reigned from 31 BC to AD 14), though, established a pattern that most of the later emperors were to follow. He encouraged the worship not of himself, but of his genius, or guardian spirit. This actually focused worship on Rome, because the emperor's genius was thought to guard the welfare of the entire state.

This notion of worshiping the Roman state was addressed in a fascinating written correspondence from the early second century AD between the emperor Trajan and Pliny the Younger, who served as a governor under the emperor Trajan. To settle a local dispute,

Pliny needed to know who among the populace was Christian. Whoever consented to worshiping the emperor in the proper manner, Pliny wrote, could not have been Christian:

Those who denied they were, or had ever been, Christians, who repeated after me an invocation to the gods, and offered adoration, with wine and frankincense, to your image, which I had ordered to be brought for that purpose, together with those of the gods, and who finally cursed Christ—none of which acts, it is said, those who are really Christians can be forced into performing—these I thought it proper to discharge. . . . They all worshipped your statue and the images of the gods, and cursed Christ. (Quoted in Kee, *The New Testament in Context,* page 44)

The Christians had obvious reasons for refusing to worship on behalf of the emperor; to do so would have contradicted their belief in only one God. The Romans, on the other hand, grew suspicious of the Christians because their refusal to worship on behalf of the emperor implied that they did not support the state. Under such circumstances it was inevitable that conflicts would arise.[K]

K
Roman worship of the genius of the emperor was really a means of expressing one's devotion to the state. In other words it was a form of patriotism. What forms of "emperor worship" do we practice today? Would you label such forms of devotion "religious"?

The Egyptian goddess Isis suckling the infant Horus.

IMAGE: RÉUNION DES MUSÉES NATIONAUX/ART RESOURCE, NY

197

Legacies from Ancient Times

In this chapter we have glimpsed many ideas and beliefs that appear strange, and many others that appear familiar. In the religions of Greece and Rome, especially, the strangeness is striking. Belief in numerous gods, many of them of questionable moral fiber; a tendency to regard religion as a means of attaining things in this world; and the likelihood that an individual would embrace more than one religion—all these features probably strike the modern Westerner as being rather odd. And yet the similarities between these traditions, born of influences passed from one to another, are equally striking. Such is the normal effect of the historical process: bits and pieces from the past are carried along, sometimes all the way from ancient times to the modern age.

We do not need to limit ourselves to a consideration of Western religions when pondering the extent of influence exercised by the religions of ancient Iran, Greece, and Rome. For instance, we can look beyond Western religions to find that Zoroastrian doctrines concerning saviors helped shape the Mahayana Buddhist pantheon of *bodhisattvas*. Nor do we need to limit ourselves to a consideration of influence in order to find meaning in a study of the ancient world. Indeed we can find as much meaning in the aspects that remain unique to that world as in the aspects it has passed along to our world, for those strange ways were the innovations of the minds and hearts of human beings, our worthy ancestors.

Chapter Review

1. When and where did Zoroastrianism begin to flourish?
2. How did Zoroastrianism spread beyond its place of origin?
3. Briefly describe the religious experience Zarathustra had at about age thirty.
4. Name the sacred text of Zoroastrianism. What is the oldest material in this text, and who wrote it?
5. Summarize the characteristics and actions associated with Ahura Mazda.
6. What is ethical dualism?
7. What is the Lie, and how does it relate to Ahura Mazda?
8. What must humans choose between in the Zoroastrian cosmic scheme?
9. Summarize Zarathustra's understanding of human destiny.

The Seven Dimensions of Religion: Ancestors of the West

Dimension	Examples
Experiential	Pythia's state of ecstasy at the oracle at Delphi, an initiate's personal encounter with the deity of a mystery religion (such as Lucius's moments within the inner sanctuary of Isis, as described by Apuleius)
Mythic	origins and doings of the Olympian pantheon, the myth of Demeter and Persephone
Doctrinal	Zoroastrian monotheism and ethical dualism, Platonic dualism
Ethical	Zoroastrian individual choice between truth and the Lie, the pure lifestyle of Orphism
Ritual	the Zoroastrian fire ritual, the Olympian Games, rites of initiation into mystery religions
Social	the Parsis within Indian society, political and social aspects of Roman emperor worship
Material	the Zoroastrian fire and tower of silence, sanctuaries like Olympia and Delphi

10. What are the general ethical demands of traditional Zoroastrian life?

11. Who are the Parsis, and where do most of them live today?

12. What are commonly regarded as having been the Bible of the ancient Greeks?

13. Explain the meaning of this sentence: The gods of the Olympian pantheon are anthropomorphic.

14. What was Aeschylus's main contribution to the understanding of the gods of the Olympian pantheon? Give an example.

15. What is an oracle? What is the most famous oracle of ancient Greece, and why was it consulted?

16. Briefly identify the three basic aspects of the mystery religions.

17. What mystery religion honored Demeter and Persephone?

18. What is the god Dionysus associated with, and how is he often depicted in Greek art?

19. Name the goal of the ascetic practices of the Orphics.

20. What is Plato's theory of knowledge?

21. What is Platonic dualism?

22. Why did Jesus seem to have much in common with the ancient Asclepius?

23. What were *numina,* and what sorts of things were they thought to inhabit?

24. Who was the most powerful Roman deity?

25. Identify the six planets of our solar system that are named after Roman deities.

26. Why did the Roman state consider it essential to maintain official worship practices?

27. Which mystery religions were the main rivals of Christianity in the later Roman Empire?

28. Briefly summarize the Egyptian myth of Isis and Osiris.

29. Briefly describe the sort of emperor worship encouraged by Augustus.

30. Why did Christians and Roman rulers clash over emperor worship?

Glossary

Ahura Mazda (ah´hoo-reh maz´dah). The Wise Lord, the one true God worshiped by Zarathustra and later by Zoroastrians.

anthropomorphic. Of human form, characteristic of the deities of ancient Greek and later Roman religion.

Avesta (a-ves´tuh). The sacred text of Zoroastrianism, which includes the very old hymns known as the Gathas, along with more recent material.

ethical dualism. The belief in universal forces of good and evil; Zoroastrianism's most distinctive feature.

Gathas (gah´thuhs). Seventeen hymns attributed to Zarathustra that constitute the oldest and most important portion of the Avesta.

mystery religions. A diverse group of beliefs and practices of ancient Greek and Roman civilization that included initiation into a specific community, a personal encounter with the deity, and hope for spiritual renewal and a better afterlife.

numen (noo´men). The ancient Roman concept of supernatural power, possessed in abundance by the gods; also believed to inhabit a wide variety of things and places, as well as human beings.

numina (noo´men-uh). Plural of *numen.* The supernatural powers that were the ancient Roman equivalent of deities.

oracle. A shrine or sanctuary at which the revelations of a god are received, often through a human medium; also, the medium or the revelation itself.

Orphism. An ancient Greek religion named for the legendary musician and singer Orpheus, which incorporated a myth of Dionysus, emphasized an ascetic lifestyle, and included belief in reincarnation, or the transmigration of the soul.

pantheon. A group of deities recognized by a society, such as the Olympian pantheon of the ancient Greeks.

Platonic dualism. Plato's highly influential perspective that true reality consists of eternal and perfect Forms, or Ideas, and that the material, bodily world is an imperfect reflection of the world of Forms, dependent on them for all its qualities.

KINGDOMS OF ISRAEL AND JUDAH, ABOUT 900 B.C.

Zobah

The Great Sea
(Mediterranean Sea)

Sidon
Damascus •
Phoenicia
Tyre •

Sea of
Chinnereth
**ARAM
(SYRIA)**

Yarmuk

Mount Carmel ▲
Megiddo • **ISRAEL**
Ramoth Gilead •
Mount Gilboa ▲

Samaria •
Succoth •

Joppa • Shiloh •
Jordan

Philistia Mizpah • Bethel

Azekah • **Jerusalem**

Gaza • Bethlehem •
Ammon

Hebron •

Beersheba • *Dead*
Sea

Zoar • **Moab**

Kadesh Barnea • Bozrah •

Teman • **Edom**

JUDAH

Ezion Geber •
Brook of Egypt
Elath •

Nile

S I N A I

EGYPT

A R A B I A

Red Sea

▢ Probable extent of Israelite control during
the Kingdom of Solomon, about 950 B.C.

▢ Kingdoms of Israel and Judah,
about 860 B.C.

--- Boundary between Israel and Judah

MAP: © 2003, SAINT MARY'S PRESS

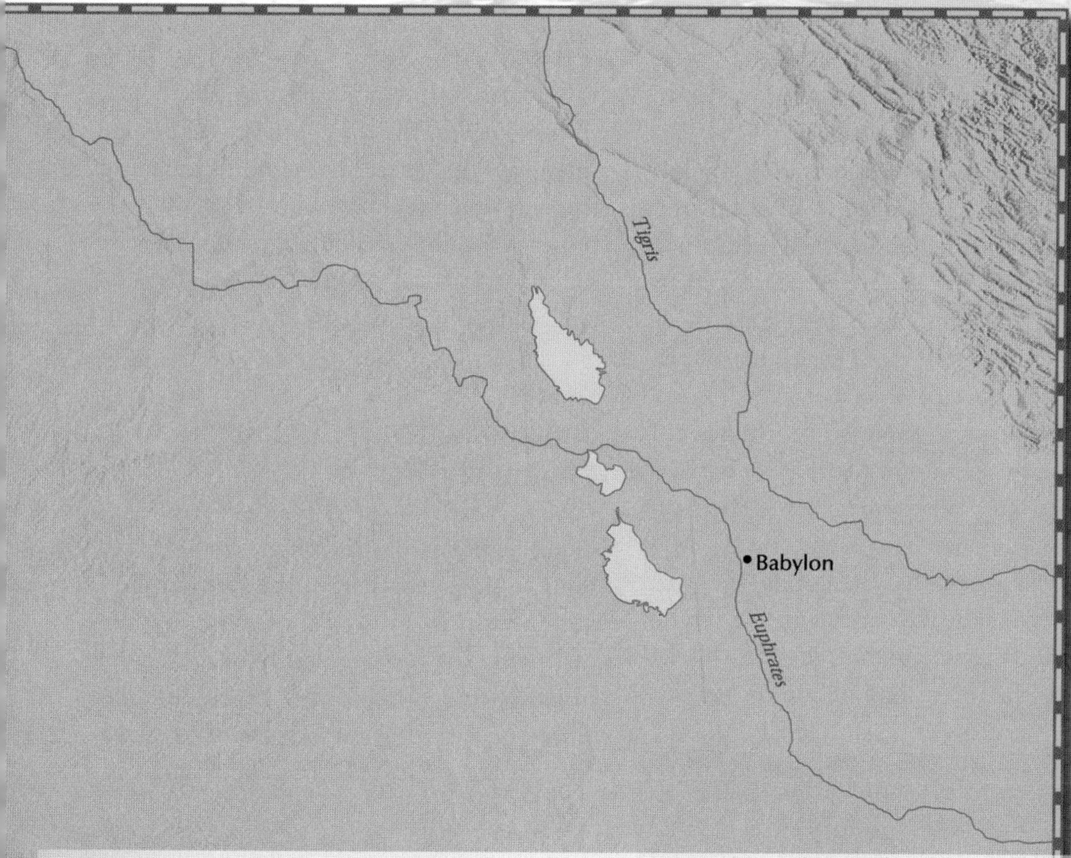

Tigris

Euphrates

• Babylon

12 Judaism

The People of the Covenant

Judaism is not only the adherence to particular doctrines and observances, but primarily living in the spiritual order of the Jewish people, the living *in* the Jews of the past and *with* the Jews of the present. . . . It is not a doctrine, an idea, a faith, but the covenant between God and the people. (Heschel, *Man's Quest for God,* page 45)

The Jewish religion can be summarized in several ways. Abraham Joshua Heschel, a renowned Jewish holy man of the twentieth century, refers to Judaism as "the covenant between God and the people." Heschel emphasizes the role of the Jewish people, both past and present.

The **Covenant** is an agreement established long ago between God and the ancient Israelites, first through Abraham and later through Moses. God spoke to Moses on Mount Sinai, promising that if the Israelites would keep the Covenant by obeying the Law (or Torah), they would be God's "treasured possession," and "a kingdom of priests and a holy nation" (Exodus 19:5–6, Tanakh).

Because of the Covenant, the Jews are understood to be God's Chosen People, a status that carries serious responsibilities. Moreover, they are forever challenged to live as befits a "holy nation," or a good and righteous people. The Covenant is between God and the people; thus Judaism places great emphasis on group identity. In modern times this emphasis has given rise to new challenges, for not all Jews are adherents of the religion Judaism. It is therefore necessary to distinguish between "religious" (or "observant") Jews, and "cultural" (or "nonobservant") Jews.

Heschel remarks that Judaism is "the living *in* the Jews of the past and *with* the Jews of the present." These notions refer to two related ways of summarizing Judaism. First, Judaism is the interpretation of the history of the Jewish people, "the Jews of the past." Second, Judaism is the sanctification of life, the means through which Jews live with "the Jews of the present." Behind each of these summary statements are Judaism's central teachings on God and on the divine revelation.

Judaism's Central Teachings: On God and Torah

God's revelation of the divine will to the Chosen People is recorded in the Hebrew Bible and in writings of rabbis from the first centuries after the Romans destroyed the Temple in Jerusalem (AD 70). This revelation, called Torah (toh´rah), is understood through the framework of Jewish teachings regarding God.

Master of the Universe: Judaism's God

Observant Jews venerate their God so deeply and constantly that they avoid pronouncing the divine name—considering it too holy to be spoken by human beings. The name is written, however, and appears in the Hebrew equivalents of the letters *YHWH*. (Hebrew had no vowels.) This name is pronounced (though not by observant Jews) as Yahweh (yah´way). When observant Jews come across the name while reading the Bible, they say "the Lord" instead of pronouncing the actual name. Often God is referred to by other phrases too, the most common being "Master of the Universe."

God has a personal name, and God is thought to be a personal being, intimately involved in the welfare of humans and the rest of the created world. But God is also transcendent of creation, and is infinitely powerful, all-knowing, and beyond the limits of space and time. And God is believed to be the one and only God. Judaism's most basic theologi-

Detail from Marc Chagall's painting *Moses Receives the Tablets of the Law*.

cal statement, called the **Shema** (shuh-mah´; Hebrew for "hear"), declares the uniqueness of God: "Hear, O Israel! The LORD is our God, the LORD alone" (Deuteronomy 6:4, Tanakh). The Shema is recited at least twice daily, in morning and evening prayers.

This basic declaration of God's uniqueness may sound obvious or commonplace today. But when it was first formulated, Israel's neighbors were all polytheists, and the Shema was a radical statement. Monotheism itself was a radical religious development, marking one of Judaism's major contributions to Western civilization.

Torah: Revelation of God's Will

Torah is among the most important terms in Judaism. It literally means "instruction" and refers to the will of God as it is revealed to humankind. It is also loosely translated as "law"; on a practical level, the revelation of God's will sets forth the Law, which guides proper human conduct. Finally, in a more specific—and more common—usage, *Torah* refers to the first five books of the Bible, which are traditionally believed to have been revealed directly by God to Moses. The five books of the Torah are the primary statement of the religious laws of Judaism.

In its more general sense, as revelation, Torah is presented in several ways, each one the extension of another. With God in the center, the divine will is revealed outward in a series of concentric circles, like the rings of a tree trunk. The first ring consists of the "written Torah," the word of God contained in the Hebrew Bible.[A]

The Written Torah: The Hebrew Bible

The Hebrew Bible contains three major parts: the Torah, the Prophets, and the Writings. In Hebrew these words are *Torah, Nevi'im,* and *Ketuvim* and begin with the letters *T, N,* and *K,* respectively. The Bible itself is sometimes referred to as the **Tanakh** (tahnakh; from *T-N-K*).

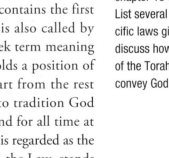

Each synagogue has an ark, which contains a scroll of the Torah, the first five books of the Bible.

The contents of the Hebrew Bible are also found in the Christian Old Testament, but the books are named and ordered somewhat differently. Of course, for Judaism the Tanakh is in no sense an "Old Testament." Nothing new has ever superseded it, and it remains the vital foundation of Jewish understanding.

The Torah. The Torah contains the first five books of the Bible. It is also called by the name *Pentateuch,* a Greek term meaning "five books." The Torah holds a position of prominence that sets it apart from the rest of the Tanakh. According to tradition God revealed its contents once and for all time at Mount Sinai to Moses, who is regarded as the Torah's author. The Torah, the Law, stands forever as Judaism's central code of holiness. It is thought to contain 613 specific laws, the most famous being the Ten Commandments, which are set forth in the Book of Exodus, chapter 20. Every synagogue (building for

A
The term *Torah* has three meanings: "God's revelation (instruction)," "the Law," and the "first five books of the Bible." One of the books of the Torah is Leviticus. Read chapter 19 of Leviticus. List several of the specific laws given. Then discuss how those laws of the Torah might also convey God's revelation.

Jewish worship) contains a scroll of the entire Torah, kept in a vessel called an ark.

The Prophets. The Prophets comprises books that include both historical accounts of ancient Israel and proclamations of the will of God spoken by those called to serve as God's mouthpieces. The Greek term *prophet* literally means "one who speaks for."

The Hebrew prophets who spoke for God are among the world's most striking religious figures. With charisma and courage, they attempted to keep Israel on its religious course through times of severe difficulty.

The prophet is called to speak for God, a role that is illustrated clearly at the beginning of the Book of Jeremiah. Jeremiah was one of the most important prophets.

> The word of the Lord came to me:
> Before I created you in the womb,
>   I selected you;
> Before you were born, I consecrated you;
> I appointed you a prophet concerning
>   the nations.
>
> (Jeremiah 1:4–5, Tanakh)

Jeremiah protests, insisting that he, a mere boy, is not capable of speaking for God. But God assures Jeremiah that he will succeed, promising to be with him. Then comes the central moment:

> The LORD put out His hand and touched my mouth, and the Lord said to me: Herewith I put My words into your mouth. (Jeremiah 1:9, Tanakh)[B]

The Writings. The books that constitute the Writings are highly diverse in both content and literary form. With the poetry of the Psalms, the wisdom literature of Proverbs and Ecclesiastes, the short stories of Esther and Ruth, and the historical accounts of the Chronicles, just to name some examples, the Writings contribute much to the overall richness of the Bible. For the most part, the Writ-

ings were composed later than the rest of the Tanakh.

Mishnah and Talmud: Teachings of the Rabbis

The Bible, or written Torah, is complemented by the vast and ingenious wealth of religious teachings of the "oral Torah." This is the material taught and transmitted by Judaism's great rabbis of antiquity. Then as now a **rabbi** (ra′b*i*) was a teacher of Torah or leader of Jewish worship. The teachings of the early rabbis were eventually written down, most notably in the Mishnah and later in the Talmud, among other texts.

The written revelation of God's will would always remain the foundational teaching of Judaism, but the varying circumstances of life demanded that the religious laws be elaborated on. The written Torah did not always say enough; also it could not directly address the continually changing situations of the Jews in a world that was always in a state of flux. The oral Torah continues the task begun by the written Torah.

Moving outward from the Bible, the next ring of interpretation is the **Mishnah** (meesh-nah′). It was written down in about AD 200, but it contains teachings that were formulated and transmitted orally by the rabbis of the preceding four centuries. Soon after it was written, it came to be regarded as a sacred text, like the Bible. It remains the starting point for rabbinic study of the oral Torah.

The **Talmud** (tahl-mood′) forms the next ring of interpretation. A great modern scholar of Judaism states, "If the Bible is the cornerstone of Judaism, then the Talmud is the central pillar, soaring up from the foundations and supporting the entire spiritual and intellectual edifice" (Steinsaltz, *The Essential Talmud,* page 3).

The Talmud is based directly on the Mishnah. Small portions of the Mishnah are cited, followed by intricate commentary, usually page after page of it. The rabbis support their

B

Read at least the entire first chapter of the Book of Jeremiah. Explain how the prophet Jeremiah is one who speaks for God. Also describe the sorts of messages Jeremiah delivers.

C

Choose a discipline or subject area that interests you, such as music, science, mathematics, or literature. Then choose a specific activity from that discipline and describe the concentric rings of creation and interpretation that surround it. For example, a certain scientific theory is formulated by one person, studied and commented on by another, revised by yet another, applied in a practical way by someone else, and so on. Be specific.

arguments by citing biblical passages. The Talmud presents a grand scheme of interpretation of God's will, blending together the oral and written forms of Torah. It is a massive work, spanning thousands of pages. Amazing though it may seem, great rabbis through the centuries are thought to have committed the entire Talmud to memory.

The Talmud itself continued to be interpreted for centuries. The most important commentary, by rabbis who lived as late as the Middle Ages, is included in modern editions. And in a real sense, the Talmud is still being interpreted; the concentric rings of the tree trunk are still growing outward. Modern Jews, like those of ancient times, strive for deeper understanding of God's will. This process of interpretation is itself a meaningful act of worship, occupying a significant place in the ongoing sanctification of life.[C]

The History of the Chosen People: Blessings and Tribulations

Earlier we noted that Judaism can be summarized as the interpretation of the history of the Jewish people. Who are the Jewish people, and why is their history of such vital importance?

IMAGE: © ANNIE GRIFFITHS BELT/CORBIS

Scholars in a yeshivah (school) discuss the meanings of passages from the Talmud.

Contents of the Hebrew Bible, or Tanakh

The Torah, or Law

Genesis, Exodus, Leviticus, Numbers, Deuteronomy

The Prophets

Joshua, Judges, Samuel (1 and 2), Kings (1 and 2), Isaiah, Jeremiah, Ezekiel; and the twelve minor prophets: Hosea, Joel, Amos, Obadiah, Jonah, Micah, Nahum, Habbakuk, Zephaniah, Haggai, Zechariah, Malachi

The Writings

Psalms, Proverbs, Job, Song of Solomon, Ruth, Lamentations, Ecclesiastes, Esther, Daniel, Ezra–Nehemiah, Chronicles (1 and 2)

Originally the Jews were the descendants of the ancient Israelites (who are also known as Hebrews). Around the time of the Exile and following it, they became known as Jews, and their religion became known as Judaism, because their country was Judah. Conversion to Judaism was quite common in ancient times, and it continues in the present day. No single Jewish "race" of genetically related people exists. It is more accurate to think of the Jews as an ethnic group that shares a common history and religion (though recently, as we have noted, some Jews do not practice Judaism).

History has great significance for Judaism because its adherents believe God is providential, or directly involved in guiding and caring for creation. The Chosen People are convinced God knows what is happening and provides for them. They therefore consider history to be a record of God's will as manifested in the events of the world.

This explains why Judaism itself can be thought of as the interpretation of Jewish history. God is loving, all-knowing, all-powerful, and providential. The Jews are the Chosen People of God. As the Chosen People, the Jews must live up to their end of the Covenant. History provides a means of measuring how adequately they have done that. To the extent that they honor the Covenant, God will reward them as a "treasured possession" (Exodus 19:6). Through the centuries the difficulties encountered by the Jews have challenged them to question over and over again just how adequately they have upheld their covenantal responsibilities.

Classical Judaism

In AD 66 Jews in Palestine initiated the Jewish War to overcome their Roman rulers. Roman armies defeated them and destroyed the Second Jerusalem Temple in AD 70. This was both an unprecedented catastrophe and a new opportunity for Judaism. The Pharisees, who focused on the study of Torah rather than on the rituals observed at the Temple, emerged from this event with their religious ways largely intact. With the impetus provided by Pharisaic Judaism, and with the compilation of the Mishnah and the Talmud over the next few

Worshipers gather at Jerusalem's Western Wall. To the left stands the Dome of the Rock, one of Islam's most sacred sites.

From the Ancient Israelites to Classical Judaism

Judaism emerged over a number of centuries, taking on its present form after the biblical period. The events of the ancient Israelites are significant for the tradition because, to begin with, Jews are descended from Abraham and the rest of the biblical patriarchs.

The Patriarchs (2000 to 1500 BC)

According to the Book of Genesis, God called forth Abraham to be the father of a great nation, leading him from his home in Mesopotamia to the Promised Land, Canaan. The males among Abraham's people were thereafter marked by circumcision, distinguishing the Israelites from people of the other nations. The stories of Abraham and his wife, Sarah, their son Isaac, and Isaac's son Jacob (who is also known as Israel) are integral to the Jewish sense of history and identity as a people.

Exodus and Revelation (c. 1280 BC)

During the centuries after the patriarchs, the Israelites moved from the land of Canaan to nearby Egypt, where food was easier to come by. Eventually they were forced into slavery by the Egyptians. This set the stage for the most important events in Israelite history: the Exodus from Egypt and the revelation on Mount Sinai. It is impossible to date the Exodus with precision; the most common estimate is about 1280 BC.

The central figure in both of these events, and the greatest prophet and most revered person in Judaism, is Moses. God called Moses to go forth to Egypt and free the Israelites from slavery. Through God's miraculous acts, including the ten devastating plagues on Egypt, and the parting of the Red Sea, Moses succeeded. In the months that followed, Moses led the people to Mount Sinai, where they agreed to enter into the Covenant with God. The Torah, with its 613 commandments, was revealed at that time to Moses.

Monarchy of David and Solomon (c. 1000 to 922 BC)

King David led the Israelite monarchy to its height of power. He managed to conquer many neighboring lands, along with the city of Jerusalem, which he made the capital. David's son Solomon built the Temple in Jerusalem, a structure of unsurpassed splendor that became the center of Israelite worship.

The kingship of David continues to hold special significance for Judaism. David has always been regarded as a prototype, or model, of the Messiah, a savior whom Jews believe will be sent by God to restore peace and justice to the world.

Babylonian Exile (587 to 538 BC)

At the end of Solomon's reign, the united monarchy was divided. The northern kingdom, Israel, endured only until 721 BC, when it fell to the Assyrians. The southern kingdom, Judah, endured until about 587 BC, when the Babylonians, led by their king, Nebuchadnezzar, conquered the land, destroyed the Temple, and carried off many of its leading citizens to exile in Babylon. The Exile lasted until 538 BC, when the Persians conquered Babylon. Many Jews returned to Judea (as Judah came to be known), where, in about 515 BC, they rebuilt the Temple. Judaism underwent further changes and revitalization about a century later, when Ezra and Nehemiah led a period of great religious reform.

Greek Conquest of Palestine (332 BC)

Under the leadership of Alexander the Great, the Greeks conquered Palestine in 332 BC, profoundly challenging the Jewish way of life. Greek language and culture quickly became established among the elite. Some Jews embraced this Greek influence and gradually lost hold of their traditional religious identity. Different forms of Judaism arose during the later period of Greek dominance. The Sadducees, members of the priestly class who enjoyed the wealth provided by Temple revenues, were generally friendly toward the foreign rulers, though the Sadducees were highly conservative about their Jewish religious ways. The Essenes actively rejected all the Greek ways and chose to live on their own in desert communities. The Pharisees adopted some facets of Greek culture but ignored its religious aspects. Put off by the Sadducees' control of the Temple, the Pharisees focused on Torah, in both its written and its oral forms.

Destruction of the Second Temple (AD 70)

In 63 BC the Romans conquered Palestine. Their rule lasted for centuries and was often harsh. The Crucifixion of Jesus of Nazareth in about AD 30 was one among many executions of Jews the Romans carried out to ensure control of the area. In AD 66 the Jews initiated a large-scale revolt, known as the Jewish War. This was eventually won by the Romans, who, in AD 70, destroyed the Jerusalem Temple for the second time. This event remains one of the greatest moments of tribulation in the history of Judaism. It was an enormous loss, removing from the Jews the physical center of their religious and cultural life. However, the Pharisees had for centuries focused on Torah rather than the Temple, so they managed to emerge from this defeat with their form of Judaism intact. It is this form that produced classical, or rabbinic, Judaism.

centuries, classical Judaism was established. It has remained the standard for Jews down to modern times.

The classical period stretched from the end of the first century AD through the seventh century, when Muslim forces conquered Palestine and the surrounding area. The Jews of the classical period were forced to live under the threat of Roman political oppression, which sometimes had violent consequences. Several decades after the Jewish War and the destruction of the Temple in AD 70, the Jews waged a second large-scale revolt against the Romans. This ended in AD 135, when the victorious Romans leveled the city of Jerusalem and issued a decree forbidding Jews to inhabit the region of Palestine. The Jews were now technically in exile from their homeland.

However, neither exile nor oppression was new to the Jewish people. Through the centuries their ancestors had endured persecution by foreign rulers: Egyptians, Assyrians, Babylonians, Persians, Greeks, and Romans. In the classical period and beyond, Jews encountered new threats: In the fourth century, Christianity arose to become the official religion of the Roman Empire. A few centuries later, many Jews found themselves living under Muslim rule.

The Jews exiled in the classical period could look to those exiled in an earlier period for a precedent. In 587 BC some of their ancestors had been forced out of their homeland and into Babylon; in 538 BC the ancestors had been allowed to return to their homeland. The Babylonian Exile had lasting significance, instilling among all Jews hope for a return from exile to a situation of peace and prosperity. It also taught the Jews how to survive without returning home. Following the Exile many remained in Babylon or elsewhere in Persia, and in Egypt. For the first time, there were Jews living away from their homeland who maintained their religious identity. This situation, known as the **Diaspora** (di-as′puh-ruh)

or Dispersion, continued throughout Jewish history. Indeed a majority of Jews have lived in the Diaspora, from the classical period to the present.

Medieval Judaism

The medieval period of Judaism spans from the eighth century to the middle of the eighteenth century. Scattered throughout a large Diaspora, Jews lived under various political and social conditions. In some places Jewish culture thrived. Medieval Spain, for example, produced both the philosophy of Maimonides (mi-mah′nuh-deez) and the mystical teachings of the Zohar.

Jewish Life in the Medieval Period

For the most part, Jews lived under the rule of Muslims (in Africa, Spain, and the Near East) and Christians (in most of Europe). Under Muslim rule Jews were generally free to practice their own religion and to conduct their own courts of law, and they were assured security of life and property. There were occasional exceptions to those principles, and Jews were required to pay certain taxes to the Muslim rulers. But overall the Jewish people fared quite well and established a large middle class.

Conditions under Christian rulers tended to vary considerably over the centuries. In the early centuries of the medieval period, European Jews emerged as successful moneylenders. (Church laws strongly discouraged Christians from participating in this profession.) This helped Europe's changing economy, and some Christians respected and appreciated the Jews with whom they had dealings. But the economic success of the Jews led to resentment among many Christians. Christians also resented the Jews for being "sons of the crucifiers" who intentionally rejected Christ.

Resentment led to open and violent persecution. Beginning in the twelfth century, Jews were commonly the victims of blood libels, which were false accusations that they had ritually murdered Christian children. Large-scale expulsions of Jews occurred in France, England, and Spain (which had come under Christian rule by the fifteenth century). Jews were also blamed for causing the Black Death, the devastating bubonic plague that killed about one-third of Europe's population in the mid–fourteenth century. For this, entire Jewish populations were massacred, mostly by wandering bands of Christians. Meanwhile the Spanish Inquisition also targeted Jews, putting many to death.

To escape persecution, many Jews migrated eastward, especially to Poland, which welcomed them. By the mid–seventeenth century, Poland had the largest population of Jews (about 150,000) of any country in the Diaspora. Here Jews enjoyed a large degree of governmental autonomy and lived in relative safety and prosperity. Polish rabbis made remarkable intellectual achievements. But even here the threat of persecution loomed. In 1648 a Cossack rebellion against Poland resulted in the brutal massacre of about one-fourth of its Jewish population.

Clearly many Jews endured great tribulation during the medieval period. But some lived in havens of relative peace and prosperity. Muslim Spain, home of the Jewish philosopher Maimonides and of the origins of Jewish mysticism, was one such refuge.[D]

Jewish Philosophy: Maimonides

Moses Maimonides (1135 to 1204) represents a great number of Jewish philosophers, teachers, and scriptural masters who contributed to the ongoing process of interpreting Torah.

Maimonides applied the philosophy of Plato and Aristotle to the biblical tradition, fashioning a new and much debated Jewish theology. His most famous book, *The Guide for the Perplexed,* has stood through the ages as an influential and challenging philosophical work.

In addition, Maimonides contributed Judaism's most famous statement of beliefs, thirteen principles that set forth the backbone of Jewish theology:

1. The belief in God's existence.
2. The belief in His unity.
3. The belief in His incorporeality.
4. The belief in His timelessness.
5. The belief that He is approachable through prayer.
6. The belief in prophecy.
7. The belief in the superiority of Moses to all other prophets.
8. The belief in the revelation of the Law, and that the Law as contained in the Pentateuch is that revealed by Moses.
9. The belief in the immutability of the Law.
10. The belief in Divine providence.
11. The belief in Divine justice.
12. The belief in the coming of the Messiah.
13. The belief in the resurrection and human immortality.

(*The Ways of Religion,* pages 261–262)

IMAGE: © PETER M. WILSON/CORBIS

Moses Maimonides applied the philosophy of Plato and Aristotle to the biblical tradition, fashioning a new Jewish theology.

D
Consider the reasons behind the persecution of medieval Jews. In general, why, do you think, did certain groups of people harass other groups? Try to name at least one example in today's world of a group persecuting another group. What seem to be the reasons behind this harassment?

E

Might the philosophy of Maimonides and the mysticism of the Kabbalah be used as two complementary approaches to God? Describe how the two approaches could work together.

The Kabbalah: Jewish Mysticism #18

Whereas Jewish philosophy emphasizes reason, Jewish mysticism, or **Kabbalah** (kab´uh-luh), teaches that God can best be known with the heart, through love. The mystics acknowledge the ultimate transcendence of God, but stress the immanence of God: they say that God can be found by looking inward.

The most famous text of Jewish mysticism is the Zohar, probably written in thirteenth-century Spain by Moses de Leon. The Zohar incorporates rich symbolism based on numbers and esoteric language, and teaches that Torah can be interpreted on different levels, each revealing hidden meanings that bring one closer to God; thus, though God is regarded as the Infinite, transcending the fallen world of humanity, the mystic can come to know God through love and understanding of the hidden truth.

Though in many ways it is an alternative to traditional Judaism, the Kabbalah does not abandon the basic forms of Jewish practice. Kabbalists observe the commandments of the

A Hasidic teenager in New York City.

IMAGE: © RICHARD T. NOWITZ/CORBIS

Torah, and are renowned for their highly ethical behavior.[E]

Modern Judaism

Great changes in European civilization began to occur in the eighteenth century. The period known as the Enlightenment, or Age of Reason, gave rise to new social theories asserting the equality of all. Monarchies began to be replaced by governments that were based on rule by the people.

These changes greatly affected religions too, including Judaism. The wide variety of reactions to the new challenges of this period gave rise to different forms of modern Judaism.

Hasidism

Hasidism (from *hasid* [ha´seed], meaning "pious") arose in the eighteenth century in eastern Europe. It draws from some of the mystical teachings of the Kabbalist tradition, holding that God is immanent and known first with the heart. Hasidism emphasizes personal relationships with God and the community, rather than study of the Torah and strict observance of its commandments.

#19 The center of each Hasidic community is the leadership of the *zaddik* (tsah´dik), a holy man who is believed to have an especially close relationship with God. Through the teachings and mere presence of the *zaddik,* Hasidic Jews are able to move closer to God. Large Hasidic communities still exist today in North America and elsewhere.

Zionism

Zionism originally referred to a movement arising in the late nineteenth century that was committed to the re-establishment of a Jewish homeland (*Zion* is a biblical name for Jerusalem). Now that the modern nation of Israel, established in 1948, exists, *Zionism* refers generally to the support of Israel.

As we have seen, throughout the centuries Jews faced persecution, a phenomenon known as **anti-Semitism.** Despite the new ideals of social equality that arose with the Enlightenment, some Jews were convinced that the only way to ensure their safety was to have their own nation. Events of anti-Semitism in the twentieth century, most tragically the Holocaust, confirmed the Zionist conviction regarding the need for a Jewish state.

The Holocaust

Of all the tribulations the Chosen People suffered through the centuries, the Holocaust is surely the most horrific. Sometimes called *Shoah* (Hebrew for "mass destruction"), the **Holocaust** refers to the persecution of Jews by German Nazis from 1933 to 1945. Culminating in the use of highly efficient extermination camps, the Holocaust resulted in the murder of an estimated six million Jews.

The tragic consequences of this immense loss of life included religious challenges for Judaism. Until this event Jews could generally make sense of their difficult history. There had been trials, of course. But some reasoned that perhaps they were the result of the Jews' own failure to live up to the Covenant. Or perhaps God would right the wrongs and bring justice to the Jews, by sending the Messiah—as had been expected since Roman times. But in the face of the Holocaust, in which one-third of the Jewish people were senselessly murdered, such answers no longer make sense to many Jews. How could God have allowed such a horrible thing to happen?

Jews have responded to these challenges in a variety of ways. Some maintain they deserved even this as punishment for their sins—most specifically, the sin of abandoning the ways of traditional Judaism. Others contend that the Holocaust can only mean God has broken the Covenant. Another response, and a prominent one, is Zionism, the ongoing support of the State of Israel.[G]

F

In "The Precious Prayer," the rabbi learns that "while humans see what is before their eyes, God looks into the heart." Compare this insight about prayer with that offered by Jesus in Matthew 6:5–6.

G

Review the opening section of this chapter, beginning with the passage from Abraham Joshua Heschel. What challenges do you think the Holocaust presents to this understanding of Judaism?

"The Precious Prayer"

The true character of Hasidism is perhaps best exposed through its many stories. This one, "The Precious Prayer," expresses the Hasidic emphasis on knowing God with the heart, through which God, in turn, knows human beings.

One Yom Kippur long ago, a rabbi was praying in the synagogue. An angel whispered in his ear about a man whose prayers had reached the highest heavens. The angel told the rabbi the man's name and hometown, and the rabbi went to find him.

When the rabbi reached that town, he asked for the man whose name the angel had given him. The only man by that name was a poor farmer. The rabbi found the farm, and the man invited him to enter the little hut in which he lived. Getting right down to business, the rabbi asked the farmer how he prayed. "But sir," replied the farmer, "I am afraid I cannot pray. For I cannot read. All I know are the first nine letters of the alphabet."

The rabbi was stunned. Could the angel have been wrong? So he asked, "What did you do on Yom Kippur?" The farmer said: "I went to the synagogue. I saw how intently everyone was praying, and my heart broke. So I began to recite the letters I know of the alphabet. And I said in my heart: 'Dear God, take these letters and form them into prayers for me, that will rise up like the scent of honeysuckle. For that is the most beautiful scent I know.' And I said that with all my strength, over and over."

When the rabbi heard this, he knew that God had sent him here to learn this: While humans see what is before their eyes, God looks into the heart. And that is why the prayers of the simple farmer were so precious.

(Adapted from Schwartz, *Gabriel's Palace,* pages 86–87)[F]

Starving Jewish concentration camp prisoners were liberated at the end of World War II in Austria. The Holocaust, or Shoah, challenged Jews to make sense of the killing of a third of their people.

The State of Israel

With the rise of the Zionist movement at the end of the nineteenth century, increasing numbers of Jews immigrated to Palestine. The Hebrew language was restored; the land was nurtured into fields fit for productive agriculture; and farming communities and cities were built. In 1948, in the wake of the Holocaust and with the sympathetic support of most of the world, Israel was granted statehood. Its political and cultural achievements since that time continue to be a source of pride for Jews. For the first time in over two millennia, the Jews have a national homeland.

Today the State of Israel provides a great deal of unity for Judaism. Most Jews, whether Israelis or not (fewer than half of the world's Jews live in Israel), and whether religiously observant or not, regard Israel as their earthly center and common cause. Much financial and political support has been provided to the state, especially by North American Jews.

Along with this unity over the State of Israel, divisive problems persist. The Palestinians also call this land their home. For both Judaism and Islam, this land is charged with sacred significance. Jews and Palestinians alike put forth claims of ownership that are based on deeply held religious convictions. Ever since the establishment of the State of Israel, wars and other violent incidents have periodically plagued the area. And so, difficult questions need to be answered. Is the development of an independent Palestinian state the optimal solution? And if so, how should control of the region be apportioned?

Deep divisions also exist between secular and religious Israeli Jews. The task of reconciling secular ideals such as Western democracy with the ways of traditional Judaism poses a great challenge to Israel.[H]

Modern Institutional Divisions

The same challenges of the modern period that prompted the development of branches

212   Judaism

of Judaism, such as Hasidism and Zionism, have also led to divisions within traditional Judaism. These divisions are most relevant in North America, where the three most prominent forms of Judaism are Reform, Orthodox, and Conservative.

Reform Judaism holds that being Jewish and being completely involved in modern society are compatible. As society changes, so must Judaism adapt to it. Reform Judaism is therefore relatively relaxed in observing the details of Jewish traditional practice. The worship liturgy is spoken in English, and the rabbi functions much like a Christian preacher, rather than a traditional scholar and teacher of Torah. About one-third of Jews in the United States adhere to Reform Judaism.

Orthodox Judaism maintains that Torah is the standard of truth and that life within society must always conform to it. Despite changes in society, Jewish life should change very little, for Torah is unchanging. This does not mean Orthodox Judaism rejects all aspects of modernity; secular education, for example, is affirmed. But compared with Reform Judaism, Orthodox Judaism is deeply traditional. In the United States, the Orthodox often live in separate communities to help maintain their traditional ways. About one-tenth of Jews in the United States adhere to Orthodox Judaism.

Conservative Judaism occupies a middle position between Reform and Orthodox. Though somewhat open to change and to modern ways, Conservative Judaism is quite strict regarding observance of traditional Jewish practices. The worship liturgy is in Hebrew, for example, and laws regulating diet and behavior on the Sabbath are strictly observed. Almost half of the Jews in the United States adhere to Conservative Judaism.

Each of these varieties of Judaism, even the Orthodox, continues to change. For example, women are becoming increasingly active in both leadership and participation. Women often now serve as rabbis in Reform and Conservative Judaism.

The Sanctification of Life: The Way of Torah

According to Judaism life is sanctified through the moment-to-moment observance of Torah. Judaism is far more concerned with correct practice than with correct belief (and differs considerably from Christianity in that respect). Judaism places little emphasis on theology or statements of belief. Rather than focusing on what God is, Judaism focuses on how to worship God. Traditionally, therefore, a Jew is not a "believer" so much as an "observer of the commandments." It could be said that for Jews, spiritual perfection is mainly a matter of perfect observance. Just what constitutes perfect observance varies depending on the type of Judaism practiced. In this section of the chapter, we will be concerned mainly with more traditional ways of being Jewish.

Daily Life

Traditionally, all aspects of Jewish life are guided by regulations derived from Torah, which categorizes acts as permitted or forbidden, obliged or free, and holy or profane. Torah thus defines both ethical conduct and worship.

Ethics

Observing Torah requires not only worshiping God but also leading an ethical life. *In The Mishnah* (in the tractate *Aboth* 1.2) an esteemed rabbi puts it this way: "By three things is the world sustained: by the Law, by the [Temple-]service, and by deeds of loving-kindness" (page 446). We have already noted

H
For some two thousand years before 1948, Jews endured without a national homeland. Imagine what your life would be like if your nation did not exist in a physical location and you were living in exile in some foreign land. What important things would be missing? How would this situation affect your religious outlook? In general, how would it affect your priorities?

People often tend to think of religion as primarily a matter of believing in certain doctrines. Drawing from your own experiences, list several examples of religious practices. In your opinion are these practices meaningful if they are independent of beliefs?

the importance of the study and interpretation of the Law, or Torah. Soon we will consider some details of service, or worship. As for deeds of loving-kindness, we need only note the prominence of the Ten Commandments in God's revelation on Mount Sinai to realize the basic significance of ethics. In addition to these famous ethical requirements (not to kill, steal, and so on), Judaism teaches many more. For example, Jews are obligated to help those who are needy, to give food and shelter to guests, and to visit those who are sick. The traditional emphasis on ethics is reflected in the charitable and philanthropic work done by the Jewish community today.

Daily Worship Through Prayer

The predominant form of daily worship is prayer, which is mandatory only for males age thirteen and older. Women are traditionally excused because of their household responsibilities (which are themselves done in accordance with Torah, and so are an integral part of the sanctification of life). However, in recent times more women have been par-

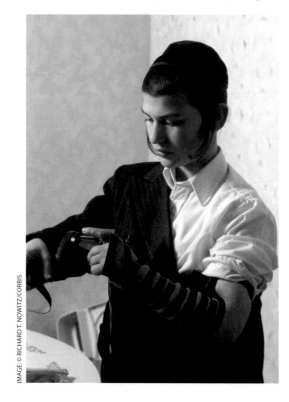

A Hasidic boy prepares for morning prayers by binding a small box containing biblical passages to his arm and by wearing a skullcap.

IMAGE: © RICHARD T. NOWITZ/CORBIS

ticipating in prayer. In any event males alone are required to wear certain ritual accessories. One is the skullcap, which is called a yarmulke (yah´muh-kuh) in Yiddish (a language derived primarily from German and Hebrew and that was commonly spoken by Jews in Europe) or *kipah* (kee-pah´) in Hebrew. A second is a set of small boxes containing biblical passages. These are secured to the forehead and to the left arm so as to be near the mind and the heart, the two primary means of serving God. A third accessory is the prayer shawl, which can be drawn over the head for privacy.

Prayers are said at least three times daily: in the morning, afternoon, and evening. They include a variety of traditional passages from the Bible and other authoritative sources. Prayers are usually recited at home but are also frequently said in public at the synagogue. Home and synagogue are the two centers of Jewish worship.

The Home and the Synagogue

The home is the most common place for Jewish worship, and it is the center of Jewish social life, which focuses on the family more than on anything else. Rules based on Torah govern family relationships, so that children honor their parents, and parents care diligently for their children.

Jewish homes are often easy to identify. On the outside, just to the right of the door, many Jews attach the *mezuzah* (muh-zoo´zuh), a small container with a scroll on which is written the Shema.

The social and religious center of the home is the dinner table. Along with festive meals in celebration of holy days and the Sabbath, ordinary meals too are important occasions. Traditionally all the food must be kosher ("proper" according to Torah), meaning that certain dietary regulations apply. Pork, for example, is prohibited, as is the mixing of meat and dairy products.

In addition to the home, the synagogue (which Reform Judaism calls the temple) is a common forum for Jewish worship. Since the Babylonian Exile (in the sixth century BC), synagogues have been centers for prayer, study, and fellowship. Though building designs vary, all synagogues contain a scroll of the five books of the Torah, which is encased in a box called an ark.

Synagogues are led by rabbis. In general, *rabbi* simply refers to one who has mastered the sacred writings of Judaism, mainly the Bible and the Talmud. The precise role of the rabbi varies among the different forms of Judaism. It also differs from the role of the Christian priest or minister, and other faith leaders, whose status tends to be more formal.[1]

Sabbath

One of the Ten Commandments states, "Remember the sabbath day and keep it holy" (Exodus 20:8, Tanakh). This the Jews have done through the centuries with both reverence and festive joy. The **Sabbath** (also commonly known by its Hebrew name, *Shabbat*) begins at sunset on Friday and lasts until sunset on Saturday. (Some Reform Jews celebrate the Sabbath on Sunday.) It is both the religious and the social high point of the week.

The Sabbath is patterned after the seventh day of Creation, on which God, according to Genesis 2:2–3, rested from labor and beheld the glory of the created world. Along with avoiding labor, Jews are required to refrain from many sorts of usual activities, such as driving, answering the phone, and (for the very observant) turning on an electric light, which would violate the biblical law prohibiting lighting a fire on the Sabbath.[J]

As well as being a day of rest, though, the Sabbath is also a day of worship and celebration. Jews devote part of the time to Torah study and Sabbath services, both at home and at the synagogue. They enjoy meals of special foods that have been prepared before the onset of the Sabbath. The Sabbath is a time of fellowship with family and other Jews of the community. It is joyful and celebratory.[K]

The Annual Calendar of Holy Days

The calendar of holy days is fundamental to Jewish life. Those annual observances ensure both the unity of the Jews and the continuity of their religious tradition. Some sixteen days are considered holy, and the first day of each month, marked by the new moon, is also honored. The most important holy days are Rosh Hashanah, Yom Kippur, and Passover. (Hanukkah, although commonly celebrated in Jewish households, is prominent primarily because it occurs during the Christmas season rather than for having great religious significance.)

Rosh Hashanah

Rosh Hashanah (rohsh hah-shah-nah´), the festival of the new year, occurs in early fall and is observed for two days. Unlike the strictly secular celebration of the New Year, Rosh Hashanah is a religious event involving both festivities and serious contemplation. Jews' celebrating God's work of creating the world is accompanied by their individual reflection on the deeds of the past year and on the need for redemption. The ram's horn, or shofar, is blown on Rosh Hashanah as a means of reminding the Jews of these spiritual needs. Rosh Hashanah marks the beginning of the Days of Awe, a ten-day period of reflection.

Rosh Hashanah is also a time to reinforce social relationships. Festive meals are held for family and friends. Visits to the graves of family members strengthen bonds with the deceased as well.

Yom Kippur

The Days of Awe conclude on the tenth day of the new year with **Yom Kippur** (yohm´ kee-poor´), the Day of Atonement, Judaism's most important holy day.

Deeply personal and solemn, Yom Kippur emphasizes repentance through confession of sin. The day is observed through prayer and through abstention from food, drink, and

J

Read Deuteronomy 6:4–9. Identify parts of this passage that relate to the Jewish worship practices you have read about in this section of your textbook. Describe how you think the Shema (Deuteronomy 6:4) relates to the rest of the passage.

K

On the Sabbath Jews celebrate the creation of the world by avoiding labor in order to rest and to worship. Do you reserve time in your life for that kind of celebration? If so, describe what that time is like. If not, reflect on what benefits it might bring.

work. The synagogue hosts services, during which prayers like this one are recited:

O my God, before I was formed, I was nothing. Now that I have been formed, it is as though I had not been formed, for I am dust in my life, more so after death. Behold I am before You like a vessel filled with shame and confusion. May it be Your will . . . that I may no more sin, and forgive the sins I have already committed in Your abundant compassion. (Translated by Neusner in "Judaism," in *Our Religions,* page 345)

Passover

The festival of **Passover** occurs early in the spring and lasts eight days. It commemorates the Exodus of the Jews from bondage in Egypt, and is a time of joyful celebration.

The high point of the festival is the Seder, which features a recitation, called the Haggadah, of the events of the Exodus as well as a meal of traditional foods that symbolize those events. Throughout the eight days of Passover, only unleavened bread (matzo) is to be eaten. The matzo is a reminder of the haste with which the Israelites had to flee from Egypt

(as noted in Exodus 12:34) and in general is symbolic of liberation and redemption.

The Passover clearly illustrates a characteristic common to most of Judaism's holy days: the events of Jewish history are commemorated as having religious significance.

Rites of Passage

Like most other religions, Judaism prescribes rites of passage, or ritual events marking life's major changes. Rites of passage serve two primary purposes. First, they reflect the inevitable changes of life, while providing a sense of permanence through their unchanging rituals and the deeply rooted values they enunciate. Second, rites of passage help to define the responsibilities of each stage of life, and to teach the means for advancing through them with appropriate maturity.

Birth and Naming

The rite of passage marking the birth of a child involves circumcision (removal of the foreskin of the penis) for boys, and naming for both boys and girls.

Throughout the eight days of Passover, only unleavened bread, called matzo, is to be eaten. The festival commemorates the Exodus of the Jews from bondage in Egypt.

Growing Up Jewish in a Christian Town

Throughout history Jews have commonly lived in situations in which they were the minority. This is still the case for many Jews today. Stuart Miller tells of his experiences growing up Jewish in a small, predominantly Christian city in Minnesota.

My parents were born overseas and immigrated to this country, my mother from Poland and my father from White Russia. Through different circumstances, they ended up in Winona, Minnesota (population twenty-five thousand), a town with only about ten Jewish families. I grew up with an older brother and a younger brother. My younger brother, Morrie, died in 1989 of cancer. My father, William, was an Orthodox Jew in the traditional sense. He observed the holidays, obeyed dietary laws, and prayed three times a day. My mother was not as religious. After my father's death, she shifted away from strict observance of Jewish Law, although she never lost her Jewish identity and remained totally devoted to Judaism.

When I was in grade school, a Jewish Sunday school teacher was brought to Winona from Minneapolis (about two hours away). There were about a dozen of us kids, of various ages. We studied Jewish history, Torah, and the Hebrew language—as much as the teacher could cram into those weekly sessions. My bar mitzvah was held in Winona, after I had received instruction from a medical student who came from Minneapolis. We celebrated the Jewish holidays in Minneapolis with my parents until my father got ill. Then we started going to synagogue in La Crosse, Wisconsin (a half hour from Winona). Through the years I received most of my learning of Hebrew, Torah, and Jewish history in La Crosse.

To a Jewish kid in a Christian community, the differences were most clear during the Christmas season. We celebrated Hanukkah, and the rest of the kids celebrated Christmas. It felt different. I was discouraged from singing Christmas songs, but I did anyway, with a compromise—I skipped certain words. The high holy days, Rosh Hashanah and Yom Kippur, also revealed differences. I missed school on those days in order to attend Jewish services. My younger brother, Morrie, was an excellent athlete. I remember a conflict when a high school football game was scheduled on Yom Kippur. Morrie missed the game that Friday. The coach was a little put off and was not able to understand my brother's decision. I was not a very good football player, so my absence never bothered my coach!

When I was in high school, a diplomat from Israel came and spoke at an assembly. Due to my upbringing, I understood what he said about Israel, and it meant a lot to me. It was obvious that my classmates did not have the same emotional involvement that I did. Most neither understood nor cared about what he said.

Not once during my high school or college years did I experience firsthand any open anti-Semitism. However, in high school I knew of two brothers who were constantly teased and harassed for being Jewish. These same harassers never did that to me or my brothers, which made me wonder, why them and not me? I recall a specific incident concerning a gas station owner with whom my family did business. A customer of ours from out of town stopped at his station to ask directions to our business. The owner told him where "the Jews'" business was—not "the Millers'" business, but "the Jews'." This astonished me. I thought I knew that station owner better than that.

Now I am older and have a family of my own. My eighteen-year-old daughter, Jessica, attends college at Penn State. My older son, Asher, is fifteen and is in high school. My younger son, Joshua, is in grade school. My wife, Sheryl, is also in school, working on a degree in dental hygiene. Sheryl and I have tried to instill in our children a love of Judaism. Jessica celebrated bat mitzvah at age thirteen. The synagogue had just changed from Orthodox to Conservative, and so she was the first woman called to publicly read the Torah. Asher celebrated bar mitzvah at age thirteen, and Joshua will as well. We usually celebrate the Jewish holidays as a family, the most important being Rosh Hashanah, Yom Kippur, Hanukkah, and Passover. I think we would agree that our favorite is Passover. The special food, the Seder night, the retelling of the Exodus from Egypt—all combine to give parents, children, and invited guests an appreciation of who they are and why their past is so important. We try to go to synagogue as much as we can, but kids (being kids) don't want to go all the time. I was much the same in my youth. I only hope that my children will have a basis of Jewish faith, and that over time they will expand upon this base on their own. Their faith can help make them aware of bad things and enable them to combat these bad things.

Growing up Jewish in a Christian town has been an experience. One lucky thing for me is that I was able to find a wonderful Jewish woman to marry. It was difficult, but as I say, I got lucky. There is anti-Semitism, but for the most part it has been covered up by a thin veneer of civility. I hope the veneer gets thicker as time goes by so that my kids can be openly proud of who and what they are, and appreciate how they differ from other kids.

Boys are circumcised and named in a ceremony that takes place on the eighth day of life, usually at the home of the parents. In the Book of Genesis, circumcision is the sign established by God when entering into the Covenant with Abraham. This ritual therefore signifies entrance into the Jewish community of descendants of Abraham.

Girls are usually named at the synagogue during a Sabbath service. However, Reform Judaism has developed a distinct ceremony for girls that is patterned after the ceremony of circumcision.

Coming of Age

The primary ritual marking the Jewish coming of age, the point at which a child takes on the religious responsibilities of an adult, is called **bar mitzvah** (bahr meets-vah´; "son of the commandment") for boys, and **bat mitzvah** (baht meets-vah´; "daughter of the commandment") for girls. At that point the young person becomes responsible for observing the detailed practices of daily Jewish life.

Bar mitzvah takes place on a boy's thirteenth birthday. During the special service,

the boy is a participant for the first time. He performs such tasks as reading from the Torah. Most Jewish girls celebrate bat mitzvah in the same manner. Orthodox Jewish girls, however, do not observe bat mitzvah.

Marriage

For Judaism marriage is the ideal human relationship. Patterned after the union between Adam and Eve, marriage celebrates God's creation by symbolically re-creating the Garden of Eden. The wedding is a most joyous and festive occasion and is almost always celebrated in a traditional manner, even by Jews who are otherwise not traditional.

Several symbols and events highlight the marriage ceremony. The bride and groom stand beneath the *huppah* (khoo-pah´), or bridal canopy, which creates a special, sacred space. Seven blessings, including the one that follows, are read over a cup of wine:

Grant perfect joy to these loving companions, as You did to the first man and woman in the Garden of Eden. Praised are You, O Lord, who grants the joy of bride and groom. (Translated by Neusner in "Judaism," in *Our Religions,* page 350)

The ceremony concludes when the groom breaks a wine glass beneath his foot. This ancient custom may have originated as a symbol of the destruction of the two Temples in Jerusalem. Today it serves to remind those present that marriage, like every aspect of life, will involve some difficulties and pain along with joy.

Death and Mourning

Death, the ultimate transition, poses unique challenges to the family of the deceased and to the community. Judaism deals with those challenges by carefully regulating the rituals and mourning activities that follow the end of a life.

Several distinct stages of mourning are prescribed. The first stage lasts from death to

With the help of a rabbi, young people prepare for their rite of passage to religious adulthood, called their bar mitzvah (for boys) or bat mitzvah (for girls).

IMAGE: MENAHEM KAHANA/AFP/GETTY IMAGES

burial, which preferably occurs on the day of death (though today that is usually not practical). When family members first learn of the death, they rip their clothes, and recite verses that acknowledge God as the "true judge." The mourners are restricted from certain activities, such as shaving and wearing leather. They are also relieved of many of the normal religious requirements, including the regular schedule of daily prayer. This allows them to attend to their grief and to special responsibilities, such as making sure the body is ritually washed and clothed in a shroud. It is buried in a plain wooden coffin.

A second stage of mourning begins after burial, with the recital of the kaddish (kah' dish), a prayer of mourning. This stage lasts seven days. During this time community members visit the family. Conversation is limited to good comments about the one who has died. Upon departing, the visitors recite a special prayer of comfort.

A third stage lasts until thirty days after burial. Throughout this period most normal activities are resumed, but social gatherings and celebrations are avoided.

If the deceased is one's parent, a fourth stage of mourning follows, this one lasting until the first anniversary of the death. During this stage the mourners avoid their usual seats at the synagogue, and they recite the kaddish during services. On the anniversary of the death, the mourners again recite the kaddish.

Note how thoroughly Judaism deals with a rite of passage, in this case, death. This same thoroughness applies to all aspects of Jewish life. Judaism is truly a religion of correct practice, from moment to moment, day in and day out.[L]

The Tradition of the Chosen People

We began this chapter by noting three ways to summarize Judaism: First, it is the Covenant between God and the Chosen People;

second, it is the interpretation of the history of the Jewish people; and third, it is the sanctification of life. Now that we have explored Judaism in some detail, it is possible to make sense of yet another summary statement, one that pulls all the others together: Judaism is the tradition of the Chosen People. To recall the words of Abraham Joshua Heschel cited at the beginning of this chapter, Judaism is "primarily living in the spiritual order of the Jewish people, the living *in* the Jews of the past and *with* the Jews of the present."

With only about fourteen million adherents worldwide, Judaism is among the smallest of the world's major religions. Many Jews today are gravely concerned that their numbers are decreasing, that the tradition is weakening, and that the Jewish people are losing their sense of identity.

Time will tell what is to become of Judaism. But given that it has endured against all odds for over two millennia, time seems to be on Judaism's side.

Chapter Review

1. Define the term *covenant* in relation to the Jews.
2. Why do observant Jews avoid pronouncing the divine name? How is the name written?
3. What is the Shema?
4. Identify the three related meanings of the term *Torah*.
5. Why is the Hebrew Bible also known as the Tanakh?
6. What is the Pentateuch?
7. Who is traditionally regarded as the author of the Torah? How many specific laws is the Torah thought to contain?
8. What is the literal meaning of the term *prophet*?
9. What is the oral Torah? How is it thought to complement the written Torah?

L
Judaism carefully observes rites of passage, as can be seen in the details involved in its mourning of the dead. How does Judaism's approach to mourning compare with secular society's approach?

10. When was the Mishnah written, and what does it contain? pg 221

11. What do the rabbis comment on in the Talmud, and how do they support their arguments?

12. Rather than describing them as a single "race" of genetically related people, what is the most accurate way to think of the Jews?

13. What does it mean to say God is providential?

14. Why did the Pharisees emerge after the destruction of the Second Jerusalem Temple in AD 70 with their religious ways intact?

15. What is the Diaspora? pg 221

16. In what areas of the world did medieval Jews live under Muslim rule? under Christian rule?

17. Briefly describe the situation of medieval Jews in Poland.

18. What does the Kabbalah teach?

19. What is believed about the *zaddik,* the leadership figure in Hasidism? pg 220

20. What is Zionism? pg 221

21. When did the Holocaust occur? What does the Hebrew term *Shoah* mean? pg 221

22. Briefly describe Reform Judaism.

23. How is Orthodox Judaism distinguishable from Reform Judaism?

24. What are the distinguishing characteristics of Conservative Judaism?

25. According to the Mishnah, what sustains the world?

26. What is the predominant form of daily worship in Judaism?

27. What are the two centers of Jewish worship?

28. What does every synagogue contain? pg 204

29. When does the Sabbath occur? What are the two main aspects of its celebration?

30. What is celebrated on Rosh Hashanah?

31. What is emphasized on Yom Kippur?

32. What does the festival Passover commemorate?

33. What is signified by the rite of passage that marks the birth of a child?

34. What are the bar mitzvah and bat mitzvah? pg 218

35. What symbols and events highlight the Jewish marriage ceremony?

36. What is the kaddish?

The Seven Dimensions of Religion: Judaism

Dimension	Examples
Experiential	knowing God inwardly through Kabbalah, Jeremiah's calling to be a prophet
Mythic	the Haggadah (recited on Passover)
Doctrinal	the Covenant, the Shema, Maimonides's thirteen principles of belief
Ethical	the Ten Commandments and other rules of Torah
Ritual	daily prayer, the Sabbath meal and observances, Passover's Seder, reciting the kaddish
Social	cohesion of the Chosen People, Hasidism's *zaddik*
Material	yarmulke, *mezuzah,* shofar, matzo, *huppah*

Glossary

anti-Semitism. Hostility toward Jews and Judaism; ranges from attitudes of disfavor to active persecution.

bar mitzvah, bat mitzvah (bahr meets-vah´, baht meets-vah´; Hebrew: "son of the commandment," "daughter of the commandment"). The ritual celebration marking the coming of age of a Jewish child, at which time the person takes on the religious responsibilities of an adult.

Covenant. The agreement established between God and the ancient Israelites, first through Abraham and later through Moses, that designates the Jews as God's Chosen People, with special rights and responsibilities.

Diaspora (di-as´puh-ruh; Greek: "dispersion"). The situation of Jews living away from their ancestral homeland, a circumstance that has been true for most Jews since the classical period.

Hasidism (from Hebrew *hasid* [ha´seed]: "pious"). A form of Judaism that arose in eastern Europe in the eighteenth century and that emphasizes mysticism, a personal relationship with God, a close-knit community, and the leadership of the *zaddik* (tsah´dik), a charismatic holy man.

Holocaust. The persecution of Jews by German Nazis from 1933 to 1945, resulting in the murder of some six million; commonly referred to by Jews as Shoah (*shoah* is Hebrew for "mass destruction").

Kabbalah (kab´uh-luh). Jewish mysticism, which teaches that God can best be known through the heart; developed mainly in the medieval period with such texts as the Zohar.

Mishnah (meesh-nah´). Written down in about AD 200; contains collected teachings of the rabbis of the preceding four centuries; along with the Talmud, is the most important text of the oral Torah.

Passover. The eight-day festival celebrated in early spring that commemorates the Exodus of the Jews from Egypt.

rabbi (ra´bi; Hebrew: "my teacher"). A teacher of Torah and leader of Jewish worship.

Rosh Hashanah (rohsh hah-shah-nah´; Hebrew: "the beginning of the year"). The festival occurring in early fall in commemoration of the new year.

Sabbath (in Hebrew, *Shabbat*). The day from sunset on Friday until sunset on Saturday (observed on Sunday by some Reform Jews) that is set aside for rest and religious celebration, as decreed by one of the Ten Commandments (Exodus 20:8).

Shema (shuh-mah´; Hebrew: "hear"). From Deuteronomy 6:4, Judaism's basic statement of monotheism: "Hear, O Israel! The Lord is our God, the Lord alone" (Tanakh).

Talmud (tahl-mood´; Hebrew: "study," "knowledge"). The vast depository of the oral Torah, based on the Mishnah with extensive rabbinic commentary on each chapter; there are two versions, the Palestinian (completed about AD 450) and the Babylonian (completed about AD 600).

Tanakh (tah-nakh). A common way of referring to the Hebrew Bible, derived from the first letters of the Hebrew names of its three sections: Torah *(T)*, Prophets *(N)*, and Writings *(K)*.

Torah (toh´rah; Hebrew: "instruction"). Generally, the revelation of God's will to the people; more specifically, the divine Law, especially as contained in the first five books of the Bible, which together are often called the Torah.

Yom Kippur (yohm´ kee-poor´; Hebrew: "day of atonement"). Judaism's most important holy day, occurring in the fall on the tenth day of the new year; spent primarily at synagogue services in prayer for forgiveness of sins and marked by abstention from food and drink (fasting).

Zionism. Originally, the movement arising in the late nineteenth century that sought to re-establish a Jewish homeland; since 1948, the general support of the State of Israel.

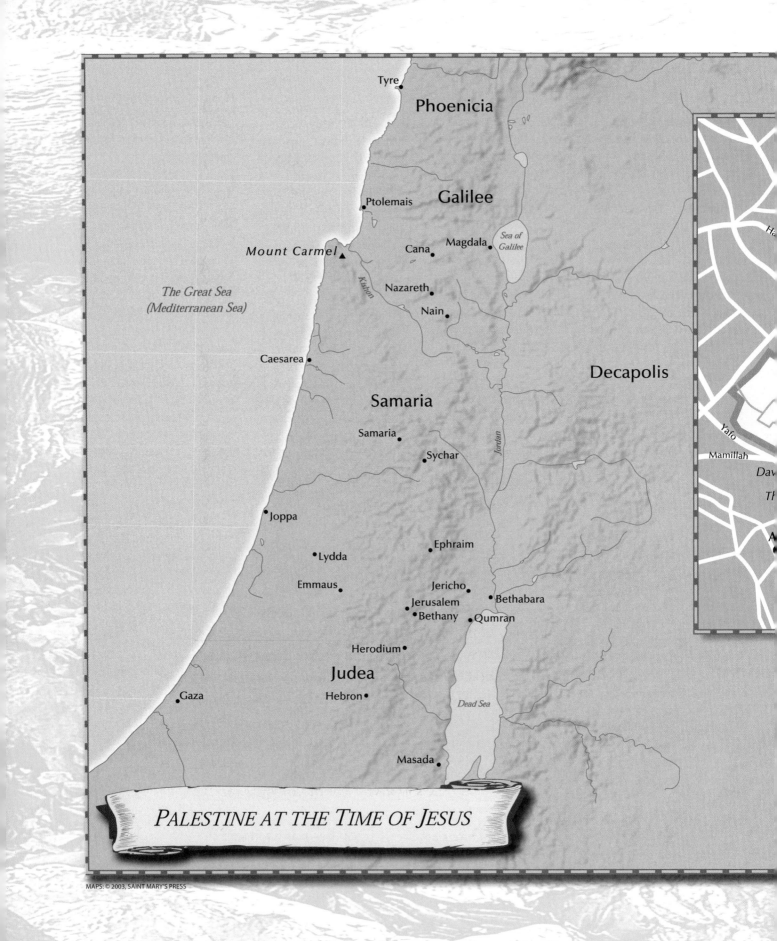

Tyre

Phoenicia

Galilee

Ptolemais

Cana • Magdala • Sea of Galilee

Mount Carmel ▲

Kishon

Nazareth

Nain

The Great Sea
(Mediterranean Sea)

Caesarea •

Decapolis

Samaria

Samaria •

Sychar •

Jordan

Joppa •

Ephraim •

Lydda •

Emmaus •

Jericho •

Bethabara •

Jerusalem •

Bethany •

Qumran •

Herodium •

Judea

Hebron •

Dead Sea

Gaza •

Masada •

PALESTINE AT THE TIME OF JESUS

Yafo

Mamillah

Dav

Th

A

MAPS: © 2003, SAINT MARY'S PRESS

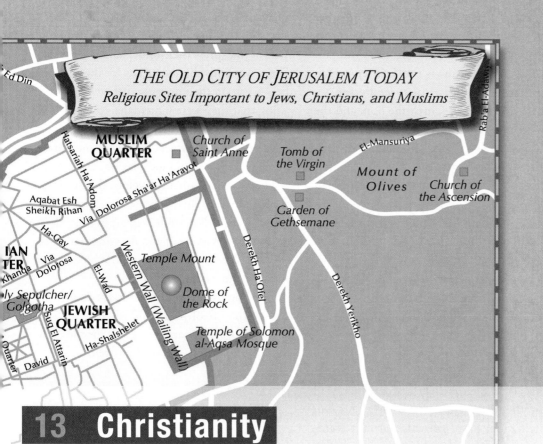

THE OLD CITY OF JERUSALEM TODAY
Religious Sites Important to Jews, Christians, and Muslims

13 Christianity

Who Is a Christian?

Nearly one-third of the world's population is Christian, making Christianity the world's largest religion. Christianity is the dominant tradition in the Americas, Europe, and Australia, and has significant followings in Asia and Africa as well.

What do the world's Christians, approximately two billion people, have in common? To put it simply, Christians share three things: Christ, creed, and Church.

To be a Christian is to acknowledge Jesus Christ as savior. The basis for knowing Christ is the New Testament, which describes the earthly life and ministry of Jesus, his Crucifixion and Resurrection, and the significance of those events for the early Church and for Christians in general.

Christian creed, based on the New Testament, consists of the essential doctrines, or beliefs, of Christianity. In the centuries following the life of Jesus, Church leaders and theologians strove to express their beliefs with ever greater precision. Classic statements such as the Nicene Creed (see page 232), formulated in the fourth century, present Christianity's core doctrines. One core doctrine is the **Incarnation,** which asserts that Christ is both fully divine and fully human. A second core doctrine is the **Trinity,** which holds that God consists of three Persons—God the Father, Jesus Christ the Son, and the **Holy Spirit**—who are at the same time one God. To be a Christian is to believe in such doctrines as the Incarnation and the Trinity, which are central elements of the Christian creed.

Finally, to be a Christian is to belong to the Church, the community of believers through which the creed is taught and Christ is celebrated. The New Testament decrees in various ways the essential role of the Church, founded by Christ and his disciples, and guided and nurtured by the Holy Spirit.

Some groups identify themselves as "Christian" although many other Christians would disagree that their beliefs and practices fall within the parameters that most Christian denominations have. For this reason it is important not to make complete generalizations about Christians, even though the chapter focuses on what *most* Christians believe and practice.

Fish have been popular Christian symbols since the days of the early Church.

IMAGE: © VANNI/ART RESOURCE, NY

Christ: Son of God, Savior

Early Christians, like some of their modern counterparts, used a concise and convenient symbol to express their understanding of who Christ was and what he meant for them. They drew a fish on their doors and elsewhere, indicating that they were Christians. In Greek the word for "fish" is *ixthus,* each letter of which begins a word (in Greek, that is) of the phrase "Jesus Christ, Son of God, Savior."

The New Testament develops this summary depiction of Christ, recounting the earthly life of Jesus of Nazareth; explaining his identity as the Son of God; and describing his role as Christ the Savior, the Messiah who came to earth for the salvation of all.

Drawing from the New Testament, we will explore the life of Jesus, and identify the significance of his life and teachings for the New Testament authors and for Christians.

The Life of Jesus

The New Testament Gospels (Matthew, Mark, Luke, and John) are the primary sources of information about the life of Jesus. They focus almost entirely on his last few years, from his baptism at around age thirty to his Crucifixion and Resurrection. One reason the Gospel authors provided little information about Jesus's early life is that they strove mainly to emphasize his teachings and to express the meaning of the events of his life, rather than to assemble a factual record. As a result we are not clear on all the details about him. Contemporary scholars who strive to overcome this shortage of ready facts and to learn about the "historical Jesus" meet with only limited success.

With these circumstances in mind, let us sketch the life of Jesus as best we can.

Judaism at the Time of Jesus

Jesus was born a Jew, and he remained a practicing Jew his entire life. His disciples were all Jews. Paul, the apostle who spread

The Sea of Galilee, known to ancient Hebrews as Lake Chinnereth and to modern Israelis as Lake Kinneret.

Jesus's message to the Gentiles (non-Jews), also was a Jew. It is therefore essential that we begin by noting a few facts about Judaism in Jesus's time.

The area of Palestine, the ancient homeland of the Jews, was conquered by the Romans in 63 BC. When Jesus was a youth, most of Palestine, including Jerusalem, came under the direct rule of a prefect, who served as a regional governor and reported directly to the Roman emperor. Pontius Pilate occupied this office from AD 26 to 36. The northern region of Galilee, where Jesus grew up and carried out most of his ministry, was ruled by Herod Antipas, a puppet king who himself was also ultimately under the rule of the Roman emperor. Being subject to the Romans placed the Jews in an extremely difficult situation. The Romans cared mainly about maintaining order and collecting taxes. The Jews, however, harbored long-standing hopes of achieving political independence. Tensions ran high, sometimes leading to conflicts and executions.

Jews responded to these difficulties in various ways. As noted in chapter 12, the Sadducees, Essenes, and Pharisees all practiced different varieties of Judaism. The Sadducees, wealthy aristocrats who controlled the Jerusalem Temple, were conservative, generally remaining on friendly terms with the rulers.

The Essenes fled from the troubles, leading lives of discipline and purity in desert communities. The Pharisees were moderate, obeying the traditional commandments of Judaism and developing the oral Torah. There was also a group known as the Zealots, who believed the only way to achieve Jewish independence was through armed rebellion.

Jesus fit none of these categories. He was not a conservative, like the Sadducees. Unlike the Essenes he chose to remain within society. He was a peaceful rebel who did not share the violent methods of the Zealots. Jesus had much in common with the Pharisees, but they did not approve of his outreach to the lower strata of the Jewish community, or of his nontraditional ways of observing Torah.

Despite these differences Jesus seems to have shared with many other Jews some aspects of a basic religious perspective of that time known by biblical scholars as **apocalypticism.** According to this perspective, the world had come under the control of evil forces that caused Jews to live in an unjust situation. However, God was still ultimately in control. The world's woes would become greater and greater until God would usher in the End Time and conquer the forces of evil. Many, though not all, Jews believed the End Time would involve the Messiah, a deliverer, who would end "this current

A

Apocalypticism continues to be an important perspective for many people. What are some ways that you have seen apocalypticism, as it is described here, manifested today?

B

The lower strata of Jewish society in Jesus's day included prostitutes, tax collectors, and others whom the Bible calls sinners and outcasts. What kinds of people make up the lower strata of society today?

age" and usher in "the age to come." The dead would be resurrected, and all would be judged, and ultimately the righteous would enjoy salvation and the rest would suffer damnation. Before the End Time, God would reveal the plan to the elect through a revelation, or apocalypse, contained in certain writings. The last book of the New Testament, the Revelation (or Apocalypse) to John, is a primary example of apocalyptic writing. Apocalypticism seems to have informed the religious outlook of Jesus, and was central to Paul and to early Christianity in general.[A]

Jesus's Early Life and Ministry

Jesus was born sometime between 6 and 4 BC (our system of dating based on Christ's birth was developed several centuries later, and scholars have now determined that it is off by at least four years). The Gospels of Matthew and Luke report that Jesus was born in Bethlehem, near Jerusalem, but he grew up in the town of Nazareth, in Galilee. Jesus likely became a carpenter, like his father, Joseph. Jesus also seems to have become well versed in the Hebrew Scriptures, the sacred texts of the Jews of that time.

Jesus's ministry lasted about two years and was carried out mainly in Galilee. It began shortly after Jesus was baptized by John the Baptist. John, clothed in animal skins and living off the land, preached the imminent coming of the judgment of God. The precise nature of Jesus and John's relationship remains unclear, but scholars think it likely that Jesus was a disciple of John's.

On beginning his ministry, Jesus attracted disciples, and eventually large crowds gathered around him. These facts alone are evidence of his charisma and of the relevance and effectiveness of his acts and teachings. The Gospels all portray Jesus as an exorcist (one who casts out demons) and a healer. He often taught in **parables,** stories cast in language and settings familiar to his listeners but proclaiming radical lessons intended to disrupt conventional

ways of thinking. Parables such as the good Samaritan and the prodigal son are among the best-known Gospel passages.

Jesus primarily ministered to fellow Jews, but unlike the Pharisees and other religious figures of his day, he constantly reached out to the lower strata of Jewish society: prostitutes, tax collectors, lepers, and other "sinners" and "outcasts."[B]

Jesus's Message

Jesus's astounding wisdom fills the Gospels, and his teachings have enriched Christians and non-Christians alike, for centuries. In conveying his message, he focused on two interrelated themes: the imminent coming of the Kingdom, or Reign, of God, and the urgent need for ethical transformation rooted in a change of heart.

The first theme is summarized in Mark 1:15, in which Jesus proclaims: "The time is fulfilled, and the kingdom of God has come near; repent, and believe in the good news." When Jesus spoke of the Kingdom of God, he referred to God's intervention in history to right the wrongs of the world. The present age of injustice was rapidly coming to an end, and a new age was beginning, one in which God's Reign would prevail. Jesus's actions and teachings were directly linked to the coming of God's Reign. In Luke 11:20, for example, Jesus remarks on the significance of his role as exorcist: "But if it is by the finger of God that I cast out the demons, then the kingdom of God has come to you."

The second theme of Jesus's ministry, ethical transformation, is also linked with the coming of God's Reign, for God's Reign would be one of righteousness. The heart of Jesus's ethical teachings can be found in his striking commandment on love:

You have heard that it was said, "You shall love your neighbor and hate your enemy." But I say to you, Love your enemies and pray for those who persecute you, so that you may be children of your Father in heaven. (Matthew 5:43–45)

The notion of loving one's enemies must have struck Jesus's listeners as radical, but parting from the norm is typical of his ethical teachings in general. Though Jesus did not reject the traditional commandments of Torah, he urged his listeners to go beyond the letter of the Law. The Reign of God demands more than legal obedience to Torah; it demands spiritual obedience as well. Love requires more than following the rules; it depends on the transformation of the individual.

Along with teaching ethical transformation through his words, Jesus also taught by his actions, focusing his ministry on the lower classes of society. Jesus consistently practiced what he preached.[C]

Jesus's Crucifixion and Resurrection

Jesus was crucified by order of the Roman prefect Pontius Pilate, probably in AD 30. The radical nature of his teachings and ministry, and the agitated crowd of followers he attracted got Jesus in trouble with the authorities. Teachings regarding a coming new "kingdom" would have struck the authorities as particularly troublesome. Some of those authorities were Jewish, though Jews may not have been as involved in Jesus's arrest and trial as the Gospels suggest. In any event only the Roman prefect had the authority to pronounce a death sentence. Jesus died the slow and painful death of crucifixion, the manner of execution reserved for those condemned as political threats to the Roman Empire.

This was by no means the end of the story. Indeed the religion of Christianity really began after the Resurrection, when Jesus's followers first experienced him as the risen Lord. The Gospels all describe the discovery of an empty tomb, from which the risen Jesus is said to have departed. Although each Gospel gives its own account, they all point to an event of profound significance and meaning. The conviction that Jesus had been raised

IMAGE: © CAMERAPHOTO/ART RESOURCE, NY

Jesus suffered the slow and painful death of crucifixion, the method of execution reserved for those condemned as political threats to the Roman Empire.

from the dead by God moved Jesus's followers to spread the news of his life and message far and wide. Some, such as Peter, were willing to die rather than deny their faith in the Resurrection.

The Good News of Christ

The Christian message is often called by the name *gospel* (in Greek, *evangelion*) which means "good news" and refers specifically to the good news regarding Jesus Christ.

Four New Testament authors have each provided a version of the **Gospel** that emphasizes certain aspects of the life and teachings of Jesus, and of his Crucifixion and Resurrection. This is a sampling of the "good news" from Paul's epistles and from three Gospels.

C
How could you apply Jesus's commandment to love your enemies in your daily life?

(When capitalized the term usually refers to the New Testament books that recount the good news of Jesus's life, death, Resurrection, and Ascension.)

The Epistles of Paul: Christ Crucified and Risen

Paul's epistles, or letters, to the churches of Corinth, Rome, Galatia, and elsewhere are of paramount importance to Christian belief and theology. Paul refers specifically to the gospel, or "good news," in his first epistle to the Corinthians:

> Now I would remind you, brothers and sisters, of the good news *[evangelion]* that I proclaimed to you, which you in turn received, in which also you stand, through which also you are being saved, if you hold firmly to the message that I proclaimed to you—unless you have come to believe in vain.
>
> For I handed on to you as of first importance what I in turn had received: that Christ died for our sins in accordance with the scriptures, and that he was buried, and that he was raised on the third day in accordance with the scriptures.
>
> (15:1–4)

Paul saw the power of Christ's Crucifixion and Resurrection as the source of salvation. Christ, in his death on the cross, carried away the consequences of humanity's sinfulness. With his Resurrection Christ overcame death. Christians, having been forgiven their sins through Christ's sacrificial death, will share in his Resurrection and experience eternal life. Thus, for Paul, salvation was the overcoming of sin and death.

Paul's perspective on resurrection and eternal life remains prominant in Christian beliefs. In keeping with his apocalyptic view of the world, Paul understood Christ's death and Resurrection as climactic moments in God's plan for salvation. Finally, when Christ returns to the world at the **second coming,** which Paul equated with the End Time, the dead will be raised, and all people—living and dead—will be judged. The good will be saved, and the evil condemned.

For Paul, salvation is not only the overcoming of death but also the restoration of friendship with God, freeing people from the bonds of sin and inspiring a newfound peace and joy. God's goodness and grace overcome the power of sin so that those freed might enjoy the "fruit of the Spirit": "love, joy, peace, patience, kindness, generosity, faithfulness, gentleness, and self-control" (Galatians 5:22–23). Paul emphasizes that this salvation comes through God's **grace**—God's presence freely given.

Like many of Jesus's parables, the one about the good Samaritan, depicted here, characterizes a social outcast in a positive light.

For Paul, God's giving of Christ ushers in the fulfillment of the divine plan for humanity, ending the era of strict obedience to the Law, in which Jews strove to be saved through observance of the Law. Now all people, Jews and Gentiles alike, can be saved through faith in Jesus Christ. Of course, Paul did not teach the abandonment of ethical behavior. But that behavior now depends on faith in Christ, which transforms the believer, rather than on observance of the Law, which God had given to the Jews to serve as a "disciplinarian until Christ came" (Galatians 3:24).

Despite his conviction that Christ signifies the end of the Law, Paul insists the Jews are still included in God's plan for salvation: "I want you to understand this mystery: a hardening has come upon part of Israel, until the full number of the Gentiles has come in. And so all Israel will be saved" (Romans 11:25–26). This remains an important statement about the relationship of Christians and Jews.D

The Gospel of Matthew: A New Revelation of Divine Law

Recall that Jesus expanded traditional ethical standards, urging a spiritual obedience to the Law. This is the main focus of the Gospel of Matthew, which presents Christ as the new Moses who reveals the fulfillment of God's Law through spiritual obedience. But Jesus made clear that his mission in no way implies that God's original revelation to the Israelites is to be disregarded: "Do not think that I have come to abolish the law or the prophets; I have come not to abolish but to fulfill" (Matthew 5:17). However, Jesus requires a new, radical obedience as illustrated by his commandment to love one's enemies, and by other statements he made, such as this: "For I tell you, unless your righteousness exceeds that of the scribes and Pharisees, you will never enter the kingdom of heaven" (Matthew 5:20).

The centerpiece of Matthew's presentation of Christ is the Sermon on the Mount (chapters 5 through 7), from which the preceding passages are drawn. The Sermon on the Mount also contains the Beatitudes, the commandment to love one's enemies, and many other specific examples of radical obedience to traditional ethical laws. It is noteworthy that in Matthew's Gospel, Jesus reveals these teachings on a mountain while in the Gospel of Luke, similar teachings are presented on a

D

For Paul, God's giving of Christ marks the end of the era of the Torah. This gift in no way releases humans from ethical responsibility. Now, however, good behavior is to be rooted in faith and the spiritual transformation it brings, rather than in obedience to the letter of the Law. Think about two or three ethical decisions you have faced. In those cases how might goodness rooted in the right spiritual perspective have differed from goodness based on rules of correct behavior?

The Beatitudes

The Beatitudes comprise the opening statements of Jesus's Sermon on the Mount and are named from the Latin term for the word with which they each open: blessed. *They are contained in Matthew 5:3–12.*

Blessed are the poor in spirit, for theirs is the kingdom of heaven.

Blessed are those who mourn, for they will be comforted.

Blessed are the meek, for they will inherit the earth.

Blessed are those who hunger and thirst for righteousness, for they will be filled.

Blessed are the merciful, for they will receive mercy.

Blessed are the pure in heart, for they will see God.

Blessed are the peacemakers, for they will be called children of God.

Blessed are those who are persecuted for righteousness' sake, for theirs is the kingdom of heaven.

Blessed are you when people revile you and persecute you and utter all kinds of evil against you falsely on my account. Rejoice and be glad, for your reward is great in heaven, for in the same way they persecuted the prophets who were before you.

E

Read the Sermon on the Mount (see Matthew, chapters 5 through 7). Find three teachings (besides those mentioned in the textbook) that you think clearly illustrate Jesus's ethical message.

F

Read the parable of the good Samaritan (see Luke 10:29–37). While keeping its basic message intact, how would you retell the parable to make it more relevant for modern society?

plain. Matthew seems to intend for his readers to recall the original revelation of Torah to Moses on Mount Sinai.[E]

The Gospel of Luke: Salvation for All People

All the Gospels portray Jesus as one whom every Christian should strive to imitate. The Gospel of Luke emphasizes this point, presenting Jesus as a role model for the perfect way to live and as offering salvation for all people. Jesus reaches out to help people in all segments of society. This Gospel gives women more attention than do the other Gospels, and many of its parables characterize outcasts in a favorable light. None does this more effectively than the parable of the good Samaritan (see Luke 10:29–37). Samaritans were historically on bad terms with the Jews, and thus were not expected to be kind toward them. But in the parable, a Samaritan aids an injured Jew who had been ignored by a priest and a Levite, members of what was supposed to be the most upstanding level of Jewish society.[F]

The Gospel of John: The Incarnation of God

The Incarnation is the focal point of the Gospel of John, in which Christ is presented as the Word, who from the beginning was with God and was God (see John 1:1). Christ, who was active in the creation of the world with his Father, is truly one with him as the Son of God, and will return to him.

In Jesus, "the Word became flesh and lived among us" (John 1:14). Human salvation comes through knowing Christ and believing in the Father who sent him. This emphasis on the saving power of knowledge and belief is evident in the following passage, in which Jesus instructs his fellow Jews: "Very truly, I tell you, anyone who hears my word and believes him who sent me has eternal life, and does not come under judgment, but has passed from death to life" (John 5:24).

Creed: What Christians Believe

The term *creed* comes from the Latin word *credo,* "I believe," which begins the Latin version of the **Apostles' Creed.** The Apostles' Creed is one of Christianity's most important statements of belief:

I believe in God,
    the Father almighty,
    creator of heaven and earth.
I believe in Jesus Christ,
    his only Son, our Lord.
He was conceived by the power of the
        Holy Spirit
    and born of the Virgin Mary.
He suffered under Pontius Pilate,
    was crucified, died, and was buried.
    He descended into hell.
On the third day he rose again.
He ascended into heaven
    and is seated at the right hand of the
        Father.
    He will come again to judge the living
        and the dead.
I believe in the Holy Spirit,
    the holy catholic Church,
    the communion of saints,
    the forgiveness of sins,
    the resurrection of the body,
    and the life everlasting.
    Amen.

Already in use by the end of the second century, the Apostles' Creed sets forth the foundations for two of Christianity's central doctrines: the Incarnation and the Trinity. Affirming both the divinity and the humanity of Christ, God incarnate, the creed also refers to each of the three Persons of the Trinity: God the Father, Jesus Christ the Son, and the Holy Spirit. Today both doctrines are defined with greater precision, thanks to the work of theologians and Church councils through the centuries.

Michelangelo's *Pietá*, in Saint Peter's Basilica at the Vatican, movingly expresses the humanity of the crucified Christ, and therefore the doctrine of the Incarnation.

The Incarnation: "The Word Became Flesh"

The Apostles' Creed asserts the divinity of Jesus while also insisting on his human nature. Like ordinary human beings, Jesus was born. But like no one else, he was born of a virgin. Mary's virginity reveals God's initiative in the incarnation and role of the Holy Spirit in Jesus's conception. The Creed returns to the emphasis on Jesus's humanity by asserting that he "suffered under Pontius Pilate, was crucified, died, and was buried." The Gospel of John does the same, clearly asserting Jesus's divinity while also emphasizing more than the other Gospels Jesus's humanness, referring to such things as his hunger and thirst, and pointing out that he wept on occasion. This focus on Jesus's humanity is in keeping with John's focus on the Incarnation. The first chapter of John establishes the foundation for the later formulations of the doctrine of the Incarnation. It identifies Christ as the Word (called Logos in Greek), who from the beginning was with God and was God (see John 1:1), active in the creation of the world. In the person of Jesus, "the Word became flesh and lived among us" (John 1:14), and because of this the salvation of humanity is possible.

For centuries the Church strove to elaborate on the words of the Gospel of John and the Apostles' Creed, in order to state precisely the doctrine of the Incarnation. It was crucial that it be made clear that the Word actually *became* flesh, rather than merely appearing to become flesh, and that this union of the divine and human natures in Jesus was permanent, affecting humanity for all time.

The **Nicene Creed,** formulated by Church leaders at the Council of Nicaea (n*i*-see'uh) in 325, states that Jesus Christ is

the only Son of God
eternally begotten of the Father,

. . . .

true God from true God,
begotten, not made, one in Being with the
　　Father.

This is obviously a much more elaborate, precise statement of the doctrine of the Incarnation than we see in the Apostles' Creed. Historically speaking, the most crucial point established at the Council of Nicaea is that

Jesus the Son and God the Father are "one in Being" (*homoousios* in Greek). God became flesh in the person of Jesus, but in no way is Jesus a lesser being. Indeed he is the *same* being.

The Trinity

The doctrine of the Trinity is the centerpiece of Christian belief and theology. By definition the Christian God is a triune God, three Persons—God the Father, Christ the Son, and the Holy Spirit—in one Godhead. To think about God is therefore to think about the Trinity. Saint Thomas Aquinas, the great medieval theologian, expresses the centrality of the Trinity this way:

It is impossible to believe explicitly in the mystery of Christ without faith in the Trinity, since the mystery of Christ includes that the Son of God took flesh, that He renewed the world through the grace of the Holy [Spirit], and again, that He was conceived by the Holy [Spirit]. (*Summa Theologiae*, volume 2, part 2, question 2, article 8)

The doctrine of the Trinity states that the three Persons of God are distinct from one another and yet of the same essence or substance. The Nicene Creed describes each Person of the triune God:

We believe in one God,
 the Father, the Almighty,
 maker of heaven and earth,
 of all that is, seen and unseen.
We believe in one Lord, Jesus Christ,
 the only Son of God
 . . . .
We believe in the Holy Spirit,
 the Lord, the giver of life,
 who proceeds from the Father and the Son.

In the Nicene Creed and later formulations, the distinctive features of the three Persons of the Trinity are precisely stated. God the Father is creator and judge, who generates the Son, and with the Son sends forth the Holy Spirit. God the Son is redeemer, begotten by, yet coeternal with, the Father. It is through the Son as Word of the Father that the Father is expressed in human history. God the Holy Spirit is reconciler and sanctifier, proceeding from the Father and the Son.

The Trinity is three Persons with distinctive features, but only one God. This is difficult for the mind to comprehend, and indeed Christians regard it as a mystery that cannot be fully grasped in this earthly life.

Church: The "One Body" of Christ

Along with belief in the Trinity and other Christian doctrines, being a Christian means belonging to the Church, the community of believers.

As Paul makes clear in his first epistle to the Corinthians, the Church is meant to be a unified body of people:

For just as the body is one and has many members, and all the members of the body, though many, are one body, so it is with Christ. For in the one Spirit we were all baptized into one body. (12:12–13)

The doctrine of the Trinity, symbolized in this stained glass window, is the centerpiece of Christian belief and theology.

IMAGE: GENE PLAISTED, THE CROSIERS

This ideal of unity is embraced by Christians, and today ecumenism, the promotion of worldwide Christian unity, is seen as a vital task. Nevertheless, differences exist among the world's Christians. We can begin to explore what it means to be One Body in Christ as ecumenism itself begins, with striving to understand the differences among Christians, as well as the historical circumstances that have fueled those differences.

The Early Church

In the years following the Resurrection, an organized Church (whose name comes from the Greek word *ekklesia* [ek-klay-see´ah], meaning "assembly") gradually took shape. The Church embodied a form of Christianity that was equipped to thrive within the wider society of the Mediterranean world and to endure through time.

In discussions about the early Church, the word **Church** commonly refers to all Christians, not just to single congregations. Even while forming one cohesive Church, however, the early Christians did not necessarily agree on everything. Some Christian communities considered the beliefs of others to be **heresies**, opinions or doctrines at variance with ac-

cepted doctrine. Occasional Church councils made important decisions that eventually led to a version of the Church that most regarded as **orthodox**, having "right doctrine."

Among the capable and courageous people who were responsible for establishing the early Church, none was more influential than the Apostle Paul.

Paul, Apostle to the Gentiles

Paul was a Pharisaic Jew from the city of Tarsus. He was passionately devoted to the study of Torah, and, by his own account, he was an adept and zealous student. Synagogues had the authority to discipline local Jews who were judged to be violating Torah, something that Paul considered the early Jewish followers of Christ to be doing. Paul, by his own account persecuted Christians (see Philippians 3:6).

Then something happened that changed Paul's life—and the history of Christianity. While traveling on a road to Damascus, Paul experienced the risen Christ. He became an **apostle** (a messenger proclaiming the Gospel of Christ), preaching primarily to Gentiles.

Paul's conversion, or call to be an apostle, occurred a few years after the Crucifixion of Jesus, perhaps as early as AD 32. Over the

IMAGE: © SCALA/ART RESOURCE, NY

Paul's mission to the Gentiles led him to preach to the people of Athens, as depicted in this fifteenth-century tapestry.

Christianity   233

One Young Catholic's Experience

Meggan L. Novotny, a college student, describes what Catholicism means to her:

To me, the most important part of being a Catholic is the personal experience of Christ at Mass. Listening to the readings and to the homily provides me with a deeper understanding of what I am called to do as a Catholic. Granted, the message may not be one that I want to hear, but it allows me to reflect personally on my strengths and weaknesses. I am always excited when the homily is finished, not because we are entering the last half of the Mass, but because the Eucharist is about to be celebrated. For me, Communion is the most serious and humbling activity.

Before receiving Communion, I always try to recollect how I have sinned, so that I can ask for forgiveness and proceed to the altar ready to receive Christ with a sense of renewed beginning. Some people watch others go up to receive Communion, but I am usually in such deep prayer and reflection that most trivial things go unnoticed. To think that Christ is present and available to me is astonishing! To know that I can do wrong and still be loved unconditionally and invited to his table sets a standard I try to achieve but can fall short of. Mass allows me to take an hour out of my day so I can examine what I have done and what I need to do to be a true follower of Christ.

next three decades, Paul traveled great distances to cities with Christian communities, such as Athens, Corinth, and Ephesus. In some places Paul himself established Christian communities. He would stay for months at a time, caring for the early churches and working to gain new converts. Meanwhile he wrote letters, or epistles, to churches elsewhere. The churches preserved some of the letters, eventually regarding them as sacred scripture. The New Testament includes several of Paul's epistles, which are the earliest New Testament books, written about ten to twenty years before the earliest Gospel.

Just as he had been a zealous Pharisee, the Apostle Paul proved to be a zealous Christian. He was also self-assured, speaking out on a variety of issues, some of them highly controversial. Eventually Paul's missionary zeal landed him in trouble with the Jewish authorities, who took his case to the Roman authorities. Because, as a Roman citizen, Paul wanted to appeal his case to Rome, he was transported there from Jerusalem. After serving two years in prison, where he continued to preach the Gospel, he was beheaded, around AD 62.

Jews and Gentiles

One decision facing Paul and other leaders of the early Church involved the relation of Christianity to Judaism. Should Gentile Christians be required, like Jews, to observe Torah, to be circumcised, to eat kosher food, and to celebrate the Sabbath and the annual Jewish holy days? Many Jews who had become Christians thought so, and Jewish Christianity flourished throughout the first century.

Paul was firmly convinced that Gentiles should be granted freedom from most requirements of Torah. His deep conviction on this matter seems to have prevailed at the Council of Jerusalem, a meeting of apostles and elders held about five to eight years after the Crucifixion. The apostles and elders decided Gentile Christians were virtually free from the requirements of the Jewish Law. It was a momentous decision, distinguishing the Christian Church from its parent, Judaism. In terms of worship, however, the Christian Church drew much from the practices of the Jewish synagogues.

Worship, Leadership, and Scripture of the First Christians

Like the Jews, early Christians gathered for weekly worship meetings. Eventually these were held on Sundays, to commemorate Christ's Resurrection and to distinguish the Church from Judaism, which celebrated the Sabbath on Saturday. Many aspects of the Christian meetings were patterned after the synagogue services: chanting psalms, singing hymns, reading from scripture, and praying. Worship also included teachings on the Gospel. The central ritual of the meetings, though, was the sacrament of the **Eucharist,** or Communion meal, a memorial of the Last Supper, which had been shared by Jesus and his Apostles the night before he was crucified. With this ritual Christians remembered the sacred mystery of Jesus's death and Resurrection as the source of all Christian life and meaning.

Baptism was also a central ritual of the early Church, functioning (as it does today) as the foundational sacrament of initiation. Its symbols illustrated the spiritual purity new Christians attained through accepting Christ. Immersion in water represented the death of their former life of sinfulness, and the emergence of new life in Christ. In addition, Baptism, like the shared meal of the Eucharist, symbolized the unity and equality of Christians, who represented a cross section of Roman society. Some were rich, many were poor, and some were even slaves, but all were brothers and sisters in Christ.

The early Church also developed a structure of leadership. By early in the second century, three distinct offices were in place: **bishops, presbyters,** and **deacons.** Bishops were seen as successors to Jesus's Apostles, and therefore were highly esteemed. Each bishop was the overseer of his church, and the bishop performed the chief task of administering the Eucharist. From early times Rome was generally regarded as the central location of the Church, and the bishop of Rome was given a special degree of authority. Eventually the bishop of Rome came to have the title **pope.** Because the Apostle Peter is traditionally thought to have been the bishop of Rome, the pope is his direct successor.

The presbyters (named after the Greek word for "elders") assisted the bishop, administering the Eucharist in the bishop's absence and taking charge of financial and disciplinary matters. Also assisting the bishop were deacons (whose name comes from the Greek word for "servants"), some of whom were women. (The Catholic Church does not regard the ancient role of deaconesses to be the same as the current ordained ministry of deacons.) The deacons helped with a variety of tasks and also linked the congregation and its bishop.

Christian scripture originally consisted of the Jewish Scriptures. By the beginning of the second century, Paul's epistles were also widely circulated and regarded as sacred or authoritative documents. Soon other writings, Gospels about the life of Jesus and various accounts of the Apostles, became known throughout the Christian communities.

IMAGE: © MATT CAMPBELL/EPA/CORBIS

Pope Benedict XVI at the United Nations General Assembly in New York City.

In the fourth century, the Church settled on a **canon** ("rule" or "standard") of twenty-seven writings. This collection is known as the **New Testament,** or New Covenant. As we have observed in the theology of Paul, Christians believed that the Gospel of Christ had fulfilled the Covenant with Israel in God's plan for the salvation of humanity.

Christ and Caesar: Christians in the Roman World

From the origins of Christianity through its first centuries of growth, its adherents lived within the political, economic, and social structures of the Roman Empire. To a large extent, Christians carried on their spiritual lives independently of Roman constraints. However, some degree of conflict between Rome and Christianity was inevitable.

In the Roman empire, worship of pagan gods and of the emperor's genius, or guardian spirit, was primarily a display of loyalty toward the Roman state. Because Christians were monotheistic, they refused to participate in such worship and this made them seem unpatriotic to the Romans. This perception is one of the reasons Romans persecuted Christians, who often died painfully as **martyrs** (named after the Greek word for "witness"), rather than violate their Christian convictions. A generally negative attitude about Christians by the Romans is chief among other reasons for persecution.

Roman attitudes and policies toward Christians changed markedly during the fourth century. As the century began, Christians were enduring the Great Persecution, begun

The Writings of the New Testament

The Gospels and the Acts of the Apostles

Matthew, Mark, Luke, John, Acts of the Apostles (the second volume of Luke's two-volume work)

Paul's Epistles

Romans, 1 Corinthians, 2 Corinthians, Galatians, Philippians, 1 Thessalonians, Philemon

"Deutero-Pauline" Epistles

(Attributed to Paul, but likely written by followers of Paul's) Ephesians, Colossians, 2 Thessalonians

Pastoral Epistles

1 Timothy, 2 Timothy, Titus

Letter to the Hebrews

Hebrews

Catholic Epistles

James, 1 Peter, 2 Peter, 1 John, 2 John, 3 John, Jude

Book of Revelation

Revelation

by the emperor Diocletian. At that time only about 5 percent of the empire was Christian. But by the end of the fourth century, Christianity was the empire's only legitimate religion, and a large majority of Roman citizens had converted. The key figure in this dramatic reversal of fortune was the emperor Constantine.

In 312 Constantine won a crucial victory that enabled him to become the uncontested emperor. He credited the victory to the intervention of Christ, and eventually he was baptized a Christian.

Constantine took significant steps that promoted Christianity in the empire. In 313 he issued a policy traditionally known as the Edict of Milan, declaring Christianity a legitimate religion and ending persecution of Christians. In 325 he convened Christian leaders to the Council of Nicaea, where they formulated the Nicene Creed to help unify the Church. The theological arguments at the council were mainly taken up by the bishops, but Constantine's presence significantly strengthened the distinction between orthodox Christianity and heresies.[G]

The Fall of Rome and *The City of God*

Among the many events leading to the fall of the Roman Empire, the sack of the city of Rome in 410 by the Visigoths was the most dramatic and alarming. Some Romans blamed Christianity, asserting that the gods were now punishing Rome for abandoning traditional pagan religion.

In response to this accusation, Bishop Augustine of Hippo, in North Africa, wrote a masterpiece of Christian theology: *The City of God*. In this work he argues that all governments and nations are corrupt and have fallen to sin. Therefore, the fall of the earthly city is of little consequence. Only the heavenly city, the Kingdom of God, truly matters.

Augustine and his theology set the stage for the great Catholic theologians of the Middle Ages, and also inspired Martin Luther, leader of the Protestant Reformation.

Medieval Christianity and the Protestant Reformation

Christianity emerged in the fourth century as the premier religion of the Roman Empire. At this time the tradition of the orthodox, or **Catholic** (named from the Greek word for "universal") Church was well established. Theological debates still raged, and occasionally those whose views varied too greatly from the orthodox position were denounced as heretics. For the most part though, the Church was a united institution.

During the next seven centuries, however, Christian unity encountered many challenges, and a gradual divide took place in the Church. By 1054 Eastern Orthodoxy, one of the three great limbs of modern Christianity, had officially become independent from the Roman Church.

The Schism Between East and West

As early as the reign of Emperor Constantine, the foundation for a schism, or split, between the Church in the East and the Church in the West was already in place. Constantine established an eastern capital, Constantinople (modern-day Istanbul, Turkey), which quickly became a second center of the Church, along with Rome. A number of problems arose. The distance between Constantinople and Rome caused communication difficulties, which were compounded by a language barrier: the Eastern Church used Greek, and the Church in Rome used Latin. Further strife resulted from a gradual loss of political unity when the western part of the Roman Empire fell, and the eastern part survived in the form of the Byzantine Empire.

Along with these divisive elements was the Eastern Christians' refusal, starting in the late fourth century, to accept the authority of the pope in Rome. The final break occurred in 1054, when Pope Leo IX excommunicated the leader of the Greek Church, the patriarch of Constantinople, who in turn excommunicated the pope. Attempts were made to rec-

G

Before Emperor Constantine legitimized Christianity in the fourth century, many Christians died as martyrs for their faith. Do you think Christian martyrdom is still possible in today's society? If so, can you think of any modern Christian martyrs?

oncile the Churches, but they failed. Eastern Orthodoxy and Roman Catholicism have been independent of each other ever since.

Catholicism in the Middle Ages

Roman Catholic Christianity was established as the dominant culture of medieval Europe. For the most part, the late Middle Ages was a period of triumph for Catholicism, though not without exceptions. Some popes and other members of the Church hierarchy engaged in corrupt practices. From 1096 to 1270, the Roman Catholic Church launched the Crusades, a series of military expeditions intended to take control of the Holy Land from the Muslims. Jerusalem was held for a time by Christians, but it soon fell back into Muslim hands. The Crusades, which were often senselessly violent, sometimes even involved Christians fighting Christians.

But medieval Catholicism also brought about much that has had lasting significance. The Church continued to fortify itself as an organized institution with spiritual authority beyond that of any monarchs or other rulers.

A modern Franciscan monk lights candles.

IMAGE: © DAVE BARTRUFF/CORBIS

Great cathedrals were constructed, sometimes over the course of centuries. Monasticism, a lifestyle emphasizing community, simplicity, celibacy, and prayer, reached a new height of influence. Established communities of monks and nuns were reformed, and new ones, such as the Dominicans and Franciscans, were founded.

Saint Francis of Assisi (1182 to 1226), founder of the Franciscan order, remains one of the most revered Christians of all time. As one who loved nature and cared for poor people, Francis for the most part shunned the organizational constraints that were so much a part of the Church. He and his loose-knit band of followers traveled the countryside in simple, coarse garments, preaching the Gospel in the streets and marketplaces. Having put aside material possessions, they worked for food, and begged when work was not available. Their rewards were being close to nature and to God, and caring for those who were less fortunate. For many people Saint Francis is the perfect example of someone living in imitation of Christ.

Medieval theology culminated in the work of the great Dominican thinker, Saint Thomas Aquinas (1225 to 1274). Drawing from the philosophy of Aristotle, Aquinas explained the relation between reason and faith, arguing that the two complement and need each other. For example, Aquinas taught that reason can prove the existence of God, but faith remains essential for full understanding of the truth, as it is revealed in the Bible and the teachings of the Church. Aquinas's final and greatest work, the *Summa Theologiae,* was controversial at first but became the standard work of Catholic theology. It remains important to the present day.[H]

The Protestant Reformation

The **Protestant Reformation** brought widespread change. It swept across much of sixteenth-century Europe, most notably in Germany, Switzerland, and England. Many Christians were frustrated with certain aspects of Catholicism and were ready for change. In Germany one man set in motion a movement that would radically change Christianity as well as European society.

Martin Luther (1483 to 1546) was born to a peasant family. He originally set out to study law, but in response to his deep religious feelings, he became a monk of the Augustinian order. He was a highly devoted monk but was unable to find freedom from his overwhelming sense of sinfulness. On a trip to Rome, Luther personally observed corruption within the hierarchy of the Church.

Gradually Luther's feelings and experiences culminated in the birth of the Reformation. Luther discovered the foundation of his Christian faith in Paul's epistles: that humans are justified (made worthy of salvation) through faith in Christ, and not through external practices, or "works." One external practice that Luther rejected was the buying and selling of **indulgences,** reductions in or pardons of the punishment due for sins committed. People believed that by giving money to the Church, they could reduce the time they would spend in the period of final purification after death, known as purgatory. Luther felt this practice completely missed the point of Christianity.

In protest against the selling of indulgences, Luther wrote the Ninety-five Theses in 1517. According to the traditional account, he nailed them to the door of the church he served, an action that at the time was considered a polite way of inviting discourse. He did not intentionally incite a major controversy, but the theses did in fact draw an enthusiastic—and highly controversial—response.

Luther defended his views with the Bible. According to him much of what the Church was doing did not conform to biblical Christianity. (Later, to help make the Bible more accessible to all Christians, including the common people, Luther translated it into German. Because the printing press had recently been invented, Luther's German Bible was widely distributed.)

Martin Luther initiated events that led to the Protestant Reformation.

The controversy Luther stirred up got him into trouble with the Church. He was eventually excommunicated but managed to evade punishment. Meanwhile local rulers chose between Protestantism (which the new movement was called, because it began as a "protest") and Catholicism. Most rulers in central and northern Germany and in the Scandinavian countries chose Protestantism. In those lands former priests, monks, and nuns could now marry. Luther himself married a former nun, and they had five children.

Elsewhere in Europe other reform movements were taking place. In England a new English translation of the Bible appeared in 1526. Its release was considered such a drastic step that its translator was condemned for heresy and burned at the stake. King Henry VIII (who reigned from 1509 to 1547) broke with the pope, who condemned his desire to remarry after divorcing his wife. King Henry declared himself head of the Church of England. Thomas More, the highest ranking government official in England other than the king, refused to renounce the pope and was beheaded. The momentum of the Reformation in England was unstoppable.

Christianity 239

Luther translated the Bible into German at about the same time the printing press was invented. Together these events greatly energized the Protestant Reformation by helping to make the Bible widely available in the language of the common people. List other technological innovations that have had a large impact on a religious tradition or traditions.

In Geneva, Switzerland, John Calvin (1509 to 1564) played a role in the Reformation that was second in importance only to Luther's. Calvin emphasized humanity's **original sin,** inherited from Adam and Eve. He believed that some would be saved from sin, but only if God had already chosen them for salvation. The rest would be damned, regardless of how they lived. This doctrine of **predestination** was coupled with the idea that one's status among the saved is shown through good works and piety. For the Calvinist, therefore, a religious life is essential, even though the issue of salvation has already been determined by predestination.

The Protestant Reformation, begun unintentionally by Martin Luther, sparked other events. For one thing, it led to the **Catholic Reformation** in 1545, an effort to clarify Roman Catholic Church doctrine on a number of fundamental issues, and cleaned up many of the corrupt practices Luther had protested against. Another effect, and a tragic one, was the Thirty Years' War (1618 to 1648), between Catholics and Protestants. In this war over half of Germany's population was killed, but nothing of real consequence was settled. Within Protestantism the motivating spirit of the Reformation itself—to protest any authority perceived to impede the Christian's relationship with God—continued to separate believers into new organized branches commonly known as denominations.[1]

Christian Divisions, Christian Unity

Today Christianity remains divided primarily into Roman Catholicism, Eastern Orthodoxy, and Protestantism. Despite differences between these and other denominations, many beliefs and practices link Christians together and form the basis of ecumenism, a movement that attempts to foster Christian unity.

Roman Catholicism

Most prevalent in central and southern Europe, Ireland, and Central and South America, and growing rapidly in Africa and Asia, Roman Catholicism today accounts for more than half of the world's Christians—slightly more than one billion people. One distinctive characteristic of Catholicism is its reliance on both the Bible and **Tradition** as the means of handing on God's revelation of Christ—means that form a single deposit of divine revelation. Tradition began with the Apostles, who handed it down to their successors, the bishops and the popes. The bishops and the popes, in turn, are responsible for carrying on and clarifying anew in every age the Tradition passed on to them. The pope, as Peter's successor, is the highest authority in the Church.

The Catholic Church understands itself to be the Body of Christ on earth. It recognizes the common baptism of all Christian churches, but does not believe a church community can possess the fullness of the faith without the seven sacraments, the adherence to Tradition as well as the Scriptures, or the recognition of the pope as the successor of Peter the Apostle. Other forms of Christianity are thought to exist in varying degrees of communion with the Catholic Church. For example, Eastern Orthodoxy is doctrinally closer to Catholicism than are most forms of Protestantism.

Catholicism recognizes seven sacraments, while most forms of Protestantism recognize only two. Each of the sacraments is an outward, physical sign of an inward, spiritual reality. The seven sacraments are Baptism, Confirmation, the Eucharist (or Holy Communion), Holy Orders (ordination of deacons, priests, and bishops), Matrimony, Anointing of the Sick, and Penance and Reconciliation. Through the sacraments—especially Baptism and the Eucharist—grace, the transforming presence of God freely given, flows forth into the person. The celebration of the Eucharist (or the Mass) is the summit of Catholic worship, and Catholics are expected to participate in the ceremony each Sunday morning or its vigil on Saturday evening.

Modern Catholicism has been strongly affected by the teaching of the **Second Vatican Council,** also called Vatican Council II or simply Vatican II. This worldwide council of bishops was convened by Pope John XXIII, and occurred from 1962 through 1965. The general aims of the Second Vatican Council were to reflect on Church teaching so the Church would respond appropriately to the needs of the modern world, and to promote Christian unity. Many landmark documents were produced out of this council, including one, *Nostra Aetate*, that acknowledges the holiness and truth that exists in non-Christian religions, and encourages dialogue with members of other religions. Other documents brought about changes in Church liturgy and encouraged Catholics to become engaged in life-giving, humanitarian struggles all over the world.

As the Catholic Church attempts to respond to the needs of the present day, it continues to take a stand on various issues, some of them quite controversial. But controversy is not new to the ancient tradition of Catholicism. Indeed the Church's strength to engage in controversy has always been a source of revitalization.

Eastern Orthodoxy

Numbering nearly 250 million adherents altogether, the various Churches of Eastern Orthodoxy are located mainly in eastern Europe, in Russia, and along the eastern coast of the Mediterranean Sea. Each of these Churches (the Greek Orthodox Church, the Russian Orthodox Church, and so on) has its own leader, but all acknowledge the patriarch of Constantinople as the one head of Eastern Orthodoxy. Unlike Roman Catholicism's pope, the patriarch of Constantinople has no special doctrinal authority. This authority is held instead by the entire Church body.

In contrast with Catholicism, which regards Tradition as the ongoing revelation of Christ, Eastern Orthodoxy limits its set of doctrines to those reached by seven ecumenical councils held prior to the year 787.

Eastern Orthodoxy observes the same seven sacraments as Catholicism, although it celebrates the sacraments somewhat differently. A distinctive practice is the great emphasis on icons, which are artistic representations of the New Testament and early Christian saints. Theologically Eastern Orthodoxy tends to focus on the Incarnation, encouraging a mystical union with God through faith in Christ. The Gospel of John is especially popular in the Eastern Church.

Recently great changes have been taking place in the world and within the Eastern Church itself. The breakup of the Soviet Union in 1991 threatened the stability of the entire Church. In North America the ethnic makeup of the various Orthodox Churches is changing, with membership among traditional groups eroding and membership among other groups building. Such changes could revitalize Eastern Orthodoxy, even as they challenge its deeply traditional ways.[J]

J
Most of the sacraments of Catholicism and Eastern Orthodoxy function in part as rites of passage, marking divisions between one stage of life and the next. Given the nature of each sacrament, identify as many such divisions as you can. How might the sacraments celebrate the passage from one life stage to the next?

IMAGE: © BENIAMINSON/ART RESOURCE, NY

This Russian Orthodox icon shows Christ holding the Bible, surrounded by biblical scenes.

Christianity 241

Protestantism

As its name suggests, Protestantism originated as a protest. Early Protestants protested specifically against any form of authority they perceived as false—anything that stood in the way of the Christian's relationship with God through Christ. In general, Protestants focus on the Bible as the primary means of knowing Christ, though different denominations vary considerably as to how they regard the Scriptures. For some Protestants, called fundamentalists, the Bible is the direct word of God, and it must be read literally. For most Protestants, however, the Bible is a human product that conveys God's truth, as long as it is read in proper context.

A second basic principle of Protestantism is justification by faith, as understood by Martin Luther. This principle states that salvation is achieved solely through the grace of God, not by works of love; as long as one has faith, good works will naturally follow. Sacraments are important too, but only as accompaniments of faith. Many Protestant Churches celebrate the sacraments of Baptism and the Eucharist, while others also celebrate Confirmation.

Protestantism is the predominant form of Christianity in northern Europe, England, Scotland, Australia, the United States, and Canada. It has four main branches, stemming from the days of the Reformation: Lutheran, Calvinist, Baptist, and Anglican (from which Methodism emerged). Today there are thousands of separate Protestant denominations, many of them derived from one of those four branches.

The shape of Protestantism continues to change. New denominations are forming, and some that were divided at one time have now reunified. Three main branches of North American Lutheranism, for example, merged in 1987 to form the Evangelical Lutheran Church in America. Changes are also occurring within the denominations. For example, the number of women in the clergy is clearly on the rise. In some denominations the majority of ministers will soon be women.

Seeking Unity amid Diversity

Some people who believe in Jesus Christ are members of religious denominations, some of which challenge the very definition of what it is to be Christian. In fact, groups identifying themselves as Christian are not always regarded as such by other Christians. The Church of Jesus Christ of Latter-day Saints (the Mormons) and the Jehovah's Witnesses are two prevalent examples of such groups. We will study each in some detail in chapter 15.

Amid this diversity within Christianity are ongoing calls for unity. Many mainline Christian denominations advocate **ecumenism**— the promotion of worldwide Christian unity. Catholicism's Second Vatican Council called for ecumenism in a paper that begins as follows:

The restoration of unity among all Christians is one of the principal concerns of the Second Vatican Council. Christ the Lord founded one Church and one Church only. However, many Christian communions present them-

Barbara Harris was ordained in 1989 as the first female bishop in the Episcopal Church.

selves to [people] as the true inheritors of Jesus Christ; all indeed profess to be followers of the Lord but they differ in mind and go their different ways, as if Christ himself were divided. (*Decree on Ecumenism,* number 1)

United in Christ

The movement toward Christian unity is generally a cause for celebration, and it seems to be gaining momentum. In 2006, for example, Pope Benedict XVI and Ecumenical Patriarchate Bartholemew I, the respective leaders of Roman Catholicism and Eastern Orthodoxy, met in Istanbul, Turkey, and issued a "Common Declaration," expressing their commitment to moving towards full union. The ideal of unity has a logical appeal, even as the many forms of Christianity exhibit a wide range of diversity. All those forms look to Christ and to the Christian creed as their common cornerstones. The Gospel of John sets forth Jesus's own prayer for Christian unity:

I ask not only on behalf of [the disciples], but also on behalf of those who will believe in me through their word, that they may all be one. As you, Father, are in me and I am in you, may they also be in us, so that the world may believe that you have sent me. (John 17:20–21)

Chapter Review

1. How much of the world's population is Christian? Where is Christianity the dominant religious tradition?
2. Define Christianity's two core doctrines.
3. What are the literal and symbolic meanings of the Greek word *ixthus?*
4. What are the primary sources of information about the life of Jesus?
5. Briefly describe the political situation in Palestine during Jesus's lifetime.
6. Name and briefly describe the varieties of Judaism at the time of Jesus, including their responses to Roman rule.
7. Explain the meaning of apocalypticism.
8. Who was John the Baptist, and how was he important in Jesus's life?
9. What are parables? Name two well-known parables.
10. To what was Jesus likely referring when he spoke of the Kingdom of God?
11. What is Jesus's radical commandment on love?

The Seven Dimensions of Religion: Christianity

Dimension	Examples
Experiential	experiencing the "fruit of the Spirit," relationship with Jesus, emotional effects of the Eucharist
Mythic	Gospel accounts of Jesus's birth and other aspects of Jesus's life (such as the Last Supper, which underlies the ritual of the Eucharist)
Doctrinal	the Incarnation, the Trinity, apocalypticism, the Apostles' Creed, the Nicene Creed, original sin, predestination
Ethical	the Beatitudes, Jesus's commandment to love one's enemies
Ritual	celebration of the Eucharist, Baptism, and other sacraments
Social	the Church, communities of monks and nuns, hierarchies within the Church (bishops, presbyters, deacons), the pope, the patriarch of Constantinople
Material	cathedrals and churches, icons

12. Why was Jesus crucified? Who ordered his execution?

13. What does the term *gospel* mean?

14. What is the primary focus of the Gospel of Matthew?

15. In what ways does the Gospel of Luke portray Jesus as reaching out to a diversity of people?

16. What is the doctrine of the Incarnation?

17. What is the focal point of the Gospel of John?

18. According to his first epistle to the Corinthians, what is Paul's Gospel message?

19. What does Paul say will happen at the second coming?

20. What does Paul emphasize about salvation?

21. What is the origin of the term *creed*?

22. How does the Gospel of John emphasize both Jesus's divinity and humanity?

23. What is Christ called in the first chapter of John's Gospel?

24. What two creeds were formulated by the year 325?

25. Historically speaking, what was the most crucial point established at the Council of Nicaea?

26. What is the doctrine of the Trinity?

27. What did Paul say the Church is meant to be?

28. What are heresies?

29. Describe how Paul came to be an Apostle of Christ.

30. What was decided at the Council of Jerusalem?

31. Why did the early Christians settle on Sunday as their primary day of worship?

32. What were the central rituals of the early Church?

33. What were the three distinct offices in the Church by the early second century? Briefly describe the role of bishop in the early Church.

34. Why did worship on behalf of the Roman emperor bring Christians into conflict with the empire?

35. Who was Augustine, and what great theological masterpiece did he write after the fall of Rome?

36. What is the meaning of the Greek word from which we get the English word *catholic?*

37. Identify the elements leading to the schism in the Church that divided the eastern and western parts of the Roman Empire.

38. What significant event occurred in the year 1054?

39. Identify some achievements of Catholicism in the Middle Ages.

40. Where, and in what century, did the Protestant Reformation take place?

41. What did Luther's Ninety-five Theses protest against?

42. What role did King Henry VIII play in the Protestant Reformation?

43. Other than the establishment of Protestantism, what were two major effects of the Protestant Reformation?

44. What is one distinctive characteristic of Roman Catholicism?

45. Identify the seven sacraments of Catholicism and Eastern Orthodoxy.

46. When was the Second Vatican Council held, and what were its general aims?

47. Name a distinctive practice of Eastern Orthodoxy and identify the tradition's theological focal point.

48. What challenges does Eastern Orthodoxy face as a result of recent changes in the world and in the Church?

49. What has Protestantism historically tended to protest against?

50. What are the four main branches of Protestantism?

51. What is ecumenism?

Glossary

apocalypticism (from Greek *apokalypsis:* "revelation"). A common Jewish religious perspective of Jesus's time, which held that the world had come under the control of evil forces and was heading toward the climactic End Time, at which point God would intervene to usher in a reign of perfect justice and goodness. Early Christianity was generally in keeping with apocalypticism.

apostle (from Greek *apostolos:* "messenger"). An early follower of Jesus's recognized as one with authority to preach the Gospel; the Apostles included the twelve original disciples (with Matthias replacing Judas after the latter's death; see Acts of the Apostles 1:15–26) and Paul.

Apostles' Creed. A short statement of Christian belief that sets forth the foundations of the central doctrines of the Incarnation and the Trinity; traditionally thought to have been composed by the Apostles.

bishops. Officials within the early Church who were regarded as successors to the Apostles. Bishops were responsible for overseeing the Church and administering the Eucharist.

canon (from Greek *kanon:* "rule" or "standard"). An authoritative set of sacred writings, such as Christianity's New Testament.

Catholic (from Greek *katholikos:* "universal"). The largest of the three major divisions of Christianity. When it is not capitalized, *catholic* is used generally to denote the universal nature of the Christian Church.

Catholic Reformation. An effort begun in 1545, initiated partly by the Protestant Reformation, to clarify Church doctrines and clean up corrupt practices.

Church (from Greek *ekklesia* [ek-klay-see´ah]: "assembly"). The community of all Christian believers.

deacons (from Greek *diakonos:* "servant"). Officials within the early Church who were like the presbyters in that they assisted the bishops, but were on closer terms with the congregation at large.

ecumenism. The promotion of worldwide Christian unity.

Eucharist. Also the Lord's Supper, or Holy Communion, a central sacrament and ritual of Christianity, a memorial of the Last Supper, which was shared by Jesus and his twelve Apostles.

gospel (from Old English *godspel:* "good news"; in Greek, *evangelion*). Referring generally to the saving power of the life, Crucifixion, and Resurrection of Jesus Christ.

grace. God's presence freely given; a key doctrine for Paul and for Christianity in general.

heresies. Opinions or doctrines at variance with accepted doctrine.

Holy Spirit. One of the three Persons of the Trinity, along with God the Father and Jesus Christ the Son. The New Testament describes the active presence in the ministry of Jesus, and later in the work of Jesus's followers (beginning with the Pentecost, described in chapter 2 of the Acts of the Apostles).

Incarnation. A core doctrine of Christianity, stating that in Jesus Christ, God became fully human while remaining fully divine.

indulgences. Reductions in, or pardons of, the punishment due for sins committed. The buying and selling of indulgences was a common practice in medieval Catholicism.

martyrs (from Greek *martys/ martyr-:* "witness"). Those who choose to die rather than violate their religious convictions.

New Testament. A collection of twenty-seven writings that, by the late fourth century AD, had been adopted by orthodox Christians as their primary sacred text.

Nicene Creed. Christianity's most important creedal statement, formulated by Church leaders at the Council of Nicaea in 325 and setting forth in precise language the doctrines of the Incarnation and of the Trinity.

original sin. Humanity's state of moral and spiritual corruption, inherited from Adam and Eve.

orthodox (from Greek *orthodoxos:* "right doctrine"). With respect to Christianity in general, the emerging version of Christianity that was deemed true by those with authority, and therefore accepted by the majority. When the word *orthodox* is capitalized, it refers to the major division of Christianity dominant in the eastern regions of Europe and the area surrounding the Mediterranean Sea.

parables. Stories that Jesus used to cast important moral lessons within the language and circumstances familiar to the common people.

pope. The title conferred on the bishop of Rome, the leader of Catholicism, who is considered by Catholics to be the direct successor of the Apostle Peter.

predestination. The doctrine, especially prevalent in Calvin's form of Protestantism, stating that God has already chosen those who will be saved from sin.

presbyters (from Greek *presbyteros:* "elder"). Officials within the early Church who assisted the bishops.

Protestant Reformation. A widespread phenomenon in sixteenth-century Europe that resulted in the emergence of Protestantism from Catholicism.

second coming. Also called parousia (pahr-*oo*-see´ah), Greek for "presence." The anticipated return of Christ to the world, on which occasion the dead will be resurrected and all people will be judged.

Second Vatican Council. Also called Vatican II. A worldwide council of Catholic bishops convened by Pope John XXIII, occurring from 1962 through 1965. The council aimed to reflect on Church teaching so that the Church would respond appropriately to the needs of the modern world, and to promote Christian unity.

Tradition. A primary means for God's revelation of Christ, beginning with the Apostles and continuing in the present day through the Church.

Trinity. A core Christian doctrine stating that God consists of three Persons—God the Father, Jesus Christ the Son, and the Holy Spirit—who are at the same time one God.

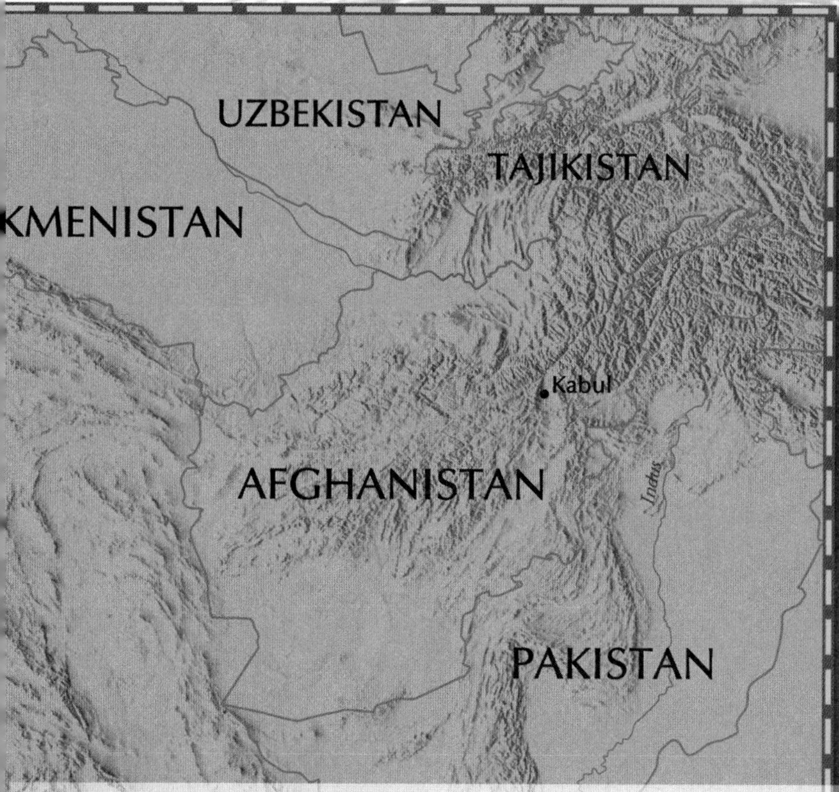

UZBEKISTAN

TAJIKISTAN

KMENISTAN

.Kabul

AFGHANISTAN

PAKISTAN

14 Islam

Submission to the One God

The name *Islam* is derived from a root word meaning "surrender" or "submission." In one simple phrase, this is the religion of Islam: submission to the one God, or Allah. The requirement of submission applies to every moment in the life of a Muslim (whose name means "one who submits").

With about 1.2 billion followers, Islam is the world's second-largest religion. It is also the fastest growing. In the United States and elsewhere, the 9-11 attacks on the World Trade Center and the Pentagon, and the subsequent warfare in Afghanistan and Iraq, gave rise to a newfound interest in Islam. Many have been surprised to learn that Islam is deeply rooted in the biblical tradition, and that it reveres the great prophets of Judaism and Jesus Christ. Islam has also played a crucial role in the shaping of Western culture, especially during the Middle Ages.

Obviously there is much to explore in the religion of Islam. Given Islam's major role in world affairs, it is now more important than ever to gain a proper understanding of the tradition and its adherents.

The Foundations of Islam

Something of the general nature of Islam can be understood simply by noting the degree of importance of each of its basic elements. First, there is the **Qur'an** (kuh-ran´; also called the Koran), the primary sacred text and Islam's earthly center. Next, there is the Prophet Muhammad, who received the contents of the Qur'an from Allah and whose life provides Muslims with an example of human perfection. The primary teachings of Islam, a third basic element, are derived from the Qur'an and from the life of Muhammad. Finally, the Muslim community, or Umma (oom´muh), bases its laws and lifestyle on those teachings.

The Qur'an: Islam's Sacred Presence

The Qur'an is the earthly center of Islam. Its role for Islam can be compared to Jesus Christ's role for Christianity. Both are considered the sacred presence in the world. Just as Christ is the source of Christianity's foundational teachings, so too is the Qur'an the source of Islam's foundational teachings.

The Qur'an is about four-fifths the size of the New Testament and is divided into 114 *suras,* or chapters. It was originally written in Arabic, and there is only one Arabic version. This is logical, for Muslims believe the Qur'an contains the direct words of Allah, revealed to the Prophet Muhammad and written down in its present form by the Prophet's earliest followers.

The term *qur'an* literally means "reading" or "recitation," and oral recitation of the text has always been favored over silent reading. Many regard the Qur'an to be the most beautiful work ever composed in the Arabic language. It is not possible to translate its full meaning into another language, owing to both its poetic quality and the subtle meaning that is conveyed visually through the Arabic

Two pages from a seventeenth-century manuscript of the Qur'an.

script. The art of calligraphy was first used in the West by Muslims to celebrate the visual splendor of the Qur'an.

The Qur'an is regarded as a miracle of God, especially because Muhammad is thought to have been illiterate. Today it is the world's most memorized book. It begins with a prayer called the Opening:

IN THE NAME OF GOD
THE COMPASSIONATE
THE MERCIFUL

Praise be to God, Lord of the Universe,
The Compassionate, the Merciful,
Sovereign of the Day of Judgement!
You alone we worship, and to You alone we
　　turn for help.
Guide us to the straight path,
The path of those whom You have favoured,
Not of those who have incurred Your wrath,
Nor of those who have gone astray.

(Qur'an 1:1–9)

The Prophet Muhammad

Islam is purely monotheistic and therefore carefully avoids regarding Muhammad as anything more than human. Even so, Islam celebrates Muhammad as the most perfect of all human beings, referring to him as a jewel among stones.

Muhammad's Life and Career

Muhammad was born about AD 570 into the leading tribe of Mecca, a city on the Arabian Peninsula that was an important center of commerce and trade. Orphaned at an early age, Muhammad grew up with his uncle. He was an honest and dependable boy who worked hard as a shepherd and later in the trading business. He became a caravan manager for a wealthy widow by the name Khadija. Eventually, when Muhammad was twenty-five and Khadija was about forty, they married. The couple had at least six children and enjoyed a long and happy union.

A tribesman in Pakistan conveys goods using a camel caravan, much as Muhammad did.

Along with raising his family and pursuing business interests, Muhammad spent much time in religious contemplation. He liked to retreat to a cave on nearby Mount Hira, where he could meditate on God in solitude. According to tradition, during one of Muhammad's visits to the cave in 610, the archangel Gabriel appeared to him in a dream and commanded him, "Recite!" Muhammad protested that he was not capable. Twice more Gabriel issued his command, pressing so hard on Muhammad's body that the man feared he would die. In desperation Muhammad asked, "What shall I recite?" Gabriel answered:

Recite in the name of your Lord who created—created man from clots of blood.

Recite! Your Lord is the Most Bountiful One, who by the pen taught man what he did not know. (Qur'an 96:1–4)

This event is celebrated as the Night of Power and Excellence. It marked the beginning of Muhammad's career as a prophet. This specific passage is the earliest "recitation" contained in the Qur'an. Muhammad would receive many more over the next twenty-two years, until his death in 632.

Muhammad told Khadija about his experience, and she became the first convert to Islam. At first Muhammad found few others who were willing to follow him. After ten years, however, several hundred families were Muslim. For the most part though, Muhammad's fellow Meccans reacted to his message with hostility. This is not surprising, for Muhammad's teachings ran counter to their accustomed ways. He taught that there was only one God, Allah, but Arabia was mostly polytheistic. In Mecca there were 360 shrines to various gods, and pilgrimages to those shrines earned much money for the city. In addition Muhammad advocated social and economic justice, and his fellow Meccans were not ready to give up their largely corrupt standards of behavior.

In the face of this hostility, Muhammad and his followers migrated northward, to the city of Yathrib, in AD 622. Leaders there knew of Muhammad's reputation as an able businessman, and they invited him to become the administrator of their city. The migration to Yathrib, of utmost significance to the history of Islam, is known as the **Hijra** (hij'ruh), or "emigration." Muslims base their system for assigning dates on this event, using the abbreviation *AH* (after Hijra); for example, AD 622 is AH 1.

Muhammad proved to be a brilliant administrator, merciful and yet firm in his justice. The city of Yathrib soon came to be known by the name Medina, a shortened form of an Arabic phrase meaning "city of the prophet." Eight years later, after several battles with his Meccan opponents, Muhammad returned in triumph to his home city, Mecca. By the time of his death two years later, most of Arabia had converted to Islam.[A]

The Seal of the Prophets

Muhammad's unique significance for Islam rests in the belief that he is the final prophet, revealing the will of Allah fully and precisely, and for all time. Muslims believe that the prophets who came before Muhammad, such as Abraham, Moses, and Jesus, also revealed God's will, but only partially. Muhammad is the Seal of the Prophets, the last of the line. There is no need for Allah to choose another.

Muhammad and Christ play very different roles within their respective religions, Islam and Christianity. Whereas Christians believe Christ *is* the sacred presence, Muslims believe Muhammad *delivered* the sacred presence, the Qur'an. Muslims regard Muhammad as nothing more than human, with no supernatural qualities. Muslims regard Christ, on the other hand, as one of only two humans (Adam is the other) conceived by God.

Muhammad is merely human, but he is revered as the best of all humans. His actions and his own teachings (which he carefully distinguished from the divine teachings of the Qur'an) together constitute the **Sunna** (soon′nuh), or "custom," of the Prophet. The Sunna of Muhammad is the second most important authority for Islam.

Muslims admire and attempt to imitate Muhammad's earthly experience, but they also value a heavenly experience, which is a focal point of Muslim piety. They believe that one night Muhammad was miraculously transported from Mecca to Jerusalem; then ascended with the archangel Gabriel through the seven heavens (the Qur'an specifies that God created seven), saw Moses, Abraham, and Jesus; and then was in the very presence of Allah. This event, the Ascension to Heaven, is one of two miracles involving Muhammad, the first being the production of the Qur'an.

Islam's Primary Teachings

The teachings of Islam are based ultimately on the Qur'an and secondarily on the Sunna of the Prophet Muhammad. Nevertheless, additional great theological achievements have come through Islam, especially during its first two centuries. A lack of consistent agreement between Muslim theologians through the ages helps to explain why Islam tends to be somewhat diverse. Its multiformity is especially dependent on location. Islam as practiced in Saudi Arabia, for example, tends to be more conservative than Islam as practiced in Egypt. Virtually all Muslims, however, agree on the following central teachings.

Allah: The One God

The Arabic name Allah literally means "the God." Allah was worshiped in Arabia before Islam. Muhammad's tribe, the Quraysh, regarded Allah as its special deity. But before Muhammad's call to be a prophet, Allah was considered one among many gods. Islam changed this decisively, for monotheism is one of the most emphasized teachings of the Qur'an.

Muslims understand Allah to be transcendent and suprapersonal, and emphasize those qualities, while at the same time seeing Allah as immanent and personal. For instance, they think of Allah as genderless because maleness and femaleness are human qualities and would thus limit God's nature. Muslims avoid artistic representations of Allah that in any way evoke human characteristics. To know the personal and immanent nature of Allah is the special achievement of a Muslim mystic, or Sufi (soo′fee), who has first experienced Allah's transcendence.

The transcendent, suprapersonal nature of Allah is made more accessible by the many names of God. Traditionally there are ninety-nine, including the Compassionate and the Real. These names provide Muslims with a variety of descriptive expressions for Allah, while maintaining their strict monotheism.

The Prophets: Messengers of Allah

Prophets provide the crucial link between Allah and human history; through them the divine will is revealed. Beginning with Adam and ending with Muhammad, Muslims believe many thousands of prophets have walked the earth. An elite few are so important that they have changed the nature of humankind's relationship with Allah.

IMAGE: © THE PIERPONT MORGAN LIBRARY/ART RESOURCE, NY

An Islamic depiction of Adam and Eve dating, from the thirteenth century.

B

Keeping in mind what you now know about Muhammad and some of Islam's other prophets, describe in your own words the function of prophecy in Islam.

C

The Cataclysm specifically describes the Day of Judgment. From that passage what can you infer about the Muslim perspective on Allah, on human nature, and on the role of Islam?

D

Muslims embrace science because it fits perfectly with their religious perspective about the natural world. From your perspective how well do science and religion go together?

Those few include Abraham, whom Muslims regard as the father of the Arabs, just as he is father of the Israelites. According to Islam, Abraham's son Ishmael moved to Mecca and became the ancestor of the Arabs. Abraham's prophecy centered on his pronouncement that there is only one God. Moses, Judaism's greatest prophet, is also revered in Islam. He pronounced Allah's ethical laws, the Ten Commandments. And then came Jesus Christ, who pronounced the Golden Rule ("Do unto others as you would have them do unto you"). Finally, Muhammad, the Seal of the Prophets, pronounced the Qur'an, and the revelation of Allah's will to humanity was complete.[B]

Human Nature and Destiny

Islam teaches that human nature is essentially good, but people are all too capable of forgetting this. Forgetfulness is a key element in the Muslim interpretation of the Fall from perfection in the Garden of Eden. When Adam and Eve ate the forbidden fruit, they caused a state of forgetfulness to come upon them. When people momentarily forget their basic goodness, their passions can lead them to sin. Herein lies the need for the Qur'an and the other revelations of the will of Allah. Human beings need directives for correct behavior so that goodness might prevail.

Human destiny is entirely dependent on the outcome of this struggle for goodness. The reward for the righteous is Paradise, and for the evildoers, Hell. The Qur'an vividly describes each realm, so that all Muslims are fully aware of the great consequences of their ethical decisions. Even more emphasis is placed on the Day of Judgment, at which time all humans will stand before Allah, and the destiny of each will be made known.

The Day of Judgment will be preceded by the coming of the Mahdi (meh'dee), a savior figure similar to Judaism's Messiah. The Mahdi will restore Islam and bring order on earth. After this Jesus Christ will return to Jerusalem and usher in the Day of Judgment.

The following passage from the Qur'an, an entire *sura* entitled the Cataclysm, gives a typical description of the Day of Judgment:

When the sky is rent asunder; when the stars scatter and the oceans roll together; when the graves are hurled about; each soul shall know what it has done and what it has failed to do.

O man! What evil has enticed you from your gracious Lord who created you, gave you an upright form, and proportioned you? In whatever shape He willed He could have moulded you.

Yet you deny the Last Judgement. Surely there are guardians watching over you, noble recorders who know of all your actions.

The righteous will surely dwell in bliss. But the wicked shall burn in Hell upon the Judgement-day: nor shall they ever escape from it.

Would that you knew what the Day of Judgement is! Oh, would that you knew what the Day of Judgement is! It is the day when every soul will stand alone and God will reign supreme. (Qur'an, *sura* 82)[C]

The Nature of the World

Muslims believe that the natural world, being the creation of Allah, is good and worthy of reverence. Indeed the world is another form of revelation of God's will, and thus it is sometimes referred to as the cosmic Qur'an. Islamic civilization's great scientific advances are undoubtedly a result of this reverence. Far from regarding science as somehow in conflict with their faith, Muslims celebrate science as a means of knowing more about Allah's perfect creation.[D]

The Umma: The Community of Muslims

Islam emphasizes the community of all Muslims. Known as the **Umma,** this community transcends the boundaries of race, ethnicity, language, and other cultural factors. The Umma is a brotherhood and sisterhood based solely in religion.

Muslim men in Houston, Texas, pray at a ceremony ending the month of Ramadan.

Practically speaking, the Umma is an ideal that is not always realized, for sometimes contention exists between certain groups of Muslims. Still, the ideal of community is a deeply held conviction and a basic element of Islam. And indeed, for most Muslims, the experience of belonging to the Umma is an everyday reality.

What is it about the religion of Islam that unites Muslims in this communal manner? It is the **Shari'a** (sha-ree'ah), or divine law. Drawn from the Qur'an and the Sunna, the Shari'a divides actions into five categories: obligatory, recommended, indifferent, disapproved, and forbidden. It is all-encompassing, setting forth in detail how to actually practice Islam—submission before Allah. To ignore the Shari'a is to stop being a Muslim.

The Shari'a was intended to be the law of the land and was this way in Islamic civilizations of the past. In modern times the Shari'a is the basis of government in several countries with Muslim majorities, including Saudi Arabia, Iran, and Pakistan.[E]

Basic Practices and Social Teachings

One of Islam's great strengths is its practical approach to religious life. The religion describes, in an orderly and clear manner, the requirements and the rewards of righteous living, and it spells out in detail how to act in order to meet the requirements and reap the rewards. The Shari'a, then, is a practical form of divine law, conceived by God but fashioned for human beings' day-to-day life.

The Five Pillars

The order and clarity of the directives for living righteously is nowhere more apparent than in the **Five Pillars** of Islam. Each pillar

E
Many Muslims live in countries governed by the Shari'a, or divine law, of Islam. Imagine what it would be like if your own country came to be ruled by a religion. What would be the most notable changes?

Islam   253

calls for specific actions, and together the Five Pillars provide a basic framework for life.

Confession of Faith

The first pillar of Islam is its central creedal statement, the confession of faith known as the **Shahada** (shuh-hah´duh): "La ilaha illa'Llah. Muhammadun rasulu'Llah" ("There is no god except God. Muhammad is the messenger of God"). Stating this freely and with conviction officially makes a person a Muslim.

The confession refers to two basic teachings of Islam: monotheism and the uniqueness of Muhammad as a prophet. Though these beliefs are essential, most of Islam's teachings, like those of Judaism, involve correct practices. The rest of the Five Pillars demonstrate Islam's emphasis on correct practice.

Prayer

The second pillar of Islam is prayer. All Muslims, women and men, are required to pray five times each day: early morning, noon, midafternoon, sunset, and evening. Muslim prayer requires ritual washing of the hands and face, prostration in the direction of Mecca, and other ritual movements. Usually the prayers are performed on a rug specifically designed for this purpose.

On Fridays public prayers are usually conducted in the **mosque,** a structure that traditionally includes a prayer hall and an enclosed courtyard, with towers called minarets at the corners. Public prayers may instead be held in an open field or in the desert, if there is no mosque nearby. Friday prayers are directed by an **imam** (i-mahm´), a "leader" who has been designated to conduct worship. The *imam* also delivers a sermon.

Fasting

The third pillar calls for fasting, which takes place during **Ramadan** (ram´uh-dahn), the ninth month of the Muslim year. Each day throughout that month, from dawn until sunset, Muslims are to avoid eating, drinking, smoking, and sex. Some are exempt from this requirement: for example, those who are sick, those who are making difficult journeys, and women who are breast-feeding.

Islam uses a calendar based on the lunar year, which has fewer days than a solar year, so Ramadan is celebrated during each season over time. When it occurs during the summer, the requirements of fasting are particularly challenging, especially in the many desert and tropical regions of Muslim lands. (When

Muslim women pray during Ramadan.

it occurs in winter, it poses difficulties for the growing number of Muslim players in the National Basketball Association.)

Fasting is believed to be beneficial in many ways. By depriving people temporarily of the material goods and sensual pleasures that are often taken for granted, it gives them insight into the situations of people who are less fortunate. Fasting also nurtures an awareness of mortality, and helps focus attention on moral and religious concerns, which fosters spiritual fortitude.

Wealth Sharing

Islam's fourth pillar, wealth sharing, helps ensure the economic welfare of the entire Muslim community. It requires that Muslims contribute 2.5 percent of the value of their possessions to a public treasury annually—that is, once every lunar year. Poor people are exempt from this requirement, and in fact are among the recipients of the shared wealth. The treasury funds can also be spent on public concerns, such as educational or cultural institutions.

Wealth sharing is considered a form of worship, and thus provides benefits beyond the economic advantages it offers the community. Along with the specific requirement of wealth sharing, Islam teaches that acts of charity should be performed regularly.

Pilgrimage

Once in their lifetime, if they can afford it and are physically able, all Muslims are to journey to Mecca. The pilgrimage, or **hajj** (haj), is the fifth pillar of Islam. The *hajj* has great religious significance, for Allah forgives the sins of those who make the journey with reverence. Any pilgrim who dies on the journey to or from Mecca is a martyr (or witness to the faith), and enters Paradise.

The pilgrimage vividly captures the communal ideal of the Umma, because Muslims from around the world gather in Mecca to celebrate their common religion, regardless of their worldly differences. Male pilgrims wear plain white clothing that signifies their basic equality, and also symbolizes ritual purity. Female pilgrims wear simple, colorful clothing

The Ka'ba is surrounded by pilgrims during the *hajj*.

F

Islam places great emphasis on its primary pilgrimage, the *hajj*. Several features of that journey have great religious significance for Muslims. Try to identify at least three of those features. Does anything in your own life have symbolic meaning similar to that of the *hajj*?

G

The Five Pillars of Islam provide a basic framework for life. State in your own words how they do so.

H

Compare Islamic teachings on the care of the body with the teachings you have received from your own religion and culture.

that is typical of their own homelands. Together the white apparel of the men and the colorful dress of the women identify Islam as a global religion that brings its diverse adherents together in the unity of the Umma.

The pilgrimage takes place during a specific month of the year and lasts for at least fifteen days. It involves several ritual acts, including the circling of the **Ka'ba** (kah'bah), a stone cubical structure in the courtyard of the Great Mosque of Mecca. This structure is believed to have been built by Abraham, and it has been a site of religious significance since pre-Islamic times. Muslims regard the Ka'ba as the navel of the earth, and as their geographic sacred center.[F][G]

The Personal and Social Life of Islam

The Shari'a, or divine law, spells out details of Muslim life that go far beyond the requirements of the Five Pillars. Its guidelines on care of the body, the status of women, and struggle are just three of the standards of personal and social behavior that contribute to Islam's clear and ordered directives for living righteously.

Care of the Body

Islam holds that the body ultimately belongs not to the individual but to God. This basic principle leads to specific teachings on the care of the body. Those teachings celebrate physical joys while controlling desires.

The body is to be kept clean; recall that washing is part of the Muslim prayer ritual. Clothing should be neither overly seductive nor overly luxurious, but there is nothing wrong with choosing clothes that are fashionable and attractive. Perfumes are especially popular. Muhammad himself once mentioned three particular joys: the company of women, prayer, and perfume. Good aromas tend to remind Muslims of Paradise.

Like Judaism, Islam regulates the diet. The Shari'a distinguishes between permitted and forbidden foods; for example, it forbids the eating of pork and the drinking of alcohol. Several passages in the Qur'an condemn wine and other intoxicants.

Sexuality is celebrated as one of Allah's greatest gifts, but one that is to be enjoyed only within marriage. Premarital and extramarital sex, and even lustful thoughts, are forbidden, as are homosexuality and prostitution. Muslims are urged to marry as early in life as possible. Marriages are traditionally arranged by parents; couples generally do not date. This custom of course contrasts sharply with the Western perspective, which places romantic love as the foundation for marriage. In Islam marriage is first and foremost a legal contract; love is expected to grow once a couple has begun married life.[H]

Women in Islam

The status of women in Islam is a controversial issue. Critics tend to accuse Islam of being chauvinistic and of denying basic rights to women. Muslims, in turn, tend to be frustrated and irritated by these accusations, dismissing them as meddlesome and unfair.

On the whole the Qur'an itself, and the ideals of Islam, regard men and women as equals, but with different roles. Often those ideals are realized in daily life. For example, though men usually have predominant roles in economic and public life, women generally have greater influence within the family, Islam's central social institution.

Three specific points of contention are commonly cited by critics: divorce, polygamy, and the wearing of the veil.

According to the Shari'a, either the husband or the wife may initiate a divorce, although traditionally it has been easier for the husband to do so. In the practice known as repudiation, a man can divorce his wife simply by stating, "I divorce you," three times. Usually, however, a waiting period is required between the utterances, to allow opportunities for reconciliation. In some Muslim countries, repudiation is no longer legal, and men and women are generally on equal footing when it comes to initiating a divorce. In any event Muhammad denounced divorce as being detested by Allah, even though it is categorized as a "permitted" act.

As for polygamy the Qur'an technically allows it, but sets limits:

You may marry other women who seem good to you: two, three, or four of them. But if you fear that you cannot maintain equality among them, marry one only. (Qur'an 4:3)[1]

This passage is open to interpretation. Some Muslims contend that it actually recommends monogamy, because being perfectly equitable toward two or more wives is nearly impossible. In most regions polygamy is rare. In some situations, however, Muslims condone the practice as the right thing. If there are many more women than men (in periods following warfare, for example), or if an older woman is widowed, it is better that men have multiple wives than that women remain alone. Muhammad himself had many wives late in life, though he was married to only Khadija for twenty-five years, until her death. Muslims hold that his practice of polygamy was mainly for the sake of political unification, and not for sensual pursuits.

Like polygamy, the wearing of the veil is referred to in a few passages of the Qur'an that have been interpreted in different ways. The most commonly cited passage is this:

Prophet, enjoin your wives, your daughters, and the wives of true believers to draw their veils close around them. That is more proper, so that they may be recognized and not be molested. (Qur'an 33:59)

Some Muslim communities require women to cover every part of their bodies and hide their faces behind veils. Others define veiling simply as covering the hair while in public. Veiling was a pre-Islamic practice in Arabia,

Some people reject the veil as a sign of oppression; others embrace it as a symbol of the Muslim tradition.

and it is no longer universal among Muslim women. In the last few decades, educated women in relatively modernized countries like Egypt have intentionally returned to wearing the veil. For them it is perceived as a means of embracing their own traditional heritage, not as a form of male domination.

Jihad: "Struggle"

Jihad (ji-had´), whose name means "exertion" or "struggle," is a principle that applies to all aspects of Islamic life, personal and social. It is sometimes counted as the sixth pillar of Islam.

On a personal level, *jihad* refers to the individual's spiritual struggle against anything that detracts from venerating Allah and from acting in accordance with the divine will. Socially *jihad* refers to the preservation of the order Allah has willed for the world. To some extent the expansion of Islam is considered part of that order.

The term *jihad* is also used in a more controversial way. In a narrow context, it refers to armed struggle, and is sometimes thought of as meaning "holy war." The Qur'an supports armed struggle for the sake of Islam if it is carried out in self-defense.

The Expansion of Islam

Islam has developed and spread rapidly since its beginnings early in the seventh century AD.

[1]
Very few Muslims practice polygamy, though it is technically allowed by the Qur'an. How do you interpret the Muslim teaching on this issue, as set forth in passage 4:3 of the Qur'an?

Islam   257

Jihad

[Jihad] is an Arabic word the root of which is Jahada, which means to strive for a better way of life. . . . The other meanings are: endeavor, strain, exertion, effort, diligence, fighting to defend one's life, land, and religion.

Jihad should not be confused with Holy War; the latter does not exist in Islam nor will Islam allow its followers to be involved in a Holy War. . . .

Jihad is not a war to force the faith on others, as many people think of it. It should never be interpreted as a way of compulsion of the belief on others, since there is an explicit verse in the Qur'an that says: "There is no compulsion in religion" Al-Qur'an: Al-Baqarah (2:256).

Jihad is not a defensive war only, but a war against any unjust regime. If such a regime exists, a war is to be waged against the leaders, but not against the people of that country. People should be freed from the unjust regimes and influences so that they can freely choose to believe in Allah.

Not only in peace but also in war Islam prohibits terrorism, kidnapping, and hijacking, when carried against civilians. Whoever commits such violations is considered a murderer in Islam, and is to be punished by the Islamic state. During wars, Islam prohibits Muslim soldiers from harming civilians, women, children, elderly, and the religious men like priests and rabbis. It also prohibits cutting down trees and destroying civilian constructions. (Muslim Student Association of the University of Southern California, Los Angeles, at *www.usc.edu/dept/MSA/ reference/glossary/term.JIHAD.html*)

The Expansion of Islamic Civilization

Following the death of Muhammad in AD 632, Muslims were led by **caliphs** (successors) chosen by the community. The first caliph was Muhammad's father-in-law Abu Bakr. These caliphs oversaw a remarkable phenomenon. First, all of Arabia, which had never managed to unite over anything in the past, embraced Islam. Soon the peoples of vast stretches of territory converted to the new religion, most often by their own free will and not because of armed force.

Within one century of Muhammad's death, Islam was the religion of the entire Middle East, Persia, North Africa, and almost all of Spain. If Muslim forces had not been defeated in the Battle of Tours / Poitiers in southern France in 732, they may well have conquered France and the rest of Europe.

The religion of Islam is, by its very nature, also a system of government and the foundation for a literary and artistic culture. In other words, Islam is also Islamic civilization. And so it was that in these vast regions, great centers of Islamic civilization developed. Muslims, Jews, and Christians lived side by side in Muslim Spain, where civilization flourished even as the rest of Europe endured the relatively stagnant Middle Ages. A mathematical system, called *al-jabar* in Arabic, was invented; in English we know it as algebra. The library of Cordoba, the main city of Muslim Spain, housed four hundred thousand titles. It is through those Arabic translations that some of the classics of ancient Greece and Rome have survived to this day.

Other Muslim empires arose, and in widely diverse regions. The Mogul Empire ruled India from 1526 to 1858. The Ottoman Empire, centered in modern-day Turkey, endured from 1326 all the way into the twentieth century.

For the most part, the flourishing of Islamic civilization came to an end during the era of European colonization. Many lands with a majority Muslim population came under the rule of European nations, and the normal functioning of Islam as a system of government within a religion was crippled. Today Islam seems to be making a rapid recovery from the effects of colonization.

The Locations of Muslims Today

Presently the nations with the greatest concentration of Muslims are located in the northern half of Africa, all of the Middle East and southwestern Asia (including Turkey, Iraq, Iran, and Afghanistan), South Asia, and the islands of Malaysia and Indonesia.

Arabia and the Muslim World

Islam crosses many boundaries of language, ethnicity, and culture. It cannot simply be equated with Arabia—which consists of Saudi Arabia, Yemen, and the Persian Gulf States—whose citizens constitute only about 20 percent of the entire Muslim population. In comparison 35 percent of the world's Muslims live in the South Asian nations of Pakistan, Bangladesh, and India. Still Arabia enjoys a special status in Islam for several reasons: Arabic involvement in Islam goes back to the earliest history of Islam, Arabia is the location of Muslim sacred sites, and Arabic is the language of Islam.

Islam in the United States

Approximately six million Muslims live in the United States, where Islam is the fastest-growing religion. About 40 percent of the U.S. Muslim population is made up of African Americans, some of whom claim a Muslim heritage. It is estimated that nearly 20 percent of Africans brought to North America as slaves were Muslim.

This heritage is one reason why some African Americans have argued that Islam is better suited for their community than Christianity, which they regard as the religion of their white oppressors. This has been the view of the Nation of Islam, a movement that began in the twentieth century and has been led by such notable men as Elijah Muhammad, Malcolm X, and Louis Farrakhan. The Nation of Islam upholds only some of the practices of traditional Islam, and most Muslims do not regard it as an authentic part of their religion. These differences were highlighted in the 1960s when Malcolm X, after making a pilgrimage to Mecca, rejected the Nation of Islam and formed a more traditional Muslim movement. For one thing, whereas the Nation of Islam teaches racial separatism, Malcolm X embraced the interracial unity he observed firsthand in Mecca.

Most Muslims in the United States, however, are immigrants or descendants of immigrants from Muslim countries. Some arrived

The Alhambra, a palace outside the city of Granada in southern Spain, shows the architectural influence of Islamic culture and art.

by the end of the nineteenth century, from the Middle East and eastern Europe. Large-scale immigration first occurred in the 1960s, caused by troubles in Muslim homelands. Immigrants from that time period tended to maintain their own ethnic ways within small communities of fellow Muslims. Their children have been more affected by Western influences. Today many of them are as typically American as they are Muslim. Islam is rapidly settling in as a common feature of the religious landscape of the United States.[J]

J
What aspects of Islam have you observed in your own nation and community? What have your observations taught you about Muslims and their religion?

Varieties of Islam

Like most religious traditions, Islam has taken various forms over the centuries. But there are only two major historical divisions: Sunnism and Shi'ism. Sufism, the mystical form of Islam, draws its adherents from both of those historical divisions, and therefore is not a separate division.

Historical Divisions Within Islam

The divisions within Islam are secondary to the theme of unity that holds together the brotherhood and sisterhood of Muslims. Various specific reasons underlie this theme of unity: Only one Arabic version of the Qur'an exists, and all Muslims regard it as the direct word of Allah. The Sunna of the Prophet allows all Muslims to share in the inspiration of Muhammad's life and teachings. And ritual practices, such as those required by the Five Pillars, are common to all.

Sunnism

Sunni (soon'nee) is drawn from a longer phrase referring to the people who follow the established custom, or sunna, meaning the Sunna of the Prophet. It is simply the common name for the form of Islam practiced by the majority (about 87 percent) of Muslims. In this respect then, it is Islam as described in the preceding pages of this chapter.

Shi'ism

Shi'i (shee'ee) comes from *shi'at 'Ali,* which means "partisans of Ali." Ali was a cousin and son-in-law of Muhammad's. Three times he was passed over before finally being named caliph, and eventually he was assassinated. These events led to the origination of the Shi'i movement by Muslims who favored Ali as the true successor of Muhammad. Shi'ism was consolidated into a distinct form of Islam when Ali's son, Husayn, was assassinated in AD 680. The martyrdom of Husayn continues to be observed within Shi'i Islam as a significant event, and Husayn himself is regarded as a great hero.

Shi'i Islam thus originated primarily from historical circumstances. Today it can be distinguished in part by geography. The nations of Iraq and Iran have Shi'i majorities. Kuwait, Afghanistan, and Pakistan also have significant Shi'i populations.

In terms of its teachings, Shi'ism is most notably distinguished by the figure of the **Imam.** Though not a prophet, the Imam is believed to have special spiritual insight, and is revered as the true earthly authority. Most Shi'is believe there have been twelve Imams, all of them descended from Muhammad through his daughter Fatima and her husband, Muhammad's cousin Ali. The twelfth Imam, Muhammad al-Mahdi, is thought to have been hidden away at a young age. At the end of time, he will return to restore Islam and to bring on the Day of Judgment.

This belief in the return of Muhammad al-Mahdi, and the general emphasis on the Imam as an authority figure, has made Shi'ism more politically volatile than Sunnism. In the Iranian Revolution of 1978 to 1979 and its aftermath, for example, the late Ayatollah Khomeini was thought to have special authority, and sometimes was even regarded as the Imam.

Islamic Mysticism: Sufism

Islam, as practiced by most Muslims, Sunni and Shi'i alike, emphasizes the transcendence and suprapersonal nature of Allah. Worship focuses on living in accordance with the divine will, through following the Shari'a. An abyss lies between the religious understanding of the individual and the great magnificence of Allah.

Sufism strives to cross that abyss, to experience Allah as immanent, dwelling within the worshiper. A Sufi saying expresses this in the words of Allah: "My Earth and My Heaven contain Me not, but the heart of My faithful servant containeth Me" (quoted in Arberry, *Sufism,* page 28).

Sufism's Place Within Islam

The term *sufism* is derived from the word *suf,* which refers to the coarse wool garment that is traditionally worn by Sufis. Despite the simplicity of the name's origin, the place of Sufism within Islam is a complicated and controversial issue.

Recall the first verse of the confession of faith, the first pillar of Islam. It declares, "There is no god except God." Sufism extends this a step further, declaring that there is *nothing* but God. If that is the case, then the worshiper too must be one with God. This is the guiding principle of Sufism. The **Sufi** experiences oneness with Allah, and through that experience gains spiritual fortitude.

Sometimes this perspective has landed Sufis in trouble with orthodox Muslims. A great Sufi by the name al-Hallaj, for example, was crucified by his fellow Muslims in 922 for having stated, "I am the Real." The Real is one of the ninety-nine names of God, so al-Hallaj was in fact claiming identity with Allah. To orthodox Muslims this was blasphemous. To Sufis it was a description of the pinnacle of religious experience.

Despite such events born of controversy, in the past Sufism generally fared well alongside orthodox Islam. In fact, it played an enor-

IMAGE: © HULTON-DEUTSCH COLLECTION/CORBIS

The late Ayatollah Khomeini, a Shi'i Muslim, was an influential and controversial leader in the Iranian revolution of 1978 to 1979.

mous role in attracting new adherents to Islam, especially in the East. Today, however, with the rise of more traditionalist forms of orthodox Islam, Sufism is commonly blamed for having caused Islam to stray from the true path, and is therefore frowned on by many.

Sufi Methods

Similar to Christian monasticism, Sufism is made up of groups known as orders. Each is led by a **shaykh** (shayk), a master and teacher. He leads his disciples through a variety of spiritual disciplines to help them achieve union with God, including recitation of sacred names and phrases, breathing exercises, and the chanting of odes. Perhaps the most famous Sufi discipline is a dance form best known in the West as the whirling dervish.

Sufis identify the aim of their disciplines as **al-fana** (ahl-fuhn'ah), or "extinction." They are referring to the extinction of the person's sense of ego, of the notion of separate existence. Once this notion is annihilated, the separation between self and God disappears, triggering the experience of union with the divine. This aspect of Sufism is similar to some of the mystical teachings of Hinduism.^K

K

Reconcile these two statements about Sufism:
- "The Sufi experiences oneness with Allah."
- "Sufis identify the aim of their disciplines as al-fana, or extinction of the person's sense of ego, of the notion of separate existence."

Islam   261

Muslim Life

Nizar Najjar is a university student in the United States. He grew up in Tunisia, a predominantly Muslim country on the Mediterranean coast of North Africa. He was asked to remark on a few topics.

What is it like to be a Muslim here, compared with in Tunisia?

There are big differences. In Tunisia, a Muslim country, we have the call to prayer, we go to the mosque, and in Ramadan everyone fasts and prays together. We can freely butcher the lamb needed for our feast at the end of Ramadan. Here, if you go to your home and butcher a lamb, you can get into trouble. Also, when I am fasting here during Ramadan, I see everyone else eating. That gives me an uncomfortable feeling. Back home, the whole community is supportive and synchronized. If a Muslim chooses not to fast, that is fine. But it is considered wrong to eat or to smoke outside, in front of others, because they are fasting, trying to resist the urge to eat or to smoke.

As for prayer, in the United States, we do not have the call to prayer. We use our watches instead. Here there is no mosque. We must find an empty, clean room for prayer, and determine the direction to Mecca before praying. We students are trying to buy a place and transform it into a mosque, so that we can at least perform our prayers.

What is involved in the practice of prayer?

Preparation for prayer involves ablution, or ritual washing. But even before ablution, you have to have good intention, by purifying your heart. Ablution is not going to do you any good if you don't purify yourself spiritually before praying. Praying is not simply a duty that you can perform just to get rid of it. What you need to do is purify yourself. You also wash yourself—your hands, face, and other parts of your body, all in a certain order. Then, if your inside is pure and your outside is clean, you are ready spiritually to perform the prayer.

In prayer we are in the presence of Allah. He is metaphorically—though not physically—in front of us. So when you are praying, it's strictly forbidden for anyone to cross in front of you. It would interrupt your sacred time of worship. It would interrupt your concentration, which is vital to prayer.

Prayer must be done with good intention. Still, it is a duty. Allah deserves our prayer. It is the least thing we can do to obey Him and to satisfy Him and to appease Him.

How would you describe the Prophet Muhammad?

Muhammad is great. Muhammad is wonderful. Muhammad had lots of accomplishments. Muhammad was successful. Muhammad transformed the whole nation. Muhammad was a political leader, he was a war strategist, he was a good economist. He was all these things. But the bottom line is, he was just a human being. He doesn't have the presence that Jesus has in the heart of Christians. We have lots of respect for Muhammad, but he was just a human being, and we do not idolize and worship him. Allah and the Qur'an are first. When we need advice, we go first to the Qur'an. If we don't find anything in the Qur'an that will guide us, then we go to the sayings of the Prophet. This is the importance of the Prophet. Some aspects of daily life and social problems were addressed by the Prophet. So we are required to follow his teachings.

What do you most want readers to know about Islam?

Just know that Muslims do not hate Christians. Actually, Muslims are the closest religion, or the closest people, to Christians. Muslims are not enemies, as the media sometimes tend to present them. Islam is the only non-Christian religion that makes it an article of faith for its followers to believe in Jesus, to believe that Jesus was one of the mightiest messengers of God, or of Allah, as we call Him. We believe in Jesus' miracle birth. We believe that he healed the blind and the lepers, by God's permission. And we believe that he is coming back. So we have lots of similarities. The only difference we have is that we do not believe that Jesus was the Son of God. But this is a separate issue. Actually, Jesus appears in the Qur'an more frequently than does Muhammad. An entire chapter in the Qur'an is dedicated to Mary, just to honor the mother of Jesus.

We have some differences with Christians, but there is no way a Muslim could hate a Christian just because he's a Christian. That's absurd. Basically we love everybody, especially Christians and Jews, who follow the Scriptures, who do good deeds. There is no difference, except in the form of worship. We love everybody. We just want everybody to love us. That's it. We don't deny that we have shortcomings. We have people who are fanatics, who want to go bomb places. But a true Muslim disagrees with these people. We don't send people to kill innocent people—that is absurd. So don't judge us based on what some bad people, some bad Muslims, do. Just judge us as persons, and judge our religion.

Islam and the World

Islam is distinctive among the great religions of the world for the extent to which it embraces the totality of life. There is simply no recognition of a division between what is religious and what is secular. The very meaning of the term *religion* in Arabic implies the need to repay one's debt to God; every aspect of life is indebted, and every action should tend to the need for repayment.

The all-encompassing nature of this, the world's second-largest religion, makes Islam an especially relevant subject of study. How does Islam see its place within our pluralistic world? Can a religion that understands itself as embracing the totality of life truly be tolerant of other religions?

The answer to such questions is twofold. Muslims regard Islam as the final revelation to all religions, just as they believe the Qur'an itself is the final revelation of the divine will. But Muslims also acknowledge that other religions include expressions of the divine will. Judaism and Christianity, especially, are favored by Islam, which regards their followers as People of the Book.

We often hear of conflicts involving Muslims: fights between Palestinian Muslims and Israeli Jews, riots pitting Hindus against Muslims in India, attacks by those labeled Muslim extremists. Like the ideals of every religion, those of Islam are not always put into practice. Nevertheless, Islam's overriding theme is the ideal of unity. This statement is from the great Sufi poet Rumi:

I am neither eastern nor western, neither
    heavenly nor earthly,
I am neither of the natural elements nor of
    the rotating spheres.
I am neither from India nor China, from
    neither Bulgaria nor Tabriz,
From neither the country of Iraq nor the
    land of Khurasan.
My sign is without sign, my locus is without
    locus,

The Sufi practice of dancing wildly to induce a mystical union with God is illustrated in this page from a sixteenth-century Persian manuscript.

It is neither body nor soul for I am myself
    the Soul of souls.
Since I expelled all duality, I see the two
    worlds as one.

I see the One, I seek the One, I know the
    One, I call upon the One.
            (Quoted in Nasr, "Islam,"
            in *Our Religions,* page 522)

Chapter Review

1. What is the root meaning of the name *Islam?*
2. Describe the Qur'an's size and structure, and identify its original language.
3. What is the literal meaning of the term *qur'an?*
4. When and where was Muhammad born?
5. Briefly describe the Night of Power and Excellence.
6. What is the Hijra, and why is it important?
7. Why is Muhammad referred to as the Seal of the Prophets?

8. What is the Sunna of the Prophet?

9. Why is Allah thought to be genderless?

10. Identify at least two of Islam's prophets other than Muhammad.

11. Who is Ishmael, and what is his place in Islam?

12. How do Muslims interpret the Fall from perfection in the Garden of Eden?

13. Briefly describe what Muslims expect to happen before and on the Day of Judgment.

14. What is the Muslim view of the natural world?

15. What determines inclusion in the Umma?

16. Identify two modern nations whose government is based on the Shari'a.

17. What is the English translation of the Muslim confession of faith?

18. Briefly describe the Muslim practice of daily prayer.

19. What is Ramadan?

20. What is required of Muslims according to the fourth pillar, wealth sharing?

21. What is the *hajj*, and what is its religious significance?

22. Summarize two Muslim teachings on the care of the body.

23. With regard to Muslim perspectives on women, what are the three specific points of contention commonly cited by Western critics?

24. Define the word *jihad.*

25. What was the extent of Islamic expansion one century after Muhammad's death?

26. What areas of the globe are presently populated with the greatest concentration of Muslims?

27. Why does Arabia enjoy a special status in Islam?

28. Why have some African Americans argued that Islam is better suited for their community than is Christianity?

29. What is Sunnism?

30. What is the meaning of the term *shi'i?*

31. Identify at least two modern nations that have a Shi'i majority or a significant Shi'i population.

The Seven Dimensions of Religion: Islam

Dimension	Examples
Experiential	fasting during Ramadan, *al-fana*
Mythic	sacred narratives of Abraham's founding of Mecca and of Muhammad's Ascension to Heaven
Doctrinal	Shahada (emphasizing monotheism), Shari'a
Ethical	wealth sharing, regulations against pork and alcohol
Ritual	prayer five times daily, various observances while on the *hajj*
Social	the Umma, the *imam,* the *shaykh*
Material	the holy cities of Mecca and Medina, the Ka'ba, mosques

32. Briefly describe the figure of the Imam in Shi'ism.
33. How does Sufism extend the first sentence of Islam's confession of faith?
34. Identify at least two Sufi methods, or disciplines.

Glossary

al-fana (ahl-fuhn´ah; Arabic: "extinction"). The extinction of one's sense of separate existence before achieving union with Allah; the aim of Sufi mystics.

caliphs (Arabic: "successors"). The military and political leaders of the Muslim community who succeeded Muhammad after his death.

Five Pillars. Specific religious and ethical requirements for Muslims: the confession of faith (Shahada), prayer or worship, fasting during Ramadan, wealth sharing, and the pilgrimage to Mecca *(hajj).*

hajj (haj). The fifth of the Five Pillars; the journey to Mecca that all Muslims are to make at least once in their lifetime, if they can afford it and are physically able.

Hijra (hij´ruh; Arabic: "emigration"). The emigration of Muhammad and his followers from Mecca to Yathrib (thereafter called Medina) in AD 622; the founding event of the Muslim community.

imam (i-mahm´; Arabic: "leader"). The leader of the Friday worship service who directs the prayers and delivers a sermon.

Imam. For Shi'i Islam, an early successor to Muhammad and leader of Islam (most Shi'is acknowledge twelve Imams), believed to have special spiritual insight.

jihad (ji-had´; Arabic: "exertion" or "struggle"). Sometimes counted as the sixth pillar of Islam, the general spiritual struggle to be a devout Muslim. In a more narrow context, *jihad* refers to armed struggle (holy war) for the sake of Islam, which the Qur'an supports only if it is carried out in self-defense.

Ka'ba (kah´bah). The stone cubical structure in the court-yard of the Great Mosque of Mecca, believed to have been built by Abraham and regarded by Muslims as the sacred center of the earth.

mosque. The Muslim place or building of worship, tradition-ally including a prayer hall and courtyard, with towers called minarets at the corners.

Qur'an (kuh-ran´; Arabic: "reci-tation"). Islam's primary sacred text, regarded by Muslims as the direct words of Allah, revealed to Muhammad through the archangel Gabriel.

Ramadan (ram´uh-dahn). The ninth month of the Islamic lunar calendar, a period during which Muslims fast, in accordance with the third of the Five Pillars.

Shahada (shuh-hah´duh; Arabic: "witnessing"). The confession of faith, the first of the Five Pillars and central creedal statement of Islam: "There is no god except God. Muhammad is the messenger of God."

Shari'a (sha-ree´ah). The divine law, derived from the Qur'an and the Sunna, encom-passing all and setting forth in detail how Muslims are to live.

shaykh (shayk). A teacher and master in Islam, such as the leader of an order in Sufism.

Shi'i (shee´ee; from *shi'at 'Ali:* "partisans of Ali"). The division of Islam dominant in Iraq and Iran, originating as a result of an early dispute over leadership; distinguishable from Sunni Islam mainly by its figure of the Imam and strong messianic expecta-tions.

Sufi (soo´fee). An adherent of Sufism, the form of Islam characterized by a mystical ap-proach to Allah, who is experi-enced inwardly.

Sunna (soon´nuh; Arabic: "custom" or "tradition"). The teachings and actions of Mu-hammad recorded in writings known as *hadith,* which provide the model for being Muslim; Islam's second most important authority (after the Qur'an).

Sunni (soon´nee). The division of Islam practiced by most Mus-lims, named after the Sunna.

Umma (oom´muh; Arabic: "community"). The community of all Muslims.

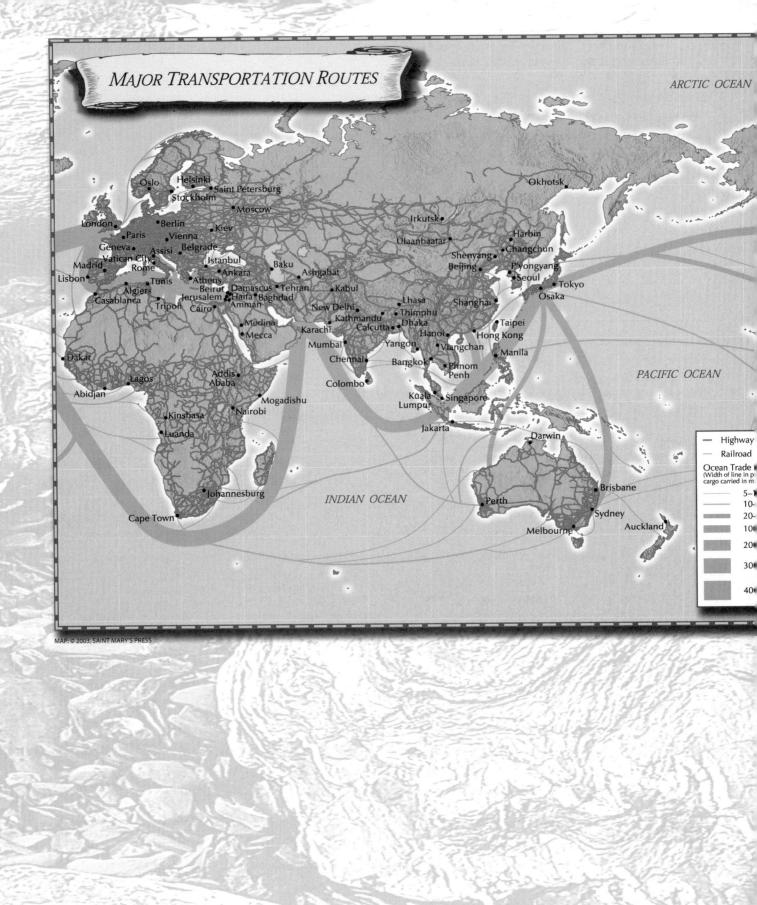

MAJOR TRANSPORTATION ROUTES

ARCTIC OCEAN

PACIFIC OCEAN

INDIAN OCEAN

Oslo
Helsinki
Stockholm
Saint Petersburg
Moscow
London
Berlin
Paris
Kiev
Vienna
Geneva
Belgrade
Assisi
Vatican City
Istanbul
Madrid
Rome
Ankara
Baku
Ashgabat
Lisbon
Athens
Tunis
Algiers
Beirut
Damascus
Tehran
Casablanca
Haifa
Baghdad
Kabul
Jerusalem
Tripoli
Amman
Cairo
New Delhi
Lhasa
Medina
Kathmandu
Thimphu
Mecca
Karachi
Calcutta
Dhaka
Mumbai
Yangon
Chennai
Bangkok
Colombo
Kuala
Lumpur
Singapore
Jakarta

Okhotsk
Irkutsk
Ulaanbaatar
Harbin
Changchun
Shenyang
Beijing
Pyongyang
Seoul
Shanghai
Tokyo
Osaka
Taipei
Hanoi
Hong Kong
Viangchan
Manila
Phnom
Penh

Dakar
Lagos
Addis
Ababa
Abidjan
Mogadishu
Kinshasa
Nairobi
Luanda
Johannesburg
Cape Town

Darwin
Perth
Brisbane
Sydney
Melbourne
Auckland

Highway
Railroad
Ocean Trade
(Width of line in p
cargo carried in m
5–1
10–
20–
100
200
300
400

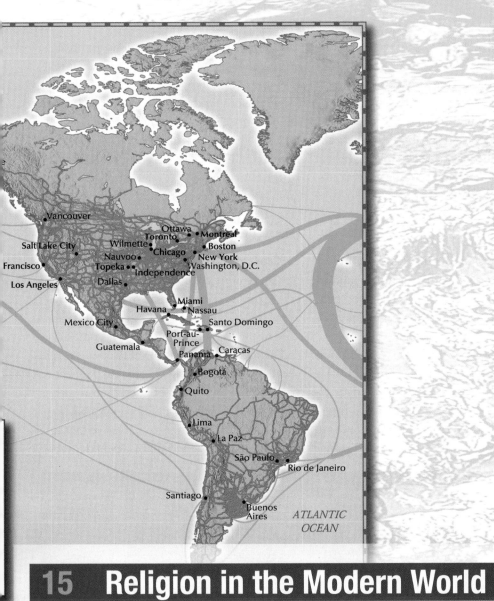

15 Religion in the Modern World

A Changing Religious Landscape

Most major world religions are centuries old, with roots reaching back to ancient times. But in the past two hundred years, a vast array of "new religious movements" have emerged, some of which have become quite large and firmly established. Major traditions such as Hinduism, Buddhism, and Christianity continue to thrive, but even those have been experiencing a new degree of change. In fact, the whole world has experienced dramatic and increasingly rapid transformations during this time, largely in response to modernization and globalization. It is no wonder religions have been swept along in the currents of those changes.

A

Think about a technology that plays a significant role in your life—for example, the cell phone. Describe how this technology affects your daily routine and your outlook.

B

Read Acts of the Apostles 2:43–47. In your own words, briefly describe the economic principles of the early Christian community. How compatible are those principles with the economic ways of today's society?

Modern Influences

The modern age is characterized by change and invention—after television came the computer and then the Internet, and now other innovative devices and capabilities. The technological revolution that has produced these is but one important aspect of the general process known as **modernization.**

Modernization

Modernization stems mainly from the Industrial Revolution, which began in England in the eighteenth century. It is the general process by which societies achieve increased literacy and education, enhanced technologies, self-sustaining economies, greater national unity, and broader participation in politics and government. Such sweeping changes affect religion. As the focus on national interests grows, the nation-state arises to become the governing authority, and the traditional authority of religious institutions diminishes. And enhanced technology and education allow the common people access to sacred texts and religious teachings that previously tended to be controlled by the religious elite.

One reason for today's varied religious landscape is that modernization has affected different societies at different times. Some small-scale societies are only today experiencing the full impact of modernization, which affects their religious ways accordingly.[A]

Capitalism and Materialism

One feature of modernization is capitalism, the economic system based on private ownership and pursuit of wealth. Along with a rapid rise of the capitalist economy has come a significant change in societal values: people have begun to embrace materialism, the perspective that private ownership of goods and wealth is a good in itself, and should be increased.

Today materialism is so pervasive that it is easy to regard it as acceptable, even desirable.

The bustle of the New York Stock Exchange symbolizes capitalism, the economic system that characterizes modernization.

IMAGE: © JUSTIN LANE/EPA/CORBIS

But traditional religious teachings tend to advise against materialism, sometimes insistently. The Christian New Testament, for example, cites Jesus as proclaiming, "It is easier for a camel to go through the eye of a needle than for someone who is rich to enter the kingdom of God" (Mark 10:25). Most other major traditions set forth similar teachings in one form or another. The widespread acceptance of materialistic values brought on by modernization and its capitalistic tendencies marks a significant change—and in some respects a challenge—to many of the religious teachings of the world.[B]

Population Growth and Urbanization

Another feature of modernization is global population growth and urbanization (the shift of population centers from rural, agricultural settings to cities). Urbanization naturally accompanies the economic changes of modernization, because capitalism thrives on manufacturing, which requires a large workforce amassed in one area.

Urbanization began to intensify during the Industrial Revolution and continues at an even more accelerated pace today. More than 50 percent of the world's population lives in cities now, compared with fewer than 10 percent in 1900. This shift has created tension with religious traditions, which through the ages have typically conformed mainly to rural settings, often punctuated by festivals and holy days scheduled in accordance with agricultural seasons.[C]

Globalization

Accompanying modernization is the process of **globalization:** the linking and intermixing of cultures. Beginning with the era of exploration and colonization, and accelerating through the centuries because of technological advances in communications and transportation, globalization has brought us to the threshold of a truly interconnected world

The globalization of the world economy has sparked protests such as this one in Richmond, California.

community. For example, fifty years ago few Westerners had heard much about Tibetan (Vajrayana) Buddhism. Today the Dalai Lama is known throughout the world, jetting from city to city, advocating freedom for his people and teaching about his tradition.

Multiculturalism

One natural result of globalization is the coexistence of different peoples and their cultures, which is called **multiculturalism**. Multiculturalism makes it impossible for followers of a particular religious tradition to regard that tradition as the one and only. Educating ourselves about other religions is a means for getting along with our neighbors in today's multicultural world.[D]

Equal Rights and Egalitarianism

Traditional religious perspectives have commonly accepted or even advocated what many today would regard as situations of inequality. One form of inequality exists in

C
Consider a religious tradition with which you are familiar. Do the various dimensions of that religious tradition (ethical, doctrinal, ritual, and so on) reflect a rural setting or an urban setting? Offer examples to support your observations.

D
Briefly describe at least one personal experience or observation of how multiculturalism affects religion.

Religion in the Modern World   269

Hinduism's caste system, for example. Another arises whenever certain people consider others inferior because they follow a different religion: for instance, Europeans who colonized the New World degraded Native Americans as heathen savages, and Muslims could regard non-Muslims as infidels (unbelievers).

Today, in most parts of the world, traditional forms of inequality are challenged. Modern societies tend to favor egalitarianism: a belief in equality between men and women, among racial and ethnic groups, and even among those who practice different religions.

Over time religious traditions have tended to accommodate these basic shifts in worldview. To some extent the egalitarian ideal and the advocacy of equal rights have become integral to most religions.

Modernization can be said to challenge religions from within, while globalization challenges them from without. Only time will tell how extensive the changes from both forms of challenges will be or what direction those changes will take. Not all the changes will head down the path toward egalitarianism. Some religious factions resist change—often rigorously—fueling the phenomenon of traditionalism.

E
Traditionalism can apply to many parts of life, not just religion. In what part of your life do you tend to be more traditional? Offer several specific examples of ways you try to maintain older beliefs and practices in that area.

Traditionalism

Within religions **traditionalism** is a common reaction to rapid changes in the surrounding world. Traditionalists maintain older forms of belief and practice regardless of new social norms. For example, Orthodox Jews maintain Torah as the standard of truth. As a result they strictly observe the Sabbath, refusing even to drive their cars while the rest of society spends Saturday going to movies or seeking other kinds of entertainment. All religions have factions that tend toward more traditionalist interpretations. Sometimes individuals choose their own degree of traditionalism, rather than following the stance of an entire group.

Certain historical eras have provoked waves of traditionalist tendencies. We seem to be in such an era today. One pronounced effect of modernization and globalization is the traditionalist phenomenon broadly identified as fundamentalism.[E]

Fundamentalism

There are basically two meanings of the term **fundamentalism.** In its strictest sense, fundamentalism emphasizes a literal interpretation of a religion's sacred texts and primary teachings—thus getting back to the "funda-

The Taliban enforced a fundamentalist interpretation of Islam during its rule in Afghanistan; for example, it required women to be completely covered in public.

IMAGE: © AFP/GETTY IMAGES

mentals." In a more general sense, *fundamentalism* refers to an intensely traditionalist form of religion, reacting against modern forces and the religious reforms they encourage. It tends to reject a diversity of interpretations in favor of an authoritarian approach that insists on one "true" interpretation.

The ambiguity brought about by these two meanings can pose problems. Consider the term *fundamentalist Islam*. If *fundamentalist* is defined in its strictest sense, it is redundant because all Muslims are expected to believe in the literal truth of the Qur'an. If *fundamentalist* is defined in its general sense, it accurately identifies Muslims who in addition advocate an intense traditionalism and an authoritarian approach.

One high-profile Muslim group that can be considered fundamentalist in the general sense is the Taliban. This group ruled much of Afghanistan in the mid-1990s and was ousted in the aftermath of the 9-11 attacks on the United States' World Trade Center and Pentagon. Reacting against such features of modernization as the movement toward equal rights for women, the Taliban enforced its own interpretation of Islam through highly authoritative means. Women were on occasion stoned to death for not wearing the veil as required by the law—the law as interpreted by the Taliban, that is.

Another fundamentalist faction operates within Hinduism. Whereas Hinduism is for the most part tolerant both toward its own diverse forms of belief and practice and toward other religions, Hindu fundamentalists support a "Hindu nation" and oppose the presence in India of Muslims and Christians.

The two meanings of *fundamentalism* are evident in Christianity as well. Some Christians consider the Bible a vehicle of human construction that conveys the religious meaning of God's Revelation, even if not every word of the Bible is literally true from a scientific and historical standpoint. Christian fundamentalists, on the other hand, regard the Bible as the literal, infallible word of God. They contend, for example, that the account of the Creation of the world in the Book of Genesis is factually accurate.

Liberalism

With traditionalism at one end of the continuum of religious thought, the other end can generally be termed **liberalism.**

Within Judaism, for example, Orthodox Judaism is more traditional and Reform Judaism is more liberal. Orthodox Judaism regards the Torah as the standard for life, while Reform Judaism holds that the religion should adapt to society's changes. As is the case with traditionalism, the world's major religions manifest their own forms of liberalism, at least to some extent. Within Christianity Catholicism's Second Vatican Council is a clear example of the Church's teaching and responding to the needs of the modern world. The effects of Vatican II have been far-reaching and enduring. Not surprisingly, one of those effects has been to motivate a more traditionalist reaction on the part of some Catholics. The continuum of the very traditional to the very liberal allows for much middle ground. Trends to one end or the other usually spur countertrends, and the religions themselves tend to be populated by a moderate majority.

Secular Humanism

If fundamentalism is traditionalism at its extreme, its liberal counterpart is **secular humanism:** the worldview that ultimate value is grounded entirely in the human realm, not in the divine or supernatural. It might appear that such a worldview is not religious at all. But modern definitions of religion seldom insist on belief in the divine or supernatural. (Zen Buddhism, for example, is also nontheistic—that is, it is not based on belief in a god or gods.) Secular humanism does provide answers to some of life's most basic questions, including questions of ethical responsibility.

Strong ethical intentions motivate secular humanists' rejection of belief in the divine. *Not* believing in supernatural assistance—either in this life or in an afterlife—leaves all responsibility for caring for the human species with humans themselves. However one might judge secular humanism, considered in the light of the history of religions, it is an extreme form of liberalism. Embracing the modern emphasis on science and on the intellectual pursuit of truth, secular humanism dismisses the traditional religious beliefs of Western culture.

The Universalist Impulse

Another notable response to modernization, and especially to globalization, might be called the universalist impulse: to regard all religious perspectives as valid. This impulse is a significant feature of some religions. Hinduism, for example, its fundamentalist faction notwithstanding, has tended to be universalist from its beginning: "God is one but men call him by many names," says the ancient Rig Veda (1.64.46). Shri Ramakrishna could go so far as to become a Muslim and then a Christian, all the while identifying himself as Hindu.

Sikhism also emphasizes a universalist impulse, having from its beginning mixed the Hindu and Islamic elements of its Indian homeland. Guru Nanak, Sikhism's founder, memorably set forth his universalist perspective: "God is neither Hindu nor [Muslim] and the path which I follow is God's" (Cole and Sambhi, *The Sikhs,* page 10).

Humanist Manifesto II

The central elements of secular humanism are set forth in "Humanist Manifesto II", a document composed in 1973 and signed by thousands. This short excerpt offers a sense for humanism's stance toward religions:

In the best sense, religion may inspire dedication to the highest ethical ideals. The cultivation of moral devotion and creative imagination is an expression of genuine "spiritual" experience and aspiration.

We believe, however, that traditional dogmatic or authoritarian religions that place revelation, God, ritual, or creed above human needs and experience do a disservice to the human species. Any account of nature should pass the tests of scientific evidence; in our judgment, the dogmas and myths of traditional religions do not do so. Even at this late date in human history, certain elementary facts based upon the critical use of scientific reason have to be restated. We find insufficient evidence for belief in the existence of a supernatural: it is either meaningless or irrelevant to the question of the survival and fulfillment of the human race. As nontheists, we begin with humans not God, nature not deity. Nature may indeed be broader and deeper than we now know; any new discoveries, however, will but enlarge our knowledge of the natural. . . .

At the present juncture of history, commitment to all humankind is the highest commitment of which we are capable; it transcends the narrow allegiances of church, state, party, class, or race in moving toward a wider vision of human potentiality. What more daring a goal for humankind than for each person to become, in ideal as well as practice, a citizen of a world community. It is a classical vision; we can now give it new vitality. Humanism thus interpreted is a moral force that has time on its side. We believe that humankind has the potential intelligence, goodwill, and cooperative skill to implement this commitment in the decades ahead.

(American Humanist Association)

IMAGE: TOM COMPAGNONI/WAX VISUAL STOCK PHOTOGRAPHY

The Baha'i House of Worship in New Delhi, India, is designed to resemble the lotus flower, which in Indian culture is a symbol of peace and purity.

Baha'i

Perhaps the religion that most fully embodies the universalist impulse is **Baha'i** (bah-hah′ ee). This tradition teaches that all founders of the world's religions have been God's divine messengers, or prophets. It thus emphasizes the unity of all religions and of all people.

Baha'i was founded in 1863 by an Iranian named Mirza Husayn ali Nuri (1817 to 1892), who is known by his followers as Baha Allah in Arabic, or Bahaullah in Persian (both names mean "glory of God"). Baha'is are, literally, "followers of Baha." When Baha Allah claimed in 1863 to be a prophet, challenging Muslim beliefs that Muhammad was the last of the prophets, he was imprisoned by Muslim authorities and then exiled for a number of years. By 1884, though, he had managed to complete the writing of the Baha'is' sacred text, Kitab al-aqdas (whose name is Arabic for "the Most Holy Book"). The administrative center of Baha'i is now in nearby Haifa, Israel; this region is considered the holy land and geographical center of the religion.

Baha'i first gained an international reputation through the travels and teachings of the son of Baha Allah, Abbas Effendi (1844 to 1921), known as Abd al-Baha (whose name is Arabic for "the servant of the glory [of God]"). Abd al-Baha's prominence as a missionary was affirmed when he was knighted by the British government in 1920. Today Baha'i is under the leadership not of one individual but of an elected body known as the International House of Justice, as was foretold in Kitab al-aqdas.

Adherents of Baha'i are required to engage in only four main practices: a communal gathering every nineteenth day (called the Feast of the Nineteenth Day); a period of fasting that lasts nineteen days (one month, according to the Baha'i calendar), corresponding to Islam's Ramadan; complete avoidance of alcoholic beverages; and daily prayer. In addition, Kitab al-aqdas encourages Baha'i communities to construct a nine-sided building that serves as a temple. Today several of these impressive structures stand in various places around the globe, including Wilmette, Illinois, and New Delhi, India. There are presently some six million Baha'is in the world.

Kitab al-aqdas proclaims that the revelations of Baha Allah are the most advanced of all religious teachings, but that even these will one day be succeeded by a new revelation, relevant for that future age. Baha'i is unique among religions in that it anticipates the day it will be superceded.

Interfaith Dialogue

Ecumenism, the promotion of Christian unity, has served as a springboard for a more general manifestation of the universalist impulse: **interfaith dialogue,** an attempt to promote greater harmony between religious traditions. Jewish-Christian dialogue is one example of this.

Interfaith dialogue can also be observed on a global scale. In 1993 the Parliament of the World's Religions convened in Chicago. It was in part a celebration of the one hundredth anniversary of the first such parliament, held in 1893. The 1893 parliament had been a milestone for interfaith dialogue because it had introduced the richness of the various traditions to a great number of people.

At the 1993 parliament, hundreds of religious leaders from around the globe approved the Declaration of a Global Ethic. Drawing on the wisdom of the world's religions, that document highlights certain principles common to all: preserving life through nonviolence, respecting all living things, dealing honestly and fairly with one another, speaking and acting truthfully, and respecting and loving one another.[F]

Postmodernism

Still another response to modernization and globalization suggests something of a new direction. **Postmodernism** arose in the late twentieth century and reflects a critical reac-

F
Reflect on the principles highlighted in the Declaration of a Global Ethic. Briefly describe the extent to which you see each principle being practiced in society.

Leaders of different religions march for peace in Lisbon, Portugal.

tion to the trends of the modern world. It incorporates the perspective that certain aspects of modernization—capitalism with its materialistic values, urbanization and a corresponding growth in population, and the technological revolution with its confidence in science—do not in fact make for a better life. Postmodernism sees globalization as also failing to improve the human condition, causing people to feel uprooted and to lack a clear sense of belonging.

The effects of postmodernism are apparent throughout the various religious perspectives. People today are generally more apt to embrace a nearness to or oneness with nature. They are more insistent on gender equality, including characterization of the divine as not necessarily male. Many reject the dominance of materialistic concerns, at least in their ideals. Finally, they tend to regard different religions as equal, thus incorporating the universalist impulse.[G]

New Religious Movements

A natural response to the modern situation has been to create new religions to fit the circumstances. Beginning especially in the nineteenth century, new religious movements became common. Frequently, though not always, new religions arise behind charismatic figures. Commonly they develop with close ties to an established tradition.

A number of new religions have gained a large following and an international reputation. As time passes the more than a thousand movements that remain relatively unknown may rise to prominence. Most of the world's established traditions, including Buddhism, Christianity, and Islam, began as new religious movements.

Two terms are often used to categorize new religious movements: *sects* and *cults.* Sociolo-gists use the word *sects* to refer to religious groups in which membership is voluntary, rather than based on birth. Sects tend to oppose the ordinary ways of society, and therefore can be described as separatist. In sociological usage the word *cults* refers to groups that are somewhat distinctive, and yet are accepted by society at large and by its predominant religion or religions. It can also be used similarly in a more traditional context. Catholicism, for example, has within it the "cult of saints": veneration of holy men and women and of their remains (called relics).

The Vedanta Society and ISKCON: Importing Religions

One result of globalization has been the importation of religions into cultures where they were previously unknown. Among many examples are two quite different imports from India that have gained a degree of prominence in the West: the Vedanta Society and ISKCON (International Society for Krishna Consciousness, popularly known as the Hare Krishna movement). Both illustrate characteristics typical of new religious movements: a charismatic founder and a connection to an established religion.[H]

The Vedanta Society

The Vedanta Society was founded by Swami Vivekananda (1863 to 1902) in the wake of his role at the World's Parliament of Religions in Chicago in 1893. Established in New York in 1894, and in San Francisco and Boston shortly thereafter, the Vedanta Society became the first Hindu organization in the United States, and has continued to play a significant role there and elsewhere in the Western world.

In 1897 Swami Vivekananda returned to India, where he founded the Ramakrishna Mission, an influential Hindu organization devoted to education, social welfare, and the

G

Would you describe yourself as a postmodernist? Why or why not?

H

Choose Buddhism, Christianity, or Islam, and think about its early years. What general features of new religious movements were present in that religion at its start?

publication of religious texts. Both the Ramakrishna Mission and the Vedanta Society were inspired by the life and teachings of Vivekananda's spiritual master, Shri Ramakrishna (1836 to 1886), who exemplified the Hindu ideal of unity.

The Vedanta Society teaches that all reality, including every individual, is essentially Brahman, the eternal, indescribable ultimate. The spiritual quest is to realize this truth, and thus to be liberated from ignorance. The Vedanta Society emphasizes philosophy, basing its approach on the Hindu path of knowledge, or *jnana marga*. It has attracted the interest of many in the West, including novelists Aldous Huxley and Christopher Isherwood.

ISKCON: The Hare Krishna Movement

While the Vedanta Society emphasizes the doctrinal dimension, the International Society for Krishna Consciousness emphasizes the ritual dimension, drawing from the Hindu path of devotion, or *bhakti marga*. This is most evident in the chanting of the names of God through a mantra well known to the counterculture of the late 1960s and the 1970s:

Hare Krishna Hare Krishna
Krishna Krishna Hare Hare
Hare Rama Hare Rama
Rama Rama Hare Hare

Rituals also include public dancing and the sharing of vegetarian meals.

ISKCON was founded in New York in 1965 by the charismatic Swami Prabhupada (1896 to 1977). Instructed by his own Hindu teacher to spread the worship of Krishna, Prabhupada arrived in the United States as a poor seventy-year-old. Soon he had attracted thousands of followers, primarily among the young. He also translated Hindu texts; his *Bhagavad-Gita As It Is*, a translation with extensive commentary, is especially popular.

The problems ISKCON has encountered since its founder's death attest the force of Prabhupada's charisma. Controversies involving leadership have led to decreased membership in North America, although the movement is still quite strong in Great Britain and elsewhere.

A group of Hare Krishna chant and dance in the streets of Gdansk, Poland.

Santeria and Voodoo: Mixing Traditions

New religious movements often result from the mixing of two or more traditions. Santeria, originating in Cuba, and Voodoo (or Vodou or Vodun), originating in Haiti, are two similar new religious movements that combine elements of African religion with elements of Christianity.

Santeria is Spanish for "the way of the saints," and the tradition's name helps explain its basic nature. After Yoruba slaves were brought to Cuba from Africa in the late eighteenth and early nineteenth centuries, they began to identify their divine beings known as *orishas* with the various saints of Catholicism. The Virgin Mary, for example, took on the identity of Oshun, the patroness of love and marriage. To ensure that the *orishas* are appeased, Santeria employs rituals similar to those of the Yoruba religion, including divination and the sharing of food with *orishas* through sacrifices.

The term *Voodoo* derives from *vodu* ("spirit" or "deity"). Although this name is accepted by scholars, it is also commonly used pejoratively and inaccurately, and Haitians often refer to their religion simply as serving the spirits. Like Santeria, Voodoo identifies traditional spirits with Catholic saints. For example, Voodoo identifies Dambala, the snake deity of the Fon people, with Saint Patrick, the fifth-century missionary who converted Ireland to Christianity—and also is renowned for having emptied Ireland of snakes. Voodoo acknowledges, along with its many spirits, a high God, who is known as Bondye (from the French *bon dieu,* "good god"). Bondye is identified with the Christian God but is thought to be disinterested in the daily concerns of human beings, which are the functions of the spirits.

The spirits are served most commonly through private rituals, although sometimes they are honored in large feasts. These celebrations can last for days, and can include animal sacrifice and ritualized drumming and dancing. Spirits are believed to enter into participants of these festivals, speaking through people's voices and thus communicating directly with the worshipers.

Catholic influence is apparent in Voodoo ritual. Voodoo incorporates Baptism, the Mass, confession, and Catholic prayers, some of them in Latin. The latter can require the expertise of a special ritual practitioner, the "bush priest," who knows the Latin form of prayers.

Owing to emigration from Cuba and Haiti to North America in recent decades, memberships in Santeria and Voodoo are large and growing rapidly in cities such as Miami, Los Angeles, Toronto, Montreal, and New York. In New York, for example, it is estimated that the followers of these two religions combined number well over one hundred thousand.

IMAGE: © CAROLINE PENN/CORBIS

Voodoo believers worship hooded figures representing resurrected ancestors.

277

Mormonism: Heeding a New Revelation

The religious movement commonly known as Mormonism arose in western New York in the 1820s in response to a new prophetic revelation. Its founding figure was Joseph Smith Jr. (1805 to 1844). A number of Mormon religious organizations consider Smith their founder, the largest being the Church of Jesus Christ of Latter-day Saints, with headquarters in Salt Lake City, Utah. The Reorganized Church of Jesus Christ of Latter-day Saints is the second largest; its headquarters are in Independence, Missouri.

The Restoration and the Book of Mormon

Mormonism began with what is known as the Restoration—namely, the restoration of

the true authority of the Christian church, which Mormons believe had been lost by the second century, after the age of the Apostles. According to the official church account, when Joseph Smith Jr. was just fourteen, he experienced a vision of two divine figures. In the following years, revelations given by an angel of a prophet named Moroni eventually led Smith to find a group of golden plates buried on a hill near his home. They contained prophecies said to have been written by Moroni's father, Mormon, some fourteen hundred years earlier. Mormon's writings also recounted the history of certain Israelites who had sailed eastward in about 600 BC and established a civilization in America. They were visited by the resurrected Christ. Eventually, at the time of Mormon and his son Moroni, their civilization was defeated in warfare.

Once Smith retrieved the plates, he translated them (from an unknown language) into English. Then Moroni took them back—though not before eleven others are said to have witnessed them. The text was published in 1830 as the Book of Mormon. Smith regarded it as a supplement to the Christian Bible, not as the Bible's replacement.

Brigham Young and Migration to the Salt Lake Valley

Joseph Smith Jr. also organized an official church in 1830. In 1838 this church was named the Church of Jesus Christ of Latter-day Saints. The following year Smith and his

Top: Joseph Smith Jr. experienced visions that led him to found the Church of Jesus Christ of Latter-day Saints. *Bottom:* A plaque commemorates Mormon pioneers who made their way to the Salt Lake Valley, led by Brigham Young.

IMAGE: TOP, © BETTMANN/CORBIS; BOTTOM, © SCOTT T. SMITH/CORBIS

followers founded Nauvoo, Illinois, which soon became the state's largest city (with about eleven thousand inhabitants by 1844). Nauvoo was governed by Mormon principles and authority. Smith and other leading figures introduced several controversial ideas, including baptism for the dead, marriage to multiple women (a form of polygamy), and the possibility of becoming divine through following Mormon teachings. Controversy led to violence. In 1844 Smith and his brother were killed by an anti-Mormon mob.

In 1847 Brigham Young (1801 to 1877) led the Church's migration to the Salt Lake Valley, which he called Zion, the biblical name for Jerusalem. Those loyal to Smith's controversial doctrines tended to join the migration; many others remained in the Midwest. The Salt Lake Valley community had grown to over one hundred thousand by the time of Young's death in 1877, and encompassed a vast territory: all of modern-day Utah, along with parts of Nevada, Idaho, Wyoming, and Arizona. Mormons dreamed of establishing their own desert nation (which they called Deseret) of Mormon rule. But in 1890 the federal government made it impossible for them to achieve that dream, and at the same time forbade the practice of polygamy.

Contemporary Teachings and Growth

Mormon teachings have evolved over the years. Polygamy was once common among members but is now rare. For more than a century, Mormons have lived by strict sexual norms, and the use of alcohol, coffee, tea, and tobacco is forbidden. Such a strict code of ethics is in keeping with their underlying belief that we live in the "latter days," a period of corruption that soon will see the second coming of Christ and the commencement of a thousand-year reign of peace and prosperity.

These elements of Mormonism's doctrinal and ethical dimensions help shape its social and ritual dimensions. Marriage ideally becomes an eternal union through a special ceremony performed in a temple. The temple itself is a special sanctuary, to which only observant members are admitted. Worship more commonly takes place in a meetinghouse.

Mormonism enjoys a high growth rate, in part because of extensive missionary work. Every male is expected to undertake a two-year missionary journey, paying his own way. Today there are about ten million members of the main organization (the Church of Jesus Christ of Latter-day Saints). The Church's emphasis on family clearly has strong appeal,

A Mormon temple in Manti, Utah.

as do the low crime rates and good schools that Mormon communities tend to maintain.

The Latter-day Saints are a well-established feature of the religious landscape of North America and elsewhere. Salt Lake City's Mormon Tabernacle and its choir are familiar to many, and Mormons and their religion are at home in communities of all sizes.[1]

Briefly describe at least three reasons why Mormonism is an especially American religion.

Jehovah's Witnesses: Focusing on a Cataclysmic End

The Bible refers to witnesses of God, who is called Yahweh or Jehovah (depending on how the Hebrew name is rendered in English). Isaiah 43:10 states, "You are my witnesses, says the LORD." Jehovah's Witnesses believe they are about to witness the end of history as we know it, brought about by God's intervention through the presence of Christ on earth.

This new religious movement arose in the wake of the predictions of Christ's return pronounced in the 1830s by a Baptist named William Miller. When he predicted Christ would return within one year of March 21, 1843, some one hundred thousand people joined in the expectation. Although Miller's specific prediction proved wrong, speculations about the return of Christ continued. The Christian movements known as the Adventists (of which the largest denomination is the Seventh-day Adventists) and the Jehovah's Witnesses took shape from these predictions.

The founding figure of the Jehovah's Witnesses was Charles Taze Russell (1852 to 1916). A successful businessman from Pennsylvania and formerly an adherent of Congregationalism (a mainstream Christian denomination), Russell initially predicted the end would come in 1878, and then revised the date to 1914. In 1879 he began to publish the *Watchtower,* and in 1884 he formed the Watchtower Bible and Tract Society. Both remain important elements of the Jehovah's Witnesses today.

The charismatic Russell built an organization of more than three million members, with headquarters in Brooklyn, New York. The organization came to be called the Jehovah's Witnesses in 1931.

Predictions of a Millennial Age

Drawing especially on the biblical book Revelation to John, Russell taught that Christ returned to earth invisibly in 1874. In 1914 Christ would initiate a radical new era that would last one thousand years and would therefore be called the **millennial age.** Only the Witnesses would be saved when the millennial age began: 144,000 of them would rule with God and Christ in heaven, and the rest would enjoy physical immortality on earth, living peacefully with one another and with the animals.

But 1914 came and went, with no clear indication of the start of the millennial age. Russell then predicted the thousand years would begin in 1925. Again nothing occurred to mark the start of the new era—and in the meantime, in 1916, Russell had died.

After 1925 the Jehovah's Witnesses pronounced 1975 as the year history would

Charles Taze Russell founded the Jehovah's Witnesses.

IMAGE: © CORBIS

end and the millennial age would begin. When that prediction proved wrong as well, some one million followers left the organization. Still the Jehovah's Witnesses remains strong, with about five million members worldwide. Scholars have found that failed predictions do not necessarily have a large negative effect on a religion. Initial feelings of disappointment and confusion tend to give way to rationalization and a renewed sense of faith, typically followed by new expectations.[J]

Worship Practices and Missionary Activities

Jehovah's Witnesses meet in buildings called Kingdom Halls. Many aspects of contemporary life are discouraged or prohibited. Higher education is opposed, for example, as is the celebration of Christmas, Easter, and birthdays. Other forms of Christianity are to be avoided, as they are thought to be controlled by Satan. During the 1940s especially, Jehovah's Witnesses needed to defend the movement in many lawsuits that were brought over their refusal to participate in the military and to express patriotism in other ways. Most often the Witnesses were successful. In 1943, for example, a U.S. Supreme Court decision allowed Jehovah's Witnesses not to salute the flag. Such cases have influenced the development of the body of constitutional law that regulates the relation between church and state.

Jehovah's Witnesses are perhaps best known because of door-to-door missionaries who distribute the *Watchtower* and *Awake!* (which was first published in 1919 as the *Golden Age*). The energy and enthusiasm with which the Witnesses undertake their missionary activities attests a depth of commitment that has always been a primary factor in the ongoing strength of the religion.

The New Age Movement: Focusing on a Rejuvenated Future

Like the Latter-day Saints and the Jehovah's Witnesses, New Agers focus on a dawning period of great significance. But for the New Age movement, this period is a rejuvenated future characterized by peace and harmony, not by the corruption of the "latter days," and no sudden end of history is anticipated.

The New Age movement has much in common with new religious movements in general. It is "new," having developed in the wake of the 1960s counterculture. It derives from

J
Think of a specific time when something you hoped for or expected did not take place. Describe similarities and differences between your experience and that of the Jehovah's Witnesses who expected the dawning of a millennial age that never came.

Jehovah's Witnesses meet in Kingdom Halls such as this one in Gloucestershire, England.

IMAGE: © EDIFICE/CORBIS

various traditions, drawing especially on Hindu notions of reincarnation and *karma,* and the Western occult or "hidden" teachings and practices involving the spiritual realm. It also exhibits its own doctrinal, experiential, ritual, and other dimensional features.

Unlike most new religious movements, the New Age movement is not based on a particular founder; rather, it is a collection of various groups, teachings, and practices, all aiming toward transforming the world by enhancing the spiritual potential of human beings. In the words of New Age author Marianne Williamson:

However disparate our personalities and interests, we all agree on one very important point: Mankind has come to a major crossroads, at which the spirit alone can lead us toward human survival. . . .

We hope to change the world into a place of grace and love. (*Illuminata,* page 4)

Common Features, Diverse Forms

The common aim of world transformation through the dawning of a New Age is vitally linked to the transformation of each individual. Often this transformation involves mystical experience, a prominent form of the experien-

A circle of stones created by New Agers stands in an "energy spot" in Coconino National Forest, Arizona.

IMAGE: © TOM BEAN/CORBIS

tial dimension of religion such as Hinduism's *moksha,* Buddhism's *nirvana,* and Islam's Sufi *al-fana,* or "extinction." Other New Agers achieve individual transformation more gradually through experiences of physical and spiritual healing brought about by a variety of techniques.

The doctrinal dimension of the New Age movement includes several beliefs that are held in common by most New Agers. The movement embraces the universalist impulse, is pervaded by Hindu beliefs in reincarnation based on *karma* (the moral law of cause and effect), and emphasizes supernatural beings who enhance the spirituality of humankind. Finally, the New Age movement regards the universe as permeated by power emanating from universal energy. This energy is typically identified as God and is given various names, such as *mind, prana, ch'i,* and Holy Spirit. This diversity of forms revolving around a common doctrinal core extends to beliefs in other powers as well. New Agers refer variously to UFOs, angels, biblical figures, and other forms of spiritual beings.

Despite its relative lack of unifying organization, the New Age movement is cohesive in the importance it places on one element of its social dimension, the teacher, who is often known as the guru (another example of South Asian influence). The movement in general reveres those who have distinguished themselves as especially effective teachers. Renowned figures include Baba Ram Dass, Swami Satchidananda, Rabbi Zalman Schachter-Shalomi, and Elizabeth Clare Prophet. Many New Agers anticipate the coming of a great teacher, someone of the category of Gautama the Buddha or Jesus, who will transform the world.

The ritual and material dimensions include a great many tools for the spiritual transformation of the individual (and, by extension, of the world). Some of those tools are ancient and familiar, such as astrology, herbs, and meditation. Channeling of disembodied spirits, rebirthing, and the use of crystals are among the numerous techniques that mark this movement.

Still more tools and techniques are part of the movement known as holistic health, which understands the body, mind, and spirit to be interrelated parts of the person. According to the holistic philosophy, treatment of any one part of the person helps heal the whole (*holistic* is derived from the Greek term for "whole," *holos*). The person, in turn, is part of nature. Many holistic health techniques—such as massage, chiropractic adjustments, fasting, and vegetarianism—aim to remove blockages of natural healing energies.

A Future for the New Age?

Scholars have mixed perspectives about the future of the New Age movement. On one hand, because it draws from well-established features of Hinduism, Western occult teachings, and other traditional forms, something akin to the New Age movement seems likely to continue to enjoy popularity. On the other hand, the movement is being forced to deal with the competitive nature of the marketplace. New Age bookstores, seminars, individual practitioners—all are in part economically motivated to succeed, and success sometimes crowds out competitors. Critics of New Age spirituality include Christians who are concerned about the common references to Christ or Christ-consciousness in a belief system that is at odds with most of Christianity.

Nature Religion: Worshiping Mother Earth

The worship of nature is part of many of the world's religious traditions. It is also part of new religious movements such as Neopaganism and Wicca, or modern witchcraft.

Neopaganism

Derived from the Latin term *paganus* (inhabitant of the country), *Neopaganism* refers to a new religious movement that finds inspiration in the various pre-Christian European and Egyptian religions. Based on reverence for nature, the movement reacts against the technology of modernization and the patriarchal tradition of Christianity.

The doctrinal dimension of the many groups that belong to the movement focuses on the sacredness of nature, which is typically personified as the Goddess (and sometimes given a name, such as Gaia, the Greek goddess Earth). But there are thought to be many goddesses and gods (Neopaganism is polytheistic), and nature itself is believed to be permeated by the divine. The rhythms of nature—such as the phases of the moon, the changing of the seasons, and the life cycle of individuals—are themselves regarded as sacred. Beyond this, though it sometimes uses certain texts, Neopaganism has little by way of dogma or doctrines. It is mainly based on experience achieved through ritual. Certain places are regarded as especially sacred, and sometimes ritual is employed to create a sacred space. Within that designated space are enacted a colorful variety of rites, including dancing, drumming, storytelling, and fire tending.

Neopaganism also emphasizes the ethical dimension, typically summarized in a basic principle of behaving responsibly, so as to bring no harm to others. Maintaining this principle, Neopagans tend to rejoice in the pleasures nature and life have to offer.

Given the diversity of Neopaganism, it is difficult to determine how many people are adherents. Probably there are more than one hundred thousand Neopagans in North America. Significant groups include the Church of All Worlds, the Covenant of the Goddess, and the EarthSpirit Community.

Wicca

Scholars typically consider Wicca a subcategory of Neopaganism. The term *wicca* in Old English means "sorcerer." Generally both male and female adherents of Wicca are called witches. Contrary to traditional witchcraft, Wicca has no association with devil worship (or Satanism). Instead, like Neopaganism generally, it focuses on reverence for nature.

This magic symbol of Wicca religion represents earth, air, fire, and spirit.

IMAGE: © REBECCA MCENTEE/CORBIS SYGMA

The Old English verb *wiccian* means "to cast a spell." Though Wicca tends not to embrace many of the ideas traditionally associated with witches and sorcerers, it does incorporate practices that are often grouped under the modern term *magick*. Based on the understanding that nature is permeated with energy, magick consists of techniques that cause natural energy to conform to a witch's will.

Wicca, like most other new religious movements, can be traced to a founding figure. Gerald Gardner (1884 to 1964), a self-taught British anthropologist, helped launch the movement in 1954 when he published *Witchcraft Today*. Many current followers of Wicca identify themselves as Gardnerian witches.

Wicca focuses worship on a goddess, usually identified as the Triple Goddess, thought to incorporate the three main stages of female life: the maiden, the mother, and the crone (or old woman). Often the Horned God is worshiped along with the Goddess. Like Neopagans generally, witches tend to practice rituals in groups and in specific places, but they usually hold to more specific norms. The group, called a coven, numbers from four to twenty, with thirteen considered optimal. The sacred place is a circle nine feet in diameter. Specific ritual items are used: the *athame* (ritual knife), the pentacle (a five-pointed star whose points are connected in a circle), a chalice, and a sword. Witches sometimes practice in the nude ("sky-clad"), although usually they are clothed, sometimes with special robes. They meet regularly, and also celebrate eight seasonal festivals, the most famous being Samhain (or Halloween). Their practices are guarded carefully; secrecy is a dominant feature of modern witchcraft.

Pentecostalism: Reinventing the Old

Pentecostalism is so closely in step with traditional forms of Christianity that it is sometimes not considered a new religious movement. It is the world's fastest growing form of Christianity, and some have estimated that by 2030 Pentecostal Christians will outnumber all other Protestants combined.

Pentecostalism gets its name from this New Testament passage:

When the day of Pentecost had come, [the Apostles] were all together in one place. And suddenly from heaven there came a sound like the rush of a violent wind, and it filled the entire house where they were sitting. Divided tongues, as of fire, appeared among them, and a tongue rested on each of them. All of them were filled with the Holy Spirit and began to speak in other languages, as the Spirit gave them the ability. (Acts of the Apostles 2:1–4)

The experience of speaking in other languages (or tongues; *glōssa* in Greek) is called **glossolalia**. It is one of the "gifts of the Spirit" referred to by the Apostle Paul in his First

Letter to the Corinthians (chapter 12). Such gifts, most notably glossolalia, are central elements of Pentecostalism, which regards them as indications of direct experience of the Holy Spirit. Such experience is the primary defining feature of the movement.

Twentieth-Century Origins

Two related incidents pinpoint the beginnings of the Pentecostal movement. On January 1, 1901, at Bethel Bible College, in Topeka, Kansas, a student named Agnes Ozman reportedly spoke in tongues. Not long afterward the college's founder and president, the Reverend Charles Fox Parham (1873 to 1929), experienced glossolalia himself and launched the Pentecostal movement.

A few years later, Parham's influence had reached California, where William Joseph Seymour, an African American minister, led his congregation to experience glossolalia. The so-called Azusa Street revival, beginning on April 9, 1906, and named for the Los Angeles location of Seymour's church, greatly influenced the growth of Pentecostalism. Many connected it with the powerful San Francisco earthquake of April 18, 1906, so that speculations about the return of Christ and the end of history ran rampant. Visitors arriving in Los Angeles experienced glossolalia and the exciting atmosphere of the new movement, and then went back to their homes across the country and around the world, spreading enthusiasm for Pentecostalism. Seymour was eventually stripped of his leadership role because of his race, and the Azusa Street revival lost its momentum after 1913, but by then Pentecostalism had taken firm root in the mainstream of Christian society.

Twenty-first-Century Growth Explosion

Pentecostalism's fast growth is mirrored by its high degree of exposure. Television evangelists Jim and Tammy Bakker, Pat Robertson, and Jimmy Swaggart are among

IMAGE: AP IMAGES/WORLD WIDE PHOTOS

Television evangelists Jim and Tammy Bakker were among the famous personalities of Pentecostalism.

its famous personalities. Scandals over sexual transgressions and financial misdealings led to the downfall of Jim Bakker and Jimmy Swaggart in the 1990s but do not seem to have harmed Pentecostalism's popularity. Today there are several million followers in the United States and hundreds of millions of followers worldwide. Growth in developing Latin American countries has been especially dramatic.

Among the more common Pentecostal denominations are the Assemblies of God and the Church of God (Cleveland, Tennessee). The basic elements of Pentecostalism form the foundation of the charismatic movement, which is now popular in other forms of Protestantism and in Catholicism as well.

Religion and Science

The scientific worldview offers an alternative to traditional religions insofar as it attempts to answer some of life's most basic questions: Where do we come from? What is the nature of human existence? What is our ultimate destiny, and what is the destiny of the universe? As a result of scientific attempts to answer these traditionally religious questions, science and religion often find themselves at odds. Religious thinkers tend to be wary of the scientific emphasis on matter as opposed to spirit. Meanwhile, science forges ahead with its experiments, discoveries, and theories, seemingly paying little regard to the concerns of the religious.

Despite this historical conflict, many today would suggest that these two areas of knowledge have the potential to complement and enrich each other. The father of modern physics, Galileo Galilei, said, "The intention of the Holy Spirit is to teach us how one goes to heaven and not how heaven goes" (quoted in *The Galileo Affair,* page 96). His comment seems to suggest that science and religion are two different ways of knowing, each best suited to helping us understand a different aspect of truth. Science is better able to explore how reality works, whereas religion is better able to explore the ultimate meaning of that reality.

Science and Scientism

For all its current influence, science as we know it today is rather young. Its origins lie mainly in the seventeenth century, with such figures as Galileo Galilei (1564 to 1642) and Sir Isaac Newton (1642 to 1727). The word *science* refers both to a method for acquiring knowledge and to the knowledge itself. The scientific method depends on the collection of empirical data and on the application of mathematics to understanding the data. Science makes certain assumptions about reality: the physical world is composed of matter and energy; truth is attained through objective experimentation rather than subjective experience; and nature, lacking anything akin to mind or spirit, is indifferent or even hostile toward humanity. The methods science uses to acquire knowledge, the type of knowledge it acquires, and the assumptions it makes about reality generally are not in keeping with traditional religious worldviews.

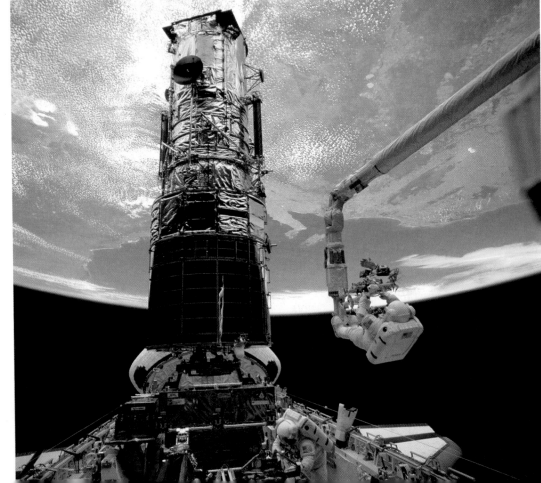

The Hubble Space Telescope orbits the earth as it probes the mysteries of the universe. The scientific worldview offers an alternative to traditional religions insofar as it attempts to answer life's most basic questions.

Scientism

When science goes so far as to become a religion, we have **scientism.** Beyond offering an alternative to traditional religions, scientism challenges religion's established role. Instead of regarding science as merely one method for acquiring knowledge, scientism insists it is the only valid method. Scientific knowledge, scientism maintains, is the only truth.

Critics fault scientism for pushing the reach of science too far and for losing sight of the bigger picture. They raise highly relevant and disturbing questions: Has not science played a major role in bringing about the environmental problems that threaten the well-being of the entire planet? Is not science partly responsible for the unthinkable possibility that the human species could be completely destroyed through nuclear or other weapons?

The problem with scientism, say its critics, is that science is not equipped to deal with ethical issues or with questions of value and meaning.[K]

Darwinism and the Search for Human Origins

Even leaving the extreme position of scientism aside, certain subjects tend to draw the scientific and the traditional religious worldviews into conflict. One such subject is the question of human origins.

In his *Origin of Species* (1859) and *Descent of Man* (1871), Charles Darwin (1809 to 1882) sets forth his evolutionary theory, commonly known as **Darwinism.** According to Darwin human life—and all other life on the planet earth—has originated from the simplest life-forms. Each generation of life passes on to the next generation the genetic traits that best enabled it to survive and reproduce, and over time this process has led to a variety of increasingly complex life-forms. Human beings, along with every other species still in existence today, are here as a result of this process of evolution.

Religious Perspectives on Darwinism

Darwinism challenges many traditional religious perspectives on human origins because it does not involve a divine agent. No mind or ordering principle directs the evolutionary process, nor is any intentional purpose at work.

Religious reactions to Darwinism have been mixed. Some fundamentalist Protestants, who hold to the literal truth of the Bible, fiercely oppose it. The fundamentalist movement known as scientific creationism attempts to prove that the Genesis account of God's creating the world in six days is scientifically true. In recent times a modified form of scientific creationism, known as intelligent design, has become quite prominent. This view insists that Creation was caused and ordered by a mind or power, commonly understood to be God.

Most other religious groups have adopted much or all of Darwinism into their perspective on human origins. The Roman Catholic perspective is an example of the positions typical among Christian groups that are

K
In a two-page essay, challenge or defend this statement: Scientific knowledge is the only truth.

Charles Darwin was a British naturalist whose theory of natural selection fundamentally altered opinions about the biology of living things.

open to aspects of Darwinism. Officially set forth by Pope Pius XII in 1950, the Catholic perspective understands physical bodies to have evolved to the point at which they were ready for God to endow them with souls. Human beings were thus set apart from the rest of creation, but still part of the evolutionary process. Catholicism asserts that though the Genesis account reveals religious truths about God, human beings, and creation, it is not necessary to believe it is scientifically accurate.

Some liberal thinkers even say Darwinism supports their religious perspectives. They note that evolutionary theory depicts an ongoing increase in the complexity of life-forms. They contend that this indicates a divine intention, offering good reason for finding life meaningful. Religious thinkers also point out that many human attributes do not necessarily improve the odds of survival. What evolutionary purpose could be served by the creative impulse that pushes a person to be a lonely philosopher or a starving artist? For that matter, what evolutionary purpose is served by religion itself? Debates over the differences between religious beliefs and evolutionary theory continue in courts and in public schools, influencing the way biology is taught.[L]

Mind, Soul, and Consciousness

Much debate between the scientific and religious worldviews centers on the question of the existence of a soul. The scientific perspective favors two general possibilities regarding mental phenomena. One, proposed by materialism, is that reality is basically matter: thoughts and feelings are manifestations of material processes. The other, asserted by naturalism, is that thoughts and feelings actually exist, but are dependent on material realities. Neither materialism nor naturalism leaves room for the existence of a soul.

L
Read the account of Creation in the Book of Genesis, chapters 1 and 2. How might a liberal religious thinker find Darwinism to be at least somewhat compatible with the biblical account?

Neurotheology

Neurotheology is a new scientific field for the psychological and biological study of religion. Neurotheologists study brain activities that accompany religious experiences and rituals such as praying, "hearing the voice of God," "being at one with the universe," and chanting or smelling incense.

Scientists have now identified areas of the brain that react in consistent ways during certain religious events. The frontal lobe is vital for achieving mental focus; during meditation it becomes more active. The parietal lobes, on the upper sides of the brain, are in charge of orienting one in space and time. When meditation induces a feeling of being in accord with reality, the parietal lobes quiet down almost completely. The temporal lobes are situated on the lower front sides of the brain; artificial electromagnetic stimulation of these lobes triggers a variety of experiences, including the sensation of being out of one's body.

Religious Responses to Neurotheology

Scientists and others point out that finding that the brain reacts to religious experiences does not imply that religion as a whole involves only the brain. Andrew Newberg, a leading figure in neurotheology, says, "It's no safer to say that spiritual urges and sensations are caused by brain activity than it is to say that the neurological changes through which we experience the pleasure of eating an apple cause the apple to exist" (quoted in Begley, "Religion and the Brain"). In other words, such brain activity could be the natural result of the encounter of the soul with the divine.

Neurotheology does not investigate religion in its entirety. It focuses mainly on the experiential dimension, with some attention to the ritual dimension. Neurotheology has little to say about the great extent of ethical commitment born of religious conviction or about the extensive organizing of society based on a culture's religious understanding.

Finally, neurotheology stops short of offering answers to one great scientific mystery: human consciousness. Even as the parietal lobes quiet to stillness, and one experiences a feeling of unity with reality, consciousness clearly remains. Both from a traditional religious point of view and from a scientific point of view, one's consciousness is, if anything, heightened and more pure during religious experiences than at other times. This suggests that perhaps religion has a good deal to teach science regarding consciousness.

Cosmology: The Origin and Destiny of the Universe

Cosmology, the understanding of the nature of the universe, encompasses some of the basic issues of both science and religion: Where did the universe come from? What is its destiny? How is it ordered? Scientific discoveries of the past hundred years have both challenged and informed religious perspectives on those questions.

Scientific Perspectives on Cosmology

The prevailing scientific cosmology has long been described by the **big bang theory,** which says that 13.7 billion years ago (although some scientists differ on the number of years), all that now makes up the universe was contained within a space smaller than an atom. Matter, energy, time, and space emerged from this tiny beginning in a huge explosion, eventually creating the universe as we know it.

Like Darwin's theory of evolution, the big bang theory does not depend on any divine action or intention to explain the origins of the universe. Whereas religious cosmologies usually offer some reason or meaning for the existence of the universe, the big bang theory does not.

Moreover, many astrophysicists paint a bleak picture of the ultimate destiny of the earth and the universe. As the sun begins to die in about a billion years, the earth will become too hot to support life, eventually being destroyed as it is engulfed by the expiring sun.

Though scientists are fairly certain about the fate of the earth, they continue to debate what the end of the universe will look like—or whether the universe will have any end at all. For many years scientists assumed the expansion of the universe caused by the big bang was slowing down owing to the gravitational pull of matter. Then in 1998 they were surprised to find that the expansion of the universe is actually accelerating. To explain this they hypothesized the existence of so-called dark energy, a force that is steadily pushing galaxies farther apart. Most scientists now believe that about 95 percent of the universe is made up of this mysterious dark energy and its cousin, dark matter, although very little is known about the properties of those elements. The discovery that dark energy and dark matter might exist led many scientists to assume the universe would continue to expand forever, until all that remained would be a void more vast than the mind can comprehend, lifeless and virtually empty.

Would this bleak death be the end of the universe? Perhaps. But many scientists say they know very little about the nature of the

IMAGE: © BETTMANN/CORBIS

Galileo Galilei represents the tension between science and religion, because his observation that the earth revolves around the sun conflicted with the prevailing religious view of his time.

universe and its ultimate destiny. In fact, a new theory suggests an alternative to the standard big bang model of the universe. According to this theory, the universe had no beginning and will have no end. Instead, it continually renews itself in cycles of big bangs that cause it to expand and "big crunches" that cause it to contract, each cycle lasting trillions of years.

What Does It All Mean?

Most traditional religious cosmologies set forth perspectives that are quite different from the ones outlined here. Commonly, such cosmologies situate our world in the center of things and endow the creation of the world with divine purpose. The relatively few religious cosmologies that do address the destiny of the universe vary a great deal—and none predict such a bleak, cold, and lonely end as does the prevailing scientific view of a forever expanding universe. For this reason some religious people might find this scientific perspective to be gloomy. Others, moved by its seemingly impenetrable mystery, might find it thrilling, and perhaps also humbling, given the almost infinitesimalness of humanity relative to the vastness of the universe. Either reaction could be considered religious in its own way.

Although many details of traditional cosmologies are incompatible with scientific views, that does not necessarily mean religion has nothing to contribute to the human investigation of existence. Science has amazed us with discoveries about how the universe works. But why does the universe exist at all? That is a question of meaning, a question perhaps best left for religion.[M]

Religion and Science: An Emerging Harmony

As our discussion so far has suggested, although religious and scientific worldviews sometimes conflict, they also have the potential to complement each other. This has been true historically, and new scientific discoveries hint at the possibility of science and religion's working together in the future as well.

The Christian Roots of Science

With good evidence on their side, philosophers of science commonly argue that science developed quite naturally *within* religion—specifically, within Christianity. For one thing, the major figures in the early development of modern science were Christian: Galileo, Newton, Nicolaus Copernicus (1473 to 1543), and Johannes Kepler (1571 to 1630). But the argument runs deeper than this.

The development of science depended on a cosmology that distinguished creation from the Creator. Such a distinction allows for the created world to be understood as material, not spiritual. Science is best applied to things that consist of matter and that are subject to the constant and impersonal laws of nature.

Christianity also regards creation as a reflection of God. Because God is believed to be all-knowing and perfectly rational, the natural world is also understood to be perfectly suited to the rational analysis of human beings. Furthermore, God is thought to have appointed human beings as the stewards, or caretakers, of nature. To care for the world, surely they need to understand it.

Other religions tend to be at least somewhat compatible with science. The Jewish cosmology and the Muslim cosmologies are similar to the Christian cosmology, and therefore also support scientific advances.

Quantum Mechanics

Religious thinkers have greeted the theory of physics called **quantum mechanics** as a great opportunity to find harmony with the scientific worldview. Quantum mechanics, developed primarily during the middle of the twentieth century, holds that the laws of nature are not so certain after all. Analyses of nature ultimately can arrive at only probabilities and predictions, not absolute facts.

M
From the material in this book, choose one religious cosmology and compare it with the scientific cosmology of the big bang theory. How are those cosmologies similar? How are they different? Do you think a follower of the religion could believe both are true? Explain your answer.

The general effect of quantum mechanics is the incorporation of such vital religious concepts as free will and moral choice within a scientific view of reality. Such circumstances invite harmony between religion and science, even as the latter forges ahead with new discoveries.

The Persistence of Mystery

At the beginning of this book, we said that religion begins with and is intimately involved with mystery. Science too is inevitably pervaded by mystery. Every new answer leads to at least one new question. And when science turns to investigating our minds, though it makes impressive strides, in the end it stands in awe of the great mystery of consciousness.

There is really nothing wrong with mystery. It is a powerful thing to behold. When looking up at the sky, some think of a heaven inhabited by God. Others think of an impersonal, vast, and ancient universe that nevertheless continues to surprise and astound the human mind.

Both perceptions of the sky conjure mystery, raising unfathomable questions. Both science and religion provide answers. However, some questions are beyond the reach of science, unanswerable through a method bound to empirical and rational procedure. This suggests an essential place for religion, even as science continues to thrive.

The psychologist Carl Jung (1875 to 1961), one of many scientifically minded people who have advocated religion, contended that human beings need to orient themselves among the many mysteries of being. The religious traditions, Jung said, help them achieve that orientation in highly effective ways. It is no accident that the great traditions have endured for centuries, and in most cases, millennia. Likely they will endure for millennia to come.[N]

N
Both science and religion explore the human experience of mystery. Use what you have learned from this book to write a two-page essay challenging or defending the following statement: Religion is essential to the human exploration of mystery because some questions are unanswerable through science alone. Defend your argument with examples from the religions described in this book.

A view of the earth from Apollo 11, with the surface of the Moon in the foreground. In recent years science has made huge strides in unlocking the secrets of the universe. However, science alone cannot provide the answers to some questions about the mystery of life, suggesting that religion will continue to be central to human concern.

IMAGE: © CORBIS

Chapter Review

1. Describe modernization. What is it? When did it begin?
2. How do the changes brought on by modernization affect religion?
3. What is materialism?
4. What is urbanization, and how does it affect religion?
5. Describe globalization, and explain how Tibet serves as an example of it.
6. What is multiculturalism, and how does it affect religions?
7. What is egalitarianism, and how does it challenge traditional religions?
8. Describe traditionalism, and explain how Orthodox Judaism serves as an example of it.
9. Briefly explain the two basic meanings of the term *fundamentalism.*
10. Define *liberalism* and briefly explain three examples of it.
11. Describe the universalist impulse, and cite three examples of religions that feature it.
12. How does Baha'i embody the universalist impulse?
13. Identify two leaders of Baha'i.
14. Identify four main practices of Baha'i.
15. Describe the Parliament of the World's Religions, and explain why it was a milestone for interfaith dialogue.
16. What is postmodernism?
17. Identify two new religious movements that are exports from India.
18. What is the meaning of the name *Santeria,* and what does this name help explain?
19. Briefly describe at least three examples of Catholic influence on Voodoo.
20. Name the two prominent leaders of Mormonism, and briefly describe their roles.
21. Briefly describe Charles Taze Russell's prediction of a millennial age.
22. How do the expectations of the New Age movement differ from those of the Jehovah's Witnesses and the Latter-day Saints?
23. In one sentence, summarize Neopaganism.
24. Who participates in Wiccan rituals? When and where are those rituals typically practiced?
25. What is glossolalia, and what makes it a central element of Pentecostalism?
26. How might science and religion complement and enrich each other?
27. Identify three basic assumptions that science makes about reality.
28. What is scientism? What do its critics say are its limitations?
29. How does Darwinism challenge traditional religious perspectives on human origins?
30. What is neurotheology?
31. How is quantum mechanics significant for religion?

In artist Margaret Carsello's *World Religions*, she portrays the diversity and interweaving of global traditions.

IMAGE: © IMAGES.COM/CORBIS

Glossary

Baha'i (bah-hah´ee). A religion emphasizing the unity of all religions and peoples, teaching that all founders of the world's religions have been God's divine messengers, or prophets. Founded in 1863 by Mirza Husayn ali Nuri (1817 to 1892), known to his followers as Baha Allah.

big bang theory. An account holding that the universe was created through an explosion about 13.7 billion years ago (although some scientists differ on the number of years) resulting in the rapid expansion of matter, energy, time, and space.

Darwinism. The evolutionary theory derived by Charles Darwin, holding that human life originated from the simplest life-forms, that each generation of life passes on to the next generation the genetic traits that best enabled it to survive and reproduce, and that over time this process has led to a variety of increasingly complex life-forms.

fundamentalism. In its strictest sense, an emphasis on a literal interpretation of a religion's sacred texts and primary teachings—thus getting back to the "fundamentals." In a more general sense, an intensely traditionalist form of religion impelled by reaction against modern forces and the religious reforms they encourage; it tends to reject diversity of interpretations in favor of an authoritarian approach that insists on one "true" interpretation.

globalization. The linking and intermixing of cultures.

glossolalia (Greek: "speaking in tongues"). One of the "gifts of the Spirit" referred to by the Apostle Paul in his First Letter to the Corinthians (chapter 12), and a common phenomenon in Pentecostalism.

interfaith dialogue. An attempt to promote harmony between religions, first inspired by ecumenism (the promotion of Christian unity).

liberalism. Within religious traditions, the counterpart to traditionalism, holding that a religion should adapt to society's changes.

millennial age. An anticipated era that is expected to last one thousand years; one of the beliefs central to Jehovah's Witnesses.

modernization. The general process by which societies transform economically, socially, and culturally to conform with the standards set by industrialized Europe.

multiculturalism. The coexistence of different peoples and their cultures; an outcome of globalization.

neurotheology. A relatively recent field incorporating psychological and biological studies of religion, focusing on the brain's involvement in religious experience and ritual.

postmodernism. A perspective that arose in the late twentieth century, reflecting a critical reaction to the trends of the modern world.

quantum mechanics. A theory of physics, developed primarily during the middle of the twentieth century, holding that the laws of nature are not entirely certain, implying that analyses of nature ultimately can arrive at only probabilities and predictions.

scientism. The worldview that science is the only valid method of acquiring knowledge.

secular humanism. The worldview that ultimate value is grounded entirely in the human realm, not in the divine or the supernatural.

traditionalism. Within religious traditions, a common reaction to rapid changes in the surrounding world, involving the maintenance of older forms of belief and practice regardless of new social norms.

Pronunciation Key

Note: Accent marks throughout the textbook appear after the syllables that are to be stressed.

Symbol	Sound
a	hat
ah	father
ahr	hard
air	hair
aw	law
ay	hay
b	box
ch	chill
d	dad
e, eh	set
ee	need
f	fine
g	gap
h	hit
hw	whether
i	sit
i	lie
ihr	ear

Symbol	Sound
j	jump
k	key
kh	ch as in German Buch
ks	hex
kw	quit
l	lamb
m	most
n	nest
ng	bing
o	tot
oh	low
oi	toy
oo	foot
oo	hoot
oor	floor
or	more
ou	cow

Symbol	Sound
p	pass
r	ring
s	sew
sh	shell
t	toe
th	thick
tw	twine
uh	ago
uhr	sir
v	van
w	water
y	yak
z	zebra
zh	vision

Index

Italicized page numbers indicate illustrations. Maps are indicated with "*m*" following the page number.

Henry VIII, King, 239
Hera, 186, *187*
Heracles/Hercules, 195
heresies, 233, 237, 239; defined, 245
Hermes, 186, *187*, 191
Herod Antipas, 225
Heschel, Abraham Joshua, 201, 202, 219
Hijra, 250; defined, 265
Hinayana Buddhism, 85
Hinduism: *avatars* of, *58*, 58–59, *59*, *63* (*see also* Krishna); Buddhism compared to, 75, 76, 77; caste system of, 48–51, *49*, *50*, 62; defined, 67; cosmology of, 45–46; fundamentalist factions of, 271; gods and goddesses, *44*, 45, *45*, *57*, 58, 59; language of, 76; life goals in, 52–53; life stages of, 51; main teachings of, 76; map locations, 40–41*m*; monism doctrine of, 43; Muslim relations with, *63*, 63–64, *64*; Nanak's response to, 110; and New Age movement, 282, 283; paths of liberation, *53*, 54–61, *57*; personal experiences, 60; polytheism of, *44*, 45, *45*; primal origins of, 22; principles of, 47–48, 52; reincarnation doctrine of, 42–43, 46–47; religious leaders and philosophers, 41–42, *42*, 49, 54–55, 60, 61–62; sacred texts of, 43, 45, 49–50, 52, 56, 76 (*see also* Bhagavad-Gita); salvation goals of, 42–43; seven dimensions of, 65; and Sikhism, 108; social order of, 48, 51, 52, 62–63; tolerance of, 41–42; as universalist, 272; Western importations of, 64, 275–276; worship practices of, 59, 60, 61, 111
Hindu women, 48, 51, 52, 62–63
Hirohito, Emperor, 170, *170*
holistic health, 283
Holocaust, 211, *212*; defined, 221
Holy Spirit, 7, 224; defined, 245, 284–285, 286
holy wars, 257, 258
Homer, 185–186, 188, 189, 190
homosexuality, 256
hope, 6
Horned God, 284
householder stage, 51
House of Best Purpose, 183
House of Hades, 190

Huai River Moon, 146
Hubble Space Telescope, *286*
Hui-neng, 154–155
hukam, 116; defined, 121
human condition: Buddhist views of, 70, 73, 76, 78–81; Confucian views of, 127; Hindu views of, 42, 45, 56, 76; Islam views of, 252; Jain views of, 97–98; Orphic views of, 192; Plato on, 192; questions concerning, 13–15; Shinto views of, 173; Sikh views of, 115; Taoist views of, 144, 145. *See also* humans; salvation
human consciousness, 289
human destiny, 15, 124, 182–183, 252
"Human Manifesto II," 272
humans: commitment to divine *versus,* 271–272; in East Asian *versus* Western religions, 140; Greek mythology on origin of, 192; as Jain life-form classification, 97; origin theories of, 287–288; religions focused on spiritual potential of, 281–283. *See also* human condition
human sacrifices, 34, *35*, 36
humility, 146–147
huppah, 218
Husayn, 260
Hygeia, 193

icons, 18, *88*, *241*
Iliad (Homer), 185–186, 188, 189, 190
imams (Islamic prayer leaders), 254; defined, 265
Imams (Shi'i spiritual authority figures), 260; defined, 265
immanent, 114, 261; defined, 121
impermanence, as religious theme, 38, 76–77, 80
Incarnation of Jesus Christ, 224, 230, 231–232; defined, 245
incarnations, *58*, 58–59
India: colonial independence of, 62; Hinduism in, 61, 66; map locations, 92–93*m*; in modern world, 65, *66*; nuclear proliferation of, 64; partitioning of, 63
individuality: art illustrating illusion of, *55*; in Buddhism, 76–78, 80;

Confucian philosophy on, 126, 133; in Hinduism, 55; in Taoism, 126; Zen Buddhism and self-centeredness of, 156, 162
indulgences, 239; defined, 245
Industrial Revolution, 268, 269
In The Mishnah, 213
initiation rituals: of Aborigines, *25*, 25–26; of Christianity, 235, 240; of Hinduism, 51; of mystery religions, 191, 196; of Sikhism loyalty order, 112–113, 117–119
Inktomi, 31
intelligent design, 287
intention, and morality, 78, 101
interfaith dialogue, *274*, 274; defined, 293
International Society for Krishna Consciousness (ISKCON), 64, 276, *276*
Iran, 180–181, 184, 253, 260
Iranian Revolution, 260
Ishmael, 252
Isis, cult of, 196–197, *197*
ISKCON (International Society for Krishna Consciousness), 64, 276, *276*
Islam: basic elements of, 248; biblical tradition connections, 247; diversity of, 251; divisions of, 260–261; expansion of, 257–260; founding of, 249–251; fundamentalist factions of, 271; and Hinduism, *63*, 63–64, *64*; locations of, 246–247*m*, 259–260; and Palestine-Israel conflict, 212; population statistics, 247; and primal religions, *26*; prophets of, 16, 249–251, 251–252; religions influencing, 182; religious conflicts, 263; root word meaning, 247; sacred texts of, 250–251 (*see also* Qur'an); and salvation, 14; seven dimensions of, 264; and Sikhism, 108; social practices of, 256–257; teachings of, 251–252; worship practices of, 17, 253–256. *See also* Muslims
Israel, 210, 211
Israelites (Hebrews): father of, 252; God's Covenant with, 201–202; history of, 207, 216; relationship to Jews, 206; monotheism of, 181; and Mormon history, 278. *See also* Jews

ixthus, 224
Izanagi, 168
Izanami, 168

J

Jainism: Buddhism compared to, 95; cosmic wheels, *97*; cosmology and wheel cycles of, 96–97; deities of, 96, 97; and destiny, 15; *karma* doctrine of, 94, 95, 98, 101, 103; life-form classifications, 97–98, 101; locations and origin of, 92–93*m*; in modern world, 104; name origins, 94; pacifism and self-defense, 101; population statistics, 94; practices of, 94, 99–102; salvation doctrine of, 93–94, 96, 97, 98–99; scriptures of, 101; sects of, *99*, 99–100; seven dimensions of, 104; *tirthankaras* of, 94–95, 97, 100, 103–104; worship practices and rituals, *98*, 100, *103*, 103–104

Janus, 195

Japan: emperors of, 170, *170*; map locations, 166–167*m*; modern transformation of, 175; mythical origins of, 168–169; state religion and native religious tradition of (*see* Shinto); Western influence on, 136; Zen's migration to, 155

Japanese Zen, 155

Japjī, 116

Jehovah's Witnesses, 242, *280*, 280–281, *281*

jen, 131; defined, 137

Jeremiah, 204

Jerusalem: as ancient capital, 207; biblical name for, 210; during Crusades, 238; Jewish oppression in, 202, 206, 207, 208; map location, 223*m*; Western Wall in, *206*

Jerusalem, Council of, 234

Jesus Christ: Asclepius compared to, 193; Christian beliefs on nature of, 230–232; Crucifixion of, 207, 224, 227, *227*, 228–229; early life of, 224–226; Gospels on, 227–230; as Islamic prophet, 250, 252, 262; on materialism, 269; ministry of, 7, 226–227; Muhammad compared to, 250; Resurrection of, 224, 227, 228, 235; salvation through, 8; second

coming of, 228, 242, 280–281; defined, 245

Jewish mysticism, 210

Jewish synagogues, 214–215

Jewish War, 206, 207

Jews: ancient homeland of, 225; ethical obligations of, 213–214; God's Covenant with, 201–202, 206, 207, 211, 236; Hasidic, 210, 211; history of, 206–209; holy days of, 215–216; as minorities in Christian communities, 208–209, 217; Muslim view of, 262; and name of God, 202; nation for, 211, 212; persecution of, 208, 209, 210–211, *212*; philosophies of, 209; religious *versus* cultural, 202; rites of passage of, 216, 218–219; worship practices of, 214–215; Zionic, 210–211. *See also* Judaism

Jiang Ziya, *146*

jihad, 257, 258; defined, 265

jinas, 94; defined, 105

jivas, 97; defined, 105

jnana marga, 54–57, *56*, 276; defined, 67

John, Gospel of, 224, 230, 231, 241, 243

John Paul II, Pope, 9

John the Baptist, 226

Judaism: apocalypticism of, 225–226; classical or rabbinic, 206, 207, 208; divisions of, 212–213, 218, 270, 271; early Christianity and, 234–235; group identity emphasis, 202; influences on, 180, 182, 183, 185; Kabbalist traditions in, 210; lifestyle and worship practices, 213–219; Maimonides theology of, 209; map locations of, 200–201*m*; medieval period of, 208; modern period, 210–213, *212*; population statistics, 219; primal origins of, 22; seven dimensions of, 220; statements and summaries reflecting, 202, 219; teachings of, 202–205. *See also* Jews

judgment, 182–183, 228, 252, 260

Jung, Carl, 291

Juno, 195

Jupiter, 195, *195*

K

Ka'ba, 256; defined, 265

Kabbalah, 210; defined, 221

Kabir, 113

kaddish, 219

Kali, 58

kama, 52; defined, 67

kami, 168–172, *171*, 173, 175; defined, 177

kamidana, 171; defined, 177

kamikaze pilots, 172

karma: asceticism benefits on, 101, 103; Buddhist doctrine of, 77–78, 82; defined, 67, 91, 105; Hindu doctrine of, 47–48, 49–50; Jain doctrine of, 94, 95, 98, 101, 103, 104; New Age beliefs of, 282

karma marga, *53*, 53–54; defined, 67

Kartarpur, 110

Kaur (Sikh name), 113

kevala, 95, 99; defined, 105

Khadija, 249, 250, 257

Khalistan, 118

Khalsa, 112–113, 116, 117–119; defined, 121

Khomeini, Ayatollah, 260, *261*

Kingdom Halls, 281, *281*

Kingdom of God, 7–8, 226, 227

Kinneret, Lake, *225*

kipah, 214

Kitab al-aqdas, 273, 274

knowledge, path of, 54–57, *56*, 276

koan, 155, 158, 159; defined, 165

kosher food, 214

Krishna: art depicting, *44*, *47*, *58*; in Hindu religion, 58–59; movements focused on, 64, 276; teachings of, to Arjuna, 47, *47*, 50–51, 54, 58

kshatriya, 49, 50; defined, 67

Kuan-yin, *86*

K'ung Fu-tzu. *See* Confucius

L

Lakota tribe, 21*m*, *29*, 29–32, *31*, *32*

Lakshmi, *45*

lamas, 82

Lame Deer, 30

Lao Tzu, 140–141, *141*. *See also Tao Te Ching* (Lao Tzu)

Law, the. *See* Torah

Laws of Manu, 52

Taoist concept of, 142–144, 145; virtues practiced in compliance with, 146–147

Taoism: founders and texts of, 140–142, *141*; individualism emphasis of, 126; map locations, 138–139*m*; philosophies of, 140, 142–145; seven dimensions of, 124, 150; strands of, 140; virtues of, 146–147, 149; in Western societies, 150

Taoist sage, 145, 146–147, 148, *148*

Tao of Pooh, The (Hoff), 150

Tao Te Ching (Lao Tzu): author of, 141–142; defined, 151; description, 141–142; on doctrines of, 145; on good government, 149; on inaction, 146; on life and death, 145; on naturalism, 147; on naturalness, 147; on noncompetition, 147; on relativity of values, 144; on Tao, 142–143, 151; as Taoism classic text, 140; translation of, 143; on warfare and nonaggression, 147, 149; on yin and yang, 144

te, 132–133; defined, 137, 142

tea ceremonies, 163

Temple of Jerusalem, 202, 206, 207, 208, 218

Ten Commandments, 203, 214, 215, 252

Tenochtitlan (*currently* Mexico City): defined, 39; fall of, 36; location and description, 21*m*, 33, 34; temples at, 34, *34*

Te of Piglet, The (Hoff), 150

Teotihuacan, 21*m*, 33, 34, *35*

Teresa of Calcutta, Mother, 7

theistic religions, 16

Theodosius I, Emperor, 189, 190

Theravada Buddhism, 85; defined, 91

Third International Jain Conference, 102

Thirty Years' War, 240

Three Jewels, 74

Three Marks of Existence, 76–77; defined, 91

Tibetan Buddhism, 82, *87*, 87–88

time, concept of, 75

tirthankaras, 94–95, 97, 100, 103–104; defined, 105

Titans (Greek mythological warriors), 192

titans (Hindu semidivine beings), 46

tolerance: of Catholic Church, 6–9; of Hinduism, 41–42; of Islam, 262, 263

Toltec, 33

Tonantzin, 36

Topiltzin Quetzalcoatl, 33, 36

Torah (the Law, *Pentateuch*): biblical books of, 205; defined, 221; and early Gentile Christians, 234; on ethics, 213–214; on family relationships, 214; as God's revelation, 202, 207; Jesus Christ's teachings and, 227; Jewish study of, 213–214; and Kabbalah, 210; Matthew on, 229; oral, 204; of Orthodox Judaism, 213; Paul on, 229; in synagogues, *203*, 203–204, 215; written, 203–204

torii, 171; defined, 177

totems, 24; defined, 39

Tours/Poitiers, Battle of, 258

towers of silence, 185, *185*

Tradition, Catholic, 240; defined, 245

traditionalism, 270; defined, 293

Trajan, Emperor, 197

transcendence, 14, 57, 210, 251, 261; defined, 19

trickster figures, 28, 31; defined, 39

Trinity, 224, 230, *232*, 232; defined, 245

Triple Goddess, 284

Twelve Vows, 103

ultimate reality: Buddhist beliefs of, 76, 80; Confucianism on, 136; Hindu beliefs of, 42, 43, 45, 76; religious questions on, 13, 15, 18

Umma, 252–253; defined, 265

United States: emigration of new religions to, 277; Islam in, 259–260, 262; Judaism divisions in, 213

unity: as Christian goal, 224, 232–233, 240, 242–243, 273; of Islam, 260; universalist impulse, 272–274, 282

universalist impulse, 272–274, 282

universe. *See* cosmology

unselfishness, 54

Untouchables, 49, *50*

Upanishads: and Buddhism development, 75, 76; defined, 67; as sacred text of Hinduism, 43, 45, 49–50, 56

urbanization, 269

vaishya, 49, *49*, *50*; defined, 67

vajra, 87

Vajrayana Buddhism, 82, *87*, 87–88; defined, 91

varna, 49

Vatican II, 241, 242–243, 271; defined, 245

Vedanta, 54–56; defined, 67

Vedanta Society, 64, 275–276

Vedas, 51

vegetarianism: as Hare Krishna ritual, 276; as Jain central principle, 94, 101, 102, 104; of New Age movement, 283; Sikh practice of, 115

veiling, 257, *257*, *270*, 271

Venus, 193

Vesta, 195

Virgin Mary, 197, 262, 277

Virgin of Guadalupe, 36

Vishnu, *45*, 58

vision quests, 30, 31; defined, 39

Vivekananda, Swami, 64, 275

Voodoo, 277, *277*

Wakan Tanka, 31; defined, 39

warfare, 147, 149, 172, 257, 258

Watchtower (publication), 280, 281

Watchtower Bible and Tract Society, 280

Waterfall (Escher), *55*

wealth sharing, 255

Wei We Wei, 80

wen, 132; defined, 137

Western Sioux (Lakota) tribe, *29*, 29–32, *31*, *32*

Western Wall (Jerusalem), *206*

wheel of rebirth. *See samsara*

whirling dervish, 261, *263*

Wicca, 283–284, *284*

widow burning, 62–63

Williamson, Marianne, 282

Wilyaru, 26

witchcraft, 284

women: Aboriginal ritual restrictions, 25, 26; as early Christian deacons, 235; as Episcopal bishops, 242, *242*; Hindu social order and, 48, 51, 52, 62–63; Islamic fundamentalist interpretations and, *270*, 271; in Islam society, 256–257; Jewish coming of age rituals and, 218; in modern Judaism, 213, 214; in Plains tribes rituals, 32; Shinto traditions and roles of, 174, 176; Sikh names for, 113

works, path of, *53*, 53–54

World Religions (Carsello), *292*

worship: Baha'i practices, 273–274; Buddhist practices, 82; of Confucian ancestors, 127; early Christian practices, 234–235; Greek practices, 188; Hindu practices, *57*, 57–61; Islamic practices, 253–256; Jain practices, *98*, 100, 103–104; Mormon practices, 279; Roman practices, 196, 197; Shinto practices, 168, *171*, 171–172, 173; Sikh practices, 116–117; Sufi practices, 261. *See also* rituals

Worst Experience, 182, 183

Wounded Knee massacre, 29

Writings, the, 204, 205

wu-wei, 146; defined, 151

Y

Yahweh, 202, 280

yang, 143–144, *144*, *150*; defined, 151

yarmulke, 214

Yathrib (*currently* Medina, Saudi Arabia), 250

yeshivah, 205

yin, 143–144, *144*, *150*; defined, 151

Yoga (philosophical school), 56–57, 97; defined, 67

yoga (spiritual practice), 56

Yom Kippur, 215–216; defined, 221

Yoruba, 20*m*, *26*, 26–28, *27*, 277

Young, Brigham, 279

Z

zaddik, 210

Zarathustra, 180–181, 183

zazen, 155, 161–162, *161*; defined, 165

Zealots, 225

Zen Buddhism: benefits of, 159, 161; cultural arts influence of, 162–163; experiential focus of, 154, 156–157; history of, 149, 153, 154–155; lifestyle and practices of, 83, 155, *161*, 161–163; map locations, 152–153*m*; as nontheistic, 271; poetry describing, 164; sects of, 155, *155*; seven dimensions of, 16, 164; symbols of, 158, *158*; teachings of, 155–159, 160. *See also* Buddhism

Zeus, 186, 188, 189, 191, 192, *195*

Zionism, 210–211, 212; defined, 221

Zohar, 208, 210

Zoroastrianism, 180–185, *184*, 198

Acknowledgments

The scriptural quotations marked Tanakh are quoted from *Tanakh: The Holy Scriptures, The New JPS translation to the Traditional Hebrew Text* (The Jewish Publication Society, 1985). Copyright ©1985 by The Jewish Publication Society. All rights reserved.

All other scriptural quotations contained herein are from the New Revised Standard Version of the Bible, Catholic Edition. Copyright © 1989 and 1993 by the Division of Christian Education of the National Council of the Churches of Christ in the United States of America. All rights reserved.

The excerpts on page 8 are from the Vatican Council II's *Declaration on the Relation of the Church to Non-Christian Religions* (*Nostra Aetate*, 1965), number 2, and *Dogmatic Constitution on the Church* (*Lumen Gentium*, 1965), number 16, as quoted in *Decrees of the Ecumenical Councils*, volume 2, edited by Norman P. Tanner, SJ (London: Sheed and Ward; Washington, DC: Georgetown University Press, 1990), pages 969 and 861. English translation copyright © 1990 by Sheed and Ward Ltd. and the Trustees for Roman Catholic Purposes Regd.

The quotation and the excerpt by Pope John Paul II on page 9 are from his document "The Challenge and the Possibility of Peace," number 2, in *Origins*, November 6, 1986, page 370.

The four excerpts on pages 11–12 are from the articles "Muslims' Veils Test Limits of Britain's Tolerance," by Jane Perlez; "A Yoga Class's Path to Serenity Leads Through Times Square," by Dalton Walker; "Niceness Counts in Ark-Building, Too," by A. O. Scott; and "In Sweep of Iraqi Town, Sectarian Fears Percolate," by Michael R. Gordon; all in the *New York Times*, June 22, 2007.

The description of a vision quest on page 30 is from *Lame Deer, Seeker of Visions: The Life of a Sioux Medicine Man*, by John Fire/Lame Deer and Richard Erdoes (New York: Simon and Schuster, 1972), pages 11 and 14–16. Copyright © 1972 by John Fire/Lame Deer and Richard Erdoes; Copyright © 1994 by Pocket Books. Reprinted with permission of Pocket Books, a division of Simon and Schuster Adult Publishing Group.

The Aztec saying on page 33 is quoted from *Religions of Mesoamerica: Cosmovision and Ceremonial Centers*, by Davíd Carrasco (San Francisco: Harper and Row, 1990), page 44. Copyright © 1990 by Davíd Carrasco.

The Aztec myth on page 33 is reprinted with permission from the *Florentine Codex: General History of the Things of New Spain*, by Fray Bernardino de Sahagún, Book 7— *The Sun, Moon, and Stars, and the Binding of the Years*, translated by Arthur J. O. Anderson and Charles E. Dibble (Santa Fe, NM: School for Advanced Research and University of Utah, 1953), part 8, page 4. Copyright © 1953 by the School for Advanced Research, Santa Fe, New Mexico.

The account of an Aztec sacrifice on pages 34 and 36 is reprinted with permission from the *Florentine Codex: General History of the Things of New Spain*, by Fray Bernardino de Sahagún, Book 2— *The Ceremonies*, translated by Arthur J. O. Anderson and Charles E. Dibble (Santa Fe, NM: School for Advanced Research and the University of Utah, 1951), part 3, page 68. Copyright © 1951, 2nd Ed. © 1981 by the School for Advanced Research, Santa Fe, New Mexico.

The Aztec riddles on page 36 are quoted from *Florentine Codex*, by Sahagún, book 6, part 7, *Rhetoric and Moral Philosophy*, translated by Dibble and Anderson (Santa Fe, NM: School of American Research and the University of Utah, 1969), pages 237 and 239. Copyright © 1969 by the University of Utah. Used with permission of the University of Utah.

The quotaton by Shri Ramakrishna on page 41 is from *The Spiritual Heritage of India*, by Swami Prabhavananda with the assistance of Frederick Manchester (Hollywood, CA: Vedanta Press, 1963), page 353. Copyright © 1963 by the Vedanta Society of Southern California.

The declaration from the Rig Veda on page 42, the two excerpts from the Laws of Manu in the sidebar on page 52, and the declaration from the Rig Veda on page 272 are quoted from *A Source Book in Indian Philosophy*, edited by Sarvepalli Radhakrishnan and Charles A. Moore (Princeton, NJ: Princeton University Press, 1957), pages xxvii, 190, 178, and xxvii, respectively. Copyright © 1957 by Princeton University Press.

The quotations by Mahatma Gandhi on pages 42 and 53–54 are from *The Moral and Political Writings of Mahatma Gandhi*, volume 1, *Civilization, Politics, and Religion*, edited by Raghavan Iyer (New York: Clarendon Press; Oxford, England: Oxford University Press, 1986), pages 542–543 and 461. Compilation copyright © 1986 by Raghavan N. Iyer.

The dialogue from the Chandogya Upanishad on pages 43 and 45 and the warning from the Katha Upanishad on page 56 are excerpted from *The Upanishads: Breath of the Eternal*, selected and translated from the original Sanskrit by Swami Prabhavananda and Frederick Manchester (New York: New American Library, Mentor Books, 1957), pages 70 and 17. Copyright © 1948 by the Vedanta Society of Southern California.

The passages from the Bhagavad-Gita on pages 47, 50–51, 54 (both), 58, and 59 are quoted from *The Bhagavad-Gita: Krishna's Counsel in Time of War*, translated by Barbara Stoler Miller (New York: Bantam Books, 1986), 2:12–13,22, 2:31–33, 5:3, 3:27, 2:47, 4:6–8, and 9:27–29, respectively. English translation copyright © 1986 by Barbara Stoler Miller. Used with permission of Bantam Books, a division of Random House.

The passage from the Chandogya Upanishad on page 50 is quoted from *The Thirteen Principal Upanishads*, second edition, revised, translated from the Sanskrit by Robert Ernest Hume (London: Oxford University Press, 1931), page 233.

The quotation by Vimla on page 51 and the study results on page 63 are paraphrased from *Dharma's Daughters: Contemporary Indian Women and Hindu Culture*, by Sara S. Mitter (New Brunswick, NJ: Rutgers University Press, 1991), pages 18 and 116. Copyright © 1991 by Sara S. Mitter.

The tale of Shankara on page 55 is from *Philosophies of India*, by Heinrich Zimmer, edited by Joseph Campbell, Bollingen Series, volume 26 (Princeton, NJ: Princeton University Press, 1951), page 20. Copyright © 1951 by Princeton University Press.

The quotations by Mahatma Gandhi on page 61 are taken from his *Young India, 1919–1922*, second edition (New York: B. W. Huebsch, 1924), page 804. Copyright © by S. Ganesan, Triplicane, Madras S.E.

The passage from the Padmapurana on page 62 is quoted from *A History of the World's Religions*, ninth edition, by David S. Noss and John B. Noss (New York: Macmillan College Publishing Co., 1994), page 119. Copyright © 1994 by Macmillan College Publishing Co.

The quotation by Gautama on pages 74–75 is taken from *Buddhism in Translations*, translated from the original Pali into English by Henry Clarke Warren (New York: Atheneum, 1984), page 109. Originally published by Harvard University Press.

The story on pages 79–80 is reprinted from *Old Path White Clouds: Walking in the Footsteps of the Buddha*, by Thich Nhat Hanh (Berkeley, CA: Parallax Press, 1991), page 407. Copyright © 1991 by Thich Nhat Hanh. Used with permission of Parallax Press, Berkeley, California, *www.parallax.org*.

The excerpt on page 80 is quoted from *Ask the Awakened: The Negative Way,* by Wei Wu Wei (London: Routledge and Kegan Paul, 1963), page 1. Copyright © 1963 by Routledge and Kegan Paul. Used with permission of Taylor and Francis Books, Ltd.

The story of compassion on page 84 is quoted from *The Hungry Tigress: Buddhist Myths, Legends, and Jataka Tales,* completely revised and expanded edition, by Rafe Martin (Cambridge, MA: Yellow Moon Press, 1999), page 143. Copyright © 1999 by Rafe Martin. Used with permission of the author.

The mantra on pages 88 is quoted from *The Buddhist Religion: A Historical Introduction,* third edition, by Richard H. Robinson and Willard L. Johnson, assisted by Kathryn Tsai and Shinzen Young (Belmont, CA: Wadsworth Publishing Co., 1982), page 94. Copyright © 1970 by Dickenson Publishing Co.

The excerpt on page 89 is from *Freedom in Exile: The Autobiography of the Dalai Lama,* by Tenzin Gyatso (San Francisco: HarperSanFrancisco, 1990), pages 11–12. Copyright © 1990 by Tenzin Gyatso, the Fourteenth Dalai Lama of Tibet. Used with permission of HarperCollins Publishers and Hodder and Stoughton.

The passage from the Acaranga Sutra on page 93 is quoted from *The Sacred Books of the East,* edited by F. Max Müller, volume 22, *Jaina Sutras,* translated by Hermann Jacobi (1884; reprint, Delhi, India: Motilal Banarsidass, 1964), page 36. Copyright © Motilal Banarsidass.

The statement from the Avashyaka Sutra on page 101 is quoted from *The Jains,* by Paul Dundas (London: Routledge, 1992), page 148. Copyright © 1992 by Paul Dundas.

Shri Nitin Mehta's words on page 102 are excerpted from *Perspectives in Jaina Philosophy and Culture,* edited by Shri Satish Kumar Jain and Dr. Kamal Chand Sogani (New Delhi, India: Ahimsa International, 1985), pages 45–46.

The words of Nanak on pages 109 and 110 (first and second), the Mool Mantra on page 114, and the words of Nanak on page 272 are quoted from *The Sikhs: Their Religious Beliefs and Practices,* second, revised edition, by W. Owen Cole and Piara Singh Sambhi (Brighton, United Kingdom: Sussex Academic Press, 1995), pages 10, 10–11, 70, and 10, respectively. Copyright © 1995 by W. Owen Cole and Piara Singh Sambhi. Used with permission of the authors and Sussex Academic Press.

The words of Nanak on page 110 (second), and the description of the Adi Granth on pages 113–114 are quoted from "Sikhism," by Khushwant Singh, in volume 13 of *The Encyclopedia of Religion,* edited by Mircea Eliade (New York: Macmillan Publishing Co., 1987), pages 316, and 319. Copyright © 1987 by Macmillan Publishing Co.

The fourth section of the Japjī in the sidebar on page 116, is quoted from *Sikhism,* by Hew McLeod (London: Penguin Books, 1997), page 272. Copyright © 1997 by W. H. McLeod. Used with permission of the author.

The excerpts from an interview with Bhai Dhanna Singh on page 118 are quoted from *Fighting for Faith and Nation: Dialogues with Sikh Militants,* by Cynthia Keppley Mahmood (Philadelphia: University of Pennsylvania Press, 1996), pages 144–145 and 150. Copyright © 1996 by Cynthia Keppley Mahmood. Used with permission of the University of Pennsylvania Press.

The words of Tu Wei-ming on page 124 are quoted from his "Confucianism," Jacob Neusner's translation of the prayers on pages 216 and 218 are quoted from his "Judaism," and Seyyed Hossein Nasr's translation of Rumi's poem on page 263 is quoted from Nasr's "Islam," all in *Our Religions,* edited by Arvind Sharma (San Francisco: HarperSanFrancisco, 1993), pages 149, 345, 350, and 522, respectively. Copyright © 1993 by HarperCollins Publishers. Used with permission of HarperCollins Publishers.

The passages from the Analects on pages 126 (all four), 127, 128, (first and second), 129 (all 3), 131 (first, second, third, fourth, and sixth), 133 (second), 134 (both), and 135 (all twelve) are quoted from *The Analects* by Confucius, translated by D. C. Lau (London: Penguin Books, 1979), pages 90, 91, 88, 86, 63, 80, 86, 73, 61, 78, 72, 72, 121, 135, 101, 63, 74, 115–116, 66, 107, 89, 69, 129, 65, 73, 128, 125, 136, 122, and 74, respectively. Copyright © 1979 by D. C. Lau. Used with permission of Penguin Books, Ltd.

The passages from the Analects on pages 128 (third), 131 (fifth), and 133 (first) are quoted from *A Source Book in Chinese Philosophy,* translated and compiled by Wing-tsit Chan (Princeton, NJ: Princeton University Press, 1963), pages 22, 42, and 22, respectively. Copyright © 1963 by Princeton University Press.

The excerpts about a teacher's position on page 130 are from *A Chinese Childhood,* by Chiang Yee (New York: W. W. Norton and Co., 1963), pages 79–80, 83, and 86, respectively. Copyright © 1952. Used with permission of Chien-fei Chiang.

The passages from the Great Learning and *Records of Rituals* on page 133 are quoted from *Chinese Religion: An Introduction,* fifth edition, by Laurence G. Thompson (Belmont, CA: Wadsworth Publishing Co., 1996), pages 12 and 11. Copyright © 1996 by Wadsworth Publishing Co.

The passage from the Book of Mencius on page 133 is from *Mencius,* translated by D. C. Lau (Middlesex, England: Penguin Books, 1970), page 102. Copyright © 1970 by D. C. Lau.

The poem "Man Is Born in Tao" on page 139 is from *The Way of Chuang Tzu,* by Thomas Merton (New York: New Directions, 1965), page 65. Copyright © 1965 by the Abbey of Gethsemani. Reprinted with permission of New Directions Publishing Corp. and Pollinger Ltd.

The words of Confucius on pages 140–141 are as told by Ssu-ma Ch'ien in *Shih Chi,* quoted in *Lao Tzu and Taoism,* by Max Kaltenmark, translated from the French by Roger Greaves (Stanford, CA: Stanford University Press, 1969), page 8. Copyright © 1969 by the Board of Trustees of the Leland Stanford Junior University.

The passages from chapter 1 of the *Tao Te Ching* on page 141, chapter 25 on page 143, chapter 34 on page 143, chapter 1 in the sidebar on page 143 (second translation of line 1), chapter 2 on page 144, chapter 70 on page 145, chapter 48 on page 146, chapter 63 on page 146, chapter 78 on page 146, chapter 22 on page 147 (both), chapter 17 on page 149, and chapter 41 on page 151 are quoted from *The Way of Lao Tzu,* translated by Wing-tsit Chan (Indianapolis: Bobbs-Merrill Co., Library of Liberal Arts Press, 1963), pages 97, 144, 160, 97, 101, 224, 184, 212, 236, 139, 130, and 174 respectively. First edition copyright © 1963. Used with permission of Pearson Education, Inc., Upper Saddle River, New Jersey.

The passages from chapter 56 of the *Tao Te Ching* on page 141 and chapter 1 in the sidebar on page 143 are quoted from *The Way and Its Power: A Study of the* Tao Te Ching *and Its Place in Chinese Thought,* by Arthur Waley (New York: Grove Press by arrangement with the Macmillan Co., 1958), pages 210 and 141.

The passages from chapter 19 of the *Tao Te Ching* on page 142, chapter 28 on page 144, chapter 70 on page 147, chapter 24 on page 147, chapter 29 on page 147, and chapter 68 on page 149 are quoted from *Tao Te Ching,* by Lao Tzu, translated by Gia-fu Feng and Jane English (New York: Random House, Vintage Books, 1989), pages 21, 30, 72, 26, 31, and 70, respectively. Copyright © 1972 by Gia-fu Feng and Jane English.

The passages from chapter 2 of the *Chuang Tzu* on pages 142 and 144–145 are quoted from *Three Ways of Thought in Ancient China,* by Arthur Waley (New York: Barnes and Noble, 1939), pages 54 and 27. Copyright © under the Berne Convention.

Frederic Spiegelberg's translation of the first line from chapter 1 of the *Tao Te Ching* in the sidebar on page 143 is quoted from his book *Living Religions of the World* (Englewood Cliffs, NJ: Prentice-Hall, 1956), page 300. Copyright © 1956 by Prentice-Hall.

Raymond B. Blakney's translation of the first line from chapter 1 of the *Tao Te Ching* in the sidebar on page 143 is quoted from his book *The Way of Life: "Lao Tzu"* (New York: New American Library, Mentor Books, 1983), page 53. Copyright © 1955 by Raymond B. Blakney. Copyright © renewed 1983 by Charles Philip Blakney.

D. C. Lau's translation of the first line from chapter 1 of the *Tao Te Ching* in the sidebar on page 143 is quoted from his translation of *Lao Tzu: Tao Te Ching* (London: Penguin Books, 1963), page 57. Copyright © 1963 by D. C. Lau.

The passage from chapter 18 of the *Chuang Tzu* on page 145 is quoted from *Chuang Tzu: Basic Writings,* translated by Burton Watson (New York: Columbia University Press), page 113. Copyright © 1964 by Columbia University Press. Used with permission of the author and Columbia University Press.

The excerpt on page 148 is from *The Monastery of Jade Mountain,* by Peter Goullart (London: John Murray Publishers, 1961), pages 30–31. Copyright © 1961 by Peter Goullart. Used with permission of Hodder and Stoughton.

The excerpts about Joshu on pages 153 and 156, about Gudo on pages 156–157, about Nan-in on page 157, about Mokurai on page 158, about the man on the vine on page 161, and from the hand of Shoun on page 161 are from *Zen Flesh, Zen Bones: A Collection of Zen and Pre-Zen Writings,* compiled by Paul Reps (Garden City, NY: Doubleday and Co., Anchor Books, 1996), pages 96, 39, 55, 5, 25, 23, and 19–20, respectively. Used with permission of Tuttle Publishing, a member of the Periplus Publishing Group.

The excerpt on page 155 is quoted from *Essays in Zen Buddhism: First Series,* by Daisetz Teitaro Suzuki (New York: Grove Press, 1961), page 13.

The excerpt about Tokusan on page 156 is from *The Three Pillars of Zen: Teaching, Practice, and Enlightenment,* twenty-fifth anniversary edition, compiled and edited by Roshi Philip Kapleau (New York: Doubleday, Anchor Books, 1989), page 195, note 27. Copyright © 1980 by the Zen Center. Copyright © 1965, 1989 by Roshi Philip Kapleau.

The quotation by Daisetz Teitaro Suzuki on page 157 and from the foreword by C. G. Jung on page 159 are from *An Introduction to Zen Buddhism,* by Daisetz Teitaro Suzuki (New York: Grove Press, Evergreen Black Cat Books, 1964), pages 38 and 10.

The *koans* about a cart, about a buffalo, and about a man hanging from a tree on pages 158–159 are excerpts from *Zen Comments on the Mumonkan,* by Zenkei Shibayama, translated into English by Sumiko Kudo (New York: New American Library, Mentor Books, 1975), pages 74, 272, and 54, respectively. Copyright © 1974 by Zenkei Shibayama.

The excerpts on page 160 are from *Pure Heart, Enlightened Mind: The Life and Letters of an Irish Zen Saint,* by Maura Soshin O'Halloran (Boston: Wisdom Publications. 2007), pages 77–79, 165, and 295. Copyright © 2007 by Katherine O'Halloran and Elizabeth O'Halloran. Used with permission of Wisdom Publications.

The haiku on page 163 is quoted from *Japanese Haiku: Two Hundred Twenty Examples of Seventeen-syllable Poems,* by Basho, Buson, Issa, Shiki, Sokan, Kikaku, and others, translated by Peter Beilenson (Mount Vernon, NY: The Peter Pauper Press), page 41. Copyright © 1955–1956 by The Peter Pauper Press.

The poem on page 164 is quoted from *Cold Mountain: One Hundred Poems by the T'ang Poet Han-Shan,* translated by Burton Watson (Grove Press, 1962; reprint, New York: Columbia University Press, 1970), page 58. Copyright © 1962 by Burton Watson. Copyright © 1970 by Columbia University Press. Used with permission of the author and Columbia University Press.

The quotations of Mootori Norinaga on pages 168 and 170 are from *Religion in the Japanese Experience: Sources and Interpretations,* by H. Byron Earhart (Encino, CA: Dickenson Publishing Co., 1974), page 10. Copyright © 1974 by Dickenson Publishing Co.

The excerpt on page 174 is quoted from *A Year in the Life of a Shinto Shrine,* by John K. Nelson (Seattle: University of Washington Press, 1996), pages 125–129. Copyright © 1996 by the University of Washington Press. Used with permission of University of Washington Press.

The first passage from the Gathas on page 182 and the passage on page 183 are quoted from *Early Zoroastrianism,* by James Hope Moulton (London: Williams and Norgate, 1913), pages 367–368 and 374.

The second passage from the Gathas on page 182 is quoted from *Textual Sources for the Study of Zoroastrianism,* edited and translated by Mary Boyce (Manchester, England: Manchester University Press, 1984), page 35. Copyright © 1984 by Mary Boyce.

The lines from Aeschylus's *Agamemnon* on page 186 are quoted from *The Oresteian Trilogy,* translated by Philip Vellacott (London: Penguin Books, 1987), page 48. Copyright © 1956 by Philip Vellacott.

The lines from Homer's *Odyssey* on page 190 are quoted from *The Odyssey,* translated by Robert Fagles (New York: Penguin Books, 1996), page 265. Copyright © 1996 by Robert Fagles.

The excerpts from Aristides's *Sacred Tales* on page 194 are quoted from *Aelius Aristides and "The Sacred Tales,"* by C. A. Behr (Amsterdam, Netherlands: Adolf M. Hakkert, Publisher, 1968), pages 224 and 261–262. Copyright © 1968 by A. M. Hakkert, Amsterdam, Netherlands.

The passage of Apuleius's *Metamorphoses* on page 196 is from *The Golden Ass,* translated by Jack Lindsay (Indiana University Press, 1962), quoted in *The Ancient Mysteries: A Sourcebook,* edited by Marvin W. Meyer (San Francisco: Harper and Row, Publishers, Perennial Library, 1987), page 158. Copyright © 1987 by Marvin W. Meyer.

The excerpt on page 197 is from *Pliny,* translated by W. M. L. Hutchinson (Cambridge, MA: Harvard University Press, 1952), quoted in *The New Testament in Context: Sources and Documents,* by Howard Clark Kee (Englewood Cliffs, NJ: Prentice-Hall, 1984), page 44. Copyright © 1984 by Prentice-Hall.

The excerpt on Judaism as the Covenant on page 201 is quoted from *Man's Quest for God: Studies in Prayer and Symbolism,* by Abraham Joshua Heschel (New York: Charles Scribner's Sons, 1954), page 45. Copyright © 1954 by Abraham Joshua Heschel.

The description of the Talmud on page 204 is quoted from *The Essential Talmud,* by Adin Steinsaltz, translated from the Hebrew by Chaya Galai (New York: Basic Books, 1976), page 3. Copyright © 1976 by Bantam Books.

Maimonides's thirteen principles on page 209 are quoted from *The Ways of Religion: An Introduction to the Major Traditions,* second edition, edited by Roger Eastman (New York: Oxford University Press, 1993), pages 261–262. Copyright © 1975 by Roger Eastman.

The story on page 211 is adapted from "The Precious Prayer," in *Gabriel's Palace: Jewish Mystical Tales,* selected and retold by Howard Schwartz (New York: Oxford University Press, 1993), pages 86–87. Copyright © 1993 by Howard Schwartz. Used with permission of Oxford University Press and Trident Media Group.

The quotation on page 213 is from *The Mishnah,* translated from the Hebrew by Herbert Danby, DD (Oxford, England: Oxford University Press, 1933), page 446.

The excerpt on page 232 is quoted from *Great Books of the Western World,* edited by Robert Maynard Hutchins, volume 20, *The "Summa Theologica" of Saint Thomas Aquinas,* volume 2, translated by fathers of the English Dominican Province and revised by Daniel J. Sullivan (Chicago: Encyclopaedia Britannica, 1952), page 398. Copyright © 1952 by Encyclopaedia Britannica.

The excerpt on pages 242–243 is from *Decree on Ecumenism (Unitatis Redintegratio)*, number 1, at *www.vatican.va/archive/hist_councils/ii_vatican_council/documents/vat-ii_decree_19641121_unitatis-redintegration_en.html*, accessed April 11, 2008.

The passages from the Qur'an on pages 249, 250, 252, and 257 (both) are quoted from *The Koran*, translated by N. J. Dawood (London: Penguin Classics, 1956; fifth revised edition, London: Penguin Books, 1990), pages 9, 429, 420, 60, and 299, respectively. Copyright © 1956, 1959, 1966, 1968, 1974, 1990, 1993 by N. J. Dawood. Used with permission of the Penguin Group UK.

The definition of *Jihad* on page 258 is quoted from the glossary of the Islamic server for the Muslim Student Association of the University of Southern California, Los Angeles, at *www.usc.edu/dept/MSA/reference/glossary/term.JIHAD.html*, accessed June 19, 2008. Used with permission of the University of Southern California Muslim Student Union.

The Sufi saying on page 261 is quoted from *Sufism: An Account of the Mystics of Islam*, by A. J. Arberry (1950; reprint, New York: Harper and Row, Publishers, Harper Torchbooks, 1970), page 28. Copyright © 1950 by A. J. Arberry.

The excerpt from the American Humanist Association's Humanist Manifesto II on page 272 is quoted from *In Defense of Secular Humanism*, by Paul Kurtz (Amherst, NY: Prometheus Books, 1983), pages 41 and 47. Copyright © 1983 by Paul Kurtz.

The quotation on page 282 is from *Illuminata: A Return to Prayer*, by Marianne Williamson (New York: Random House, 1994; reprint, New York: Riverhead Books, 1995), page 4. Copyright © 1994 by Marianne Williamson.

The quotation by Galileo Galilei on page 286 is from *The Galileo Affair: A Documentary History*, edited and translated by Maurice A. Finocchiaro (Berkeley, CA: University of California Press, 1989), page 96. Copyright © 1989 by the Regents of the University of California.

The quotation by Andrew Newberg on page 288 is from "Religion and the Brain," by Sharon Begley, in *Newsweek*, May 7, 2001, page 52.

To view copyright terms and conditions for Internet materials cited here, log on to the home pages for the referenced Web sites.

During this book's preparation, all citations, facts, figures, names, addresses, telephone numbers, Internet URLs, and other pieces of information cited within were verified for accuracy. The authors and Saint Mary's Press staff have made every attempt to reference current and valid sources, but we cannot guarantee the content of any source, and we are not responsible for any changes that may have occurred since our verification. If you find an error in, or have a question or concern about, any of the information or sources listed within, please contact Saint Mary's Press.